英国经典文学作品选读

（注释加译文版）

姜晓瑜　董妍妍　邓纯旭　主　编

知识产权出版社

全国百佳图书出版单位

图书在版编目（CIP）数据

英国经典文学作品选读: 英文 / 姜晓瑜, 董妍妍, 邓纯旭主编. —北京 : 知识产权出版社, 2017.8
ISBN 978-7-5130-5080-7

Ⅰ. ①英… Ⅱ. ①姜… ②董… ③邓… Ⅲ. ①英语 - 阅读教学 - 高等学校 - 教材②英国文学 - 作品 - 介绍 Ⅳ. ①H319.4：I

中国版本图书馆CIP数据核字(2017)第 201303 号

内容提要

本书是供普通高等学校学生使用的英国文学教材，涵盖了英国从 Anglo-Saxon 时期到 20 世纪的主要作家作品。本书共 20 个单元，可供上下学期使用。本书在介绍文学作品的同时，巧妙地融合了作家及文学史的内容，体系更完整。将文学批评方法融入每一单元，帮助学生提高文学欣赏水平。每单元设有课后问答题，便于学生更好地理解内容，也有助于学生形成批判性思维，激发学生的学习积极性，活跃课堂气氛。

责任编辑：田　姝　　　　　　　　　　责任出版：孙婷婷

英国经典文学作品选读

YINGGUO JINGDIAN WENXUE ZUOPIN XUANDU

姜晓瑜　董妍妍　邓纯旭　主　编

出版发行：知识产权出版社 有限责任公司		网　　址：http : // www.ipph.cn	
电　　话：010 - 82004826		http : //www.laichushu.com	
社　　址：北京市海淀区气象路50号院		邮　　编：100081	
责编电话：010 - 82000860转8598		责编邮箱：tianshu@cnipr.com	
发行电话：010 - 82000860转8101		发行传真：010 - 82000893	
印　　刷：虎彩印艺股份有限公司		经　　销：各大网上书店、新华书店及相关专业书店	
开　　本：880mm×1230mm　1/16		印　　张：19.75	
版　　次：2017年8月第1版		印　　次：2017年8月第1次印刷	
字　　数：200千字		定　　价：49.00元	

ISBN 978 - 7 - 5130 - 5080 - 7

编 委 会

姜晓瑜　董妍妍　邓纯旭　主　编

张文政　尹雪梅　高　娜　副主编

前　言

本书是根据英国文学历史的顺序结合作品选读所编写的一套适合我国普通高等院校及职业院校的非英语专业学生使用的教材。本教材力求做到内容丰富、观点正确，选文具有代表性，为学习者提供一个学习英国文学作品的平台。

本教材的整体框架包含三个部分。

第一部分：作家简介。通过对重要作家生平的简介，了解其人生经历对文学作品的影响，进而体会文学作品的深刻意义。

第二部分：作品选读。这一部分为本教材的核心部分。本教材选择了最具代表性的篇章段落，并附有中文翻译。学习者可在阅读的同时，学习英语单词，了解文化历史，领会文学作品的魅力。

第三部分：练习部分。这一部分主要是针对所选篇章段落的文学作品提出一些思考性的问题，指引学生把握文学作品的精髓。

本教材适用于广大的英语学习者，包括大中专院校的学生、各类英语自学者。学生可以在本教材的指引下，逐步提高自身的文化及文学修养。

在教材的编写中，我们参考了互联网、报刊和书籍的相关文献，由于篇幅有限，不能一一列出，在此向这些文献的所有者表示诚挚的谢意和敬意。

本教材是集体智慧的结晶，编写过程中得益于全体编委的努力工作。特别感谢大连医科大学的姜晓瑜、董妍妍、邓纯旭、张文政、尹雪梅以及朝阳市卫生学校高娜老师付出的辛劳，他们在出版过程中做了一次次的深入探索与尝试，力图做到细致入微、精益求精。尽管如此，其中必定还有疏漏之处，敬请各位同仁和广大使用者批评指正。

CONTENTS

Unit 1   Geoffrey Chaucer (1340?—1400)

Life

Geoffrey Chaucer was born in London sometime around 1343, though the precise date and location of his birth remain unknown. His father and grandfather were both London vintners; several previous generations had been merchants in Ipswich. In 1324 John Chaucer, Geoffrey's father, was kidnapped by an aunt in the hope of marrying the twelve-year-old boy to her daughter in an attempt to keep property in Ipswich. The aunt was imprisoned and the £250 fine levied suggests that the family was financially secure–bourgeois, if not elite. John Chaucer married Agnes Copton, who, in 1349, inherited properties including 24 shops in London from her uncle.

While records concerning the lives of his contemporary poets, William Langland and the Pearl Poet are practically non-existent, since Chaucer was a public servant, his official life is very well documented, with nearly five hundred written items testifying to his career. The first of the "Chaucer Life Records" appears in 1357, in the household accounts of Elizabeth de Burgh, the Countess of Ulster, when he became the noble woman's page through his father's connections, a common medieval form of apprenticeship for boys into knighthood or prestige appointments. The countess was married to Lionel, Duke of Clarence, the second surviving son of the king, Edward III, and the position brought the teenage Chaucer into the close court circle, where he was to remain for the rest of his life. He also worked as a courtier, a diplomat, and a civil servant, as well as working for the king from 1389 to 1391 as Clerk of the King's Works.

In 1359, in the early stages of the Hundred Years' War, Edward III invaded France and Chaucer travelled with Lionel of Antwerp, 1st Duke of Clarence, Elizabeth's husband, as part of the English army. In 1360, he was captured during the siege of Rheims. Edward paid £16 for his ransom, a considerable sum, and Chaucer was released.

After this, Chaucer's life is uncertain, but he seems to have travelled in France, Spain, and Flanders, possibly as a messenger and perhaps even going on a pilgrimage to Santiago de Compostela. Around 1366, Chaucer married Philippa (de) Roet. She was a lady-in-waiting to Edward III's queen, Philippa of Hainault, and a sister of Katherine Swynford, who later became the third wife of John of Gaunt. It is uncertain how many children Chaucer and Philippa had, but three or four are most commonly cited.

According to tradition, Chaucer studied law in the Inner Temple (an Inn of Court) at this time. He became a member of the royal court of Edward III as avarlet de chambre, yeoman, or esquire on 20 June 1367, a position which could entail a wide variety of tasks. His wife also received a pension for court employment. He travelled abroad many times, at least some of them in his role as a valet. In 1368, he may have attended the wedding of Lionel of Antwerpto Violante Visconti, daughter of Galeazzo II Visconti, in Milan. Two other literary stars of the era were in attendance: Jean Froissart and Petrarch. Around this time, Chaucer is believed to have written *The Book of the Duchess* in honour of Blanche of Lancaster, the late wife of John of Gaunt, who died in 1369.

A possible indication that his career as a writer was appreciated came when Edward III granted Chaucer "a gallon of wine daily for the rest of his life" for some unspecified task. This was an unusual grant, but given on a day of celebration, St George's Day, 1374, when artistic endeavours were traditionally rewarded, it is assumed to have been another early poetic work. It is not known which, if any, of Chaucer's extant works prompted the reward, but the suggestion of him as poet to a king places him as a precursor to later poets laureate. Chaucer continued to collect the liquid stipend until Richard II came to power, after which it was converted to a monetary grant on 18 April 1378. Chaucer obtained the very substantial job of comptroller of the customs for the port of London, which he began on 8 June 1374. He must have been suited for the role as he continued in it for twelve years, a long time in such a post at that time. His life goes undocumented for much of the next ten years, but it is believed that he wrote (or began) most of his famous works during this period. He was mentioned in law papers of 4 May 1380, involved in the raptus of Cecilia Chaumpaigne. What raptus means is unclear, but the incident seems to have been resolved quickly and did not leave a stain on Chaucer's reputation. It is not known if Chaucer was in the city of London at the time of the Peasants' Revolt, but if he was, he would have seen its leaders pass almost directly under his apartment window at Aldgate.

While still working as comptroller, Chaucer appears to have moved to Kent, being appointed as one of the commissioners of peace for Kent, at a time when French invasion was a possibility. He is thought to have started work on The Canterbury Talesin the early 1380s. He also became a Member of Parliament for Kent in 1386. On 15 October that year, he gave a deposition in the case of Scrope v. Grosvenor. There is no further reference after this date to Philippa, Chaucer's wife, and she is presumed to have died in 1387. He survived the political upheavals caused by the Lords Appellants, despite the fact that Chaucer knew some of the men executed over the affair quite well.

On 12 July 1389, Chaucer was appointed the clerk of the king's works, a sort of foreman organising most of the king's building projects. No major works were begun during his tenure, but he did conduct repairs on Westminster Palace, St. George's Chapel, Windsor, continue building the wharf at the Tower of London, and build the stands for a tournament held in 1390. It may have been a difficult job, but it paid well: two shillings a day, more than three times his salary as a comptroller. Chaucer was also appointed keeper of the lodge at the King's park in Feckenham, which was a largely honorary appointment.

He is believed to have died of unknown causes on 25 October 1400, but there is no firm evidence for this date, as it comes from the engraving on his tomb, erected more than one hundred years after his death. There is some speculation—most recently in Terry Jones' book *Who Murdered Chaucer? : A Medieval Mystery*—that he was murdered by enemies of Richard II or even on the orders of his successor Henry IV, but the case is entirely circumstantial. Chaucer was buried in Westminster Abbey in London, as was his right owing to his status as a tenant of the Abbey's close. In 1556, his remains were transferred to a more ornate tomb, making Chaucer the first writer interred in the area now known as Poets' Corner.

The Canterbury Tales

The Canterbury Tales is a collection of 24 stories that runs to over 17000 lines written in Middle English by Geoffrey Chaucer. In 1386, Chaucer became Controller of Customs and Justice of Peace and, three years later, Clerk of the King's work in 1389. It was during these years that Chaucer began working on his most famous text, *The Canterbury Tales*. The tales (mostly written in verse, although some are in prose) are presented as part of a story-telling contest by a group of pilgrims as they travel together on a journey from London to Canterbury to visit the shrine of Saint Thomas Becket at Canterbury Cathedral.

It has been suggested that the greatest contribution of *The Canterbury Tales* to English literature was the popularization of the English vernacular in mainstream literature, as opposed to French, Italian or Latin. English had, however, been used as a literary language centuries before Chaucer's time, and several of Chaucer's contemporaries—John Gower, William Langland, the Pearl Poet, and Julian of Norwich—also wrote major literary works in English. It is unclear to what extent Chaucer was seminal in this evolution of literary preference.

While Chaucer clearly states the addressees of many of his poems, the intended audience of The Canterbury Tales is more difficult to determine. Chaucer was a courtier, leading some to believe that he was mainly a court poet who wrote exclusively for nobility.

The Canterbury Tales is generally thought to have been incomplete at the end of Chaucer's life. In the General Prologue, some thirty pilgrims are introduced. According to the *Prologue*, Chaucer's intention was to write two stories from the perspective of each pilgrim on the way to and from their ultimate destination, St. Thomas Becket's shrine (making for a total of four stories per pilgrim). Although perhaps incomplete, *The Canterbury Tales* is revered as one of the most important works in English literature. Not only do readers find it entertaining, but it is also open to a wide range of interpretations.

Comments on *The Canterbury Tales*

The Canterbury Tales was written during a turbulent time in English history. The Catholic Church was in the midst of the Western Schism and, though it was still the only Christian authority in Europe, was the subject of heavy controversy. Lollardy, an early English religious movement led by John Wycliffe, is mentioned in the *Tales*, which also mention a specific incident involving pardoners (sellers of indulgences, which were believed to relieve the temporal punishment due for sins that were already forgiven in the Sacrament of Confession) who nefariously claimed to be collecting for St. Mary Rouncesval hospital in England. *The Canterbury*

Tales is among the first English literary works to mention paper, a relatively new invention that allowed dissemination of the written word never before seen in England. Political clashes, such as the 1381 Peasants' Revolt and clashes ending in the deposing of King Richard II, further reveal the complex turmoil surrounding Chaucer in the time of the Tales' writing. Many of his close friends were executed and he himself moved to Kent to get away from events in London.

While some readers look to interpret the characters of *The Canterbury Tales* as historical figures, other readers choose to interpret its significance in less literal terms. After analysis of Chaucer's diction and historical context, his work appears to develop a critique of society during his lifetime. Within a number of his descriptions, his comments can appear complimentary in nature, but through clever language, the statements are ultimately critical of the pilgrim's actions. It is unclear whether Chaucer would intend for the reader to link his characters with actual persons. Instead, it appears that Chaucer creates fictional characters to be general representations of people in such fields of work. With an understanding of medieval society, one can detect subtle satire at work.

The Prologue

The *Prologue* is the key to *The Canterbury Tales* that narrates about the gathering of a group of people in an inn that intend to go on a pilgrimage to Canterbury next morning.

In the *Prologue*, the narrator of *The Canterbury Tales*, who is one of the intended pilgrims, provides more or less accurate depictions of the members of the group and describes why and how *The Canterbury Tales* is told. If we trust the *General Prologue*, Chaucer determined that each pilgrim should tell two tales on the way to Canterbury and two tales on the way back. The host of the inn offers to be and is appointed as judge of the tales as they are told and is supposed to determine the best hence winning tale. As mentioned before, *The Canterbury Tales* was never finished.

It provides a framework for the tales. It contains a group of vivid sketches of typical medieval figures. All classes of the English feudal society, except the royalty and the poorest peasant, are represented by these thirty pilgrims.

Every figure is drawn with the accuracy of a portrait. It is no exaggeration to say that *The Prologue* supplies a miniature of the English society of Chaucer's time. Looking at his word-pictures, we know at once how people live in that era. That is why Chaucer has been called "the founder of English realism."

The Prologue [1]

Whan that Aprille with his shoures soote,

The droghte of March hath perced to the roote,

And bathed every veyne in swich licóur

Of which vertú engendred is the flour;

Whan Zephirus[2] eek with his swete breeth

Inspired hath in every holt and heeth

The tendre croppes, and the yonge sonne

Hath in the Ram[3] his halfe cours y-ronne,

And smale foweles maken melodye,

That slepen al the nyght with open ye,

So priketh hem Natúre in hir corages,

Thanne longen folk to goon on pilgrimages,

And palmeres[4] for to seken straunge strondes,

To ferne halwes, kowthe in sondry londes;

And specially, from every shires ende

Of Engelond, to Caunterbury they wende,

The hooly blisful martir for to seke,

That hem hath holpen whan that they were seeke.

 N o t e s

[1] In the modern English-translation by Theodore Morrison, Chaucer's ogiginal metrical form, the heroic coupletis, is used.

[2] zephyrs: the west wind

[3] Ram: sign of the Zodiac; the Sun is the Ram from March 12 to April 11.

[4] Palmers: pilgrims, who, originally, brought back palm leaves from the Holy Land.

 Q u e s t i o n s

1. Can you enjoy the beautiful scenery written by Chaucer?

2. What is Heroic couplets?

3. What are the characteristics of the description of the prologue?

Analysis of *The Prologue*

The Prologue is actually a gallery of all walks of people. Chaucer widely selected his materials from English society of that age. Except the top of royal and the lowest salves, we can nearly find the representative of all social classes. Though reading the book, we can have a better understanding and broaden our eyesight of English society in 14th century, as well as enjoy the feature of art.

The prologue is rich in content. There is the knight who has participated in no less than fifteen of the great crusades of his era; the wife of Bath who has been married five times and well practiced in the art of love; the pardoner who is associated with shiftiness and gender ambiguity; just name a few. They belong to different parts of the society, living in different background, thus had different life styles, habits and custom. They charted, joked, quarreled, and compromised; they discussed, praised, criticized, and persuaded. They adopted their particular way to present their life experience, providing a vivid series of narratives which differ in content and style.

 中文译文

序诗

夏雨给大地带来了喜悦，

送走了土壤干裂的三月，

沐浴着草木的丝丝经络，

顿时百花盛开，生机勃勃。

西风轻吹留下清香缕缕，

田野复苏吐出芳草青青；

碧蓝的天空腾起一轮红日，

青春的太阳洒下万道金辉。

小鸟的歌喉多么清脆优美，

迷人的夏夜怎好安然入睡。

美丽的自然撩拨万物的心弦，

多情的鸟儿歌唱爱情的欣欢。

香客盼望膜拜圣徒的灵台，

僧侣立愿云游陌生的滨海。

信徒来自全国东西南北，

众人结伴奔向坎特伯雷，

去朝谢医病救世的恩主，

以缅怀大恩大德的圣徒。

References

[1] 常耀信 . 英国文学简史 [C]. 天津：南开大学出版社，2006.

[2] 王守仁 . 英国文学选读 [C]. 北京：高等教育出版社，2005.

Unit 2   William Shakespeare (1564—1616)

Life

William Shakespeare was an English poet, playwright, and actor, widely regarded as the greatest writer in the English language and the world's pre-eminent dramatist. He is often called England's national poet, and the "Bard of Avon."His extant works, including collaborations, consist of approximately 38 plays, 154 sonnets, two long narrative poems, and a few other verses, some of uncertain authorship. His plays have been translated into every major living language and are performed more often than those of any other playwright.

Shakespeare was born and brought up in Stratford-upon-Avon, Warwickshire. At the age of 18, he married Anne Hathaway, with whom he had three children: Susanna, and twins Hamnet and Judith. Sometime between 1585 and 1592, he began a successful career in London as an actor, writer, and part-owner of a playing company called the Lord Chamberlain's Men, later known as the King's Men. He appears to have retired to Stratford around 1613, at age 49, where he died three years later. Few records of Shakespeare's private life survive, which has stimulated considerable speculation about such matters as his physical appearance, sexuality, and religious beliefs, and whether the works attributed to him were written by others.

Shakespeare produced most of his known work between 1589 and 1613. His early plays were primarily comedies and histories, and these are regarded as some of the best work ever produced in these genres. He then wrote mainly tragedies until about 1608, including Hamlet,

Othello, King Lear, and Macbeth, considered some of the finest works in the English language. In his last phase, he wrote tragicomedies, also known as romances, and collaborated with other playwrights.

Many of his plays were published in editions of varying quality and accuracy during his lifetime. In 1623, however, John Heminges and Henry Condell, two friends and fellow actors of Shakespeare, published a more definitive text known as the *First Folio*, a posthumous collected edition of his dramatic works that included all but two of the plays now recognised as Shakespeare's. It was prefaced with a poem by Ben Jonson, in which Shakespeare is hailed, presciently, as "not of an age, but for all time."

In the 20th and 21st centuries, his works have been repeatedly adapted and rediscovered by new movements in scholarship and performance. His plays remain highly popular, and are constantly studied, performed, and reinterpreted in diverse cultural and political contexts throughout the world.

Plot of *Hamlet*

Act I

The protagonist of Hamlet is Prince Hamlet of Denmark, son of the recently deceased King Hamlet, and nephew of King Claudius, his father's brother and successor. Claudius hastily married King Hamlet's widow, Gertrude, Hamlet's mother, and took the throne for himself. Denmark has a long-standing feud with neighboring Norway, which culminated when King Hamlet slew King Fortinbras of Norway in a battle years ago. Although Denmark defeated Norway, and the Norwegian throne fell to King Fortinbras's infirm brother, Denmark fears that an invasion led by the dead Norwegian king's son, Prince Fortinbras, is imminent.

On a cold night on the ramparts of Elsinore, the Danish royal castle, the sentries Bernardo and Marcellus and Hamlet's friend Horatio encounter a ghost that looks like the late King Hamlet. They vow to tell Prince Hamlet what they have witnessed.

As the Court gathers the next day, while King Claudius and Queen Gertrude discuss affairs of state with their elderly adviser Polonius, Hamlet looks on glumly. After the Court exits, Hamlet despairs of his father's death and his mother's hasty remarriage. Learning of the Ghost from Horatio, Hamlet resolves to see it himself.

As Polonius's son Laertes prepares to depart for a visit to France, Polonius gives him contradictory advice that culminates in the ironic maxim "to thine own self be true." Polonius's daughter, Ophelia, admits her interest in Hamlet, but both Polonius and Laertes warn her against seeking the prince's attention. That night on the rampart, the Ghost appears to Hamlet, telling the prince that he was murdered by Claudius and demanding that Hamlet avenge him. Hamlet agrees and the Ghost vanishes. The prince confides to Horatio and the sentries that from now on he plans to "put an antic disposition on" and forces them to swear to keep his plans for revenge secret. Privately, however, he remains uncertain of the Ghost's reliability.

Act II

Soon thereafter, Ophelia rushes to her father, telling him that Hamlet arrived at her door the prior night half-undressed and behaving crazily. Polonius blames love for Hamlet's madness and resolves to inform Claudius and Gertrude. As he enters to do so, the king and queen finish welcoming Rosencrantz and Guildenstern, two student acquaintances of Hamlet, to Elsinore. The royal couple has requested that the students investigate the cause of Hamlet's mood and behavior. Additional news requires that Polonius wait to be heard: messengers from Norway inform Claudius that the King of Norway has rebuked Prince Fortinbras for attempting to re-fight his father's battles. The forces that Fortinbras conscripted to march against Denmark will instead be sent against Poland, though they will pass through a portion of Denmark to get there.

Polonius tells Claudius and Gertrude his theory regarding Hamlet's behavior, and speaks to Hamlet in a hall of the castle to try to uncover more information. Hamlet feigns madness but subtly insults Polonius all the while. When Rosencrantz and Guildenstern arrive, Hamlet greets his friends warmly, but quickly discerns that they are spies. Hamlet becomes bitter, admitting that he is upset at his situation but refusing to give the true reason why, instead commenting on "what a piece of work" humanity is. Rosencrantz and Guildenstern tell Hamlet that they have brought along a troupe of actors that they met while traveling to Elsinore. Hamlet, after welcoming the actors and dismissing his friends-turned-spies, plots to stage a play featuring a death in the style of his father's murder, thereby determining the truth of the Ghost's story, as well as Claudius's guilt or innocence, by studying Claudius's reaction.

Act III

Polonius forces Ophelia to return Hamlet's love letters and tokens of affection to the prince while he and Claudius watch from afar to evaluate Hamlet's reaction. Hamlet is walking alone in the hall as the King and Polonius await Ophelia's entrance, musing whether "to be or not to be." When Ophelia enters and tries to return Hamlet's things, Hamlet accuses her of immodesty and cries "get thee to a nunnery," though it is unclear whether this, too, is a show of madness or genuine distress. His reaction convinces Claudius that Hamlet is not mad for love. Shortly thereafter, the court assembles to watch the play Hamlet has commissioned. After seeing the Player King murdered by his rival pouring poison in his ear, Claudius abruptly rises and runs from the room: proof positive for Hamlet of his uncle's guilt.

Gertrude summons Hamlet to her room to demand an explanation. Meanwhile, Claudius talks to himself about the impossibility of repenting, since he still has possession of his ill-gotten goods: his brother's crown and wife. He sinks to his knees. Hamlet, on his way to visit his mother, sneaks up behind him, but does not kill him, reasoning that killing Claudius while he is praying will send him straight to heaven while the Ghost is stuck in purgatory. In the queen's bedchamber, Hamlet and Gertrude fight bitterly. Polonius, spying on the conversation from behind a tapestry, makes a noise. Hamlet, believing it is Claudius, stabs wildly, killing Polonius, but pulls aside the curtain and sees his mistake. In a rage, Hamlet brutally insults his mother for her apparent ignorance of Claudius's villainy, but the Ghost enters and reprimands Hamlet for his inaction and harsh words. Unable to see or hear the Ghost herself, Gertrude takes Hamlet's conversation with it as further evidence of madness. After begging the queen to stop sleeping with Claudius, Hamlet leaves, dragging Polonius's corpse away. Hamlet jokes with Claudius about where he has hidden Polonius's body, and the king, fearing for his life, sends Rosencrantz and Guildenstern to accompany Hamlet to England with a sealed letter to the English king requesting that Hamlet be executed immediately.

Act IV

Demented by grief at Polonius's death, Ophelia wanders Elsinore. Laertes arrives back from France, enraged by his father's death and his sister's madness. Claudius convinces Laertes that Hamlet is solely responsible, but a letter soon arrives indicating that Hamlet has returned to Denmark, foiling Claudius's plan. Claudius switches tactics, proposing a fencing match between Laertes and Hamlet to settle their differences. Laertes will be given a poison-tipped foil, and Claudius will offer Hamlet poisoned wine as a congratulation if that fails. Gertrude interrupts to report that Ophelia has drowned, though it is unclear whether it was suicide or an accident exacerbated by her madness.

Act V

Horatio has received a letter from Hamlet, explaining that the prince escaped by negotiating with pirates who attempted to attack his England-bound ship, and the friends reunite offstage. Two gravediggers discuss Ophelia's apparent suicide while digging her grave. Hamlet arrives with Horatio and banters with one of the gravediggers, who unearths the skull of a jester from Hamlet's childhood, Yorick. Hamlet picks up the skull, saying "alas, poor Yorick" as he contemplates mortality. Ophelia's funeral procession approaches, led by Laertes. Hamlet and Horatio initially hide, but when Hamlet realizes that Ophelia is the one being buried, he reveals himself, proclaiming his love for her. Laertes and Hamlet fight by Ophelia's graveside, but the brawl is broken up.

Back at Elsinore, Hamlet explains to Horatio that he had discovered Claudius's letter with Rosencrantz and Guildenstern's belongings and replaced it with a forged copy indicating that his former friends should be killed instead. A foppish courtier, Osric, interrupts the conversation to deliver the fencing challenge to Hamlet. Hamlet, despite Horatio's advice, accepts it. Hamlet does well at first, leading the match by two hits to none, and Gertrude raises a toast to him using the poisoned glass of wine Claudius had set aside for Hamlet. Claudius tries to stop her, but is too late: she drinks, and Laertes realizes the plot will be revealed. Laertes slashes Hamlet with his poisoned blade. In the ensuing scuffle, they switch weapons and Hamlet wounds Laertes with his own poisoned sword. Gertrude collapses and, claiming she has been poisoned, dies. In his dying moments, Laertes reconciles with Hamlet and reveals Claudius's plan. Hamlet rushes at Claudius and kills him. As the poison takes effect, Hamlet, hearing that Fortinbras is marching through the area, names the Norwegian prince as his successor. Horatio, distraught at the thought of being the last survivor, says he will commit suicide by drinking the dregs of Gertrude's poisoned wine, but Hamlet begs him to live on and tell his story. Hamlet dies, proclaiming "the rest is silence." Fortinbras, who was ostensibly marching towards Poland with his army, arrives at the palace, along with an English ambassador bringing news of Rosencrantz and Guildenstern's deaths. Horatio promises to recount the full story of what happened, and Fortinbras, seeing the entire Danish royal family dead, takes the crown for himself.

Comments on *Hamlet*

From the early 17th century, the play was famous for its ghost and vivid dramatisation of melancholy and insanity, leading to a procession of mad courtiers and ladies in Jacobean and Caroline drama. Though it remained popular with mass audiences, late 17th-century Restoration critics saw Hamlet as primitive and disapproved of its lack of unity and decorum. This view changed drastically in the 18th century, when critics regarded Hamlet as a hero—a pure, brilliant young man thrust into unfortunate circumstances. By the mid-18th century, however, the advent of Gothic literature brought psychological and mystical readings, returning madness and the Ghost to the forefront. Not until the late 18th century did critics and performers begin to view Hamlet as confusing and inconsistent. Before then, he was either mad, or not; either a hero, or not; with no in-betweens. These developments represented a fundamental change in literary criticism, which came to focus more on character and less on plot. By the 19th century, Romantic critics valued Hamlet for its internal, individual conflict reflecting the strong contemporary emphasis on internal struggles and inner character in general. Then too, critics started to focus on Hamlet's delay as a character trait, rather than a plot device. This focus on character and internal struggle continued into the 20th century.

Major Characters

Hamlet

He is the Prince of Denmark; he is son of the late King Hamlet; and nephew of the present King Claudius.

Claudius

She is the King of Denmark, elected to the throne after the death of his brother, King Hamlet. Claudius has married Gertrude, his brother's widow.

Gertrude

She is the Queen of Denmark, and King Hamlet's widow, now married to Claudius, and mother to Hamlet.

Polonius

He is Claudius's chief counsellor, and the father of Ophelia and Laertes.

Laertes

He is the son of Polonius, and has returned to Elsinore from Paris.

Ophelia

She is the daughter of Polonius, and Laertes's sister, who lives with her father at Elsinore. She is in love with Hamlet.

Hamlet

To be, or not to be, that is the question; whether 'tis nobler in the mind to suffer. The slings[1] and arrows of outrageous[2] fortune, or to take arms against a sea of troubles, and by opposing end them?

To die, to sleep, no more; and by a sleep to say we end the heart-ache and the thousand natural shocks. That flesh is heir to, 'tis a consummation[3]. Devoutly to be wish'd. To die, to sleep. To sleep, perchance to dream. Ay, there's the rub. For in that sleep of death what dreams may come. When we have shuffled[4] off this mortal coil. Must give us pause: there's the respect. That makes calamity of so long life;

For who would bear the whips and scorns of time, the oppressor's wrong, the proud man's contumely, the pangs of despised love, the law's delay, the insolence[5] of office and the spurns. That patient merit of the unworthy takes, when he himself might his quietus make with a bare bodkin?

Thus conscience does make cowards of us all; and thus the native hue of resolution is sicklied o'er with the pale cast of thought, and enterprises of great pith and moment with this regard their currents turn awry, and lose the name of action.

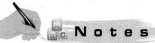 **Notes**

[1] 吊索
[2] 愤怒的
[3] 完成
[4] 拖着走
[5] 傲慢、无理的行为

1.Do you agree with Hamlet's understanding of death?

2.How do you understand Hamlet's character according to this monologue?

Analysis of Hamlet's Character

He has a complex personality. Firstly, he is smart but indecisive. He has planed a play which showed the reasons of his father's death to the king and his mother, and told Horatio observe the expression of his uncle. He is smart but when he had the chance to kill his uncle, he gave up because he thought if he killed his uncle when his uncle wass praying, his uncle would go to the Heaven after he was dead but his poor father can only stay in the Hell. Finally, his hesitation leads to the deaths of his mother, uncle and Laertes. Secondly, he is kind but sometimes cold-blooded. He is filial. When he heard that his father was murdered by his uncle, he decided to kill his uncle. And even his mother did an incestuous thing, Hamlet is still filial to his mother, he listened to his mother to stay in the Denmark. But Hamlet is also cold-blooded. He ignored the death of Rosencrantz and Guildenstern who were his classmates in University. He killed Polonius by mistake, but he didn't feel regretful and put the dead body in a lobby just anyhow. He even cheated his beloved girl that he was mad and cruel-hearted.

Hamlet has a strong sense of social responsibility. When he found that his father was murdered by his uncle, he decided to avenge his father's death. It is not only because his father was a good king but also because his uncle wasscheming and many officials would sacrifice principle for profit. He thought about not only his misfortune but also the social misfortune. The society was in chaos and confusion. Even Hamlet faced the strong feudal forces; he bravely fought against the feudal forces. But Hamlet fought against the forces alone from the beginning to the end of the play, so it is impossible for him to win. The conflict between Hamlet and Claudius is the biggest conflict in the play, and it represents the conflict between the humanism and feudalism, the conflict between the humanist ideals and the real gloomy society.

Hamlet's views sometimes are rather extreme. The murder made him think that the society is so gloomy and he neglected the other good things in the world. He said some bad words to Ophelia, He also told Ophelia to get to a nunnery. Hamlet also abused his mother with some bad words. Even though his mother married his uncle and forgot his father's true love, she loves Hamlet truly. She was really happy when she saw his son won in the battle.

Hamlet is good at thinking but sometimes his views are parochial. Hamlet was thinking from the beginning of the play. He thought about the reasons why his mother was so heartless that she can forget his father so quickly and married his uncle, he thought about why the king sent Rosencrantz and Guildenstern to him, he even thought about the problem of life. But sometimes his views are parochial. When his fellows stopped him following the ghost because they thought the ghost would do something bad to Hamlet, but Hamlet already didn't care about the life. But as a prince, he should live not because he will avenge his father's death but because he will ascend to the throne and govern the country in the future.

Hamlet has a so complex character. He is smart and indecisive, kind and cold-blooded. He has a strong sense of social responsibility. He represents the humanism and fought against the king who represents the feudalism. And his bad ending also represents the tragic destiny of that age.

 中文译文

哈姆雷特

生存还是毁灭，这是一个值得考虑的问题；默然忍受命运的暴虐的毒箭，或是挺身反抗人世的无涯的苦难，通过斗争把它们扫清，这两种行为，哪一种更高贵？

死了，睡着了，什么都完了；要是在这种睡眠之中，我们心头的创痛，以及其他无数血肉之躯所不能避免的打击，都可以从此消失，那正是我们求之不得的结局。死了，睡着了，睡着了也许还会做梦。嗯，阻碍就在这儿：因为当我们摆脱了这一具朽腐的皮囊以后，在那死的睡眠里，究竟将要做些什么梦，那不能不使我们踌躇顾虑。人们甘心久困于患难之中，也就是为了这个缘故。

谁愿意忍受人世的鞭挞和讥嘲、压迫者的凌辱、傲慢者的冷眼、被轻蔑的爱情的惨痛、法律的迁延、官吏的横暴和费尽艰辛所换来的小人的鄙视，要是他只要用一柄小小的刀子，就可以清算他自己的一生？

这样，重重的顾虑使我们全变成了懦夫，决心的炽热的光彩，被审慎的思维盖上了一层灰色，伟大的事业在这一种考虑之下，也会逆流而退，失去了行动的意义。

References

[1] 王佐良，等. 英国文学选注 [C]. 北京：商务印书馆，1983.

Unit 3   Francis Bacon (1561—1626)

Life

Francis Bacon, 1st Viscount St Alban, was an English philosopher, statesman, scientist, jurist, orator, and author. He served both as Attorney General and as Lord Chancellor of England. After his death, he remained extremely influential through his works, especially as philosophical advocate and practitioner of the scientific method during the scientific revolution.

Bacon has been called the father of empiricism. His works argued for the possibility of scientific knowledge based only upon inductive and careful observation of events in nature. Most importantly, he argued this could be achieved by use of a skeptical and methodical approach whereby scientists aim to avoid misleading themselves. While his own practical ideas about such a method, the Baconian method, did not have a long lasting influence, the general idea of the importance and possibility of a skeptical methodology makes Bacon the father of scientific method. This marked a new turn in the rhetorical and theoretical framework for science, the practical details of which are still central in debates about science and methodology today.

Bacon was generally neglected at court by Queen Elizabeth, but after the accession of King James I in 1603, Bacon was knighted. He was later created Baron Verulam in 1618 and Viscount St. Alban in 1621. Because he had no heirs, both titles became extinct upon his death in 1626, at 65 years of age. Bacon died of pneumonia, with one account by John Aubrey stating that he had contracted the condition while studying the effects of freezing on the preservation of meat.

Bacon's seminal work *Novum Organum* was influential in the 1630s and 1650s among scholars, in particular Sir Thomas Browne, who in his encyclopaedia Pseudodoxia Epidemica

(1646—1672) frequently adheres to a Baconian approach to his scientific enquiries. During the Restoration, Bacon was commonly invoked as a guiding spirit of the Royal Society founded under Charles II in 1660. During the 18th-century French Enlightenment, Bacon's non-metaphysical approach to science became more influential than the dualism of his French contemporary Descartes, and was associated with criticism of the ancien regime. In 1733 Voltaire introduced him to a French audience as the "father" of the scientific method, an understanding which had become widespread by the 1750s. In the 19th century his emphasis on induction was revived and developed by William Whewell, among others. He has been reputed as the "Father of Experimental Philosophy."

He also wrote a long treatise on *Medicine, History of Life and Death*, with natural and experimental observations for the prolongation of life.

One of his biographers, the historian William Hepworth Dixon, states: "Bacon's influence in the modern world is so great that every man who rides in a train, sends a telegram, follows a steam plough, sits in an easy chair, crosses the channel or the Atlantic, eats a good dinner, enjoys a beautiful garden, or undergoes a painless surgical operation, owes him something."

In 1902 Hugo von Hofmannsthal published a fictional letter addressed to Bacon and dated 1603, about a writer who is experiencing a crisis of language. Known as The Lord Chandos Letter, it has been proposed that Bacon was identified as its recipient as having laid the foundation for the work of scientists such as Ernst Mach, notable both for his academic distinction in the history and philosophy of the inductive sciences, and for his own contributions to physics.

Comments on Bacon's Essays

The *Essays* is the first writing English essay and plays an important role in the history of world literature. It has been translated into many languages as the enduring best seller. It was also named as "one of the 20 best books in human history" by American magazine Life in 1985. The book depicts a wide range of things in the world, showing the vicissitudes of life. It is said that many people are edified by the book's influence. As for today's young readers, the Essays is like a wise old man speaking with fervor and assurance, because it contains the essence of the sage. The main content of the book is some short comments telling Bacon's attitudes and ideas of different perspective of things. It involves politics, economy, religion, love, marriage, friendship, art, education, ethics and many other aspects. From *Of Truth*, *Of Death*, and *Of Nature in Men*, we can see he is a lover of philosophy; from *Of Empire*, *Of Ambition*, and *Of Boldness*, we can see he is a sophisticate of officialdom; from *Of Love*, *Of Friendship*, and *Of Marriage* and *Single Life*, we can see he is a man of taste; from *Of Adversity, Of Happiness*, and

Of Deformity, we can see he is a powerhouse of self-improvement; from *Of Discourse*, and *Of Simulation and Dissimulation*, we can see he is a wit of worldliness. Having such a positive and fulfilling political career, Bacon seems no time to do any other things. But his immortal fame and well reputation will be in place by his philosophical and literary works, rather than his political activities. The *Essays* is concise and comprehensive, wise and attractive. It contains many of the wise remarks of an experienced person, which not only refers to the politics but also explores many life philosophies.

In the Essays, there are many famous sayings such as "Histories make men wise; poets witty; the mathematics subtitle; natural philosophy deep; moral grave; logic and rhetoric able to contend."and "Travel, in the younger sort, is a part of education; in the elder, a part of experience. " Both of them and many other remarks in the book could reveal one aspect of the philosophy of life which can enlighten different groups of people in the society. Nevertheless, in my opinion young people are the largest beneficiaries, because their outlook on life, value and world is still in the formation stage and they need the correct direction to lead them. Nearly every significant entry point has been mentioned in the book which reminds and encourages us when we go through ups and downs in the life. We all need a lamp to illuminate the road and the *Essays* is just the lamp. It shows the great wisdom of the writer after experiencing so many hardships of life, and meanwhile it also shows the great wisdom of the world which is never plain sailing.

People can say Francis Bacon is a true modern philosopher. The whole set of his world outlook is secular rather than religious. He is a rationalist rather than a superstitious admirer, an empiricist rather than a sophist, a realist rather than a theorist. His profound knowledge, wonderful language together with science and technology resonate in a perfect way. Although Bacon is a loyal Englishman, his vision far exceeded his own borders. His scientific conjecture is intended as a starting point for the further discussion but not as the final conclusion. He is a sign of the times. The depth and breadth of his life is the eternal pursuit of us today.

Of Studies

Studies serve for delight, for ornament[1], and for ability. Their chief use for delight, is in privateness and retiring; for ornament, is in discourse; and for ability, is in the judgment and disposition of business. For expert and execute, and perhaps judge of particulars, one by one; but the general counsels, and the plots and marshalling[2] of affairs, come best form those that are learned.To spend too much time in studies is sloth[3]; to use them too much for ornament, is affectation; to make judgement wholly by their rules, is the humour of a scholar.

They perfect nature, and are perfected by experience: for natural abilities are like natural plants, that need proyning by study; and studies themselves do give forth directions too much at large, except they be bounded in by experience.

Crafty men contemn studies, simple men admire them, and wise men use them; for they teach not their own use; but that is a wisdom without them, and above them, won by observation.

Read not to contradict and confute[4]; nor to believe and take for granted; nor to find talk and discourse; but to weigh and consider.

Some books are to be tasted, others to be swallowed, and some few to be chewed and digested; that is, some books are to be read only in parts;

Others to be read, but not curiously; and some few to be read wholly, and with diligence[5] and attention. Some books also may be read by deputy, and extracts made of them by others; but that would be only in the less important arguments, and the meaner sort of books; else distilled books are, like common distilled waters, flashy things.

Reading maketh a full man; conference a ready man; and writing an exact man. And therefore, if a man write little, he had need have a great memory; if he confer little, he had need have a present wit; and if he read little, he had need have much cunning[6], to seem to know that he doth not.

Histories make men wise; poets witty; the mathematics subtile; natural philosophy deep; moral grave; logic and rhetoric able to contend. Abeunt studia in morse.

Nay there is no stand or impediment[7] in the wit, but may be wrought out by fit studies: like as diseases of the body may have appropriate exercises.

Bowling is good for the stone and reins; shooting for the lungs and breast; gentle walking for the stomach; riding for the head; and the like. So if a man's wit be wandering, let him study the mathematics; for in demonstrations, if his wit be called away never so little, he must begin again. If his wit be not apt to distinguish or find differences, let him study the schoolmen; for they are cymini sectores. If he be not apt to beat over matters, and to call up one thing to prove and illustrate another, let him study the lawyers' cases. So every defect of the mind may have a special receipt.

Notes

[1] 装饰品，点缀物

[2] 整理

[3] 怠惰，懒惰

[4] 驳斥，驳倒

[5] 勤奋，勤勉

[6] 狡猾的，巧妙的，可爱的

[7] 口吃，妨碍，阻止

 Questions

1.According to Bacon, why do people read books?

2.Do you agree with Bacon about his idea of reading?

 **中文译文**

论读书

读书足以怡情，足以博彩，足以长才。其怡情也，最见于独处幽居之时；其博彩也，最见于高谈阔论之中；其长才也，最见于处世判事之际。练达之士虽能分别处理细事或一一判别枝节，然纵观统筹、全局策划，则非好学深思者莫属。读书费时过多易惰，文采藻饰太盛则矫，全凭条文断事乃学究故态。读书补天然之不足，经验又补读书之不足；因为天生才干犹如自然花草，读书之后方知如何修剪移接。而书中所示，如不以经验范之，则大而无当。有手艺者鄙读书，无知者羡读书，唯明智之士用读书，然书并不以用处告人，用书之智不在书中，而在书外，全凭观察得之。读书时不可存心诘难作者，不可尽信书上所言，亦不可只为寻章摘句，而应推敲细思。书有可浅尝者，有可吞食者，少数则须咀嚼消化。换言之，有只需读其部分者，有只需大体涉猎者，少数则需全读，读时需全神贯注、孜孜不倦。书亦可请人代读，摘要也可请人代作，但只限题材较次或价值不高者，否则书经提炼犹如水经蒸馏，淡而无味矣。

读书使人充实，讨论使人机智，笔记使人准确。因此不常动笔者须记忆特强，不常讨论者须天生聪颖，不常读书者须欺世有术，始能无知而显有知。读史使人明智，读诗使人灵秀，数学使人周密，科学使人深刻，伦理学使人庄重，逻辑修辞使人善辩。凡有所学，皆成性格。人之才智如有滞碍，无不可读适当之书使之顺畅，一如身体百病，皆可借相宜之运动除之。保龄利睾肾，射箭利胸肺，慢步利肠胃，骑马利头脑，诸如此类。如智力不集中，可令读数学，因为演题须全神贯注，稍有分散即须重演；如不能辨异，可令读经院哲学，因为研究经院哲学者吹毛求疵者也；如不善分析论证，不善以一物阐证另一物，可令读律师之案卷。头脑中凡有缺陷，皆有特药可医。

References

[1] Drabble, Margaret. *The Oxford Companion to English Literature*[M]. Beijing: Foreign Language Teaching and Research Press, 2005.

[2] Rogers, Pat. *An Outline of English Literature*[M]. Oxford University Press, 1998.

Unit 4   John Milton (1608—1674)

Life

John Milton (1608—1674) was an English poet, polemicist, man of letters, and civil servant for the Commonwealth of England under Oliver Cromwell. He wrote at a time of religious flux and political upheaval, and is best known for his epic poem *Paradise Lost* (1667), written in blank verse.

Milton's poetry and prose reflect deep personal convictions, a passion for freedom and self-determination, and the urgent issues and political turbulence of his day. Writing in English, Latin, Greek, and Italian, he achieved international renown within his lifetime, and his celebrated Areopagitica (1644)—written in condemnation of pre-publication censorship—is among history's most influential and impassioned defences of free speech and freedom of the press.

William Hayley's 1796 biography called him the "greatest English author", and he remains generally regarded "as one of the preeminent writers in the English language", though critical reception has oscillated in the centuries since his death (often on account of his republicanism). Samuel Johnson praised *Paradise Lost* as "a poem which...with respect to design may claim the first place, and with respect to performance, the second, among the productions of the human mind", though he described Milton's politics as those of an "acrimonious and surly republican."

Paradise Lost

Milton's magnum opus, the blank-verse epic poem *Paradise Lost*, was composed by the blind and impoverished Milton from 1658 to 1664 (first edition), with small but significant revisions published in 1674 (second edition). As a blind poet, Milton dictated his verse to a series of aides in his employ. It has been argued that the poem reflects his personal despair at the failure of the Revolution, yet affirms an ultimate optimism in human potential. Some literary critics have argued that Milton encoded many references to his unyielding support for the "Good Old Cause."

On 27 April 1667, Milton sold the publication rights for *Paradise Lost* to publisher Samuel Simmons for £5, equivalent to approximately £7,400 income in 2008, with a further £5 to be paid if and when each print run sold out of between 1,300 and 1,500 copies. The first run was a quarto edition priced at three shillings per copy, published in August 1667, and it sold out in eighteen months.

Milton followed up the publication *Paradise Lost* with its sequel *Paradise Regained,* which was published alongside the tragedy Samson Agonistes in 1671. Both of these works also resonate with Milton's post-Restoration political situation. Just before his death in 1674, Milton supervised a second edition of Paradise Lost, accompanied by an explanation of "why the poem rhymes not", and prefatory verses by Andrew Marvell. In 1673, Milton republished his 1645 Poems, as well as a collection of his letters and the Latin prolusions from his Oxford days. A 1668 edition of *Paradise Lost*, reported to have been Milton's personal copy, is now housed in the archives of the University of Western Ontario.

Comments on *Paradise Lost*

The writer and critic Samuel Johnson wrote that Paradise Lost shows off "[Milton's] peculiar power to astonish" and that "[Milton] seems to have been well acquainted with his own genius, and to know what it was that Nature had bestowed upon him more bountifully than upon others: the power of displaying the vast, illuminating the splendid, enforcing the awful, darkening the gloomy, and aggravating the dreadful."

Milton scholar John Leonard interpreted the "impious war" between Heaven and Hell as civil war :

Paradise Lost is, among other things, a poem about civil war. Satan raises "impious war in Heav'n" (i 43) by leading a third of the angels in revolt against God. The term "impious war" implies that civil war is impious. But Milton applauded the English people for having the courage to depose and execute King Charles I. In his poem, however, he takes the side of "Heav'n's awful Monarch'" (iv 960). Critics have long wrestled with the question of why an antimonarchist and defender of regicide should have chosen a subject that obliged him to defend monarchical authority.

The editors at the Poetry Foundation argue that Milton's criticism of the English monarchy was being directed specifically at the Stuart monarchy and not at the monarchy system in general.

In a similar vein, critic and writer C.S. Lewis argued that there was no contradiction in Milton's position in the poem since "Milton believed that God was his natural superior and that Charles Stuart was not." Lewis interpreted the poem as a genuine Christian morality tale.

Other critics, like William Empson, view it as a more ambiguous work, with Milton's complex characterization of Satan playing a large part in that perceived ambiguity. Empson argued that "Milton deserves credit for making God wicked, since the God of Christianity is 'a wicked God." Leonard places Empson's interpretation "in the [Romantic interpretive] tradition of William Blake and Percy Bysshe Shelley." As Blake famously wrote, "The reason Milton wrote in fetters when he wrote of Angels & God, and at liberty when of Devils & Hell, is because he was a true Poet and of the Devil's party without knowing it." This quotation succinctly represents the way in which the 18th- and 19th-century English Romantic poets viewed Milton.

Characters

Satan

Satan is the first major character introduced in the poem. Formerly called Lucifer, he was the most beautiful of all angels in Heaven, and is a tragic figure who describes himself with the now-famous quote "Better to reign in Hell than serve in Heaven." He is introduced to Hell after he leads a failed rebellion to wrest control of Heaven from God. Satan's desire to rebel against his creator stems from his unwillingness to be subjugated by God and his Son, claiming that angels are "self-begot, self-raised," and thereby denying God's authority over them as their creator.

Satan is deeply arrogant, albeit powerful and charismatic. Satan's persuasive powers are evident throughout the book; not only is he cunning and deceptive, but he is also able to rally the fallen angels to continue in the rebellion after their agonizing defeat in the Angelic War. He argues that God rules as a tyrant and that all the angels ought to rule as gods. Though commonly understood to be the antagonizing force in Paradise Lost, Satan may be best defined as a tragic or Hellenic hero. According to William McCollom, one quality of the classical tragic hero is that he is not perfectly good and that his defeat is caused by a tragic flaw, as Satan causes both the downfall of man and the eternal damnation of his fellow fallen angels despite his dedication to his comrades. In addition, Satan's Hellenic qualities, such as his immense courage and perhaps, lack of completely defined morals, compound his tragic nature.

Satan's status as a protagonist in the epic poem is debatable; Milton arguably characterizes him as such, but Satan lacks several key traits that would otherwise make him the definitive protagonist in the work. One deciding factor that insinuates his role as the protagonist in the story is that most often a protagonist is heavily characterized and far better described than the other characters, and the way the character is written is meant to make him seem more interesting or special to the reader For that matter, Satan is both well described and is depicted as being quite versatile in that he is shown as having the capacity to do evil whilst retaining his characteristic sympathetic qualities and thus it is this complex and relatable nature makes him a likely candidate for the story's overarching protagonist.

According to Ibrahim Taha's definition of a protagonist the protagonist must be able to exist in and of himself or herself and that the secondary characters in the work exist only to further the plot for the protagonist. Because Satan does not exist solely for himself, as without God he would not have a role to play in the story, he may not be viewed as protagonist because of the continual shifts in perspective and relative importance of characters in each book of the work. Satan's existence in the story involves his rebellion against God and his determination to corrupt the beings he creates in order to create evil so that there can be a discernable balance and justice for both himself and his fallen angels. Therefore, it is more probable that he exists in order to combat God, making his status as the definitive protagonist of the work relative to each book.

Satan's status as a traditional hero in the work is similarly up to debate as the term "hero" evokes different meanings depending on the time and the person giving the definition and is thus a matter of contention within the text. According to Aristotle, a hero is someone who is "superhuman, godlike, and divine" but is also human. A hero would have to either be a human with God-like powers or the offspring of God. While Milton gives reason to believe that Satan is superhuman, as he was originally an angel, he is anything but human. Therefore, according to Aristotle's definition of a hero alone, Satan is not a hero. Torquato Tasso and Francesco Piccolomini expanded on Aristotle's definition and declared that for someone to be considered heroic one has to be perfectly or overly virtuous. Satan repeatedly demonstrates a lack of virtue throughout the story as he intends to tempt God's creations with evil in order to destroy the good God is trying to create. Satan goes against God's law and therefore becomes corrupt and lacking of virtue and, as Piccolimini warned, "vice may be mistaken for heroic virtue." Satan is very devoted to his cause, although that cause is evil but he strives to spin his sinister aspirations to appear as good ones. Satan achieves this end multiple times throughout the text as he riles up his band of fallen angels during his speech by deliberately telling them to do evil to explain God's hypocrisy and again during his entreaty to Eve. He makes his intentions seem pure and positive even when they are rooted in evil and according to Steadman, this is the chief reason that readers often mistake Satan as a hero.

Although Satan's army inevitably loses the war against God, Satan achieves a position of power and begins his reign in Hell with his band of loyal followers, composed of fallen angels, which is described to be a "third of heaven." Satan's characterization as the leader of a failing cause folds into this as well and is best exemplified through his own quote, "to be weak is to be miserable; Doing or Suffering", as through shared solidarity espoused by empowering rhetoric, Satan riles up his comrades in arms and keeps them focused towards their shared goal. Similar to Milton's republican sentiments of overthrowing the King of England for both better representation and parliamentary power, Satan argues that his shared rebellion with the fallen angels is an effort to "explain the hypocrisy of God", and in doing so, they will be treated with the respect and acknowledgement that they deserve. As scholar Wayne Rebhorn argues, "Satan insists that he and his fellow revolutionaries held their places by right and even leading him to claim that they were self-created and self-sustained" and thus Satan's position in the rebellion is much like that of his own real world creator.

Adam

Adam is the first human created by God. Though initially alone, Adam demands a mate from God. Considered God's prized creation, Adam, along with his wife, rules over all the creatures of the world and resides in the Garden of Eden. He is more gregarious than Eve, and yearns for her company. His complete infatuation with Eve, while pure in and of itself, eventually contributes to his joining her in disobedience to God.

Unlike the Biblical Adam, before he leaves Paradise this version of Adam is given a glimpse of the future of mankind (including a synopsis of stories from the *Old and New Testaments*) by the Archangel Michael.

Eve

Eve is the second human created by God, taken from one of Adam's ribs and shaped into a female form of Adam. Far from the traditional model of a good wife, she is often unwilling to be submissive towards Adam. She is more intelligent and curious about external ideas than her husband. Though happy, she longs for knowledge and, more specifically, self-knowledge. Her first act in existence is to turn away from Adam and look at and ponder her own reflection. Eve is extremely beautiful and thoroughly in love with Adam, though may feel suffocated by his constant presence. One day, she convinces Adam that it would be good for them to split up and work different parts of the Garden. In her solitude, she is tempted by Satan to sin against God. Adam shortly follows along with her.

The Son of God

The Son of God is the spirit who will become incarnate as Jesus Christ, though he is never named explicitly, since he has not yet entered human form. Milton's God refers to the Son as "My word, my wisdom, and effectual might", but Milton believed in a subordinationist doctrine of Christology that regarded the Son as secondary to the Father. The poem is not explicitly anti-trinitarian, but is consistent with Milton's convictions. The Son is the ultimate hero of the epic and is infinitely powerful, single-handedly defeating Satan and his followers and driving them into Hell. The Son of God tells Adam and Eve about God's judgment after their sin. He sacrificially volunteers to journey to the World, become a man himself, and redeem the Fall of Man through his own death and resurrection. In the final scene, a vision of Salvation through the Son of God is revealed to Adam by Michael. Still, the name, Jesus of Nazareth, and the details of Jesus' story are not depicted in the poem.

God the Father

God the Father is the creator of Heaven, Hell, the world, and of everyone and everything there is, through the agency of His Son. He desires glory and praise from all his creations. He is an all-powerful, all-knowing, infinitely good being who cannot be overthrown by even the great army of angels Satan incites against him. The stated purpose of the poem is to justify the ways of God to men, so God often converses with the Son of God concerning his plans and reveals his motives regarding his actions. The poem portrays God's process of creation in the way that Milton believed it was done, with God creating Heaven, Earth, Hell, and all the creatures that inhabit these separate planes from part of Himself, not out of nothing. Thus, according to Milton, the ultimate authority of God derives from his being the "author" of creation. Satan tries to justify his rebellion by denying this aspect of God and claiming self-creation, but he admits to himself this is not the case, and that God "deserved no such return/ From me, whom He created what I was."

Raphael

Raphael is an archangel whom God sends to warn Adam about Satan's infiltration of Eden and to warn him that Satan is going to try to curse Adam and Eve. He also has a lengthy discussion with the curious Adam regarding creation and events which transpired in Heaven.

Michael

Michael is a mighty archangel who fought for God in the Angelic War. In the first battle, he wounds Satan terribly with a powerful sword that God designed to even cut through the substance of angels. After Adam and Eve disobey God by eating from the Tree of Knowledge, God sends the angel Michael to visit Adam and Eve. His duty is to escort Adam and Eve out of Paradise. Before he does this, Michael shows Adam visions of the future which cover an outline of the Bible, from the story of Cain and Abel in Genesis, up through the story of Jesus Christ in the *New Testament*.

Introduction to *Paradise Lost*

Paradise Lost was written in such a historical period. The theme of *Paradise Lost* was chosen from the foundation of American literary−Bible. Some of these theological concepts and terminology related to human nature is essential for understanding the epic. The theme of *Paradise Lost* was chosen from the "Genesis." He gave the only 100 words bizarre story twists and turns and made it a new epic.

Paradise Lost is consisted of 12 parts. Part 1, the reasons and results of the events; part 2, Satan and angles discuss how to fight against God; part 3, God decides how to give human a gift; part 4, Satan meets with Adam and Eve and his temptation; part 5, the angels warn Adam about

Satan's temptation; part 6, the angels and Satan fight against God; part 7, Adam asks angles about world problems, and gets answers; part 8, Adam asks angles about how celestial bodies run, but he is not satisfied with the answers; part 9, Satan pretends as a snake and ask Adam and Eve to eat the forbidden fruit; part 10, God is so angry and Adam also regrets; part11, Adam and Eve are expelled from the Paradise; part 12, Adam and Eve leave the paradise and then lost the paradise.

Paradise Lost describes that: after escaping the dungeon, Satan went to the God to establish the Garden of Eden for human ancestors—Adam and Eve. They ate the forbidden fruit tree due to the temptation of Satan. Therefore, because of their ignorance and depravity, God expelled Adam and Eve from the Garden of Eden. Their fault was the original sin of human which caused death, suffering, famine, pestilence on Earth. However, God still gave human the chance to salvation. God sent Jesus Christ to do redemption price, so that mankind could return to paradise with tough faith and sincere repentance. Milton revealed the failure of State and the Church through the research of history. Many of his controversial works reflect this phenomenon. Many commentators have analyzed the works of Milton. The commentators who convinced the Marxist said that: in society, all undertakings of the literature who were keen on promoting the development of cultural were ultimately based on economic change. John Milton is a British progressive camp and a typical representative of the bourgeoisie. His literary thought reflected in his works fully reflects the status of the English bourgeois revolution in that period.

Paradise Lost

Torments him; round he throws his baleful[1] eyes

That witness'd huge affliction and dismay

Mixt with obdurate pride and stedfast hate:

At once as far as Angels kenn he views

The dismal Situation waste and wilde,

A Dungeon horrible, on all sides round

As one great Furnace flam'd, yet from those flames

No light[2], but rather darkness visible

Serv'd only to discover sights of woe,

Regions of sorrow, doleful shades, where peace

And rest can never dwell, hope never comes

That comes to all; but torture without end

Still urges, and a fiery Deluge, fed

With ever-burning Sulphur unconsum'd:

Such place Eternal Justice had prepar'd

For those rebellious, here their Prison ordain'd

In utter darkness, and their portion set

As far remov'd from God and light of Heav'n

As from the Center [3]thrice to th' utmost Pole.

O how unlike the place from whence they fell!

There the companions of his fall, o'rewhelm'd

With Floods and Whirlwinds of tempestuous fire,

He soon discerns, and weltring by his side

One next himself in power, and next in crime,

Long after known in PALESTINE, and nam'd

BEELZEBUB.[4] To whom th' Arch-Enemy,

And thence in Heav'n call'd Satan, with bold words

Breaking the horrid silence thus began.

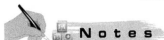 **N o t e s**

[1]malignant, as well as suffering

[2]as far as angels can see

[3]The earth Milton makes use in Paradise Lost of two images of the cosmos: first, the earth is the center of the created cosmos of nine concentric spheres; but second, the earth and the whole created cosmos are a mere appendage, hanging from Heaven by a golden chain, in the larger, aboriginal, and less shapely cosmos. In the present passage, the fall from Heaven to Hell through the aboriginal universe is described as thrite as far as the distance (in the created universe) from the center (earth) to the outermost sphere.

[4]In Christian and Biblical sources, Beelzebub is another name for the devil, similar to Satan. In Christian demonology, he is one of the seven princes of Hell according to Catholic views on Hell. The Dictionnaire Infernal describes Beelzebub as a demonic fly who is also known

as the "Lord of the Flies." The god of the Philistine city of Ekron, a Canaanite god. The name Beelzebub is linked with the Caananite god Baal.

Questions

1. How do you understand the character of Satan?
2. What does Milton want to express in this poem?
3. As a college student, should we have the spirit of rebellion or obedience?

Analysis

Paradise Lost which played a powerful role in promoting the development of the epic was the product of Puritanism, as well as rooted in Milton's personal beliefs and faith. The creative style of Milton was different from any writers after him. Although Milton was involved in Puritan movement, his religious ideas and political arguments all promoted he development of capitalism. Therefore, we can saw that secular humanism which provided a new way to deal with social problems was the combination of the thoughts of humanist and religious doctrine. It can be said, *Paradise Lost* was the epic of mankind, but also an epic display of human nature. Milton understood the true meaning of truth and his own environment in which he used to express the epic figures of the revolutionary ideas and his fighting spirit. And he also expressed the despair and anguish brought by the restoration.

Milton was progressive bourgeoisie in fact, and his advanced thinking related to social progress. He believed that social progress, as well as the doctrine of God was the rational laws of nature. Therefore, the advanced productive forces will eventually replace the bourgeois which hindered the pace of capitalist development. That was a perfect reflection of historical inevitability. In *Paradise Lost,* the Satan fought against God and the feudal kingdom of heaven that was the civil war between the two classes. Justice would eventually prevail over evil. The King Charles I was brought to the guillotine. However, with the Republic of depravity and corruption, the bourgeoisie compromised with the House of Stuart king Charles II, and they broke the revolutionary movement the restoration together. Representatives of the advanced productive forces went against the law of social development. Milton used Adam and Eve to map the historical events. Its meaning was very clear. From an objective point of view, the masses were the driving force of historical progress and the ultimate source of social progress. But the bourgeoisie ignored the power of people. Milton expressed his own political position and revolutionary consciousness by *Paradise Lost*. He made a series of thinking about human nature. This was why he used human degradation to be the creative theme. Therefore, we could say that his epic was based on history. He was a devout Puritan, but his political views were applicable to the materialist outlook on life.

In *Paradise Lost*, the Satan was the most successful image the author shaped, especially in the first two volumes. He was an image of a rebel. The romantic poet, Blake Byron Shelley, highly praised for this image of heroism. He said: "Satan was on behalf of the imaginative soul of mankind." The reason why the character Satan could get admiration of many romantic poets and readers was mostly that this image reflected the will of freedom.

First of all, the epic praised Satan's spirit of resistance.

In traditional concepts, Satan was the devil from hell, the scum of angels, human enemies. Because of his ambition and rebellion he was thrown into the abyss of misery by God. However, in *Paradise Lost*, the poet portrayed Satan as a brave hero that went against the usual religious beliefs.

The intention of describing this extraordinary momentum and power of Satan was to emphasis his courageous and prudent and his spirit of hating tyrants and resisting God. Although the struggle was failed, but he had never doubted that his struggle was a justice action, he had never regretted to fall into hell where he suffered in the flames and he had never been desperate and hopeless. He convinced that his spirit of resistance would never disappear and his revolutionary willing would never depress.

It should be said that: this was the reflection of the revolutionary spirit of the bourgeois and a song of all revolutionary fighters.

The epic also describes that, after being expelled from heaven and thrown into the flames of hell, Satan was even still full of the indomitable fighting spirit. He vowed to continue the confrontation with God. When reading those words filled with courage, all readers could see his will to overcome all the difficulties and accomplish all his plans.

Second, the epic had also criticized the autocratic rule of God. Whether in the ancient Greek myth, or religious traditions, God had always been portrayed as the ruler of the universe and the absolute authority. Even in Dante's famous work Divine Comedy filled with modern spirit, God was still praised as a true, good, and kind image. While in *Paradise Lost,* God was a typical image of tyranny. The poet condemned God through Satan's words. On the surface, God had given human free will; in fact, he had suppressed the true freedom.

Obviously, the poet's criticism and condemnation of God were out from the social reality of United Kingdom. The tyrant was the embodiment of Stuart. Milton laid his own political tendencies in the great Satan. He portrayed Satan's resistance as the justice resistance to authoritarian rule and a bold challenge to the violent regime.

In *Paradise Lost*, Lenovo was rich and metaphor was innovative. This was another artistic characteristic of Paradise Lost. This was mainly reflected in the psychological description of Adam and Eve when they were driven out after eating the forbidden fruit. The story of Adam and Eve in *Bible* was just a few words and very specific. There was no document about their life and inner feelings. But in *Paradise Lost*, the story was written vivid, flesh and colorful. In Milton's imagination and description, the worldly things seemed to have feelings and emotions.

Milton had made the most powerful cry for freedom and equality. He attempted to suggest that the heaven paradise had lost, but the earth paradise would begin. The poet's unique writing style created a new poetry generation. This was also the most important contribution of *Paradise Lost* to British literary language

In short, *Paradise Lost* combined the political, ideological, religious, artistic elements, and achieved the perfect unity of arts. This epic gives use a wonderful art pleasure.

 中文译文

失乐园

他以邪恶的眼神望向四周

只看到巨大的痛苦和沮丧

混合着冷酷的骄傲和笃实的憎恨

旋以天使之眼看到

荒芜凄惨的境遇

四周皆是恐怖的地牢

如巨大的洪炉，那火焰之中

没有光，只有看得见的黑暗

只为让你看见悲哀的景象

悲痛的领域，阴沉的影子，

永无和平与休息，人人都有的希望在这里

永不来临，只有无穷的折磨

仍在以燃烧不尽的硫黄，

持续那烈火的狂潮

这样的地方是永恒的正义

为反叛者所准备，这里注定是他们的监狱

在绝对的黑暗中，他们的身体

被置于离神和天堂的光明的玄远之地

三倍于天堂的中心到最远支柱的距离

与他们坠落的地方多么的不同

那和他一起坠落的，是无法抗拒的

有如洪水旋风般的狂暴的火焰

他很快辨认出，在他之旁

和他一样具有权力和罪行的

那以后很久才在巴勒斯坦被名以

别卜西以及他们头号敌人的

当时在天堂被称作撒旦的，

以大胆言辞打破恐怖的沉默的魔王

Sonnet[1]

On His Blindness [2]

When I consider how my light [3]is spent,

Ere half my days, in this dark world and wide,

And that one talent which is death to hide

Lodged with me useless, though my soul more bent

To serve there with my Maker[4], and present

My true account, lest he returning chide,

"Doth God exact day labor, light denied?"

I fondly ask; but Patience, to prevent

That murmur, soon replies: "God doth not need"

Either man's work or his own gifts; who best;

Bear his mild yoke[5], they serve him best. His state

Is kingly: thousands at his bidding speed

They also serve who only stan[6]

Notes

[1] 这是一首十四行诗，属彼得拉克体，韵式为 ABBA，ABBA，CDE，CDE，仍是由意大利式的前八行（octave）和后六行 (sestet) 两个部分组成。前八行描写诗人对失明的沮丧、悲观情绪，甚至怀疑上帝的不公待遇。（费了这么多行才转到正题："质问上帝"，但想到那是跟上帝说话，而且弥尔顿那么虔诚，他说话一定是小心的、委婉的。一个 fondly 就能充分说明他战战兢兢、谨慎谦卑的心情。）后六行用对话的形式，描写内心争斗，并在这个过程中，让自己从郁闷的心情中解脱出来。自己与自己的斗争往往是一种最残酷的斗争，这种纠结往往会使人痛苦不堪。然而，从弥尔顿的诗行中，我们看到的是坦然，是面对，是希望。这种对生命的积极向上的态度体现了弥尔顿是多么伟大！失明并不是侍奉上帝的障碍，而是侍奉上帝的必然部分，只有耐心地接受这个事实，才能做出更大的成就，来感谢上帝的恩赐。人生固然有很多痛苦，具有大智大勇的人，在默默忍受命运折磨的时候，永远不会放弃希望和等待。华兹华斯称赞十四行诗在弥尔顿的笔下"变成了战斗号角，他从中吹出生机蓬勃的曲调"。

[2] 弥尔顿从 1644 年视力就开始下降，1652 年因《为英国人民声辩》(A Defense of the English People) 的写作过度劳累而导致双目失明，这时他才 44 岁。此诗在 1655 年写成，当时弥尔顿 47 岁。弥尔顿在文学上的地位仅次于莎士比亚。实际上，他大名鼎鼎的 12 卷史诗《失乐园》也是在失明状态下写成的。

[3] 诗歌的主调是黑暗与光明的对照，通过对比和头韵的写作手法，让读者体会到他失明的痛苦。比如 mind 和 soul 的对比；days, dark 及 world, wide 的头韵，等等。

[4] 诗歌涉及不少典故，比如，他不但几次提到上帝（Maker, God），而且还提到那时当货币使用的 talent。这个 talent 本意是才能、天赋，但在《圣经》里是这样的：《马太福音》第二十五章的故事，说主人要到远方去，把三位仆人叫来，按每人的才能派给银子去赚更多的钱。他用 talent 做单位，古时 talent 是衡量金子、银子的重量单位。第一位仆人拿到五千 talent 银子，第二个拿到二千，第三个拿到一千。第一和第二个仆人都去做生意，只有第三个仆人，把一千 talent 银子埋在了地里。等主人回来算账时，第一个人赚了一倍，有一万，第二个人也赚了一倍，有四千，他却仍是一千。主人便发怒，夺过他的

一千给了第一个仆人；并且把这个废物仆人丢在黑暗里，哀哭切齿。因此，"one talent"，"一千银子"，意思是说："天赋最低的（才能）""庸才"。所以，后面的 account 显然指代的是这三个人的账面所得的财富。而恰恰中文的"才"和"财"同音。

[5] "mild yoke" 的典故也是出于《马太福音》第十一章：*11:29 Take my yoke upon you, and learn of me; for I am meek and lowly in heart: and ye shall find rest unto your souls.（我心里柔和谦卑，你们当负我的轭，学我的样式，这样，你们心里就必得享安息。）*11:30 For my yoke is easy, and my burden is light.（因为我的轭是宽适的，我的担子是轻省的。）

[6] 诗歌用了大量跨行手法，使得全诗有一种近乎散文的婉转语调，读者一直读到最后一行，才感觉舒了一口气，因为最后一行是独立完整的诗行，直截了当，清晰得很。这种手法也使得全诗浑然一体，你不得不读下去，直到最后看到结论。

 中文译文

十四行诗

我想到，在这黑暗的茫茫世界上

人生尚未过半，就耗尽英光

想到，我这点小财（才）埋起来就等于死亡

可它却在我这闲置荒废，虽然我的灵魂

多么想用它为造物主服务，并悉数供奉

我全部的财富，以免遭他的责骂，

于此，我不禁傻问："上帝不给光明却要人白日劳作？"

"忍耐"为阻止我喃喃地抱怨，

立刻过来答道："上帝不要求"

人的劳作，也不要你还他礼物；只要你

能忍受一点点痛苦，架起他的车辕，就是最好的侍奉。上帝

就像是一位国王，臣民千计，都听他调遣，他们努力奉献

不停地奔波忙碌于沧海桑田。

坚定不移地站立和等待也是侍奉。

References

[1] 苏煜. 英国诗歌赏析 [C]. 北京：新华出版社，2006.

Unit 5   John Bunyan (1628—1688)

Life

John Bunyan was an English writer and Baptist preacher best remembered as the author of the Christian allegory *The Pilgrim's Progress*. In addition to *The Pilgrim's Progress*, Bunyan wrote nearly sixty titles, many of them expanded sermons.

Bunyan came from the village of Elstow, near Bedford. He had some schooling and at the age of sixteen joined the Parliamentary army during the first stage of the English Civil War. After three years in the army he returned to Elstow and took up the trade of tinker, which he had learned from his father. He became interested in religion after his marriage, attending first the parish church and then joining the Bedford Meeting, a nonconformist group in Bedford, and becoming a preacher. After the restoration of the monarch, when the freedom of nonconformists was curtailed, Bunyan was arrested and spent the next twelve years in jail as he refused to undertake to give up preaching. During this time he wrote a spiritual autobiography, *Grace Abounding to the Chief of Sinners*, and began work on his most famous book, *The Pilgrim's Progress*, which was not published until some years after his release.

Bunyan's later years, in spite of another shorter term of imprisonment, were spent in relative comfort as a popular author and preacher, and pastor of the Bedford Meeting. He died aged 59 after falling ill on a journey to London and is buried in Bunhill Fields. *The Pilgrim's Progress* became one of the most published books in the English language; 1,300 editions having been printed by 1938, 250 years after the author's death.

He is remembered in the Church of England with a Lesser Festival on 30 August, and on the liturgical calendar of the United States Episcopal Church on 29 August. Some other churches of the Anglican Communion, such as the Anglican Church of Australia, honour him on the day of his death (31 August).

The Pilgrim's Progress

The Pilgrim's Progress from *This World to That Which Is to Come; Delivered under the Similitude of a Dream* is a 1678 Christian allegory written by John Bunyan. It is regarded as one of the most significant works of religious English literature, has been translated into more than 200 languages, and has never been out of print.

Bunyan began his work while in the Bedfordshire county prison for violations of the *Conventicle Act*, which prohibited the holding of religious services outside the auspices of the established Church of England. Early Bunyan scholars such as John Brown believed *The Pilgrim's Progress* was begun in Bunyan's second, shorter imprisonment for six months in 1675, but more recent scholars such as Roger Sharrock believe that it was begun during Bunyan's initial, more lengthy imprisonment from 1660 to 1672 right after he had written his spiritual autobiography, *Grace Abounding to the Chief of Sinners*.

The English text comprises 108,260 words and is divided into two parts, each reading as a continuous narrative with no chapter divisions. The first part was completed in 1677 and entered into the Stationers' Register on 22 December 1677. It was licensed and entered in the "Term Catalogue" on 18 February 1678, which is looked upon as the date of first publication. After the first edition of the first part in 1678, an expanded edition, with additions written after Bunyan was freed, appeared in 1679. The Second Part appeared in 1684. There were eleven editions of the first part in John Bunyan's lifetime, published in successive years from 1678 to 1685 and in 1688, and there were two editions of the second part, published in 1684 and 1686.

Plot of The *Pilgrim's Progress*

First Part

The entire book is presented as a dream sequence narrated by an omniscient narrator. The allegory's protagonist, Christian, is an everyman character, and the plot centres on his journey from his hometown, the "City of Destruction" ("this world"), to the "Celestial City" ("that which is to come": Heaven) atop Mount Zion. Christian is weighed down by a great burden—the knowledge of his sin—which he believed came from his reading "the book in his hand" (the Bible). This burden, which would cause him to sink into Hell, is so unbearable that Christian must seek deliverance. He meets Evangelist as he is walking out in the fields, who directs him to the "Wicket Gate" for deliverance. Since Christian cannot see the "Wicket Gate" in the distance, Evangelist directs him to go to a "shining light," which Christian thinks he sees. Christian leaves his home, his wife, and children to save himself: he cannot persuade them to accompany him. Obstinate and Pliable go after Christian to bring him back, but Christian refuses. Obstinate returns disgusted, but Pliable is persuaded to go with Christian, hoping to take advantage of the Paradise that Christian claims lies at the end of his journey. Pliable's journey with Christian is cut short when the two of them fall into the Slough of Despond, a boggy mire-like swamp where pilgrims' doubts, fears, temptations, lusts, shames, guilts, and sins of their present condition of being a sinner are used to sink them into the mud of the swamp. It is there in that bog where Pliable abandons Christian after getting himself out. After struggling to the other side of the slough, Christian is pulled out by Help, who has heard his cries and tells him the swamp is made out of the decadence, scum, and filth of sin, but the ground is good at the narrow Wicket Gate. Finally Christian has a rough time because of his past sins wearing him down, but Hopeful helps him over; and they are welcomed into the Celestial City.

Second Part

The Second Part of *The Pilgrim's Progress* presents the pilgrimage of Christian's wife, Christiana; their sons; and the maiden, Mercy. They visit the same stopping places that Christian visited, with the addition of Gaius' Inn between the Valley of the Shadow of Death and Vanity Fair, but they take a longer time in order to accommodate marriage and childbirth for the four sons and their wives. The hero of the story is Great-Heart, a servant of the Interpreter, who is the pilgrims' guide to the Celestial City. He kills four giants called Giant Grim, Giant Maul, Giant Slay-Good, and Giant Despair and participates in the slaying of a monster called Legion that terrorizes the city of Vanity Fair.

The passage of years in this second pilgrimage better allegorizes the journey of the Christian life. By using heroines, Bunyan, in the Second Part, illustrates the idea that women as well as men can be brave pilgrims.

Comments on *The Pilgrim's Progress*

The Pilgrim's Progress is a book that combines with theology and literature, but at first it is a work of religious literature. Bunyan is a religious fanaticism at that time. At this point, his work can't put up without his religion. So the *Bible* becomes his original to create this masterpiece. Also the life experience of Bunyan gives him a lot of creation material. What's more, the English *Bible* is the model of it. He makes *The Pilgrim's Progress* with his genius. In this book, you can find the shadow and lingering charm of the *Bible*.

Characters

First Part

Christian, who was born named Graceless, the protagonist in the First Part, whose journey to the Celestial City is the plot of the story.

Evangelist, the religious man who puts Christian on the path to the Celestial City. He also shows Christian a book, which readers assume to be the Bible.

Obstinate, one of the two residents of the City of Destruction, who run after Christian when he first sets out, in order to bring him back. Like his name, he is stubborn and is disgusted with Christian and with Pliable for making a journey that he thinks is nonsense.

Pliable, the other of the two, who goes with Christian until both of them fall into the Slough of Despond, (a boggy mire composed of the decadence and filthiness of sin and a swamp that makes the fears and doubts of a present and past sinner real). Pliable escapes from the slough and returns home. Like his name, he is insecure and goes along with some things for a little while but quickly gives up on them.

Help, Christian's rescuer from the Slough of Despond.

Second Part

Mr. Sagacity, a guest narrator who meets Bunyan himself in his new dream and recounts the events of the Second Part up to the arrival at the Wicket Gate.

Christiana, wife of Christian, who leads her four sons and neighbour Mercy on pilgrimage.

Matthew, Christian and Christiana's eldest son, who marries Mercy.

Samuel, second son, who marries Grace, Mr. Mnason's daughter.

Joseph, third son, who marries Martha, Mr. Mnason's daughter.

James, fourth and youngest son, who marries Phoebe, Gaius's daughter.

Mercy, Christiana's neighbour, who goes with her on pilgrimage and marries Matthew.

Mrs. Timorous, relative of the Timorous of the First Part, who comes with Mercy to see Christiana before she sets out on pilgrimage.

Mrs. Bat's-Eyes, a resident of The City of Destruction and friend of Mrs. Timorous. Since she has a bat's eyes, she would be blind or nearly blind, so her characterization of Christiana as blind in her desire to go on pilgrimage is hypocritical.

Mrs. Inconsiderate, a resident of The City of Destruction and friend of Mrs. Timorous. She characterizes Christiana's departure "a good riddance" as an inconsiderate person would.

The Pilgrim's Progress[1]

Then I saw in my dream, that when they were got out of the wilderness, they presently saw a town before them, and the name of that town is Vanity, and at the town there is a fair kept, called Vanity Fairy it is kept all the year long; it bearth the name of Vanity Fair because the town where it is kept is lighter than vanity, and also because all that is there sold, or that cometh thither, is vanity.As is the saying of the wise, "All that cometh is vanity."

This fair is no new-erected business, but a thing of ancient standing, I will show you the original of it.

Almost five thousand years ago, there were pilgrims walking to the Celestial City[2], as these two honest persons are,and Beelzebub, Apollyon, and Legion, with their companions,perceiving by the path that the pilgrims made, that their way to the city lay through this town of Vanity, they contrived to set up a fair, a fair wherein should be sold all sorts of vanity, and that it should last all the year long. Therefore at this fair are all such merchandise sold, as houses, lands, trades, places, honors,preferments, titles, countries, kingdoms, lusts, pleasures, and delights of all sorts, as whores, bawds, wives, husbands,children, masters, servants, lives, blood, bodies, souls, silver,gold, pearls, precious stones, and what not.

And, moreover, at this fair there is at all times to be seen jugglings, cheats, games, plays, fools, apes, knaves, and rogues, and that of every kind. Here are to be seen, too, and that for nothing, thefts, murders, adulteries, false swearers, and that of a blood-red colour.

And as in other fairs of less moment, there are the several rows and streets, under their proper names, where such and such wares are vended, so here likewise you have the proper places,rows, streets (viz. countries and kingdoms), where the wares of this fair are soonest to be found. Here is the Britain Row, the French Row, the Italian Row, the Spanish Row, the German Row, where several sorts of vanities are to be sold. But, as in other fairs, some one commodity is as the chief of all the fair, so the ware of Rome and her merchandise is greatly promoted in this fair, only our English nation, with some others, have taken a dislike thereat.

Now, as I said, the way to the Celestial City lies just through this town where this lusty fair is kept; and he that will go to the city, and yet not go through this town, must needs go out of the world. The Prince of princes himself, when here, went through this town to his own country, and that upon a fair-day, too, yea,and as I think, it was Beelzebup, the chief lord of this fair, that invited him to buy of his vanities, yea, would have made him lord of the fair, would he but have done him reverence as he went through the town. Yea, because he was such a man of honour, Beelzebub had him from street to street, and showed him all the kingdoms of the world in a little time, that he might, if possible,allure the Blessed One to cheapen and buy some of his vanities;but he had no mind to the merchandise, and therefore left the town,without laying so much as one farthing upon these vanities. This fair,therefore, is an ancient thing, of long standing, and a very great fair.

Now these pilgrims, as I said, must needs go through the fair. Well, so they did, but behold, even as they entered into the fair, all the people in the fair were moved, and the town itself as it were in a hubbub about them, and that for several reasons: for First, The pilgrims were clothed with such kind of raiment as was diverse from the raiment of any that traded in the fair. The people, therefore, of the fair, made a great gazing upon them: some said they were fools, some they were bedlams, and some they were outlandish men.

Secondly, And as they wondered at their apparel, so they did likewise at their speech, for few could understand what they saids they naturally spoke the language of Canaan, but they that kept the fair were the men of this world, so that, from one end of the fair to the other, they seemed barbarians each to the other.

Thirdly, But that which did not a little amuse the merchandisers was that these pilgrims set very light by all their wares, they cared not so much as to look upon them, and if they called upon them to buy, they would put their fingers in their ears, and cry, "Turn away mine eyes from beholding vanity," and look upwards, signifying that their trade and traffic was in heaven.

One chanced mockingly, beholding the carriages of the men, to say unto them, What will we buy? But they, looking gravely upon him, said, "We buy the truth." At that there was an occasion taken to despise the men the more, some mocking, some taunting, some speaking reproachfully, and some calling upon others to smite them. At last things came to a hubbub and great stir in the fair, insomuch that all order was confounded. Now was word presently brought to the great one of the fair, who quickly came down, and deputed some of his most trusty friends to take these men into examination, about whom the fair was almost overturned. So the men were brought to examination, and they that sat upon them asked whence they came, whither they went, and what they did there, in such an unusual garb? The men told them that they were pilgrims and strangers in the world, and that they were going to their own country, which was the Heavenly Jerusalem[3], and that they had given no occasion to the men of the town, nor yet to the merchandisers, thus to abuse them, and to let them in their journey, except it was for that, when one asked them what they would buy, they said they would buy the truth. But they that were appointed to examine them did not believe them to be any other than bedlams and mad, or else such as came to put all things into a confusion in the fair. Therefore they took them and beat them, and besmeared them with dirt, and then put them into the cage, that they might be made a spectacle to all the men of the fair.

 **N o t e s**

[1]This is perhaps the best-known episode in the book, Bunyan characteristically turns one of the most familiar institutions in contemporary England—annual fairs—into an allegory of universal spiritual significance. Christian and his companion Faithful pass through the town of vanity at the season of the local fair. "Vanity" means emptiness or worthlessness and hence the fair is an allegory of worldliness and the corruption of the religious life throught the attractions of the world. From earliest times numerous fairs were held for stated periods throughout Britain; to them the most important merchants from all over Europe brought their wares. The serious business of buying and selling was accompanied by all sorts of diversions—eating, drinking, and other fleshly pleasures, as well as spectacles of strange animals, acrobats, and other wonders.

[2]Celestial City is the Holy City of the Celestial Church of Christ (CCC). It is located in the Imeko AfonLocal Government Area of Ogun State, Nigeria, very close to the border with Benin. Celestial City is known as "Jerusalem" by the celestials. The city has potential as a tourist location.

[3]In the Book of Ezekiel, New Jerusalem is Ezekiel's prophetic vision of a city centered on the rebuilt Holy Temple, the Third Temple, to be established in Jerusalem, that will be the capital of the Messianic Kingdom, the meeting place of the twelve tribes of Israel, during the Messianic era. The prophecy is recorded by Ezekiel as having been received on Yom Kippur of the year 3372 of the Hebrew calendar. It will be inhabited by people to live eternally in spirit form, created by God as a gift to mankind. Not everyone will reside in New Jerusalem, as most will possibly stay on Earth. In the *New Testament* it is also titled Heavenly Jerusalem in the *Book of Revelation* as well as Zion in other books of the Christian Bible.

 Questions

1. In this book, what kind of metaphor did the author use?
2. What does "vanity fair" mean?
3. What is the significance of this writing technique?

 中文译文

天路历程

接着，我在梦境中看到他们走出荒原。不久，他们就看到了前面的一个小镇，小镇的名字叫浮华镇。在这个小镇，有个常年不散的集市，名为"浮华集市"。起此名字，是由于这个小镇比浮华还要轻浮，同时，也是由于集市上所买卖的东西都是奢侈浮华的东西。正如智者所言："索要来的都是虚空的。"

这个集市并不是刚刚建立的，而是由来已久了；接下来，我就给你讲一讲它的由来。

大约五千年前，有一批朝圣者，就像这两个忠实的人一样，要到天国去朝拜。恶魔亚玻伦、魔鬼比埃兹巴伯以及众喽啰，对朝见者去天国的路进行了研究后发现，他们在朝见的途中，必然要取道浮华镇，于是他们谋划在这里建立一个集市，在这个集市上出卖各种浮华的东西，并常年开放。因此，在这个集市上所经营的商品就包括房子、土地、职业、地盘、荣耀、特权、名位、国家、王国、欲望、幸福以及各种快乐；比如，妓院、老鸨、老婆、丈夫、孩子、主人、奴仆、生命、血液、肉体、灵魂、银子、金子、珍珠、宝石等。

而且，在这个集市上，你不时地会看到变戏法的人、骗子、赌博者、游戏者、傻子、模仿者及各色人等。在这儿，不用花一个子儿，你就会看到，偷盗、谋杀、通奸、虚假的宣誓，每一样都令人触目惊心。

另有一些不是很重要的集市也有大大小小的各种街道，通过名字就知道他们所经营的东西，这个集市和其他集市一样，也有自己固有的地方、道路和街市（比如，国家街市或王国街市），在这儿，这些东西更容易被找到。这个集市里有英国街、法国街、意大利街、西班牙街，还有德国街，这些街上卖好多种浮华的东西。但是，正如在其他街上看到的一样，这条街上也有某种商品特别畅销，比如，罗马的货物及其商品在这里就备受推崇，仅有英国人和少数几个国家的人不太喜欢他们。

正如刚才我所提到的，通往天国的道路恰恰要穿过这个拥有浮华集市的小镇。那些想要到天国朝见却又不经过这个小镇的人是必须"离开这个世界的"。当初，耶稣本人也是取道此镇而回到自己的国家。耶稣到的那一天，正是赶集的日子。是的，我想，是这个集市的主要创办人，魔鬼比埃兹巴伯，邀请耶稣去购买他的浮华商品；他还许诺，只要耶稣在路过集市的时候，向他表示敬意，他就会让耶稣成为集市的主人。当时，魔鬼带他走遍了集市所有的街道，不一会儿的工夫，就向他展示了世界各国的领土。是的，耶稣是一个如此荣耀的人，倘若可能的话，魔鬼就会引诱他同自己讨价还价，并买走他的某些浮华商品，但是耶稣并没有把这些放在心上，一分钱没花便离开了那个小镇。由此可见，这个古老的集市，可谓是由来已久，规模庞大。

正如刚才我说的，现在，这两个朝见者必须要穿过这个集市。而且，他们也这样做了。但是，当他们走进集市的时候，集市上所有人都骚动起来，整个小镇也好像因他们的到来而开始了一片喧哗！这是为什么呢？第一，两位朝圣者身上穿的衣物和集市上所卖的任何一件都不同。因而，集市上的人便盯着他们看，有人说他们是傻子，有人说他们是疯子，也有人说他们简直就是外地来的怪人。

第二，当他们在大街上闲逛的时候，不仅服饰奇异，而且他们的语言也与集市上的人不同；几乎没人能听懂他们的话。他们很自然地操着应许之地的迦南语，但是，集市上的经营者们，却是生活在这个凡俗的世界上，根本听不懂这两个人的话。因而，当这两个人从这个集市走向另一个集市时，他们在这些经营者眼里，仿佛都是蛮荒之人。

第三，但是，令那些商人所不高兴的是，这两位朝见者对他们所卖的物品并不感兴趣。这俩人在看那些商人的时候，也是不屑一顾的样子。假若商人要招呼他们买东西，他们便用手指堵住自己的耳朵，喊道："我们不看虚假的东西。"然后，便抬头看天，好像他们的生意是在天上。

　　一个商人看着朝见者手里的烟卷，想碰碰运气，便操着愚弄的口气对他们说："你们想要买什么？"他们却表情严肃地看着他说："我们要买真理。"这好像又给了商人们嘲笑他们的机会，有人讥讽他们，有人奚落他们，有人责备他们，甚至有人招呼别人来揍他们一顿。终于，集市上一片喧哗，因为他们想要的东西实在是令人迷惑不解。很快这些话就传到了集市首领的耳朵里，他立刻赶了过来，并委托他最信任的几个朋友对这两人进行了审问。因为正是他们使整个集市几乎闹翻了天。于是，这两人就被带去接受审问。审理他们的人问他们从哪里来，要到哪里去，穿着这种奇怪的服饰在那里做什么。他们回答，他们是朝见者，是寄居在这凡俗世上的，他们要回自己的国家去，他们的国家是天上的耶路撒冷；他们还说，镇上的人和集市上的人没有理由这么羞辱他们，还妨碍他们的旅程。在有人问他们想买什么的时候，他们说要买真理。但是，审讯他们的人根本就不相信这些，认为他们不是疯子就是傻子，抑或，他们根本就是存心来捣乱的。于是，他们逮捕了这两个朝见者，还殴打了他们，给他们身上涂满脏兮兮的泥土，还把他们关进笼子里，让集市上所有人都来羞辱他们。

Unit 6   Daniel Defoe (1660—1731)

Life

Daniel Defoe born Daniel Foe, was an English trader, writer, journalist, pamphleteer, and spy, most famous for his novel *Robinson Crusoe*. Defoe is noted for being one of the earliest proponents of the novel, as he helped to popularise the form in Britain with others such as Samuel Richardson, and is among the founders of the English novel. He was a prolific and versatile writer, producing more than five hundred books, pamphlets, and journals on various topics,  including politics, crime, religion, marriage, psychology, and the supernatural. He was also a pioneer of economic journalism.

Defoe's first notable publication was *An Essay upon Projects*, a series of proposals for social and economic improvement, published in 1697. From 1697 to 1698, he defended the right of King William III to a standing army during disarmament, after the *Treaty of Ryswick* (1697) had ended the Nine Years' War (1688—1697). His most successful poem, *The True-Born Englishman* (1701), defended the king against the perceived xenophobia of his enemies, satirising the English claim to racial purity. In 1701, Defoe presented the Legion's Memorial to the Speaker of the House of Commons, later his employer Robert Harley, flanked by a guard of sixteen gentlemen of quality. It demanded the release of the Kentish petitioners, who had asked Parliament to support the king in an imminent war against France.

Not all of Defoe's pamphlet writing was political. One pamphlet was originally published anonymously, entitled "A True Relation of the Apparition of One Mrs. Veal the Next Day after her

Death to One Mrs. Bargrave at Canterbury the 8th of September, 1705." It deals with interaction between the spiritual realm and the physical realm and was most likely written in support of Charles Drelincourt's *The Christian Defense against the Fears of Death* (1651). It describes Mrs. Bargrave's encounter with her old friend Mrs. Veal after she had died. It is clear from this piece and other writings that the political portion of Defoe's life was by no means his only focus.

From 1719 to 1724, Defoe published the novels for which he is famous (see below). In the final decade of his life, he also wrote conduct manuals, including *Religious Courtship* (1722), *The Complete English Tradesman* (1726) and *The New Family Instructor* (1727). He published a number of books decrying the breakdown of the social order, such as *The Great Law of Subordination Considered* (1724) and *Everybody's Business is Nobody's Business* (1725) and works on the supernatural, like *The Political History of the Devil* (1726), *A System of Magick* (1727) and *An Essay on the History and Reality of Apparitions* (1727). His works on foreign travel and trade include *A General History of Discoveries and Improvements* (1727) and *Atlas Maritimus and Commercialis* (1728). Perhaps his greatest achievement with the novels is the magisterial *A tour thro' the whole island of Great Britain* (1724—1727), which provided a panoramic survey of British trade on the eve of the Industrial Revolution.

Plot of *Robinson Crusoe*

As Defoe's masterpiece, *Robinson Crusoe* is one of the few books in English literature that have been enjoying an undiminished popularity for centuries. The novel consists of three parts, but only the first part has been widely read. The plot of the novel is based upon the real experience of Alexander Seilkirk, a Scottish sailor, who was ever deserted on an uninhabited island after he had quarreled with the captain. He had lived there in solitude for five years before he was rescued by a passing ship. On his return to England in 1709, his experience became widely known after it was reported in many periodicals.

Inspired by the adventurous experience of this Scottish sailor, Defoe successfully characterizes Robinson Crusoe as the protagonist of the novel. The whole story of Robinson Crusoe covers three parts. In the first part, Crusoe, a slave trader meets with his most unfortunate shipwreck. He is cast by the cold waves upon the shore of an uninhabited island, where he manages to live for 28 years because there is no possible opportunity for him to escape. In order to live in the wilderness, he swim back to the ship to search and bring back the remaining food, clothing, household tools and guns, and then builds a simple cottage to shelter himself against the possible attacks of wild animals. He grows barley and rice in spring and harvests when the autumn comes. He rescues a savage, whom he names Friday and makes his servant. Crusoe tries his best to teach Friday to speak and read English, while Friday serves his teacher and master in every possible way. After having lived on the island for 28 years, they are rescued by a passing ship, which carries them back to England. The first part of story ends with Crusoe sending women and supplies to the island to establish a regular colony there.

The second part is a series of adventures of Crusoe on his 11 year business trip to different parts of the world, especially his return to the island where he lived for 28 years to set up a colony and simultaneously spread English views of religion and morality. Because of its less unified and more monotonous plot, the second part has been considered as inferior to the first part, and together with the third part, another dull narration of Crusoe's adventures have few readers.

Comments on *Robinson Crusoe*

The novel can be read in different ways. Most simple, it is a story of sea adventures. Its thrilling incidents:the shipwreck, the earthquake, the meeting with Friday, the clash with the savage naives—have attracted millions of readers, including young children. To read it politically, we may interpret the story as a process of colonial expansion. Crusoe, supported by advanced technology represented by gun, conquers a less civilized people represented by Man Friday. Though they become good friends, Friday has remained a servant to his master—Crusoe since the first day they met.

To read it socially, we find that Crusoe's adventures imply different Western Cultural values. The novel sings a song of "the dignity of labor", a slogan as a disguise to justify the bourgeoisie's bloody accumulation of wealth. Robinson is a self-made man. He succeeds in creating a new life all through his own efforts.

The novel also explores the theme of "back to nature." Industrialization brought England material wealth, but it also ended the peaceful life in the countryside and created poverty and disturbance in the city. The novel expresses a desire to go back to a more economic and humble life style. After four years on the island, Robinson starts to like its idyllic life: "I looked now upon the (civilized) world as a thing remote, which I had nothing to do with, no expectation from, and indeed no desire about…"

There is also the theme of "religious devotion". Completely separated from civilization, Crusoe reflects upon man's frailty and God's mercy. He has a fuller understanding of the power of religion. Crusoe find the need, after being thrown into the deserted island, for prayer and repentance, and finds that inner peace does not come from material possessions in civilized world but from communication with God.

Robinson Crusoe is written in almost colloquial language. Though it is a novel of 18th century, we have no difficulties in understanding its story. It is narrated in the first person singular. The narration of this novel is true and realistic to life, like a person telling his own experience to his friends. Simple language, realistic narration and real background of the story, for it is based on a sailor's real experience, all these elements make Robinson Crusoe's adventures more believable, convincing and exciting.

Symbolism pervades in this novel. In general, the whole story symbolizes the whole process of human development: from the primitive stage, to feudal period to the capital society. The tools fetched by Crusoe and offering him great help symbolize the civilization, which is necessary to the survival of a person on a desolate island. The island itself has symbolic significance because it is the physical conditions, which changed Crusoe to stop wandering (Crusoe is a merchant, loving sailing adventures). The confinement on the island is mostly responsible for the physical and mental growth, which took place within Crusoe. In the case of Robinson Crusoe, it was this solitude that essentially changed him and made him less of a wanderer, both spiritually and physically, for he found faith in God and no longer was able to aimlessly wander due to the confinement on the island.

In *Robinson Crusoe*, the narrator develops to form an optimistic outlook towards an unfortunate situation, however, that a man isolated himself from society and lived on an uninhabited island for 28 years is still a myth, as Aristotle said such as man, if he exists, is either a beast or a God.

In 1905, Chinese translator Lin Shu translated *Robinson Crusoe* with simple language, concise description and well-knit plot construction. In the Chinese version, it is narrated in the first singular person with realistic psychological description. Therefore, the Chinese readers have a chance to read it and think about it.

Major Characters

Robinson Crusoe

He is one of the protagonists most successfully portrayed in English novels. Through his characterization of Crusoe, Defoe depicts him as a hero struggling against nature and human fate with his strong will and hand, and Defoe eulogize the creative physical and mental labor. From an individual laborer to a master and colonizer, Crusoe seems to have gone through various phases of human civilization—primitive stage, feudal society and the capitalistic in 18th century, creating a picture of how man's history has developed. That is the vital significance of the novel.

However Crusoe is not portrayed as a great hero in epic adventurer to win readers of generations. He does not boast of his courage in getting rid of the difficulties and fear on the uninhabited island, and he is always in an un-heroic feeling of fear or panic, as when he first finds the footprint on the beach. Crusoe prefers to depict himself as an ordinary sensible man, never as an epic hero. It is his perseverance in spending months making a canoe that makes his adventures praiseworthy. Additionally, his resourcefulness in building a home, dairy, grape arbor, country house, and goat stable from practically nothing is clearly remarkable. The Swiss philosopher Jean-Jacques Rousseau applauded Crusoe's do-it-yourself independence, and he recommends that children be taught to imitate Crusoe's life.

Crusoe is very interested in possessions and power. He has an ambition of possessions and power. When he first calls himself king of the island, he really does consider himself king, so he describes the Spaniard as his subject. His teaching Friday to call him "Master", even before teaching him words for "yes" or "no" is annoying for any grown-up, who is taught in that way. In conclusion, Crusoe's virtues tend to be private: his industry, resourcefulness, courage and do-it-yourself independence make him an excellent individual. His vices are social, and his urge to control others is highly objectionable. By bringing both sides together into one complex character, Defoe gives us a fascinating glimpse into the contradictions of a modern man.

Friday

He is probably the first nonwhite character to be given a realistic and humane portrayal in the English novel. Crusoe represents the first colonial mind in fiction, and Friday represents all the natives of America, Asia, and Africa who would later be oppressed in the age of European imperialism. At the moment when Crusoe teaches Friday to call him "Master", Friday becomes an enduring political symbol of racial injustice in a modern world.

Friday is a key figure within the context of the novel. In *Robinson Crusoe*, he is much more charming and colorful than his master. Indeed, Defoe stresses the contrast between Crusoe's and Friday's personalities. In his joyful reunion with his father, Friday exhibits far more emotion toward his family than Crusoe who never mentions missing his family or dreams about the happiness of seeing them again. Friday's expression of loyalty in asking Crusoe to kill him rather than leave him is more touching than anything Crusoe ever says or does. In short, Friday's emotional directness has a sharp contrast with Crusoe's emotional numbness.

Introduction to Chapter IV

The most successful and significant portion of the novel is the story of the hero's first adventures on the uninhabited island, especially when he is alone and before he has Friday as his servant (Chapter IV). Here the hero is not a colonizer or a foreign trader but is depicted as a man struggling against nature and living through a seemingly primitive environment. Here we see the glorification of the new bourgeois man who has the will and courage to face hardships and the determination to preserve himself and improve on his living conditions. Here we even see the glorification of physical and mental labor, which enable the hero to gradually create a favorable environment for himself. This part provides the possible conditions for the probability of a single man managing to live on in a deserted place and soon to improve his living conditions. Without many useful things (stand for products of human civilization of many centuries), which he got from the wrecked ship, he could not even have survived at all. It is told in a simple, straightforward style, and this adds to the realistic effect of the story.

Chapter IV

My thoughts were now wholly employed about securing myself against either savages, if any should appear, or wild beasts, if any were in the island; and I had many thoughts of the method how to do this, and what kind of dwelling to make, whether I should make me a cave in the earth, or a tent upon the earth; and, in short, I resolved upon both, the manner and description of which it may not be improper to give an account of.

I soon found the place I was in was not for my settlement, particularly because it was upon a low moorish ground[1] near the sea, and I believed would not be wholesome[2]; and more particularly because there was no fresh water near it. So I resolved to find a more healthy and more convenient spot of ground.

I consulted several things in my situation, which I found would be proper for me. First, health and fresh water, I just now mentioned. Secondly, shelter from the heat of the sun. Thirdly security from ravenous[3] creatures, whether men or beasts. Fourthly, a view to the sea, that if God sent any ship in sight I might not lose any advantage for my deliverance, of which I was not willing to banish all my expectation yet.

In search of a place proper for this, I found a little plain on the side of a rising hill, whose front towards this little plain was steep as a house — side, so that nothing could come down upon me from the top; on the side of this rock there was a hollow place, worn a little way in, like the entrance or door of a cave; but there was not really any cave, or way into the rock at all.

On the flat of the green, just before this hollow place, I resolved to pitch my tent. This plain was not above a hundred yards broad, and about twice as long, and lay like a green before my door, and at the end of it descended irregularly every way down into the low grounds by the seaside. It was on the NNW[4]. side of the hill, so that I was sheltered from the heat every day, till it came to a W.[5] and by S[6]. sun, or thereabouts, which in those countries is near setting.

Before I set up my tent, I drew a half circle before the hollow place, which took in about ten yards in its semi — diameter from the rock, and twenty yards in its diameter from its beginning and ending. In this half circle I pitched two rows of strong stakes[7], driving them into the ground till they stood very firm like piles[8], the biggest end being out of the ground about five feet and a half, and sharpened on the top. The two rows did not stand above six inches from one another.

Then I took the pieces of cable which I had cut in the ship, and laid them in rows one upon another, within the circle, between these two rows of stakes, up to the top, placing other stakes in the inside leaning against them, about two feet and a half high, like a spur to a post; and this fence was so strong that neither man or beast could get into it, or over it. This cost me a great deal of time and labor, especially to cut the piles in the woods, bring them to the place, and drive them into the earth.

The entrance into this place I made to be not by a door, but by a short ladder to go over the top; which ladder, when I was in, I lifted over after me, and so I was completely fenced in, and fortified, as I thought, from all the world, and consequently slept secure in the night, which otherwise I could not have done; though as it appeared afterward, there was no need of all this caution from the enemies that I apprehended danger from.

Into this fence or fortress, with infinite labor, I carried all my riches, all my provisions, ammunition, and stores, of which you have the account above; and I made me a large tent, which, to preserve me from the rains that in one part of the year are very violent there, I made double, viz.[9], one smaller tent within, and one larger tent above it, and covered the uppermost with a large tarpaulin[10], which I had saved among the sails. And now I lay no more for a while in the bed which I had brought on shore, but in a hammock[11], which was indeed a very good one, and belonged to the mate of the ship[12].

Into this tent I brought all my provisions, and everything that would spoil by the wet; and having thus enclosed all my goods I made up the entrance, which, till now, I had left open, and so passed and repassed, as I said, by a short ladder.

When I had done this, I began to work my way into the rock; and bringing all the earth and stones that I dug down out through my tent, I laid them up within my fence in the nature of a terrace, so that it raised the ground within about a foot and a half; and thus I made me a cave just behind my tent, which served me like a cellar to my house.

It cost me much labor, and many days, before all these things were brought to perfection, and therefore I must go back to some other things which took up some of my thoughts. At the same time it happened, after I had laid my scheme for the setting up my tent, and making the cave, that a storm of rain falling from a thick dark cloud, a sudden flash of lightning happened, and after that a great clap of thunder, as is naturally the effect of it. I was not so much surprised with the lightning, as I was with a thought which darted into my mind as swift as the lightning itself. O my powder! My very heart sunk within me when I thought that at one blast all my powder might be destroyed, on which, not my defence only, but the providing me food, as I thought, entirely depended. I was nothing near so anxious about my own danger; though had the powder took fire, I had never known who had hurt me.

Such impression did this make upon me, that after the storm was over I laid aside all my works, my building, and fortifying, and applied myself to make bags and boxes to separate the powder, and keep it a little and a little in a parcel, in hope that whatever might come it might not all take fire at once, and to keep it so apart that it should not be possible to make one part fire another[13]. I finished this work in about a fortnight; and I think my powder, which in all was about

240 pounds weight, was divided in not less than a hundred parcels. As to the barrel that had been wet, I did not apprehend any danger from that, so I placed it in my new cave, which in my fancy I called my kitchen, and the rest I hid up and down and in holes among the rocks, so that no wet might come to it, marking very carefully where I laid it.

In the interval of time while this was doing, I went out once, at least, every day with my gun, as well to divert myself, as to see if I could kill anything fit for food, and as near as I could to acquaint myself with what the island produced. The first time I went out, I presently discovered that there were goats in the island, which was a great satisfaction to me; but then it was attended with this misfortune to me, viz., that they were so shy, so subtle, and so swift of foot, that it was the difficultest thing in the world to come at[14] them. But I was not discouraged at this, not doubting but I might now and then shoot one, as it soon happened; for after I had found their haunts a little, I laid wait in this manner for them. I observed if they saw me in the valleys, though they were upon the rocks, they would run away as in a terrible fright; but if they were feeding in the valleys, and I was upon the rocks, they took no notice of me, from whence I concluded that, by the position of their optics, their sight was so directed downward, that they did not readily see objects that were above them. So afterward I took this method: I always climbed the rocks first to get above them, and then had frequently a fair mark. The first shot I made among these creatures I killed a she－goat, which had a little kid by her, which she gave suck to[15], which grieved me heartily; but when the old one fell, the kid stood stock still by her till I came and took her up; and not only so, but when I carried the old one with me upon my shoulders, the kid followed me quite to my enclosure; upon which I laid down the dam[16], and took the kid in my arms, and carried it over my pale[17], in hopes to have bred it up tame[18]; but it would not eat, so I was forced to kill it, and eat it myself. These two supplied me with flesh a great while, for I eat sparingly, and saved my provisions, my bread especially, as much as possibly I could.

Having now fixed my habitation, I found it absolutely necessary to provide a place to make a fire in, and fuel to burn; and what I did for that, as also how I enlarged my cave, and what conveniences I made, I shall give a full account of in its place. But I must first give some little account of myself, and of my thoughts about living, which it may well be supposed were not a few. I had a dismal prospect of my condition; for as I was not cast away upon that island without being driven, as is said, by a violent storm, quite out of the course of our intended voyage, and a great way, viz., some hundreds of leagues out of the ordinary course of the trade of mankind[19], I had great reason to consider it as a determination of Heaven, that in this desolate place, and in this desolate manner, I should end my life. The tears would run plentifully down face when I made these reflections, and sometimes I would expostulate with myself, why Providence[20] should thus completely ruin its creatures, and render them so absolutely miserable, so without help abandoned, so entirely depressed, that it could hardly be rational to be thankful for such a life.

But something always returned swift upon me to check these thoughts, and to reprove[21] me; and particularly one day, walking with my gun in my hand by the seaside, I was very pensive[22] upon the subject of my present condition, when reason, as it were, expostulated[23] with me t' other way, thus: "Well, you are in a desolate condition it is true, but pray remember, where are the rest of you? Did not you come eleven of you in the boat? Where are the ten? Why were not they saved, and you lost? Why were you singled out? Is it better to be here, or there?" And then I pointed to the sea. All evils are to be considered with the good that is in them, and with what worse attends them.

Then it occurred to me again, how well I was furnished[24] for my subsistence, and what would have been my case if it had not happened, which was a hundred thousand to one, that the ship had floated from the place where she first struck and was driven so near to the shore that I had time to get all these things out of her; what would have been my case, if I had been to have lived in the condition in which I first came on shore, without necessaries of life, or necessaries to supply and procure them? "Particularly," said I aloud (though to myself), "what should I have done without a gun, without ammunition, without any tools to make anything or to work with, without clothes, bedding, a tent, or any manner of covering?" and that now I had all these to a sufficient quantity, and was in a fair way to provide myself in such a manner, as to live without my gun when my ammunition was spent; so that I had a tolerable view of subsisting without any want as long as I lived. For I considered from the beginning how I would provide for the accidents that might happen, and for the time that was to come, even not only after my ammunition should be spent, but even after my health or strength should decay.

I confess I had not entertained any notion of my ammunition being destroyed at one blast— I mean, my powder being blown up by lightning; and this made the thoughts of it so surprising to me when it lightened and thundered, as I observed just now.

And now being to enter into a melancholy relation of a scene of silent life[25], such, perhaps, as was never heard of in the world before, I shall take it from its beginning and continue it in its order. It was by my account, the 30th of September when, in the manner as above said, I first set foot upon this horrid island, when the sun being to us in its autumnal equinox[26], was almost just over my head, for I reckoned myself, by observation, to be in the latitude of 9 degrees 22 minutes north of the line.

After I had been there about ten or twelve days it came into my thoughts that I should lose my reckoning of time for want of books and pen and ink, and should even forget the Sabbath days[27] from the working days; but to prevent this, I cut it with my knife upon a large post, in capital letters; and making it into a great cross, I set it up on the shore where I first landed, viz., "I came on shore here the 30th of September 1659." Upon the sides of this square post I cut every day a notch[28] with my knife, and every seventh notch was as long again as the rest, and every first day of the month as long again as that long one; and thus I kept my calendar, or weekly, monthly, and yearly reckoning of time.

 Notes

[1] 低洼的沼泽地

[2] healthy

[3] 饥饿的

[4] north-north west 的缩写

[5] west 的缩写

[6] south 的缩写

[7] 木桩

[8] 桥桩

[9] 也就是；即

[10] 防水油布

[11] 吊床

[12] 大副

[13] 一部分火药引爆另一部分火药

[14] 接近

[15] 喂奶，哺乳

[16] 母羊

[17] 栅栏，及鲁滨逊的家

[18] 把它（羔羊）驯养大

[19] 人迹罕至之处

[20] 上帝

[21] 严厉谴责

[22] 沉思的

[23] 规劝；告诫

[24] 提供

[25] 预想到将来的生活忧郁而寂寞

[26] 秋分；秋分点

[27] 安息日

[28] 凹痕

 Questions

1. How does Robinson keep himself secure and find a proper place for living?

2. How difficult is it to hunt a goat?

3. If you were thrown on a deserted island in 17th century, what would your feelings and thoughts be and what would you do?

4. What is the psychological development of *Robinson Crusoe*?

5. What do you learn from reading this passage?

Analysis of Chapter IV

This chapter gives some details to the readers about how Robinson, by sheer will power, hard manual labor, perseverance and resourcefulness, begins to build up a new life for himself on the desolate island.

Chapter IV is not only a vivid description of Crusoe's manual labor but also his psychological description. How he built a shelter for himself and how he relieved himself from depression and desperation and formed a realistic idea and plan for his future life are realistically presented in this selection. Being abandoned on an uninhabited island, Crusoe was in great depression and upset. "*I had a dismal prospect of my condition.*" For this accident had cut his normal connection with the outside human world. Robinson rebuked the determination of Heaven. It was the determination of Heaven that made him so miserable, helpless and depressed. So "*It could hardly be rational to be thankful for such a life.*"

But "*something always returned swift upon me to check these thoughts and reprove me.*" Robinson suddenly realized what he thought before was mistaken. He began to blame himself for what in his mind. In his reconsideration, he found God/ Providence had offered him a lot of mercy. He compared the destiny of his fellow men on the ship and his destiny. Though thrown on the island, he survived rather than be drowned.

"*Then it occurred to me again, how well I was furnished for my subsistence and what would have been my case if it had not happened, which was a hundred thousand to one, that the ship floated from the place where she first struck, and was driven so near the shore that I had time to get all these things out of her?*" "a thousand to one" refers so small a chance for the ship to float from the place, so near the shore. The use of the feminine pronoun "she", not "it" proves Robinson's affectionate feelings for the ship and what the ship offers him. Therefore Robinson feels lucky to be able to fetch many things from the wrecked ship, such as an iron bar, a cask of gunpowder, any guns, boards, etc, all of which are well employed and furnished. Thus he blames no more. "*So that I had a tolerable view of subsisting, without any want, as long as I lived.*" Robinson became realistic and considered how to deal with future accidents such as the exhaustion of ammunition and the decay of health and strength.

A lightning destroys his gunpowder. Such an accident made Crusoe decide to put everything into order. "*I shall take it from its beginning, and continue it in its order.*" According to the sun position, he settled the date, the time.

This chapter focuses a psychological development of Robinson Crusoe, from depression to confidence by finding comfort from God. Then he holds a tolerable view towards the unfavorable conditions. Finally because of accidents, he made a pragmatic and realistic decision to settle everything in order.

 中文译文

《鲁滨孙漂流记》 第四章

首先，我感到目前居住的地方不太合适。一则因离海太近，地势低湿，不大卫生；二则附近没有淡水。我得找一个比较卫生、比较方便的地方建造自己的住所。

我根据自己的情况，拟定了选择住所的几个条件：第一，必须如我上面所说的，要卫生，要有淡水；第二，要能遮阴；第三，要能避免猛兽或人类的突然袭击；第四，要能看

到大海，万一上帝让什么船只经过，我就不至于失去脱险的机会，因为我始终存有一线希望，迟早能摆脱目前的困境。

我按上述条件去寻找一个合适的地点，发现在一个小山坡旁，有一片平地。小山靠平地的一边又陡又直，像一堵墙，不论人或野兽都无法从上面下来袭击我。在山岩上，有一块凹进去的地方，看上去好像是一个山洞的进口，但实际上里面并没有山洞。

在这山岩凹进去的地方，前面是一片平坦的草地，我决定就在此搭个帐篷。这块平地宽不过一百码，长不到二百码。

若把住所搭好，这块平坦的草地犹如一块草皮，从门前起伏连绵向外伸展形成一个缓坡，直至海边的那块低地。这儿正处小山西北偏北处，日间小山正好挡住阳光，当太阳转向西南方向照到这儿时，也就快要落下去了。

搭帐篷前，我先在石壁前面划了一个半圆形，半径约十码，直径有二十码。

沿这个半圆形，我插了两排结实的木桩；木桩打入泥土，仿佛木橛子，大头朝下，高约五尺半，顶上都削得尖尖的。两排木桩之间的距离不到六英寸。然后，我用从船上截下来的那些缆索，沿着半圆形，一层一层地堆放在两排木桩之间，一直堆到顶上，再用一些两英尺半高的木桩插进去支撑住缆索，仿佛柱子上的横茶。这个篱笆十分结实，不管是人还是野兽，都无法冲进来或攀越篱笆爬进来。这项工程，花了我不少时间和劳力，尤其是我得从树林里砍下粗枝做木桩，再运到草地上，又一一把它们打入泥土，这工作尤其费力费时。

至于住所的进出口，我没有在篱笆上做门，而是用一个短梯从篱笆顶上翻进来，进入里面后再收好梯子。这样，我四面都受保护，完全与外界隔绝，夜里就可高枕无忧了。不过，我后来发现，对我所担心的敌人，根本不必如此戒备森严。我又花了极大的力气，把前面讲到的我的全部财产，全部粮食、弹药武器和补给品，一一搬到篱笆里面，或者可以说搬到这个堡垒里来。我又给自己搭了一个大帐篷用来防雨，因为这儿一年中有一个时期常下倾盆大雨。我把帐篷做成双层的；也就是说，里面一个小的，外面再罩一个大的，大帐篷上面又盖上一大块油布。那油布当然也是我在船上搜集帆布时一起拿下来的。现在我不再睡在搬上岸的那张床上了，而是睡在一张吊床上，这吊床原是船上大副所有，质地很好。我把粮食和一切可能受潮损坏的东西都搬进了帐篷。完成这些工作后，就把篱笆的出入口堵起来。此后，我就像上面所说，用一个短梯翻越篱笆进出。

做完这些工作后，我又开始在岩壁上打洞，把挖出来的土石从帐篷里运到外面，沿篱笆堆成一个平台，约一英尺高。这样，帐篷算是我的住房，房后的山洞就成了我的地窖。

这些工作既费时又费力，但总算一一完成了。现在，我再回头追述一下其他几件使我煞费苦心的事情。在我计划搭帐篷打岩洞的同时，突然乌云密布，暴雨如注，雷电交加。在电光一闪、霹雳突至时，一个思想也像闪电一样掠过我的头脑，使我比对闪电本身更吃惊："哎哟，我的火药啊！"想到一个霹雳就会把我的火药全部炸毁时，我几乎完全绝望了。因为我不仅要靠火药自卫，还得靠其猎取食物为生。当时，我只想到火药，而没有想到火药一旦爆炸自己也就完了。假如火药真的爆炸，我自己都不知道死在谁的手里呢。

这场暴风雨使我心有余悸。因此，我把所有其他工作，包括搭帐篷、筑篱笆等都先丢在一边。等雨一停，我立刻着手做一些小袋子和匣子，把火药分成许许多多个小包。这样，万一发生什么情况，也不致全部炸毁。我把一包包的火药分开贮藏起来，免得一包着火危及另一包。这件工作我足足费了两个星期的时间。火药大约有二百四十磅，我把它们分成一百多包。至于那桶受潮的火药，我倒并不担心会发生什么危险，所以我就把它放到新开的山洞里；我把这山洞戏称为我的厨房，其余的火药我都藏在石头缝里，以免受潮，并在储藏的地方小心地做上记号。

在包装和储藏火药的两星期中，我至少每天带枪出门一次。这样做可以达到三个目的：一来可以散散心；二来可以猎获点什么东西吃；三来也可以了解一下岛上的物产。第一次外出，我便发现岛上有不少山羊，使我十分满意。可我也发现这于我来说并非是件大好事。因为这些山羊胆小而又狡猾，而且跑得飞快，实在很难靠近他们。但我并不灰心，我相信总有办法打到一只的。不久我真的打死了一只。我首先发现了山羊经常出没之地，就采用打埋伏的办法来获取我的猎物。我注意到，如果我在山谷里，哪怕它们在山岩上，它们也准会惊恐地逃窜；但若它们在山谷里吃草，而我站在山岩上，它们就不会注意到我。我想，这是由于小羊眼睛生的部位，使它们只能向下看，而不容易看到上面的东西吧。因此，我就先爬到山上，从上面打下去，往往很容易打中。我第一次开枪，打死了一只正在哺小羊的母羊，使我心里非常难过。母羊倒下后，小羊呆呆地站在它身旁；当我背起母羊往回走时，那小羊也跟着我一直走到围墙外面。于是我放下母羊，抱起小羊，进入木栅，一心想把它驯养大。可是小山羊就是不肯吃东西，没有办法，我只好把它也杀了吃了。这两只一大一小的山羊肉，供我吃了好长一段时间，因为我吃得很省，我要尽量节省粮食，尤其是面包。

住所建造好了，我就想到必须要有一个生火的地方，还得准备些柴火来烧。至于我怎样做这件事，怎样扩大石洞，又怎样创造其他一些生活条件，我想以后在适当的时候再详谈。

现在想先略微谈谈自己，谈谈自己对生活的看法。在这些方面，你们可以想象，确实有不少感触可以谈的。

我感到自己前景暗淡。因为，我被凶猛的风暴刮到这荒岛上，远离原定的航线，远离人类正常的贸易航线有数百海里之遥。我想，这完全是出于天意，让我孤苦伶仃，在凄凉中了却余生。想到这些，我眼泪不禁夺眶而出。有时我不禁犯疑，苍天为什么要这样作践自己所创造的生灵，害得他如此不幸，如此孤立无援，又如此沮丧寂寞呢！在这样的环境中，有什么理由要我们认为生活于我们是一种恩赐呢？

可是，每当我这样想的时候，立刻又有另一种想法出现在我的脑海里，并责怪我不应有上述这些念头。特别有一天，当我正带着枪在海边漫步时，我思考着自己目前的处境。这时，理智从另一方面劝慰我："的确，你目前形单影只，孑然一身，这是事实。可是，你不想想，你的那些同伴呢？他们到哪儿去了？你们一同上船时，不是有十一个人吗？那么，其他十个人到哪儿去了呢？为什么他们死了，唯独留下你一个人还活着呢？是在这孤岛上强呢，还是到他们那儿去好呢？"说到去他们那儿时，我用手指了指大海——"他们都已葬身大海了！真是，我怎么不想想祸福相倚和祸不单行的道理呢？"这时，我又想到，我目前所拥有的一切，殷实充裕，足以维持温饱。要是那只大船不从触礁的地方浮起来飘近海岸，并让我有时间从船上把一切有用的东西取下来，那我现在的处境又会怎样呢？要知道，像我现在的这种机遇，真是千载难逢的。假如我现在仍像我初上岸时那样一无所有；既没有任何生活必需品，也没有任何可以制造生活必需品的工具，那我现在的情况又会怎么样呢？"尤其是，"我大声对自己说，"如果我没有枪，没有弹药，没有制造东西的工具，没有衣服穿，没有床睡觉，没有帐篷住，甚至没有任何东西可以遮身，我又该怎么办呢？"可是现在，这些东西我都有，而且相当充足，即使以后弹药用尽了，不用枪我也能活下去。我相信，我这一生绝不会受冻挨饿，因为我早就考虑到各种意外，考虑到将来的日子；不但考虑到弹药用尽之后的情况，甚至想到我将来体衰力竭之后的日子。

我得承认，在考虑这些问题时，并未想到火药会被雷电一下子炸毁的危险；因此雷电交加之际，忽然想到这个危险，着实使我惊恐万状。这件事我前面已叙述过了。

现在，我要开始过一种寂寞而又忧郁的生活了；这种生活也许在这世界上是前所未闻的。因此，我决定把我生活的情况从头至尾，按时间顺序一一记录下来。我估计，我是九月三十日踏上这可怕的海岛的；当时刚入秋分，太阳差不多正在我头顶上。所以，据我观察，我在北纬九度二十二分的地方。

上岛后十一二天，我忽然想到，我没有书、笔和墨水，一定会忘记计算日期，甚至连安息日和工作日都会忘记。为了防止发生这种情况，我便用刀子在一根大柱子上用大写字母刻上以下一句话："我于一六五九年九月三十日在此上岸。"我把柱子做成一个大十字架，立在我第一次上岸的地方。

References

[1] 张伯香，龙江 . 英美经典小说赏析 [C]. 武汉：武汉大学出版社，2005.

Unit 7   Jonathan Swift (1667—1745)

Life

Jonathan Swift (1667—1745) was an Anglo-Irish satirist, essayist, political pamphleteer (first for the Whigs, then for the Tories), poet and cleric who became Dean of St Patrick's Cathedral, Dublin.

Swift is remembered for works such as *A Tale of a Tub* (1704), *An Argument Against Abolishing Christianity* (1712), *Gulliver's Travels* (1726), and *A Modest Proposal* (1729). He is regarded by the Encyclopædia Britannica as the foremost prose satirist in the English language, and is less well known for his poetry. He originally published all of his works under pseudonyms– such as Lemuel Gulliver, Isaac Bickerstaff, Drapier's Letters as MB Drapier – or anonymously. He is also known for being a master of two styles of satire, the Horatian and Juvenalian styles.

His deadpan, ironic writing style, particularly in *A Modest Proposal*, has led to such satire being subsequently termed "Swiftian."

Swift had residence in Trim, County Meath after 1700. He wrote many of his works during this time period. In February 1702, Swift received his Doctor of Divinity degree from Trinity College, Dublin. That spring he travelled to England and then returned to Ireland in October, accompanied by Esther Johnson–now 20–and his friend Rebecca Dingley, another member of William Temple's household. There is a great mystery and controversy over Swift's relationship with Esther Johnson, nicknamed "Stella." Many, notably his close friend Thomas Sheridan, believed that they were secretly married in 1716; others, like Swift's housekeeper Mrs Brent and Rebecca Dingley (who lived with Stella all through her years in Ireland) dismissed the story as absurd. Swift certainly did not wish her to marry anyone else: in 1704, when their mutual friend William Tisdall informed Swift that he intended to propose to Stella, Swift wrote to him to dissuade him from the idea. Although the tone of the letter was courteous, Swift privately expressed his disgust for Tisdall as an "interloper", and they were estranged for many years.

During his visits to England in these years, Swift published *A Tale of a Tub and The Battle of the Books* (1704) and began to gain a reputation as a writer. This led to close, lifelong friendships with Alexander Pope, John Gay, and John Arbuthnot, forming the core of the Martinus Scriblerus Club (founded in 1713).

Swift became increasingly active politically in these years. From 1707 to 1709 and again in 1710, Swift was in London unsuccessfully urging upon the Whig administration of Lord Godolphin the claims of the Irish clergy to the First-Fruits and Twentieths which brought in about £2,500 a year, already granted to their brethren in England. He found the opposition Tory leadership more sympathetic to his cause, and, when they came to power in 1710, he was recruited to support their cause as editor of The Examiner. In 1711, Swift published the political pamphlet *The Conduct of the Allies*, attacking the Whig government for its inability to end the prolonged war with France. The incoming Tory government conducted secret (and illegal) negotiations with France, resulting in the Treaty of Utrecht (1713) ending the War of the Spanish Succession.

Swift was part of the inner circle of the Tory government, and often acted as mediator between Henry St John (Viscount Bolingbroke), the secretary of state for foreign affairs (1710—1715), and Robert Harley (Earl of Oxford), lord treasurer and prime minister (1711—1714). Swift recorded his experiences and thoughts during this difficult time in a long series of letters to Esther Johnson, collected and published after his death as A Journal to Stella. The animosity between the two Tory leaders eventually led to the dismissal of Harley in 1714. With the death of Queen Anne and accession of George I that year, the Whigs returned to power, and the Tory leaders were tried for treason for conducting secret negotiations with France.

Also during these years in London, Swift became acquainted with the Vanhomrigh family (Dutch merchants who had settled in Ireland, then moved to London) and became involved with one of the daughters, Esther. Swift furnished Esther with the nickname "Vanessa", and she features as one of the main characters in his poem Cadenus and Vanessa. The poem and their correspondence suggest that Esther was infatuated with Swift, and that he may have reciprocated her affections, only to regret this and then try to break off the relationship. Esther followed Swift to Ireland in 1714, and settled at her old family home, Celbridge Abbey. Their uneasy relationship continued for some years; then there appears to have been a confrontation, possibly involving Esther Johnson. Esther Vanhomrigh died in 1723 at the age of 35, having destroyed the will she had made in Swift's favour. Another lady with whom he had a close but less intense relationship was Anne Long, a toast of the Kit-Cat Club.

Plot of *Gulliver Travels*

Gulliver's Travels can be ranked among the greatest satirical works of world literature. It was published anonymously in 1726 after his 6-year labor at it since 1720. It consists of four voyages of Gulliver, the protagonist, respectively to Lilliput, to Brobdingnag, to Laputa and other strange lands, and to the country of the Houyhnhnms, four major remote and fantastic countries after he has met with shipwrecks or pirates or other unfortunate happenings on the sea.

In the first part Lemuel Gulliver, a surgeon on Lilliput, where the inhabitants are six inches high. But they are greedy and vicious. The Emperor thinks himself the terror of the world, though he is only as big as Gulliver's thumb. The English political parties and religious dissension are satirized in the description of the wearers of high heels and low heels and of the controversy on the fantastic question whether eggs should be broken at the big or small end.

In the second part Gulliver comes to Brobdingnag, where he finds himself among wise giants sixty feet high. The king of Brobingnag makes the observation that European history is "only a heap of conspiracies, rebellions, murders, massacres, revolutions, banishments; the very worst effects that avarice, faction, hypocrisy, cruelty, madness, hatred, envy, lust, malice, and ambition could produce." His conclusion: "I can not but conclude the bulk of your natives to be the most pernicious race of little odious vermin that nature ever suffered to crawl upon the surface of the earth." That is to say the people lived in England is so harmful a race. Because of their devastating effects, the nature is greatly suffered. "Crawl upon" is employed to compare human being to disgusting beasts or insects or worms. So it is a sharp satire on the society in times.

The third part provides readers a series of adventures at several places. Again on a ship, captured by pirates and set adrift in a small canoe, he lands on the floating island of Laputa. This visit to the flying island of Laputa and other strange lands offer him chances of meeting the king and the nobles who are described as a group of absent-minded philosophers and astronomers engrossed in extremely abstract and absurd discussions. It is a skillful satire upon philosophers, men of science, historians, and projectors. Their behavior is abstract and laughable because the projectors are engaged in projects such as extracting sun-shines out of cucumbers, turning ice into gunpowder and making cloth from cobweb (the net work made by spiders).

The satire in the fourth part is the sharpest and bitterest. Again, Gulliver as captain of a ship was cast upon an unknown island, the land of Houyhnhnms (so named because the word sounds like the long-pitched cry or neighing of a horse). Here are horses born with reason and possessed of all good and admirable qualities, and they are the ruling class. The rest of the inhabitants are Yahoos, a species of hairy, naked and wild animals, disgusting creatures shaped like human beings, who are the embodiment of every conceivable evil. Then after learning the language of the Houyhnhnms, Gulliver is asked to tell about the conditions of England and Europe. First he remarks on the causes of furious and bloody wars, and then he tells about the unjust legal system and self-seeking lawyers in England. The greed for money prevalent in the English society of his time, and the exploitation of human labor as well as the idle life led by the noble men in his country are mentioned in his talk. He admires the Houyhnhnms. Finally Gulliver expresses his wish to stay forever with the Houyhnhnms, but it is not granted him. So he builds a canoe and sails to an uninhabited island, and there he is seized and carried by force into a Portuguese ship. Eventually he returns to England. Because he is so disgusted with the Yahoos that when he returns to England he looses consciousness when his wife kisses him. For he recognizes his wife as a vicious Yahoo in the shape of the human, so disgusting to him. Gulliver's illusion is getting worse and worse: he has difficulty in figuring out human beings and he thinks that horses speak to him.

Comments on *Gulliver Travels*

In *Gulliver Travels*, from different angles, Swift's social satire touches upon the political, religious, legal, military, scientific, philosophical as well as literary institutions in his England and the men who made their careers there.

It exposes the ugly appearances of the English ruling classes, showing their hypocrisy and greed, their intrigue and corruption, their ruthless oppression and exploitation of the common people. It criticizes the declining feudalism and the new capitalist relations, ridiculing the predominance of money in human relations in that society. It also attacks the aggressive wars and colonialism in the 18th century.

Satire, as a most distinct feature of Swift's *Gulliver Travels*, is a kind of writing that holds up to ridicule or contempt the weakness and wrong doings of individuals, groups, institutions, or humanity in general. The aim of satirists is to set a moral standard for society, and they attempt to persuade the readers to see their point of view through the force of laughter.

The most famous and representative satirical work in English literature is Jonathan Swift's *Gulliver Travels*. In the distant land of Brobdingnag, where the people are twelve times as tall as a normal human being, Gulliver is brought before the King to describe the English people. Swift satirizes the English people through the King's response: *He (the king) was perfectly astonished with the historical account I gave him of our affairs during the last century, protesting it was only a heap of conspiracies, rebellions, murders, massacres, revolutions, banishments; the very worst effects that avarice, faction, and so many evils could produce.* A similar expression will be read in part IV from our selections.

Major Characters

Lemuel Gulliver

He is the narrator and protagonist of the story. Gulliver is a bold, intelligent and well educated adventurer who visits a multitude of strange lands. He has courage for he undergoes some experiences of nearly being devoured by a giant rat, taken captive by pirates, shipwrecked on faraway shores, and shot in the face with poison arrows. His sixteen–year isolation from humanity is really hard to bear, however, he rarely shows such feeling and emotional attachment to family. In addition, Gulliver is quite different from other great travelers, such as Odysseus, who get themselves out of dangerous situations by exercising their wit and ability to trick others. He seems too dull for any battles of wit and too unimaginative to think up tricks, and thus he ends up with passive situations.

Houyhnhnms

They are rational horses and masters of land. The are the ruling class. They process all the virtues—reason, wisdom, knowledge, manners and self-control. Their thoughts and behavior are wholly governed by reason and truthfulness—they do not even have a word for "lie" in their language. They maintain a simple, and peaceful society. Houyhnhnms are like ordinary horses, except that they are highly intelligent and deeply wise. They live in a sort of socialist republic, with the needs of the community put before individual desires. They are the masters of the Yahoos, the savage humanlike creatures in Houyhnhnmland. In all, the Houyhnhnms have the greatest impact on Gulliver throughout all his four voyages. The meeting with Houyhnhnms becomes Gulliver a "human-hater" and he is grieved and unwilling to leave them. Even when he goes back in England he relates better with his horses than with his human family. He is certainly, in the end, a horse lover.

Yahoos

They are a species of hairy, naked, filthy and wild animals, disgusting creatures who are shaped like human beings. The men are characterized by their hairy bodies, and the women by their low-hanging breasts. They are extremely primitive in their eating habits. They are servants to Houyhnhnms, pulling their carriages and performing manual tasks. Though they are in the shape of human but behave exactly like animals. They have all the conceivable beastly qualities that Gulliver's own countrymen have—violent, evil and base. Despite Gulliver's disgust for these creatures, he ends his writings referring to himself as a Yahoo, just as what the Houyhnhnms do in the end— expel him from their realm. Thus, "Yahoo" becomes another term for human, at least in the mind of Gulliver at the end of his fourth journey.

Introduction to Chapter VI

This selection is from the fourth part of the novel, in which Gulliver tells, in the first person singular, his experiences when traveling in the land of Houyhnhnms, the noble horses. The Houyhnhnms, who are moral, intelligent, and noble-minded, stand in striking contrast to the Yahoos who are hairy, uncultivated, and infamous for their savagery, although they inhabit the same land with the Houyhnhnms. It is obvious that Swift throws his acid satire upon the corruption, hypocrisy, avarice, treachery , and other kinds of social evils of early 18th century England in Chapter VI. More over, he not only pours his antipathy to the realities, but also exhibits a strong desire for an ideal society, as is clearly illustrated by his description of the sharp contrast between the Houyhnhnms and Yahoos in Chapter VIII.

Part IV Chapter VI

[A continuation of the state of England under Queen Anne. The character of a first minister of state in European courts.]

My master was yet wholly at a loss to understand what motives could incite this race of lawyers to perplex, disquiet, and weary themselves, and engage in a confederacy of injustice[1], merely for the sake of injuring their fellow-animals; neither could he comprehend what I meant in saying, they did it for "hire." Whereupon I was at much pains to describe to him the use of "money" , the materials it was made of, and the value of the metals; that when a Yahoo had got a great store of this precious substance, he was able to purchase whatever he had a mind to; the finest clothing, the noblest houses, great tracts of land, the most costly meats and drinks, and have his choice of the most beautiful females. Therefore since "money" alone was able to perform all these feats, our Yahoos thought they could never have enough of it to spend, or to save, as they found themselves inclined, from their natural bent[2] either to profusion or avarice; that the rich man enjoyed the fruit of the poor man's labour, and the latter were a thousand to one in proportion to the former; that the bulk of our people were forced to live miserably, by labouring every day for small wages, to make a few live plentifully.I enlarged myself much on these, and many other particulars to the same purpose; but his Honour was still to seek[3]; for he went upon a supposition, that all animals had a title[4] to their share in the productions of the earth, and especially those who presided over the rest. Therefore he desired I would let him know, what these costly meats were, and how any of us happened to want[5] them? Whereupon I enumerated as many sorts as came into my head, with the various methods of dressing them[6], which could not be done without sending vessels by sea to every part of the world, as well for liquors to drink as for sauces and innumerable other conveniences[7]. I assured him that this whole globe of earth must be at least three times gone round before one of our better female Yahoos could get her breakfast, or a cup to put it in. He said that must needs be a miserable country which cannot furnish food for its own inhabitants. But what he chiefly wondered at was, how such vast tracts of ground as I described should be wholly without fresh water, and the people put to the necessity of sending over the sea for drink. I replied, that England (the dear place of my nativity) was computed to produce three times the quantity of food more than its inhabitants are able to consume, as well as liquors extracted from grain, or pressed out of the fruit of certain trees, which made excellent drink, and the same proportion in every other convenience of life. But, in order to feed the luxury and intemperance of the males, and the vanity of the females, we sent away the greatest part of our necessary things to other countries, whence, in return, we brought the materials of diseases, folly, and vice, to spend among ourselves. Hence it follows of necessity, that vast numbers of our people are compelled to seek their livelihood by begging, robbing, stealing, cheating, pimping, flattering, suborning, forswearing, forging[8], gaming[9], lying, fawning[10], hectoring[11], voting[12], scribbling[13], stargazing[14] poisoning, whoring, canting, libeling, freethinking[15], and the like occupations: every one of which terms I was at much pains to make him understand.

That "wine" was not imported among us from foreign countries to supply the want of water or other drinks, but because it was a sort of liquid which made us merry by putting us out of our senses, diverted all melancholy thoughts, begat wild extravagant imaginations in the brain, raised our hopes and banished our fears, suspended every office[16] of reason for a time, and deprived us of the use of our limbs, till we fell into a profound sleep; although it must be confessed, that we always awaked sick and dispirited; and that the use of this liquor filled us with diseases which made our lives uncomfortable and short.

But beside[17] all this, the bulk of our people supported themselves by furnishing the necessities or conveniences of life to the rich and to each other. For instance, when I am at home, and dressed as I ought to be, I carry on my body the workmanship of a hundred tradesmen; the building and furniture of my house employ as many more, and five times the number to adorn my wife.

I was going on to tell him of another sort of people, who get their livelihood by attending the sick, having, upon some occasions, informed his honour that many of my crew had died of diseases. But here it was with the utmost difficulty that I brought him to apprehend what I meant. He could easily conceive, that a Houyhnhnm, grew weak and heavy a few days before his death, or by some accident might hurt a limb; but that nature, who works all things to perfection, should suffer any pains to breed in our bodies, he thought impossible, and desired to know the reason of so unaccountable an evil. I told him, we fed on a thousand things which operated contrary to each other; that we ate when we were not hungry, and drank without the provocation of thirst; that we sate[18] whole nights drinking strong liquors, without eating a bit, which disposed us to sloth, inflamed our bodies, and precipitated or prevented digestion[19]; that prostitute female Yahoos acquired a certain malady, which bred rottenness in the bones of those who fell into their embraces; that this, and many other diseases, were propagated from father to son; so that great numbers came into the world with complicated maladies upon them; that it would be endless to give him a catalogue of all diseases incident to human bodies, for they would not be fewer than five or six hundred, spread over every limb and joint -in short, every part, external and intestine, having diseases appropriated to itself. To remedy which, there was a sort of people bred up among us in the profession, or pretence, of curing the sick. And because I had some skill in the faculty, I would, in gratitude to his honour, let him know the whole mystery and method by which they proceed.

But, besides real diseases, we are subject to many that are only imaginary, for which the physicians have invented imaginary cures; these have their several names, and so have the drugs that are proper for them; and with these our female Yahoos are always infested.

One great excellency in this tribe, is their skill at 'prognostics', wherein they seldom fail; their predictions in real diseases, when they rise to any degree of malignity, generally portending death, which is always in their power, when recovery is not: and therefore, upon any unexpected signs of amendment, after they have pronounced their sentence, rather than be accused as false prophets, they know how to approve their sagacity to the world, by a seasonable dose.

They are likewise of special use to husbands and wives who are grown weary of their mates; to eldest sons, to great ministers of state, and often to princes.

I had formerly, upon occasion[20], discoursed with my master upon the nature of government in general, and particularly of our own excellent constitution, deservedly the wonder and envy of the whole world. But having here accidentally mentioned a minister of state, he commanded me, some time after, to inform him, what species of Yahoo I particularly meant by that appellation.

I told him that a "first" or "chief minister of state", who was the person I intended to describe, was the creature wholly exempt from joy and grief, love and hatred, pity and anger; at least, makes use of no other passions, but a violent desire of wealth, power, and titles; that he applies his words to all uses, except to the indication of his mind; that he never tells a truth but with an intent that you should take it for a lie; nor a lie, but with a design that you should take it for a truth; that those he speaks worst of behind their backs are in the surest way of preferment; and whenever he begins to praise you to others, or to yourself, you are from that day forlorn. The worst mark you can receive is a promise, especially when it is confirmed with an oath; after which, every wise man retires, and gives over all hopes.

There are three methods, by which a man may rise to be chief minister. The first is, by knowing how, with prudence, to dispose of a wife, a daughter, or a sister; the second, by betraying or undermining his predecessor; and the third is, by a furious zeal, in public assemblies, against the corruption's of the court. But a wise prince would rather choose to employ those who practise the last of these methods; because such zealots prove always the most obsequious and subservient to the will and passions of their master. That these ministers, having all employments[21] at their disposal, preserve themselves in power, by bribing the majority of a senate or great council; and at last, by an expedient, called an "act of indemnity" [22] (whereof I described the nature to him), they secure themselves from after-reckonings[23], and retire from the public laden with the spoils of the nation.

The palace of a chief minister is a seminary to breed up others in his own trade: the pages, lackeys[24], and porters, by imitating their master, become ministers of state in their several districts, and learn to excel in the three principal ingredients, of insolence, lying, and bribery. Accordingly, they have a subaltern court paid to them by persons of the best rank[25]; and sometimes by the force of dexterity and impudence, arrive, through several gradations, to be successors to their lord.

He is usually governed by a decayed wench[26], or favourite footman, who are the tunnels through which all graces are conveyed[27], and may properly be called, in the last resort, the governors of the kingdom.

One day, in discourse, my master, having heard me mention the "nobility" of my country, was pleased to make me a compliment which I could not pretend to deserve: that he was sure I must have been born of some noble family, because I far exceeded in shape, colour, and cleanliness, all the Yahoos of his nation, although I seemed to fail in strength and agility, which must be imputed to my different way of living from those other brutes; and besides I was not only endowed with the faculty of speech, but likewise with some rudiments of reason, to a degree that, with all his acquaintance, I passed for a prodigy.

He made me observe, that among the Houyhnhnms, the white, the sorrel, and the iron-gray, were not so exactly shaped as the bay, the dapple-gray, and the black; nor born with equal talents of mind, or a capacity to improve them; and therefore continued always in the condition of servants, without ever aspiring to match out of their own race[28], which in that country would be reckoned monstrous and unnatural.

I made his honour my most humble acknowledgments for the good opinion he was pleased to conceive of me, but assured him at the same time, that my birth was of the lower sort, having been born of plain honest parents, who were just able to give me a tolerable education; that nobility, among us, was altogether a different thing from the idea he had of it; that our young noblemen are bred from their childhood in idleness and luxury; that, as soon as years will permit, they consume their vigour, and contract odious diseases among lewd females[29]; and when their fortunes are almost ruined, they marry some woman of mean birth, disagreeable person, and unsound constitution (merely for the sake of money), whom they hate and despise. That the productions of such marriages are generally scrofulous, rickety, or deformed children; by which means the family seldom continues above three generations, unless the wife takes care to provide a healthy father, among her neighbours or domestics, in order to improve and continue the breed. That a weak diseased body, a meagre countenance, and sallow complexion, are the true marks of noble blood; and a healthy robust appearance is so disgraceful in a man of quality, that the world concludes his real father to have been a groom or a coachman. The imperfections of his mind run parallel with those of his body, being a composition of spleen, dullness, ignorance, caprice, sensuality, and pride.

Without the consent of this illustrious body[30], no law can be enacted, repealed, or altered: and these nobles have likewise the decision of all our possessions, without appeal.

 **N o t e s**

[1]series of unlawful injustice

[2]natural inclination or tendency(天性)

[3]but still my master was to seek an answer, i.e., he still did not understand; his Honour, his majesty, the title of emperor, here refers to master in the land of Houyhnhnm

[4]right, claim

[5]lack

[6]preparing them for cooking, i.e., adding spices such as ginger, pepper, cinnamon, etc

[7]material comforts, goods, here, articles of food

[8]making counterfeit money (造假币)

[9]gambling

[10] 奉承

[11]threatening

[12]to vote for money or manipulate elections

[13]writing carelessly as a hack writer

[14]the occupation of an astrologer

[15]rejecting traditional religious belief, hence, in this context, behaving oneself loosely, immorally

[16]function

[17]besides

[18]sate-sat

[19]caused us to suffer from loose bowels or constipation （便秘）

[20]on suitable opportunity or sometimes

[21]official posts, here implying profitable jobs

[22]An act of this sort was usually passed at each session of Parliament, to protect holders of public office from the possible consequences of any official acts done illegally but in good faith（赦免条例）.

[23]later reckonings, i.e., reckonings of illegal gains after retirement from public office

[24]low servants; men servants

[25]they, of inferior rank themselves and their court are subjected to those of the highest ranks for they and their court are paid by them

[26]an immoral, corrupt young woman, perhaps a servant girl who is getting old

[27]the secret channels through which all favours are handed out

[28]to marry outside of their own race

[29]unchaste women

[30]the nobility

 Questions

1. What social evils and what professions are attacked by the author in Chapter VI?

2. How does a chief minister achieve his position?

3. How is the "nobility" described by the author?

4. According to your understanding, what are the similarities between Gulliver's native countrymen and Yahoos?

Analysis of Chapter VI

Chapter VI, from Part IV of *Gulliver's Travels* is to give Gulliver's master "master in the land of Houyhnhnms" a continual accounts of the state of England and England's first prime minister. All these descriptions have deeply confused the master.

Gulliver's natives are yahoo-like human beings. They are crazy about "hire." Here it means promotion of position and they are also crazy for money with which they can buy whatever they want. Their nature is profusion and avarice. The rich men are the minority of society depending on the fruit of the poor. After Gulliver's description, the master did not understand why the man of England are so greedy and horrible like that. Therefore, Gulliver go on explaining to the Master what these "costly meats(In Chapter VI, 1st paragraph, Line8, it means human being or natives of England)" were—such as: How the female cook breakfast; how they get water and make excellent drink (wine); the inequality between the poor and rich can be read. The poor provide the greatest part of our necessary things to other countries so as to feed the "luxury and intemperance of the males, and the vanity of the females", however in return, we brought the materials of disease, folly, and vice. In order to live we have to beg, rob, steal, cheat, pimp, forswear, flatter... and so on. Gulliver lists more than 20 words of evils. These parallel words make readers at tense reading it, feeling horrible to live in the world where evils are prevalent in every corner and Gulliver himself "was at much pains to make him understand." (In Chapter VI last line of 1st paragraph)

Gulliver's "Introduction of wine" in next paragraph is impressive and profound. It is a sort of liquid which made us merry, get rid of melancholy thoughts by putting us out of our senses; get wild extravagant imaginations in brain, raised our hopes and banish our fears, make us unreasonable for a time, result in unconscious limb and sound sleep. Eventually, wine made our lives uncomfortable and short.

Above all, English natives live an extravagant life. Though at home, one will dress as he ought to be, "I carry on my body the workmanship of a hundred tradesmen.(In Chapter VI 3rd paragraph)" In social intercourse, one must be able to use different arts to communicate with different persons, which makes one person a hundred tradesman. In result, one becomes hypocritical person of diverse personalities. In the following words "the building and furniture of my house employ as many more, and five times the number to adorn my wife." The structure "as many more" and the number "5 times to adorn" are a little exaggerated and absurd. However, to some extent, it is a satire reflecting the sick psychology of his contemporary Englishmen, a kind of wine and extravagant life.

"I was going on to tell himself of another sort of people." Here, "another sort of people" refers the diseased people. It is difficult for Master of Houyhnhnm to understand; because on the land of Houynhnhns, a Houyhnhnm grew weak and heavy a few days before his death or by accident might hurt a limb. According to the master, if making good use of our natural organs, it is impossible for us to suffer pains. Gulliver illustrates instances to satisfy master's curiosity about causes of diseases in human body. E.g. we feed on a thousand things, which operated contrary to each other; such as bad habits, amoral behavior (the propagation of malady from female prostitute) thus, numerous and endless diseases permeate in human world. Statistics have been employed to specify the seriousness of malady: *could not be fewer than 5 or 6 hundred spread over every limb and joint; those diseases are incurable* though a sort of people—doctors pretend to cure the sick.

Besides real diseases, they have imaginary disease and imaginary cures. Doctors are good at predictions. When they predict that somebody is of malignity (of fatal disease) and going to die, they are in the power, while the patients are at doctor's mercy.

In the latter part of Chapter VI, Gulliver explained the *nature of government and Minister of state was a creature wholly exempt from joy and grief, love and hatred, pity and anger.* The Minister is emotionless and passionless. What he pursues is wealth, power and titles. He is a liar, *whenever he begins to praise you to others or to yourself, you are from that day forlorn.* That is to say when you are praised in front of others by the prime minister, from that moment on, you are deserted or wrecked, and you are devastated. The prime minister is unreliable. If a wise man receives his promise, he will give up hopes and withdraw.

Gulliver presents three methods of seizing the position of Minister. One way is to dispose of a wife, a daughter or a sister (abandon wife, daughter or sister to devote to the scheme of rising to chief minister's position) ; another way is betraying or undermining the predecessors and the third way is to be enthusiastic or crazy about the public assemblies against the corruption of the court. "A wise prince", king or governor will choose those who practice the last of three methods, because such zealots prove always obedient and loyal to the will and passions of their master. Moreover, these "ministers" have their official authoritative posts. These posts are profitable. In order to preserve their power, they bribe the majority of a senate or great council. If the ministers preserved their office, they still have preserved ways of making money—"(at the bottom the 10th paragraph) *by an expedient called an 'act of indemnity'"...they secured themselves from after reckoning.* "after reckoning" means later reckoning. The ministers make sure that they could be free from reckoning of illegal gains after their retirement from the governmental offices.

Therefore, the ministers retired with wealth and the nation was burdened with the spoils.

For the ministers had set bad examples, their subordinates would follow them, imitate them and become the "ministers of street." The persons who are inferior to the ministers follow their master's footprints and even excel them in three principal ingredients of insolence, lying and bribery. *They have a subaltern court paid to them by persons of the best rank*(In Chapter VI 11th paragraph). They, still, refer to the inferior officers. These officers and their court are subjected to those of higher ranks, who pay them and their court. Someday in the future, the inferior officers may be successors to their masters through several grades of promotion. However, Gulliver himself is considered as man from noble, so from many aspects, he is different from what Yahoos look like. Yahoos, in the land of Houyhnhnms, are servants of Houyhnhnms. They are lower than Houyhnhnms, because Yahoos are different from Houyhnhnms in the aspects of appearance, talents and capacity. The Houyhnhnms are forbidden to marry out of their race. For other races are considered monstrous and unnatural. This rule keeps the Houyhnhnms pure and unpolluted.

At the end of the conversation between Gulliver and Master of Houyhnhnms, Gulliver makes a distinct explanation of the different connotation of "nobility" in English and in the language of the Houyhnhnms. The concept of nobility in English is so superficial and shallow. In the last paragraph of this chapter, the author points out this noble race, the Houyhnhnms is the truly ruling class on the land.

Gulliver's Travels, Swift's achievement in literature, is thus a satire on the whole English society of 18th century. Especially in this part, English life is shown to resemble the despicable social life of the Yahoos and to contrast with the nobility of the Houyhnhnm.

 **中文译文**

《格列佛游记》 第四部分（第六章）

（再谈女王统治下的英国——欧洲宫廷中一位首相大臣的性格。）

我的主人还是完全不能明白这一帮律师为什么仅仅为了迫害自己的同类而不厌其烦地组织这么一个不义的组织？他们究竟有什么目的呢？对于我说的他们干这事是受人之雇，它也搞不明白究竟又是怎么回事。于是我又只好不厌其烦地向它说明钱的作用。解释钱是由哪些材料制成的，各种不同金属的价值如何。我对它说，当一只"野胡"储有大量这样的贵重物质时，它想买什么就都能买到，比如最好的衣服、最华丽的房屋以及大片的土地，最昂贵的肉食和酒类，还可以挑选到最漂亮的女人。所以，既然金钱一项就能建立这种种功劳，我们的"野胡"就认为，不论是用钱还是储蓄，钱总是越多越好，永远也不会有满足的时候，因为他们发现自己天性就是这样，不是挥霍浪费就是贪得无厌。富人享受着穷人的劳动成果，而穷人和富人在数量上的比例是一千比一。我们的大多数人民被迫过悲惨的日子，为了一点点报酬每天都得辛苦劳作，为的是能让少数人过富裕的生活。我在这些问题以及许多别的类似的细节上谈了很多，可主人阁下还要往下问，因为它是这样推想的：地球上出产的东西，所有动物都有权享受一份，尤其是主宰其他动物的统治者更有享受的权利。因此它要我告诉它，那些昂贵的肉食到底是些什么肉？我们怎么偏偏就吃不到？我于是就把能想得到的各种肉类一一列举出来，同时还列举了各种不同的烹调的方法；如果不是派船只航海到世界各地去采办酒类、调料以及数不清的其他食品，这一切是办不到的。我对他讲，给我们的一只境况较好的雌"野胡"做一顿早餐或者弄一只盛早餐的杯子，至少得绕地球转三圈才能办到。它说，一个国家连自己居民的饭都供不起，肯定是个悲惨的国家。但更使它感到奇怪的是，在像我描述的这么大片的土地上怎么竟然完全没有淡水，人们必须到海外去弄饮料？我回答说，英国（那是我亲爱的出生地）生产的粮食据估算是那里居民消费需求的三倍；从谷物和某种树木的果实中提取或榨取的液体可制成极好的饮料，它们和每一样别的日常用品一样，也都是居民消费需求的三倍。但是，为了满足男人的奢侈无度和女人的虚荣，我们都把绝大部分的必需品送到国外去，而由此换回疾病、愚蠢、罪恶的材料供自己消费。于是我们大多数人就没有生存的依靠，只好靠讨饭、抢劫、偷窃、欺骗、拉皮条、作伪证、谄媚、教唆、伪造、赌博、说谎、奉承、威吓、搞选举、滥作文、星象占卜、放毒、卖淫、侈谈、诽谤、想入非非以及各种相似的事来糊口过日子。这其中的每一个名词我都费了不少劲来解释，最后它终于明白了。

我又说，我们从国外进口酒类倒并不是因为我们缺少淡水或其他饮料，而是因为酒是一种喝了可以使人麻木而让人高兴的液体；它可以消遣我们所有的忧愁，在脑海中唤起狂野奔放的想象，增加希望，驱除恐惧，使每一点理智暂时都失去效用，四肢不能运动，直到我们昏睡过去。可是我们必须承认，一觉醒来总是精神萎靡，而总喝这种流体只会给我们带来种种疾病，使我们的生命痛苦而短暂。

然而除了所有这一切之外，我们的大多数人民还得靠向富人提供日常必需品或者互相之间提供这些东西来维持自己的生活。比如我在家的时候，身上穿得像模像样，那一身衣服就是一百名工匠的手艺；我的房子和房子里的家具也同样需要这么多人来制造，而把我的妻子打扮一下，则需要五百名工匠付出劳动。

接下来我又跟他谈到另一类人，他们是靠侍候病人来维持生活的，我在前面也曾有几次跟主人说过，我船上有许多水手就是因生病才死的。可是我真是费了九牛二虎之力才使它明白了我的意思。一个"慧骃"在临死前几天会慢慢变得衰弱无力、行动迟缓，或者遇上什么意外会弄伤一条腿，这对于它都是很容易就能理解的。可是，为什么大自然将万事万物都创造得非常完美，竟会让我们的身体遭受痛苦？它不相信这些，所以它就想知道造成如此不可解释的灾难，究竟是什么原因呢？我就对它说，我们吃的东西不下千种，吃下去却互不相容；还有，我们肚子不饿却还要吃，嘴巴不渴却只管喝；通宵达旦坐在那儿喝烈性酒，东西却不吃一点儿，喝得人懒慵松散，身体发烧，不是消化太快就是无法消化。卖淫的女"野胡"身上有一种病，谁要是投进她们的怀抱就得烂骨头，而这种病和许多别的病一样，都是遗传的，所以许多人生到这个世上来，身上就已经带有种种复杂的疾病了。要是把人身上的所有疾病全都讲给它听，一时还真说不完，因为这些病不下五六百种，人的四肢和每一个关节——总之，身体的每一部分都各有毛病。为了治疗这些疾病，我们中间就培养了一类专以治病为业的人，不过也有冒充的。因为我在这一行上有点本事，为了感谢主人对我的恩德，我愿意把那些人行医的秘密和方法全都说给它听。

但是，除了这些真正的疾病之外我们还会生许多仅仅是空想的病，对此医生们则发明了空想的治疗的方法；这些病各有其不同的名称，并且也有对症的药品。我们的女"野胡"们就老是会染上这样的空想病。

这帮人有超人的本事，他们能预测病症的后果，这方面难得会弄错。真正的疾病症状恶化，通常死亡就在眼前了，没有办法治好，那他们的预言就总是有把握的。所以，要是他们已经宣判了病的死刑，而病人却出乎意料地渐有好转的迹象，他们也不会就这样任人去骂他们是骗子；他们知道如何及时地给病人用上一剂药就可以向世人证明，他们还是有先见之明的。

对自己的配偶已感到厌倦的丈夫或妻子，对长子、大臣，尤其是对君王，他们也都有特别的用处。我前面已经跟我的主人谈过政府的一般性质，特别是我们那优越的宪法，那真是值得全世界赞叹和美慕的。这里我又偶然提到了"大臣"这个词，它就要我跟它说说，我所称的"大臣"到底是一种什么样的"野胡"。

我说，我要描述的这位首相大臣是这样一个人：他整个儿是哀乐无动于衷、爱恨不明、不同情不动怒；至少你可以说，他除了对财富、权力和爵位有强烈的欲望外，别的一概不动感情。他说的话当什么用都可以，就是不表明他的心。他每说一句实话，却总要想你会把它当成谎言，而每次说谎又都以为你会信以为真。那些被他在背后说得一塌糊涂的人，实际上是他最喜欢的人，而每当他向别人或当你的面夸奖你时，从那天起你就要倒霉。最糟糕的标志是你得到了他的一个许诺，如果他在向你许诺时还发了誓，那就更为糟糕；他这么做，每一个聪明人都会自行引退，一切希望全都放弃。

　　一个人可以通过三种办法爬上首相大臣的位置。第一，要知道怎么样以比较慎重的方式出卖自己的妻女和姐妹；第二，背叛或者暗杀前任首相大臣；第三，在公开集会上慷慨激昂地抨击朝廷的各种腐败。但是英明的君王一定愿意挑选惯于采用第三种办法的人，因为事实证明，那些慷慨激昂的人总是最能顺从其主子的旨意和爱好。这些大臣一旦控制了所有的要职，就会贿赂元老院或者大枢密院中的大多数人，以此来保全自己的势力。最后，他们还借一种"免罚法"（我向它说明了这条法令的性质）以保证自己事后免遭不测，满载着从国民身上贪污来的赃物从公职上悄然引退下来。

　　首相官邸是他培养同伙的学校。他的随从、仆人和看门人通过效仿其主子，也都在各自的区域内做起大官来。他们向主人学习蛮横、说谎和贿赂这三种主要本领而能更胜一筹，于是他们也就有了自己的小朝廷，受到贵族的奉承。有时他们还靠机巧和无耻，一步步往上爬，终于做上了他们老爷的继承人。

　　首相大臣往往受制于色衰的荡妇或者自己的亲信仆人，趋炎附势、企求恩宠的人都得通过这个渠道，所以说到底，讲他们是王国的统治者，倒是很恰当的。

　　有一天，我的主人听我谈到我国的贵族，它倒是说了我一句好话，不过我是不敢当。它说，它敢肯定我是出身于贵族家庭，因为我模样好，肤色白，身上干净，这几方面都远远超过它们国内所有的"野胡"；虽然我似乎不及它们那样身强力壮、动作敏捷，可那是因为我的生活方式与那些畜生完全不一样。除此之外，我不但具有说话的能力，而且还有几分理性，以致它所有的相识都认为我是一个难得的人才。

　　它叫我注意，"慧骃"中的白马、栗色马和铁青马样子长得跟火红马、深灰色斑纹马和黑马并不完全一样，这是天生的，也没有变好的可能，所以它们永远处在仆人的地位。它们如果妄想出人头地，那样的话，在这个国家中就会被认为是一件可怕而反常的事。

　　我的主人十分看重我，对此我向它表示万分的感激；不过我同时又告诉它，我其实出身低微，父母都是普普通通的老百姓，只能供我接受一些还说得过去的教育。我说我们那里的贵族可跟它想象的完全不一样；我们的年轻贵族从孩提时代起就过着游手好闲、奢侈豪华的生活；一到成年，他们就在淫荡的女人中鬼混，消耗精力，并染上一身恶病；等到自己的财产所剩无几时，就娶一个出身卑贱、脾气乖戾而身体还不好的女人做妻子，那只是因为她有几个钱，其实他对这个女人是既恨又瞧不起。这种婚姻的产物，生下来的孩子通常不是患瘰疬病、佝偻病，就是残废。做妻子的如果不注意在邻居或佣人中给她的孩子找一个身体强健的父亲以改良品种传宗接代的话，那这家人一般是传不到三代就要断子绝孙。身体虚弱多病，面貌瘦削苍白，是一个常见的贵族的标志。健康强壮的外表在一位贵族看来反倒是一种极大的耻辱，因为世人会认为他真正的父亲一定是个马夫或者车夫。他的头脑也和他的身体一样大有缺陷，那是古怪、迟钝、无知、任性、荒淫和傲慢的合成品。

不得到这一帮贵族的同意，任何法令都不能颁布，既不能废除，也不能修改。这些贵族还对我们所有的财产拥有决定权，而不用征求我们的意见。

References

[1] 斯威夫特. 格列佛游记 [M]. 孙予，译，上海：上海译文出版社，2006.

Unit 8   Richard Brinsley Sheridan (1751—1816)

Life

Sheridan was born in 1751 in Dublin, Ireland, where his family had a house on the fashionable Dorset Street. While in Dublin Sheridan attended the English Grammar School in Grafton Street. The family moved permanently to England in 1758 when he was aged seven. He was a pupil at Harrow School from 1762 to 1768.

His mother, Frances Sheridan, was a playwright and novelist. She had two plays produced in London in the early 1760s, though she is best known for her novel *The Memoirs of Miss Sidney Biddulph* (1761). His father, Thomas Sheridan,

was for a while an actor-manager at the Smock Alley Theatre in Dublin, but following his move to England in 1758 he gave up acting and wrote several books on the subject of education, and especially the standardisation of the English language in education. After Sheridan's period in Harrow School, his father employed a private tutor, Lewis Ker, who directed his studies in his father's house in London, while Angelo instructed him in fencing and horsemanship.

In 1772 Sheridan fought two duels with Captain Thomas Mathews, who had written a newspaper article defaming the character of Elizabeth Ann Linley, the woman Sheridan intended to marry. In the first duel, they agreed to fight in Hyde Park, but finding it too crowded they went first to the Hercules Pillars tavern and then on to the Castle Tavern in Henrietta Street, Covent Garden. Far from its romantic image, the duel was short and bloodless. Mathews lost his sword and, according to Sheridan, was forced to "beg for his life" and sign a retraction of the article. The apology was made public and Mathews, infuriated by the publicity the duel had received, refused to accept his defeat as final and challenged Sheridan to another duel. Sheridan was not obliged to accept this challenge, but could have become a social pariah if he had not. The second duel, fought in July 1772 at Kingsdown near Bath, was a much more ferocious affair. This time both men broke their swords but carried on fighting in a "desperate struggle for life and honour." Both were wounded, Sheridan dangerously, being "borne from the field with a portion of his antagonist's weapon sticking through an ear, his breast-bone touched, his whole body covered with wounds and blood, and his face nearly beaten to jelly with the hilt of Mathews' sword." His remarkable constitution pulled him through, and eight days after this bloody affair the Bath Chronicle was able to announce that he was out of danger. Mathews escaped in a post chaise.

The School for Scandal

Sheridan's famous comedy *The School for Scandal,* written in 1777, is condidered his masterpiece. This play presents a brilliant protryal of England's high society and a biting satire on the morals and manners of that age.

Plot

Act I

Scene I: Lady Sneerwell, a wealthy young widow, and her hireling Snake discuss her various scandal-spreading plots. Snake asks why she is so involved in the affairs of Sir Peter Teazle, his ward Maria, and Charles and Joseph Surface, two young men under Sir Peter's informal guardianship, and why she has not yielded to the attentions of Joseph, who is highly respectable. Lady Sneerwell confides that Joseph wants Maria, who is an heiress, and that Maria wants Charles. Thus she and Joseph are plotting to alienate Maria from Charles by putting out rumors of an affair between Charles and Sir Peter's new young wife, Lady Teazle. Joseph arrives to confer with Lady Sneerwell. Maria herself then enters, fleeing the attentions of Sir Benjamin Backbite and his uncle Crabtree. Mrs. Candour enters and ironically talks about how "tale-bearers are as bad as the tale-makers." Soon after that, Sir Benjamin and Crabtree also enter, bringing a good deal of gossip with them. One item is the imminent return of the Surface brothers' rich uncle Sir

Oliver from the East Indies, where he has been for fifteen years; another is Charles' dire financial situation.

Scene II: Sir Peter complains of Lady Teazle's spendthrift ways. Rowley, the former steward of the Surfaces' late father, arrives, and Sir Peter gives him an earful on the subject. He also complains that Maria has refused Joseph, whom he calls "a model for the young men of the age," and seems attached to Charles, whom he denounces as a profligate. Rowley defends Charles, and then announces that Sir Oliver has just arrived from the East Indies.

Act II

Scene I: Sir Peter argues with his wife, Lady Teazle, refusing to be "ruined by [her] extravagance." He reminds her of her recent and far humbler country origins. Lady Teazle excuses herself by appealing to "the fashion", and departs to visit Lady Sneerwell. Despite their quarrel, Sir Peter still finds himself charmed by his wife even when she is arguing with him.

Scene II: At Lady Sneerwell's, the scandal-mongers have great fun at the expense of friends not present. Lady Teazle and Maria arrive; Lady Teazle joins in, but Maria is disgusted. So is Sir Peter, when he arrives, and rather breaks up the party with his comments. He departs, the others retire to the next room, and Joseph seizes the opportunity to court Maria, who rejects him again. Lady Teazle returns and dismisses Maria, and it is revealed that she is seriously flirting with Joseph, who doesn't want her, but cannot afford to alienate her.

Scene III: Sir Oliver calls on his old friend Sir Peter. He is amused by Sir Peter's marriage to a young wife. Their talk turns to the Surface brothers. Sir Peter praises Joseph's high morals but Sir Oliver suspects that he might be a hypocrite.

Act III

Scene I: Sir Oliver describes his plan to visit each of the brothers incognito to test their characters. He will disguise himself as their needy relative Mr. Stanley, and ask each for his help. Rowley also brings in the "friendly Jew" Moses, a moneylender who has tried to help Charles, to explain Charles' position. Moses mentions that he is to introduce Charles to yet another moneylender ("Mr. Premium") that very evening. Sir Oliver decides that with Moses' assistance, he will pose as Premium when visiting Charles (still intending to visit Joseph as Stanley).

Sir Peter is left alone and when Maria enters, he tries to convince her to marry Joseph expressing him as a worthier match than Charles, whom she favours. When she is not persuaded, he threatens her with "the authority of a guardian." She goes, and Lady Teazle enters asking her husband for two hundred pounds. Sir Peter and Lady Teazle argue again, and conclude that they should separate.

Scene II: Sir Oliver (as Mr. Premium) arrives with Moses at Charles' house. While they are waiting in the hall, Trip, the servant, tries to negotiate a loan on his own account from Moses. Sir Oliver concludes that "this is the temple of dissipation indeed!"

Scene III: Charles and his raucous guests drink heavily and sing merry songs, as they prepare for a night of gambling. Charles raises a toast to Maria. Moses and "Premium" enter, and Sir Oliver is dismayed at the scene. Charles does not recognise his long-lost uncle. Charles frankly asks "Premium" for credit, noting that Sir Oliver (whom he believes is in India) will soon leave him a fortune. "Premium" discounts this possibility, noting that Sir Oliver could live many years, or disinherit his nephew. He asks if Charles has any valuables of his own to sell for immediate cash. Charles admits that he has sold the family silver and his late father's library, and offers to sell "Premium" the family portrait collection. "Premium" accepts, but Sir Oliver is silently outraged.

Act IV

Scene I: Charles goes on to sell all of the family portraits to "Premium", using the rolled-up family tree as an auction-hammer. However, he refuses to sell the last portrait, which is of Sir Oliver, out of respect for his benefactor; Charles will not sell it even when "Premium" offers as much for it as for all the rest. Moved, Sir Oliver inwardly forgives Charles. Sir Oliver and Moses leave, and Charles sends a hundred pounds of the proceeds for the relief of "Mr. Stanley", despite Rowley's objection.

Scene II: Sir Oliver, reflecting on Charles's character with Moses, is met by Rowley, who has brought him the hundred pounds sent to "Stanley." Declaring "I'll pay his debts, and his benevolence too", Sir Oliver plans to go meet his other nephew in the person of Stanley.

Scene III: Joseph, anxiously awaiting a visit from Lady Teazle, is told by a servant that she has just left "herchair at the milliner's next door" and so has the servant draw a screen across the window (his reason: "my opposite neighbour is a maiden lady of so curious a temper"). On her entrance, Joseph forswears any interest in Maria, and flirts in earnest with Lady Teazle, perversely suggesting that she should make a "faux pas" for the benefit of her reputation. The servant returns to announce Sir Peter, and Lady Teazle hides in panic behind the screen. Sir Peter enters and tells Joseph that he suspects an affair between Charles and Lady Teazle (due to the rumours spread by Joseph and Lady Sneerwell). Joseph hypocritically professes confidence in Charles' and Lady Teazle's honour. Sir Peter confides his intention to give his wife a generous separate maintenance during his life and the bulk of his fortune on his demise. He also urges Joseph to pursue his suit with Maria (much to Joseph's annoyance, as Lady Teazle is listening behind the screen).

Charles's arrival is announced. Sir Peter decides to hide, and have Joseph sound Charles out about his relationship with Lady Teazle. He starts behind the screen, but sees the corner of Lady Teazle's petticoat there already. Joseph "confesses" that he is not as virtuous as he seems: "a little French milliner, a silly rogue that plagues me" is hiding there to preserve her own reputation. Sir Peter then hides in the closet.

Charles now enters and Joseph questions him about Lady Teazle. Charles disclaims any designs on her, noting that Joseph and the lady seem to be intimate. To stop Charles, Joseph whispers to him that Sir Peter is hiding in the closet, and Charles hauls him forth. Sir Peter tells Charles he now regrets his suspicions about him. Charles passes off his comments about Joseph and Lady Teazle as a joke.

When Lady Sneerwell is announced, Joseph rushes out to stop her from coming up. Meanwhile, Sir Peter tells Charles about the "French milliner." Charles insists on having a look at her and flings down the screen as Joseph returns, discovering Lady Teazle. Charles, very amused, leaves the other three dumbstruck individuals. Joseph concocts an explanation for Sir Peter of why he and Lady Teazle are together. But she refuses to endorse it and admits that she came to pursue an affair with Joseph; however, having learned of Sir Peter's generosity, she has repented. She denounces Joseph and exits, and the enraged Sir Peter follows as Joseph continues trying to pretend innocence.

Act V

Scene I: Sir Oliver (as Mr. Stanley) now visits Joseph. Joseph, like Charles, does not recognise his long-lost uncle. He greets "Stanley" with effusive professions of goodwill, but refuses to give "Stanley" any financial assistance, saying he has donated all his money to support Charles. "Stanley" suggests that Sir Oliver would help him if he was here, and that Joseph might pass on some of what Sir Oliver has given him. But Joseph tells "Stanley" that Sir Oliver is in fact very stingy, and has given him nothing except trinkets such as tea, shawls, and "Indian crackers." Furthermore, Joseph has lent a great deal to his brother, so that he has nothing left for "Stanley." Sir Oliver is enraged, as he knows both statements are flat lies, he sent Joseph 12,000 pounds from India. He stifles his anger, and departs amid further effusions. Rowley arrives with a letter for Joseph announcing that Sir Oliver has arrived in town.

Scene II: At Sir Peter's house, Lady Sneerwell, Mrs. Candour, Sir Benjamin, and Crabtree exchange confused rumours about the Teazle affair. Sir Benjamin says Sir Peter was wounded in a swordfight with Joseph Surface, while Crabtree insists it was a pistol duel with Charles. When Sir Oliver enters, they take him for a doctor and demand news of the wounded man. At that moment Sir Peter arrives to prove the report wrong, and orders the scandalmongers out of his house. Sir Oliver says he has met both of his nephews and agrees with Sir Peter's (former) estimate of Joseph's high character, but then acknowledges with laughter that he knows the story of what happened at Joseph's with the closet and screen. When he leaves, Rowley tells Sir Peter that Lady Teazle is in tears in the next room, and Sir Peter goes to reconcile with her.

Scene III: Lady Sneerwell complains to Joseph that Sir Peter, now that he knows the truth about Joseph, will allow Charles to marry Maria. They plot to use Snake as a witness to a supposed relationship between Charles and Lady Sneerwell, and she withdraws.

Sir Oliver arrives. Joseph takes him for "Stanley" and orders him out. Charles arrives and recognises "Premium." Despite the identity confusion, both brothers want the man out before Sir Oliver comes. As Charles and Joseph try to eject their incognito uncle, Sir Peter and Lady Teazle arrive with Maria, ending Sir Oliver's pretense. Sir Oliver, Sir Peter, and Lady Teazle together condemn Joseph, but Sir Oliver forgives Charles because of his refusal to sell Sir Oliver's picture and his generous aid to his uncle "Stanley." Maria, however, declines to give Charles her hand, citing his supposed involvement with Lady Sneerwell. Joseph now reveals Lady Sneerwell. Charles is baffled, and Rowley then summons Snake. Snake, however, has been bribed to turn against Sneerwell, so her lie is exposed. After Lady Teazle tells her that she (Lady Teazle) is withdrawing from the School for Scandal, Lady Sneerwell leaves in a rage, and Joseph follows, supposedly to keep her from further malicious attacks. Charles and Maria are reconciled. Charles makes no promises about reforming, but indicates that Maria's influence will keep him on a "virtuous path." The concluding line assures the audience that "even Scandal dies, if you approve."

Comments on *The School for Scandal*

The School for Scandal has been widely admired. The English critic William Hazlitt was particularly effusive in his praise of Sheridan's comedies in general and of this play in particular:

The School for Scandal is, if not the most original, perhaps the most finished and faultless comedy which we have. When it is acted, you hear people all around you exclaiming, "Surely it is impossible for anything to be cleverer." Besides the wit and ingenuity of this play, there is a genial spirit of frankness and generosity about it, that relieves the heart as well as clears the lungs. It professes a faith in the natural goodness as well as habitual depravity of human nature.

Edmund Gosse called the play "perhaps the best existing English comedy of intrigue", while Charles Lamb wrote that "This comedy grew out of Congreveand Wycherley", but criticised "sentimental incompatibilities" even while admitting that "the gaiety upon the whole is buoyant."

Samuel Barber composed his first full orchestral work as an overture programmed for the play. On the other hand, the play has also in modern times been criticised for some hints of anti-Semitism, specifically "the disparaging remarks made about moneylenders, who were often Jewish." It is true that the moneylender Moses is portrayed in a comparatively positive light, but the way he is described suggest that he is in some way to be considered an exception to Jews in general; also, his own usurious business practices as stated to Sir Peter are clearly less than exemplary. It may be significant that in Johann Zoffany's portrait of Robert Baddeley as Moses, we find that "Under his arm Moses holds a rolled parchment of the Surface family tree that is used as an auction hammer, and he seems to be ticking off pictures in the catalogue", although in the play Careless is the auctioneer in the relevant scene and Moses has a relatively minor role.

Another criticism that has been made of the play involves the characterisation. A writer in the 19th century periodical Appleton's Journal states that:

The great defect of *The School for Scandal*, the one thing which shows the difference between a comic writer of the type of Sheridan and a great dramatist like Shakespeare, is the unvarying wit of the characters. And not only are the characters all witty, but they all talk alike. Their wit is Sheridan's wit, which is very good wit indeed; but it is Sheridan's own.

Another reviewer in Variety noted of a 1995 production starring Tony Randall as Sir Peter Teazle that Sheridan's play was "such a superbly crafted laugh machine, and so timeless in delivering delectable comeuppance to a viper's nest of idle-rich gossipmongers, that you'd practically have to club it to death to stifle its amazing pleasures"

But in the hands of a talented director and cast, the play still offers considerable pleasure. A New York production of 2001 prompted praise in the New York Times for being "just the classy antidote one needs in a celebrity-crazed world where the invasion of privacy is out of control, but the art of gossip is nonexistent."

The School for Scandal

Act I (Excerpt)

(Lady Sneerwell at her dressing table with Lappet)

(Miss Verjuice drinking chocolate)

Lady Sneerwell: The Paragraphs, you say, were all inserted?

Verjuice: They were, Madam, and as I copied them myself in a feigned[1] Hand, there can be no suspicion whence they came.

Lady Sneerwell: Did you circulate[2] the Report of Lady Britfle's intrigue with Captain Boastall?

Verjuice: Madam, by this time Lady Brittle is the talk of half the town, and I doubt not in a week the men will toast her as a demirep[3].

Lady Sneerwell: What have you done as to the insinuation as to a certain Baronet's Lady and a certain Cook.

Verjuice: That is in as fine a train as your ladyship could wish. I told the story yesterday to my own maid with directions to communicate it directly to my hairdresser. He I am informed has a brother who courts a Milliners' Prentice in pallmall whose mistress has a first cousin whose sister is feme de Chambre to Mrs Clackit-so that in the common course of things it must reach Mrs Clackit's ears within flour-and-twenty hours and then, you know, the business is as good as done.

Lady Sneerwell: Why, truly, Mrs Clackit has a very pretty talent, a great deal of industry-yet-yes-been tolerably successful in her way. To my knowledge, she has been the cause of breaking off six matches, of three sons being disinherited and four daughters being turned out of doors, of three several elopements, as many close confinements, nine separate maintenances and two divorces, Nay I have more than once traced her causing a tete-a-tete in the town and country magazine-when the parties perhaps had never seen each other's faces before in the course of their lives.

Verjuice: She certainly has talents.

Lady Sneerwell: But her manner is gross[4].

Verjuice: This very true. She generally designs well, has a free tongue and a bold invention; but her colouring is too dark and her outline often extravagant. She wants that delicacy of tint, and mellowness of sneer, which distinguish your Ladyship's Scandal.

Lady Sneerwell: Ah! You are partial, Verjuice.

Verjuice: Not in the least; everybody allows that lady Sneerwell can do more with a word or a look than many can with the most laboured detail, even when they happen to have a little truth on their side to support it.

Lady Sneerwell: Yes, my dear Verjuice. I am no hypocrite to deny the satisfaction I reap from the success of my efforts. Wounded myself, in the early part of my life, by the envenomed tongue of slander, I confess I have since known no to the reducing others to the level of my own injured pleasure equal reputation.

Verjuice: Nothing can be more natural. But, my dear lady Sneerwell, there is one affair in which you have lately employed me, wherein, I confess I am at a loss to guess your motives.

Lady Sneerwell: I conceive you mean with respect to my neighbour, Sir Peter Teazle, and his family-Lappet. And has my conduct in this matter really appeared to you so mysterious?

Verjuice: Entirely so.

Lady Sneerwell: An old Batchelor as sir Peter was, having taken a young wife from out of the country—as Lady Teazle is—are certainly fair subjects for a little mischievous raillery; but here are two young men, to whom sir Peter has acted as a kind of guardian since their father's death, the eldest possessing the most amiable character and universally well spoken of, the youngest, the most dissipated and extravagant young fellow in the kingdom, without friends or character-the former one an avowed admirer of yours and apparently your favourite, the latter attached to Maria sir Peter's ward, and confessedly beloved by her.

Verjuice: Now on the face of these circumstances, it is utterly unaccountable to me, why you, a young widow with no great jointure, should not close with the passion of a man of such character and expectations as Mr Surface;and more so why you should be so uncommonly earnest to destroy the mutual attachment subsisting between his brother Charles and Maria.

Lady Sneerwell: Then at once to unravel this mistery.1 must inform you that love has no share whatever in the intercourse between Mr Surface and me.

Verjuice: No!

Lady Sneerwell: His real attachment is to Maria, or her fortune;but finding in his brother a favoured rival, He has been obliged to mask his pretensions, and profit by my assistance.

Verjuice: Yet still I am more puzzled why you should interest yourself in his success.

Lady Sneerwell: Heavens! How dull you are! Cannot you surmise the weakness which I hitherto, thro' shame have concealed even from you?Must I confess that Charles-that Libertine, that extravagant, that bankrupt in fortune and reputation-that he it is for whom I am thus anxious and malicious and to gain whom I would sacrifice eveything.

Verjuice: Now indeed, your conduct appears consistent and I no longer wonder at your enmity to Maria, but how came you and Mr Surface so confidential?

Lady Sneerwell: For our mutual interest-but I have found out him a tong time since, altho' he has contrived to deceive everybody beside. I know him to be artful selfish and malicious-while with sir Peter, and indeed with all his acquaintance, he passes for a youthful miracle of prudence-good sense and benevolence.

Verjuice: Yes, yes, I know sir Peter vows he has not his equal in England;and, above all, He praises him as a man of sentiment.

Lady Sneerwell: True and with the assistance of his sentiments and hypocrisy[5] he has brought sir Peter entirely in his interests with respect to Maria and is now I believe attempting to flatter Lady Teazle into the same good opinion towards him—while poor Charles has no friend in the house-though I fear he has a powerful one in Maria's heart, against whom we must direct our schemes.

Lady Sneerwell: Show him up. He generally calls about this time. I don't wonder at people's giving him to me for a lover.

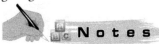 **N o t e s**

[1] 伪造的

[2] 传播，扩散

[3] 娼妓，情妇

[4] 粗鄙的

[5] 虚伪

1. How did the ladies in the play circulate the rumor?

2. Why did the author want to express by the play?

3. How do you understand the play?

 中文译文

造谣学校

（史妮薇女士和女仆拉匹特在她的梳妆台前）

（沃竺思小姐在喝巧克力饮料）

史妮薇女士：你把那些段落都加进去了吗？

沃竺思：都加进去了，女士。我亲自抄的，笔迹都是模仿的，看到那些段落谁也不会怀疑它们的出处。

史妮薇女士：你散播了布丽泰尔小姐跟波斯特尔上尉的绯闻了吗？

沃竺思：夫人，现在大半个镇子都在议论布丽泰尔小姐的事了，我相信用不了一个星期，男人们都会为她这个婚妓干杯了。

史妮薇女士：你是怎么把那位男爵和那位厨师的事偷偷传出去的？

沃竺思：正如夫人您的料想，昨天我把这事和我的女仆说了，也暗示她跟我的理发师交流交流。听说理发师有个兄弟正在追求帕尔莫帽店的一个学徒，那个学徒的女主人有位很近的堂妹，刚好是克拉吉特夫人的女相好。照这样发展下去，用不了二十四小时就会传到克拉吉特夫人的耳朵里。那时候，就正如所愿，一切就大功告成了。

史妮薇女士：真的，这个克拉吉特夫人真是个了不起的天才啊，干了一大堆的好事，而且，她办的那点事啊，还挺成功的。据我所知，就因为她，六对恋人分手了，三个儿子被剥夺了继承权，四个女儿被逐出家门，三五个私奔了，还有那么几个给关禁闭了，九家维持分居，两家离婚了。不仅如此，我还多次听说她在镇上和《国家杂志》引起对质，可当时双方还都素昧平生。

沃竺思：在那些方面，她真是个天才。

史妮薇女士：可她太粗俗了。

沃竺思：那倒是真的。她通常盘算得很周全，而且快人快语、大胆创新，可是，色泽太晦暗，轮廓往往太夸张。她的线条不够细致，讥讽的手法也欠圆滑。这才显示出夫人您造谣的水平啊。

史妮薇女士：哈，沃竺思，这倒是真的。

沃竺思：还不止啊。大家都知道，别人即使有事实支持，也得费上九牛二虎之力。而您，史妮薇女士，只需开个口，瞧一眼就行。

史妮薇女士：是啊，亲爱的沃竺思，我可不是伪君子，我不否认能从努力中收获成功，我挺满足的。前半生，在诽谤的毒害中自己也受过伤害。我承认，从我名誉被败坏的那时起，就想把别人都糟蹋得跟我一样，没有什么比这更快乐的了。

沃竺思：这是最自然不过的了。可是我尊敬的史妮薇女士，您最近找我去办的那件差事，老实说，我实在猜不透你的动机何在？

史妮薇女士：你指的是我的邻居——彼德·狄索爵士和他家人，拉匹特吧？这件事上我的表现，让你真的觉得那么神秘？

沃竺思：就是的啊。

史妮薇女士：像彼德·狄索爵士这样的老光棍，从农村娶回来一个年轻的妻子，就是狄索女士，当然是搞恶作剧、开玩笑的好素材了。但是还有两个年轻人，自从他们父亲去世后，彼德·狄索爵士就担起监护人的角色。老大个性温厚，口碑又那么好；那小的呢，是王国里最浪荡放纵的家伙，既没朋友也没气质。前者公开承认拜倒在您的石榴裙下，也显然是您的意中人。小的喜欢上了玛丽娅，彼德爵士的护士。大家都知道她爱他。

沃竺思：面对这一切，我绝对接受不了，你说你一个没什么遗产的寡妇，为什么就不能热情地靠近像索菲斯先生这样有个性和前途的年轻人呢？更可气的是，为什么你要如此出奇的热心去破坏他弟弟查理和玛丽娅两人之间的感情？

史妮薇女士：现在马上给你揭晓答案。我必须告诉你：爱是不能分享的，无论我和索菲斯先生如何交往。

沃竺思：不会吧！

史妮薇女士：他真正爱着的是玛丽娅，或者说是她的财产。可是，当他发现他兄弟是个强劲对手时，只好掩饰企图，靠我的协助。

沃竺思：这，我就更糊涂了，你为什么会对他的成功有那么大的兴趣？

史妮薇女士：天啊！好笨啊你！现如今你都猜不出我的弱点，多丢人啊！要不我怎么连你都隐瞒啊，非要我承认，查尔斯，那个放荡、奢侈、穷困潦倒、声名狼藉的家伙，就是他搞得我心神不宁、耿耿于怀的，为把他搞到手，我愿意牺牲一切。

沃竺思：这么说，你的行为看起来就一致了，我也不再怀疑你对玛丽娅的敌意了。但是你和索菲斯又怎么能如此推心置腹呢？

史妮薇女士：为了我们相互的利益啊，我可已经注意他很久了。他这个人狡猾、自私而且恶毒。简单地说，是个满嘴道德的无赖；彼德爵士和认识他的人竟然以为他是个谨慎、有良知、心肠慈善的青年楷模。

沃竺思：是的，是的，我知道彼德爵士曾说：英国找不到像他这样的人。而且，最重要的是，他还自诩是个多愁善感的人。

史妮薇女士：真的，在他的多愁善感和伪善的帮助下，他彻底赢得了彼德爵士的欢心和玛丽娅的尊重。我现在相信他又在企图讨好狄索女士对他产生同样的好感。但是，可怜的查尔斯在那家里没有朋友，尽管我害怕他在玛丽娅心中很有分量，我们必须把矛头对准玛丽娅。

仆人：索菲斯先生来了。

史妮薇女士：请他进来。他通常在这个时候来看我。别人把他当作我的情人，我并不觉得奇怪。

References

[1] 徐晓东 . 英文观止 [C]. 北京：世界图书出版公司，2006.

Unit 9 George Gordon, Lord Byron
(1788—1824)

Life

Lord Byron is the English Romantic poet and satirist whose poetry and personality captured the imagination of Europe. Renowned as the "gloomy egoist" of his autobiographical poem Childe Harold's Pilgrimage (1812—1818) in the 19th century, he is now more generally esteemed for the satiric realism of *Don Juan* (1819—1824).

Byron was celebrated in life for aristocratic excesses including huge debts, numerous love affairs, rumors of a scandalous incestuous liaison with his half-sister, and self-imposed exile. It has been speculated that he suffered from manic depression.

He married twice. He had a legitimate daughter and rumored to had another three children from his affairs. He enjoyed adventure, expecially relating to the sea. Byron had a great love of animals, most notably for a dog. He died at 36 years of age from a fever contracted while in Greece. His life is depicted in fiction, plays and films.

Don Juan

Don Juan is a satiric poem by Lord Byron, based on the legend of Don Juan, which Byron reverses, portraying Juan not as a womaniser but as someone easily seduced by women. It is a variation on the epicform. Byron himself called it an "Epic Satire." Byron completed 16 cantos, leaving anunfinished 17th canto before his death in 1824. Byron claimed he had no ideas in his mind as to what would happen in subsequent cantos as he wrote his work.

When the first two cantos were published anonymously in 1819, the poem was criticised for its "immoral content", though it was also immensely popular.

Synopsis

The Argument

The story, told in seventeen cantos, begins with the birth of Don Juan. As a young man he is precocious sexually, and has an affair with a friend of his mother. The husband finds out, and Don Juan is sent away to Cadiz. On the way, he is shipwrecked, survives, and meets the daughter of a pirate, whose men sell Don Juan as a slave. A young woman who is a member of a Sultan's harem, sees that this slave is purchased. She disguises him as a girl and sneaks him into her chambers. Don Juan escapes, joins the Russian army, and rescues a Muslim girl named Leila. Don Juan meets Catherine the Great, who asks him to join her court. Don Juan becomes sick, is sent to England, where he finds someone to watch over the young girl, Leila. Next, a few adventures involving the artistocracy of Britain ensue. The poem ends with Canto XVII.

Comments on *Don Juan*

At the turn of 18th and 19th century's romanticism appeared in England as a new trend in literature. Byron is one of the best-known English poets. He is famous for his masterpiece called Don Juan.

Don Juan was written in Italy during the year 1818-1823. The story of the poem describes a hero who was called Don Juan, is a Spanish youth of noble birth. At the beginning of the poem, Don Juan lived in a carefree and type without any worry. But something unexpected always happen any time. His lover Julia was shut up and he survied by a beautiful girl who was pirate's daughter and her father fought against their love. They had no choice but separate from each other. Don Juan suffered many a setback during his life.

Don Juan

7

That is the usual method, but not mine;

My way is to begin with the beginning.

The regularity of my design

Forbids all wandering as the worst of sinning,

And therefore I shall open with a line

(Although it cost me half an hour in spinning)

Narrating somewhat of Don Juan's father

And also of his mother, if you'd rather.

8

In Seville[1] was he born, a pleasant city,

Famous for oranges and women. He

Who has not seen it will be much to pity;

So says the proverb, and I quite agree.

Of all the Spanish towns is none more pretty;

Cadiz[2] perhaps, but that you soon may see.

Don Juan's parents lived beside the river,

A noble stream, and called the Guadalquivir[3].

9

His father's name was Jose—Don, of course.

A true Hidalgo, free from every stain

Of Moor[4] or Hebrew blood, he traced his source

Through the most Gothic[5] gentlemen of Spain.

A better cavalier ne'er mounted horse,

Or, being mounted e'er got down again,

Than Jose, who begot our hero, who

Begot—but that's to come. Well, to renew:

10

His mother was a learned lady, famed

For every branch of every science known,

In every Christian language ever named,

With virtues equalled by her wit alone.

She made the cleverest people quite ashamed,

And even the good with inward envy groan,

Finding themselves so very much exceeded

In their own way by all the things that she did.

Notes

[1] 塞维尔（Seville）：西班牙南部塞维拉（Sevilla）省城。

[2] 卡提斯（Cadiz）：西班牙西南部省份。

[3] 瓜达尔奎弗（the Guadalquivir）：西班牙南部河流，长约 374 英里，通往大西洋。唐·璜父母就在这条河边生息。

[4] 摩尔人（Moor）：北非的穆斯林民族，曾于 8 世纪时渡海征服了西班牙。

[5] 哥特人（Gothic）：条顿民族之一部。

Questions

1. From the above lines, can you figure out the family background of Don Juan?

2. What did the author want to express in the poem?

3. What is the significance of the poem?

中文译文

唐·璜

7

此乃通常诗法，而我的却不是

按照我的路子是要从头起始；

谋篇布局，我有规律性的设置

散漫的七攀八扯一概须禁止，

因之，我要写一段开场的序诗

（尽管我为此耗费了半个小时）

关于唐·璜的父亲，我得要讲讲，

假如你也想，就再说说他亲娘。

8

可爱的塞维尔，他在那里降生，

出美女和柑橘——该城遐迩闻名，

谁若没见过它，那可真是不幸，

谚语就这么说，我也深表赞成；

西班牙再没有比它更美之城，

卡提斯，还可能——不久可看分明；

唐·璜的父母亲在河岸边居住，
好一条名川，它叫瓜达尔奎弗。

9

他的父亲名叫约瑟，姓唐，当然
西班牙的贵族，属于正宗世传，
与摩尔人或犹太人丝毫无染，
哥特人缙绅之后，可追本溯源；
与约瑟相比，好骑士从未上鞍，
或是被抱上去，又跨回了地面。
这约瑟生养了我们的主人公，
又有了孙辈，那是后来的内容。

10

他的母亲可是位博学的夫人，
通晓科学的每一个分支别门，
基督教的语言她能如数家珍，
且德行之高，唯其才学可相称；
她羞煞了那些最聪颖的人们，
善良人也会嫉妒得心痛阵阵，
因他们发觉凡是自己的方法，
在所有的事情上都远不如她。

References

[1] 苏煜. 英国诗歌赏析 [C]. 北京：新华出版社，2006.

Unit 10   Jane Austen (1775—1817)

Life

As a great novelist of realism, Jane Austen, the sixth child of the family of seven was born in a small village in 1775. Her father was a churchman, a learned man who encouraged his daughter both in her reading and writing. She received a good education at home. She is a vigorous reader and her family spent much time in group reading and performing theatricals. In such environment, Jane Austen's literary talent was being cultivated and developed. She never married in her life and she never lived apart from her family. She lived a quiet and uneventful life. Her closed friend was her sister, who also remained unmarried. Aside from doing  domestic chores at home, Austen spent nearly all her time composing and revising. So because of many times of her revision, the year of the publication usually is not correspondent with the year when she wrote the work. However, almost every novel produced by her is very impressive, especially on the mind of women readers.

Sense and Sensibility was published in 1811. It relates the story of two sisters and their love affairs. Elinor is a woman of good sense, while Marianne is the creature of sensibility. When they find the men they love have other lovers, one controls her emotion and the other lets the emotion control her action. It seems that Austen was offering her advice to young girls that they should never lose their reasoning power in dealing with men. She also criticized the selfish and irresponsible behaviors of both men and women in choosing marriage partners.

Mansfield Park (1814), *Emma* (1816), and *Persuasion* (1818) deal with the romantic entanglements of their strongly characterized heroines. *Mansfield Park* is more solemn and moralistic than Austen's early novels. Poor Fanny Price is adopted by her rich uncle, the stern but kind-hearted Sir Thomas Bertram. In the Mansfield Park, Fanny finds her cousin Edmund an only friend. When the sophisticated Henry Crawford and his sister Mary visit the Mansfield neighborhood, the moral sense of each marriageable member in the Bertram family is tested in various ways. Fanny proves herself an honest and virtuous woman and finally wins the heart of Edmund.

Emma, presents the story of the beautiful, charming and clever Emma Woodhouse in a more relaxed atmosphere. She is eager to plan a future for Harriet Smith, an orphan girl. The Woodhouse treat her as a member of the family. Emma first prevents her from marrying Robert Martin, an eligible young farmer, and then helps her in several failed attempts to pursue an ideal husband. She herself becomes the victim of her "clever" plan when she is surprised to learn that Harriet intends to marry Mr. Knightly, with whom Emma is in love. Eventually, Emma realizes how she again and again ruined Harriet chances to happiness, and she has learned her lesson through the events. In the end Mr. Knightly proposes to Emma and Harriet happily accepts Robert Martin as her husband.

Persuasion has more psychological depth than her previous novels. *Northanger Abbey* (1818) tells the story of the unsophisticated and sincere Catherine Morland, who learns to distinguish between the excessively emotional life in Gothic novels and the realities of ordinary human existence. The novel voiced Austen's subtle criticism of the highly popular Gothic romances of the late 18th century.

Another two, published posthumously are fragments and early drafts of Jane Austen including *Lady Susan* (1871) *The Watsons* (1871) and *Sanditon* (1925), which are less known to readers.

Pride and Prejudice (1813) is the most popular of her novels. The characters are remarkably portrayed and they come alive under her pen: the long-winded (talkative) mother; the flattering churchman; the clever and quick-minded Elizabeth, whose "prejudice" is matched with Darcy's "Pride"; the empty-headed and flirtatious Kitty and Lydia; the modest and unselfish Jane; and the good natured Mr. Bennet. The conflict between Elizabeth and Darcy is the conflict between two equally wrong views on people's worth. Elizabeth is not the ideal woman to be Darcy's wife at first sight because she does not have a pretty face. But a woman's value should not be judged from the surface. Darcy will soon find her a woman with special charm and beauty. He loves her for her intelligence and integrity. But his proposal is rejected. His pride hurt, yet he had learned his lesson. Elizabeth finally discards her prejudice and accepts the man as her husband.

Plot of *Pride and Prejudice*

The first sentence of the novel sets the tone of it: It is *truth universally acknowledged, that a single man in possession of a good fortune must be in want of a wife*. Mr. and Mrs. Bennet are the parents of five unmarried daughters. The only aim of Mrs. Bennet is to find a husband for each. Mr. Bennet, is a gentleman of bookish nature, is disdainful of his wife and indifferent to his daughters, except Elizabeth, because she is intelligent and witty. An estate near the Bennets is leased by Mr Bingley, a wealthy bachelor, who brings with him his friend Mr. Darcy, likewise wealthy and unmarried. Bingley makes a good impression, but the arrogant Darcy is much disliked, especially by Elizabeth. Bingley and Sweet-tempered Jane Bennet fall in love, but Darcy temporarily frustrates their courtship. The fact is, however, that Darcy and Elizabeth also love each other, though neither realizes it. Darcy is blinded by his pride and Elizabeth is blinded by her prejudice against Darcy. Finally after Darcy has saved the reputation of silly Lydia, who has eloped with a never-do-well officer (Wickham), Darcy and Elizabeth realize their errors of judgment and become engaged, and Jane and Bingley are reunited.

The plot, like Austen's others works such as *Emma* and *Persuasion*, is simple and naturally grown out of the characters and their ordinary relations. It deals with the everyday life of small and big landlords and their families in the English countryside, particularly with the love and marriage of the younger members of those families. The story centers round the heroine Elizabeth Bennet (who stands for "Prejudice") and the hero Fitzwilliam Darcy (who stands for "pride") and a minor couple, her sister Jane and his friend Charles Bingley. The incidents of the lives of these characters, including teas and visits and walks and dances and conversations and other expected or unexpected happenings, finally lead to the happy unions of the two couples.

Comments on *Pride and Prejudice*

The novel begins with a conversation at Longbourn, the Bennet household, regarding the arrival of Mr. Bingley, "a single man of large fortune" to Netherfield Park, a nearby estate. *Mrs. Bennet* sees Mr. Bingley as a potential suitor for her daughters, and attempts to persuade Mr. Bennet to visit him. There are five daughters in the Bennet family. *Mr. Bennet* seems to prefer Elizabeth, the second oldest, because of her intelligence, while Mrs. Bennet seems fonder of the oldest, Jane, because of her beauty, and the middle child, Lydia, because of her good humor.

The first line of the novel —"It is a truth universally acknowledged, that a single man in possession of a good fortune, must be in want of a wife" – is among the most famous first lines in literature. It not only calls the reader's attention to the central place that marriage will have in the plot of the story, but also introduces the reader immediately Jane Austen's use of **irony**. While the focus of the line is on "a single man . . . in want of a wife," the real emphasis in the novel and in the society of the late-eighteenth and early-nineteenth centuries is the need for young women to find a husband in possession of a good fortune. The purely economic, utilitarian motive for marriage will come under attack in the novel. This strange social trend in marriage leaves many women with little choice but to marry for the sake of economic survival.

Our first glimpse of the Bennett family is enough to provide us with a fairly accurate sketch of their characters. Mrs. Bennett is chatty, frivolous and obsessed with marrying off her daughters, while Mr. Bennett is rather detached and ironic, not overly involved with the cares of the family. Jane is beautiful, amiable and good-natured, and always assumes that others are as good-natured as she. Elizabeth, good-looking but not as beautiful as her sister, however she has a sharp wit and prides herself on her keen perception of others' characters.

From the very first pages of the novel Austen's tendency to favor dialogue over narration is clearly manifested. Critics have acclaimed Austen has ability to bring characters to life by having them reveal themselves to the reader through their actions and dialogue, not through detailed narrative descriptions. Critic George Henry Lewes, a contemporary of Jane Austen, praises her because *"instead of description, the common and easy resource of novelists, she has the rare and difficult art of dramatic presentation instead of telling us what her characters are, and what they feel, she presents the people, and they reveal themselves."*

Her skillful art of the treatment of conversation is shown in this opening chapter. The characters are made to reveal themselves through their own words, and Jane Austen is always able to find the precise expression that accurately fits the character and the occasion. She is possessed of a neat humor and a satirical touch.

Her style is an almost perfect instrument for her purpose—simple, clear, quiet, precise, keen, suggestive and mildly ironical.

Major Characters

Elizabeth Bennet

The protagonist of the novel and the second oldest of five sisters, Elizabeth is lively, quick-witted, sharp-tongued, bold and intelligent. Elizabeth is good-looking, and is especially distinguished by her fine eyes. The importance of her eyes may be symbolic of her abilities of perception. She has pride in her abilities to perceive the truth of situations and of people's characters. However, her perceptive abilities fail her frequently because she judges people so rashly. By the end of the novel she overcomes her prejudice through her dealings with Darcy. Elizabeth is concerned with propriety, good manners, and virtue, but is not impressed by mere wealth or titles.

Mr. Darcy

An extremely wealthy aristocrat, Darcy is proud, haughty and extremely conscious of class differences at the beginning of the novel. He does, however, have a strong sense of honor and virtue. His first proposal to Elizabeth is refused. Elizabeth's rebukes help him to recognize his faults. It is, in fact, precisely because Elizabeth is not so fearful of his high social status and she is not afraid to criticize his character that he is attracted to her. The self-knowledge acquired from Elizabeth's rebukes and the desire to win Elizabeth's love spur him to change and judge people more by their character than by their social class.

Jane Bennet

Jane is the oldest in the family. Beautiful, good-tempered, sweet, amiable, humble and selfless, Jane is universally well liked. She refuses to judge anyone badly, always making excuses for people. Jane is a static character as she is basically a model of virtue from the beginning, there is no room for her to develop in the novel.

Charles Bingley

Mr. Bingley, much like Jane, is an amiable and good-tempered person. He is not overly concerned with class differences, and Jane's poor family connections are not a serious obstruction to his attachment to her. Bingley is very modest and easily swayed by the advice of his friends, as seen in his decision not to propose to Jane as a result of Darcy's belief that Jane does really love him. Also like Jane, Bingley lacks serious character faults and is thus static throughout the novel.

Mr. Wickham

An officer in the regiment stationed at Meryton, Wickham is quickly judged to be a perfectly good and amiable man because of his friendliness and the ease of his manners. He initially shows a preference for Elizabeth, and she is pleased by his attentions and inclined to believe his story about Darcy. Yet while Wickham has the appearance of goodness and virtue, this appearance is deceptive. His true nature begins to show itself through his attachment to Miss King for purely mercenary purposes and then through Darcy's exposition of his past and through his elopement with Lydia, deceiving her to believe that he intends to marry her. But for Elizabeth's maturity and intelligence, she may also have been the prey of Wickham.

Mrs. Bennet

Mrs. Bennet is a foolish and frivolous woman. She lacks all sense of propriety and virtue. She has no concern for the moral or intellectual education of her daughters. She is a totally illiterate housewife. From the beginning of the novel her sole obsession is to marry off her daughters. She is perfectly happy with Lydia's marriage, and never once blames her daughter for her shameful conduct or for the worry she has caused her family. Her impropriety is a constant source of mortification (侮辱, 悔恨, 遗恨) for the Elizabeth, and the inane nature of her conversation makes her society so difficult to bear that even Jane and Bingley decide to move out of the neighborhood a year after they are married.

Mr. Bennet

An intelligent man with good sense, Mr. Bennet made the mistake of marrying a foolish woman. He takes shelter in his books and seems to want nothing more than to be bothered as little as possible by his family. That is to say for Mr. Bennet, anything is better than being bothered by the trivial family matters. His indolence leads to the neglect of the education of daughters. Even when Elizabeth warns him not to allow Lydia to go to Brighton because of the moral danger of the situation, he does not listen to her because he does not want to be bothered with Lydia's complaints.

Lydia Bennet

The youngest of the Bennet sisters, Lydia is foolish and flirtatious. She is given up to indolence and the gratification of every strange idea. She is the favorite of Mrs. Bennet, because the two have something in common. Lydia is constantly obsessed with the officers in the regiment, and sees no purpose to life beyond entertainment and diversion. She lacks no sense of virtue, propriety or good-judgment, which can be observed in her elopement with Wickham and her complete lack of remorse afterward.

Catherine (Kitty) Bennet

Kitty seems to have little personality of her own, but simply to act as a shadow to Lydia, following Lydia's lead in whatever she does. The end of the novel provides hope that Kitty's character will improve by leaving from the society of Lydia and her mother and being taken care of primarily by Jane and Elizabeth.

Mary Bennet

The third oldest of the Bennet sisters, Mary is strangely solemn and pedantic (迂腐的，学究式的). She dislikes going out into society, and prefers to spend her time studying. In conversation, Mary is constantly moralizing or trying to make profound observations about human nature and life in general.

Introduction to Chapter I

Chapter I is the opening chapter of *Pride and Prejudice* and it is also the most well-known beginning of British classics. In this chapter, all major characters leave a rough impression on readers mind and the theme of the novel does appear in the first chapter. This is rare in novel. Reading chapter I, readers learn the author is good at conversation and she presents a vivid picture of 19th century life of middle class.

Chapter I

It is a truth universally acknowledged, that a single man in possession of a good fortune must be in want of a wife.

However little known the feelings or views of such a man may be on his first entering a neighbourhood, this truth is so well fixed in the minds of the surrounding families, that he is considered as the rightful property of some one or other of their daughters.

"My dear Mr. Bennet," said his lady to him one day, "have you heard that Netherfield Park[1] let at last?"

Mr. Bennet replied that he had not.

"But it is," returned she; "for Mrs. Long has just been here, and she told me all about it."

Mr. Bennet made no answer.

"Do not you want to know who has taken it?" cried his wife impatiently.

"You want to tell me, and I have no objection to hearing it."

This was invitation enough.

"Why, my dear, you must know, Mrs. Long says that Netherfield is taken by a young man of large fortune from the north of England; that he came down on Monday in a chaise and four[2] see the place, and was so much delighted with it that he agreed with Mr. Morris[3] immediately; that he is to take possession before Michaelmas[4] and some of his servants are to be in the house by the end of next week."

"What is his name?"

"Bingley."

"Is he married or single?"

"Oh! single, my dear, to be sure! A single man of large fortune; four or five thousand a year. What a fine thing for our girls!"

"How so? How can it affect them?"

"My dear Mr. Bennet," replied his wife, "how can you be so tiresome! You must know that I am thinking of his marrying one of them."

"Is that his design in settling here?"

"Design! nonsense, how can you talk so! But it is very likely that he may fall in love with one of them, and therefore you must visit him as soon as he comes."

"I see no occasion for that[5]. You and the girls may go, or you may send them by themselves, which perhaps will be still better; for, as you are as handsome as any of them, Mr. Bingley might like you the best of the party."

"My dear, you flatter me. I certainly have had my share of beauty, but I do not pretend to be any thing extraordinary now. When a woman has five grown up daughters, she ought to give over thinking of her own beauty."

"In such cases, a woman has not often much beauty to think of."

"But, my dear, you must indeed go and see Mr. Bingley when he comes into the neighbourhood."

"It is more than I engage for, I assure you.[6]"

"But consider your daughters. Only think what an establishment[7] it would be for one of them. Sir William and Lady Lucas are determined to go, merely on that account, for in general, you know they visit no new comers. Indeed you must go, for it will be impossible for us to visit him, if you do not.[8]"

"You are over-scrupulous, surely. I dare say Mr. Bingley will be very glad to see you; and I will send a few lines by you to assure him of my hearty consent to his marrying which ever he chases of the girls; though I must throw in a good word for my little Lizzy[9]."

"I desire you will do no such thing. Lizzy is not a bit better than the others; and I am sure she is not half so handsome as Jane[10], nor half so good humoured as Lydia[11]. But you are always giving her the preference."

"They have none of them much to recommend them," replied he; "they are all silly and ignorant like other girls; but Lizzy has something more of quickness than her sisters."

"Mr. Bennet, how can you abuse your own children in such way? You take delight in vexing me. You have no compassion on my poor nerves."

"You mistake me, my dear. I have a high respect for your nerves. They are my old friends. I have heard you mention them with consideration these twenty years at least."

"Ah! you do not know what I suffer."

"But I hope you will get over it, and live to see many young men of four thousand a year come into the neighbourhood."

"It will be no use to us if twenty such should come, since you will not visit them."

"Depend upon it, my dear, that when there are twenty I will visit them all."

Mr. Bennet was so odd a mixture of quick parts[12], sarcastic humour, reserve, and caprice, that the experience of three and twenty years had been insufficient to make his wife understand his character. Her mind was less difficult to develop[13]. She was a woman of mean understanding, little information, and uncertain temper. When she was discontented, she fancied herself nervous. The business of her life was to get her daughters married; its solace was visiting and news.

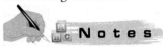

Notes

[1]an estate in the neighbourhood of the home of the Bennets

[2]a carriage drawn by four horses

[3]the estate-agent

[4]a festival celebrated on Sep. 29, the feast day in honor of the archangel St. Michael. Usually on this day, a contract will be signed

[5]I see no need for that

[6]It is more than I can promise

[7]what a marriage (多好的一门亲事)

[8]This is because it was the etiquette of the time for the male head of a family to pay the first visit to a newly-moved-in neighbour. It would have been a shocking breach of etiquette for a mother and her daughters to call first.

[9]Elizabeth, Mr. Bennet's second daughter

[10]Mr. Bennet's eldest daughter

[11] Mr. Bennet's youngest daughter

[12] abilities or intelligence

[13] unwrap; unfold; hence in the present context, understand

Questions

1. How do you understand the first sentence of this chapter?

2. What had happened to Mrs. Bennet?

3. According to this chapter, can you imagine Bennets' daughters' appearance?

4. Describe the personality of Mr. Bennet and Mrs. Bennet in your own words.

Analysis of Chapter I

The selection given here is the first chapter of the novel in which the parents of the Bennet girls are busy considering the prospects of their daughter's marriages, shortly after hearing of the arrival of a rich, unmarried young man as their neighbor. Mild satire may be found here in the author's seemingly matter-of-fact description of a very ordinary, practical family conversation, though unmistakable sympathy is given here to both Mrs. Bennet and Mr. Bennet.

 中文译文

《傲慢与偏见》 第一章

凡是有钱的单身汉，总想娶位太太，这已经成了一条举世公认的真理。这样的单身汉，每逢新搬到一个地方，四邻八舍虽然完全不了解他的性情如何，见解如何，可是，既然这样的一条真理早已在人们心目中根深蒂固，因此人们总是把他看作自己某一个女儿理所应得的一笔财产。

有一天班纳特太太对她的丈夫说："我的好老爷，尼日斐花园终于租出去了，你听说过没有？"

班纳特先生回答道，他没有听说过。

"的确租出去了，"她说，"朗格太太刚刚上这儿来过，她把这件事的底细，一五一十地告诉了我。"

班纳特先生没有理睬她。

"你难道不想知道是谁租去的吗？"太太不耐烦地嚷起来。

"既是你要说给我听，我听听也无妨。"

这句话足够鼓励她讲下去了。

"哦！亲爱的，你得知道，朗格太太说，租尼日斐花园的是个阔少爷，他是英格兰北部的人；听说他星期一那天，乘着一辆驷马大轿车来看房子，看得非常中意，当场就和莫理斯先生谈妥了；他要在"米迦勒节"以前搬进来，打算下个周末先叫几个佣人来住。"

"这个人叫什么名字？"

"彬格莱。"

"有太太的呢，还是单身汉？"

"噢！是个单身汉，亲爱的，确确实实是个单身汉！一个有钱的单身汉；每年有四五千英镑的收入。真是女儿们的福气！"

"这怎么说？关女儿们什么事？"

"我的好老爷，"太太回答道，"你怎么这样叫人讨厌！告诉你吧，我正在盘算，他要是挑中我们一个女儿做老婆，可多好！"

"他住到这儿来，就是为了这个打算吗？"

"打算！胡扯，这是哪儿的话！不过，他万一看中我们的某一个女儿呢。他一搬来，你就得去拜访拜访他。"

"我不用去。你带着女儿们去就得啦，要不你干脆打发她们自己去，那或许倒更好些，因为你跟女儿们比起来，她们哪一个都不能胜过你的美貌，你去了，彬格莱先生倒可能挑中你呢？"

"我的好老爷，你太捧我啦。从前也的确有人赞赏过我的美貌，现在我可不敢说有什么出众的地方了。一个女人家有了五个成年的女儿，就不该对自己的美貌再转什么念头。"

"这样看来，一个女人家对自己的美貌也转不了多少念头喽。"

"不过，我的好老爷，彬格莱一搬到我们的邻近来，你的确应该去看看他。"

"老实跟你说吧，这不是我分内的事。"

"看在女儿的份儿上吧。只请你想一想，不论她们哪一个，要是攀上了这样一个人家，该多么好。威廉爵士夫妇已经决定去拜望他，他们也无非是这个用意。你知道，他们通常是不会拜望新搬来的邻居的。你的确应该去一次，要是你不去，叫我们怎么去。"

"你实在过分花心思啦。彬格莱先生一定高兴看到你的；我可以写封信给你带去，就说随便他挑中我哪一个女儿，我都心甘情愿地答应他把她娶过去；不过，我在信上得特别替小丽莎吹嘘几句。"

"我希望你别这么做。丽莎没有一点儿地方胜过别的几个女儿；我敢说，论漂亮，她抵不上吉英一半；论性子，她抵不上丽迪雅一半。可你老是偏爱她。""她们没有哪一个值得夸奖的，"他回答道，"她们跟人家的姑娘一样，又傻，又无知；倒是丽莎要比她的几个姐妹伶俐些。"

"我的好老爷，你怎么舍得这样糟蹋自己的亲生女儿？你是在故意叫我气恼，好让你自己得意吧。你半点儿也不体谅我的神经衰弱。"

"你真错怪了我，我的好太太。我非常尊重你的神经。它们是我的老朋友。至少在最近二十年以来，我一直听你郑重其事地提到它们。"

"啊！你不知道我怎样受苦呢！"

"不过我希望你这毛病会好起来，那么，像这种每年有四千镑收入的阔少爷，你就可以眼看着他们一个个搬来做你的邻居了。"

"你既然不愿意去拜访他们，即使有二十个搬了来，对我们又有什么好处！"

"放心吧，我的好太太，等到有了二十个，我一定去一个个拜访到。"

班纳特先生真是个古怪人，他一方面喜欢插科打诨，爱挖苦人，同时又不苟言笑，变幻莫测，即使他那位太太积二十三年之经验，还摸不透他的性格。太太的脑子是很容易分析的。她是个智力贫乏、不学无术、喜怒无常的女人，只要碰到不称心的事，她就以为神经衰弱。她生平的大事就是嫁女儿；她生平的安慰就是访友拜客和打听新闻。

References

[1] 奥斯汀. 傲慢与偏见 [M]. 张玲，张扬，译. 北京：人民文学出版社，1993.

[2] 范存忠. 英国文学史提纲 [C]. 成都：四川人民出版社，1983.

Unit 11   Charles Dickens (1812—1870)

Life

Charles John Huffam Dickens (1812—1870) was an English writer and social critic. He created some of the world's best-known fictional characters and is regarded as the greatest novelist of the Victorian era. His works enjoyed unprecedented popularity during his lifetime, and by the twentieth century critics and scholars had recognised him as a literary genius. His novels and short stories enjoy lasting popularity.

Born in Portsmouth, Dickens left school to work in a factory when his father was incarcerated in a debtors' prison. Despite his lack of formal education, he edited a weekly journal for 20 years, wrote 15 novels, five novellas, hundreds of short stories and non-fiction articles, lectured and performed extensively, was an indefatigable letter writer, and campaigned vigorously for children's rights, education, and other social reforms.

Dickens' literary success began with the 1836 serial publication of *The Pickwick Papers*. Within a few years he had become an international literary celebrity, famous for his humour, satire, and keen observation of character and society. His novels, most published in monthly or weekly instalments, pioneered the serial publication of narrative fiction, which became the dominant Victorian mode for novel publication. The instalment format allowed Dickens to evaluate his audience's reaction, and he often modified his plot and character development based on such feedback. For example, when his wife's chiropodist expressed distress at the way Miss Mowcher in *David Copperfield* seemed to reflect her disabilities, Dickens improved the character with positive features. His plots were carefully constructed, and he often wove elements from topical events into his narratives. Masses of the illiterate poor chipped to have each new monthly episode read to them, opening up and inspiring a new class of readers.

Dickens was regarded as the literary colossus of his age. His 1843 novella, *A Christmas Carol*, remains popular and continues to inspire adaptations in every artistic genre. *Oliver Twist* and *Great Expectations* are also frequently adapted, and, like many of his novels, evoke images of early Victorian London. His 1859 novel, *A Tale of Two Cities*, set in London and Paris, is his best-known work of historical fiction. Dickens's creative genius has been praised by fellow writers—from Leo Tolstoy to George Orwell and G. K. Chesterton—for its realism, comedy, prose style, unique characterisations, and social criticism. On the other hand, Oscar Wilde, Henry James, and Virginia Woolf complained of a lack of psychological depth, loose writing, and a vein of saccharine sentimentalism. The term Dickensian is used to describe something that is reminiscent of Dickens and his writings, such as poor social conditions or comically repulsive characters.

Oliver Twist

Oliver Twist, or The Parish Boy's Progress, is the second novel by English author Charles Dickens, and was first published as a serial 1837—1839. The story is of the orphan Oliver Twist, who starts his life in a workhouse and is then sold into apprenticeship with an undertaker. He escapes from there and travels to London, where he meets the Artful Dodger, a member of a gang of juvenile pickpockets led by the elderly criminal, Fagin.

Oliver Twist is notable for its unromantic portrayal by Dickens of criminals and their sordid lives, as well as for exposing the cruel treatment of the many orphans in London in the mid-19th century. The alternate title, *The Parish Boy's Progress*, alludes to Bunyan's *The Pilgrim's Progress*, as well as the 18th-century caricature series by William Hogarth, *A Rake's Progress* and *A Harlot's Progress*.

In this early example of the social novel, Dickens satirizes the hypocrisies of his time, including child labour, the recruitment of children as criminals, and the presence of street children. The novel may have been inspired by the story of Robert Blincoe, an orphan whose account of working as a child labourer in a cotton mill was widely read in the 1830s. It is likely that Dickens's own youthful experiences contributed as well.

Oliver Twist has been the subject of numerous adaptations for various media, including a highly successful musical play, Oliver!, and the multiple Academy Award-winning 1968 motion picture.

Plot of *Oliver Twist*

Workhouse years

Oliver Twist was born into a life of poverty and misfortune in a workhouse in an unnamed town (although when originally published in Bentley's Miscellany in 1837, the town was called Mudfog and said to be within 70 miles north of London – in reality this is the location of the town of Northampton). Orphaned by his mother's death in childbirth and his father's unexplained absence, Oliver is meagrely provided for under the terms of the Poor Law and spends the first nine years of his life living at a baby farm in the 'care' of a woman named Mrs. Mann. Oliver is brought up with little food and few comforts. Around the time of Oliver's ninth birthday, Mr. Bumble, the parish beadle, removes Oliver from the baby farm and puts him to work picking and weaving oakum at the main workhouse. Oliver, who toils with very little food, remains in the workhouse for six months. One day, the desperately hungry boys decide to draw lots; the loser must ask for another portion of gruel. The task falls to Oliver, who at the next meal tremblingly comes up forward, bowl in hand, and begs Mr. Bumble for gruel with his famous request: "Please, sir, I want some more."

A great uproar ensues. The board of well-fed gentlemen who administer the workhouse hypocritically offer £5 to any person wishing to take on the boy as an apprentice. Mr. Gamfield, a brutal chimney sweep, almost claims Oliver. However, when he begs despairingly not to be sent away with "that dreadful man", a kindly old magistrate refuses to sign the indentures. Later, Mr. Sowerberry, an undertaker employed by the parish, takes Oliver into his service. He treats Oliver better and, because of the boy's sorrowful countenance, uses him as a mourner at children's funerals. However, Mr. Sowerberry is in an unhappy marriage, and his wife takes an immediate dislike to Oliver – primarily because her husband seems to like him – and loses few opportunities to underfeed and mistreat him. He also suffers torment at the hands of Noah Claypole, an oafish but bullying fellow apprentice and "charity boy" who is jealous of Oliver's promotion to mute, and Charlotte, the Sowerberrys' maidservant, who is in love with Noah.

In trying to bait Oliver, Noah insults Oliver's biological mother, calling her "a regular right-down bad 'un' ". Oliver flies into a rage, attacking and beating the much bigger boy. Mrs. Sowerberry takes Noah's side, helps him to subdue, punch, and beat Oliver, and later compels her husband and Mr. Bumble, who has been sent for in the aftermath of the fight, to beat Oliver once again. Once Oliver is sent to his room for the night, he breaks down and weeps, upset at the events which he had faced. The next day, Oliver escapes from the Sowerberrys' house and decides to run away to London instead.

London, the Artful Dodger, and Fagin

During his journey to London, Oliver encounters Jack Dawkins, a pickpocket more commonly known by the nickname the "Artful Dodger", and his sidekick, a boy of a humorous nature, named Charley Bates, but Oliver's innocent nature prevents him from recognizing any hint that the boys may be dishonest. Dodger provides Oliver with a free meal and tells him of a gentleman in London who will "give him lodgings for nothing, and never ask for change." Grateful for the unexpected assistance, Oliver follows Dodger to the "old gentleman's" residence. In this way, Oliver unwittingly falls in with an infamous Jewish criminal known as Fagin, the so-called gentleman of whom the Artful Dodger spoke. Ensnared, Oliver lives with Fagin and his gang of juvenile pickpockets in their lair at Saffron Hill for some time, unaware of their criminal occupations. He believes they make wallets and handkerchiefs.

Later, Oliver naïvely goes out to "make handkerchiefs" (because there is no income) with the Artful Dodger and Charley Bates. Oliver realises too late that their real mission is to pick pockets. Dodger and Charley steal the handkerchief of an old gentleman named Mr. Brownlow, and promptly flee. When he finds his handkerchief missing, Mr. Brownlow turns round, sees Oliver running away in fright, and pursues him. Others join the chase and Oliver is caught and taken before the magistrate. Curiously, Mr. Brownlow has second thoughts about the boy – he seems reluctant to believe he is a pickpocket. To the judge's evident disappointment, a bookstall holder who saw Dodger commit the crime clears Oliver, who, by now actually ill, faints in the courtroom. Mr. Brownlow takes Oliver home and, along with his housekeeper Mrs. Bedwin, cares for him.

Oliver stays with Mr. Brownlow, recovers rapidly, and blossoms from the unaccustomed kindness. His bliss, however, is interrupted when Fagin, fearing Oliver might "peach" on his criminal gang, decides that Oliver must be brought back to his hideout. When Mr. Brownlow sends Oliver out to pay for some books, one of the gang, a young girl named Nancy, whom Oliver had previously met at Fagin's, accosts him with help from her abusive lover, a brutal robber named Bill Sikes, and Oliver is quickly bundled back to Fagin's lair. The thieves take the five-pound note Mr. Brownlow had entrusted to him, and strip him of his fine new clothes. Oliver, dismayed, flees and attempts to call for police assistance, but is ruthlessly dragged back by the Artful Dodger, Charley and Fagin. Nancy, however, is sympathetic towards Oliver and saves him from beatings by Fagin and Sikes.

In a renewed attempt to draw Oliver into a life of crime, Fagin forces him to participate in a burglary. Nancy reluctantly assists in recruiting him, all the while assuring the boy that she will help him if she can. Sikes, after threatening to kill him if he does not cooperate, sends Oliver through a small window and orders him to unlock the front door. The robbery goes wrong, however, and Oliver is shot and wounded in his left arm at the targeted house. After being abandoned by Sikes, the wounded Oliver makes it back to the house and ends up under the care of the people he was supposed to rob: Miss Rose and her guardian Mrs. Maylie.

Mystery

A mysterious man named Monks has found Fagin and is plotting with him to destroy Oliver's reputation. Monks denounces Fagin's failure to turn Oliver into a criminal, and the two of them agree on a plan to make sure he does not find out about his past. Monks is apparently related to Oliver in some way, although this is not mentioned until later. Back in Oliver's home town, Mr. Bumble has married Mrs. Corney, the wealthy matron of the workhouse where the story first began, only to find himself in an unhappy marriage, constantly arguing with his domineering wife. After one such argument, Mr. Bumble walks over to a pub, where he meets Monks, who questions him about Oliver. Bumble informs Monks that he knows someone who can give Monks more information for a price, and later Monks meets secretly with the Bumbles. After Mrs. Bumble has told Monks all she knows, the three arrange to take a locket and ring which had once belonged to Oliver's mother and toss them into a nearby river. Monks relates this to Fagin as part of the plot to destroy Oliver, unaware that Nancy has eavesdropped on their conversation and gone ahead to inform Oliver's benefactors.

Now ashamed of her role in Oliver's kidnapping and fearful for the boy's safety, Nancy goes to Rose Maylie and Mr. Brownlow to warn them. She knows that Monks and Fagin are plotting to get their hands on the boy again and holds some secret meetings on the subject with Oliver's benefactors. One night, Nancy tries to leave for one of the meetings, but Sikes refuses permission when she declines to state exactly she is going. Fagin realises that Nancy is up to something and resolves to find out what her secret is. Meanwhile, Noah has fallen out with the undertaker Mr. Sowerberry, stolen money from him, and fled to London. Charlotte has accompanied him—they are now in a relationship. Using the name "Morris Bolter", he joins Fagin's gang for protection and becomes a practicer of "the kinchin lay" (kidnapping of children), and Charlotte (it is implied) becomes a prostitute. During Noah's stay with Fagin, the Artful Dodger is caught with a stolen silver snuff box, convicted (in a very humorous courtroom scene), and transported to Australia. Later, Noah is sent by Fagin to "dodge" (spy on) Nancy, and discovers her secret: she has been meeting secretly with Rose and Mr. Brownlow to discuss how to save Oliver from Fagin and Monks.

Fagin angrily passes the information on to Sikes, twisting the story just enough to make it sound as if Nancy had informed on him. Believing Nancy to be a traitor, Sikes beats her to death in a fit of rage and flees to the countryside to escape from the police. There, Sikes is haunted by visions of Nancy's ghost and increasingly alarmed by news of her murder spreading across the countryside. He returns to London to find a hiding place, only to die by accidentally hanging himself while attempting to flee across a rooftop from an angry mob.

Resolution

Monks is forced by Mr. Brownlow to divulge his secrets: his real name is Edward Leeford, and he is Oliver's paternal half-brother and, although he is legitimate, he was born of a loveless marriage. Oliver's mother, Agnes, became their father's true love after Monks witnessed his parents' divorce. Mr. Brownlow has a picture of Agnes, and began making inquiries when he noticed a marked resemblance between her and Oliver. Monks has spent many years searching for his father's child – not to befriend him, but to destroy him. Brownlow asks Oliver to give half his inheritance (which proves to be meagre) to Monks because he wants to give him a second chance; and Oliver, being prone to giving second chances, is more than happy to comply. Monks later moves to America, where he squanders his money, reverts to crime, and ultimately dies in prison.

Fagin is arrested and condemned to the gallows. On the eve of his hanging, in an emotional scene, Oliver, accompanied by Mr. Brownlow, goes to visit the old reprobate in Newgate Gaol, where Fagin's terror at being hanged has caused him to lose himself in daydreams and develop a fever.

On a happier note, Rose Maylie turns out to be the long-lost sister of Agnes, and therefore Oliver's aunt. She marries her long-time sweetheart Harry, and Oliver lives happily with his saviour, Mr. Brownlow. Noah becomes a paid, semi-professional police informer. The Bumbles lose their jobs and are reduced to great poverty, eventually ending up in the same workhouse where they originally lorded it over Oliver and the other orphan boys. Charley Bates, horrified by Sikes's murder of Nancy, becomes an honest citizen, moves to the country, and works his way up to prosperity.

Comments on *Oliver Twist*

In *Oliver Twist*, Dickens mixes grim realism with merciless satire to describe the effects of industrialism on 19th-century England and to criticise the harsh new Poor Laws. Oliver, an innocent child, is trapped in a world where his only options seem to be the workhouse, a life of crime symbolized by Fagin's gang, a prison, or an early grave. From this unpromising industrial/institutional setting, however, a fairy tale also emerges. In the midst of corruption and degradation, the essentially passive Oliver remains pure-hearted; he steers away from evil when those around him give in to it, and in proper fairy-tale fashion, he eventually receives his reward-leaving for a peaceful life in the country, surrounded by kind friends. On the way to this happy ending, Dickens explores the kind of life an outcast, orphan boy could expect to lead in 1830s London.

Poverty and social class

Poverty is a prominent concern in *Oliver Twist*. Throughout the novel, Dickens enlarged on this theme, describing slums so decrepit that whole rows of houses are on the point of ruin. In an early chapter, Oliver attends a pauper's funeral with Mr. Sowerberry and sees a whole family crowded together in one miserable room.

This ubiquitous misery makes Oliver's few encounters with charity and love more poignant. Oliver owes his life several times over to kindness both large and small. The apparent plague of poverty that Dickens describes also conveyed to his middle-class readers how much of the London population was stricken with poverty and disease. Nonetheless, in *Oliver Twist* he delivers a somewhat mixed message about social caste and social injustice. Oliver's illegitimate workhouse origins place him at the nadir of society; as an orphan without friends, he is routinely despised. His "sturdy spirit" keeps him alive despite the torment he must endure. Most of his associates, however, deserve their place among society's dregs and seem very much at home in the depths. Noah Claypole, a charity boy like Oliver, is idle, stupid, and cowardly; Sikes is a thug; Fagin lives by corrupting children; and the Artful Dodger seems born for a life of crime. Many of the middle-class people Oliver encounters—Mrs. Sowerberry, Mr. Bumble, and the savagely hypocritical "gentlemen" of the workhouse board, for example—are, if anything, worOn the other hand, Oliver—who has an air of refinement remarkable for a workhouse boy—proves to be of gentle birth. Although he has been abused and neglected all his life, he recoils, aghast, at the idea of victimising anyone else. This apparently hereditary gentlemanliness makes Oliver Twist something of a changeling tale, not just an indictment of social injustice. Oliver, born for better things, struggles to survive in the savage world of the underclass before finally being rescued by his family and returned to his proper place—a commodious country house.

One early 21st century film adaptation of the novel dispenses with the paradox of Oliver's genteel origins by eliminating his origin story completely, making him just another anonymous orphan like the rest of Fagin's gang.

Symbolism

Dickens makes considerable use of symbolism. The many symbols Oliver faces are primarily good versus evil, with evil continually trying to corrupt and exploit good, but good winning out in the end. The "merry old gentleman" Fagin, for example, has satanic characteristics: he is a veteran corrupter of young boys who presides over his own corner of the criminal world; he makes his first appearance standing over a fire holding a toasting-fork; and he refuses to pray on the night before his execution. The London slums, too, have a suffocating, infernal aspect; the dark deeds and dark passions are concretely characterised by dim rooms and pitch-black nights, while the governing mood of terror and brutality may be identified with uncommonly cold weather. In contrast, the countryside where the Maylies take Oliver is a bucolic heaven.

The novel is also shot through with a related motif, social class, which calls attention to the stark injustice of Oliver's world. When the half-starved child dares to ask for more, the men who punish him are fat. A remarkable number of the novel's characters are overweight.

Toward the end of the novel, the gaze of knowing eyes becomes a potent symbol. For years, Fagin avoids daylight, crowds, and open spaces, concealing himself most of the time in a dark lair. When his luck runs out at last, he squirms in the "living light" of too many eyes as he stands in the dock, awaiting sentence. Similarly, after Sikes kills Nancy, he flees into the countryside but is unable to escape the memory of her dead eyes. In addition, Charley Bates turns his back on crime when he sees the murderous cruelty of the man who has been held up to him as a model.

Major Characters

Oliver Twist

He is the main character of the story. Oliver is an affection-starved little boy who will not commit crimes. He was abused as a young child, and only wants to be loved. His adventures make him the best of friends and the worst of enemies.

Fagin

He is the main antagonist in the story. "The Jew" takes Oliver under his wing and tries to make a pickpocket out of him. He is a powerful crime leader who has an affection for only money and will kill anyone who stands in his way.

Nancy

She is a woman who works for Fagin and tries to help Oliver which eventually leads to her death. She is passionate, caring, and loves Sikes, who eventually kills her.

Mr. Brownlow

He is a man who Oliver's thief friends rob on the street. He takes Oliver in, and discovers his true parentage.

Chapter 1 Oliver's Early Life

Oliver Twist was born in a workhouse, and when he arrived in this hard world, it was very doubtful whether he would live beyond the first three minutes. He lay on a hard little bed and struggled to start breathing.

Oliver fought his first battle without much assistance from the two people present at his birth. One was an old woman, who was nearly always drunk, and the other was a busy local doctor, who was not paid enough to be very interested in Oliver's survival. After all, death was a common event in the workhouse[1], where only the poor and homeless lived.

However, Oliver managed to draw his first breath, and then announced his arrival to the rest of the workhouse by crying loudly. His mother raised her pale young face from the pillow and whispered, "Let me see the child, and die."

The doctor turned away from the fire, where he had been warming his hands. "You must not talk about dying yet," he said to her kindly. He gave her the child to hold. Lovingly, she kissed the baby on its forehead with her cold white lips, then stared wildly around the room, fell back-and died. "Poor dear!" said the nurse, hurriedly putting a green glass bottle back in the pocket of her long skirt.

The doctor began to put on his coat.

"The baby is weak and will probably have difficulties," he said.

"If so, give it a little milk to keep it quiet." The he looked at the dead woman. "The mother was a good-looking girl. Where did she come from?"

"She was brought here last night," replied the old woman. "She was found lying in the street. She'd walked some distance, judging by her shoes, which were worn to pieces. Where she came from, where she was going to, or what her name was, nobody knows."

The doctor lifted the girl's left hand. "The old story," he said sadly, shaking his head.

"No wedding ring[2], I see. Ah! Good night."

And so Oliver was left with only the drunken nurse. Without clothes, under his first blanket, he could have been the child of a king or a beggar. But when the woman dressed him later in rough cotton clothes, yellow with age, he looked exactly what he was - an orphan in a workhouse, ready for a life of misery, hunger, and neglect.

Oliver cried loudly. If he could have known that he was a workhouse orphan, perhaps he would have cried even more loudly.

There was no one to look after the baby in the workhouse, so Oliver was sent to a special "baby farm" nearby. There, he and thirty other children rolled around the floor all day, without the inconvenience of too much food or too much clothing. Mrs Mann, the old woman who "looked after" them, was very experienced. She knew what was good for children, and a full stomach was very dangerous to their health. She also knew what was good for herself, so she kept for her own use the money that she was given for the children's food. The board responsible for the orphans sometimes checked on the health of the children, but They always sent the beadle, a kind of local policeman, to announce their visit the day before. So whenever the board arrived, of course, the children were always neat and clean.

This was the way Oliver was brought up. Consequently, at the age of nine he was a pale, thin child and short for his age. But despite frequent beatings by Mrs Mann, his spirit was strong, which was probably the reason why he managed to reach the age of nine at all.

On Oliver's ninth birthday, Mr Bumble the beadle came to the house to see Mrs Mann. Through the front window Mrs Mann saw him at the gate, and turned quickly to the girl who worked with her.

"Quick ! Take Oliver and those others upstairs to be washed ! " she said. Then she ran out to unlock the gate. (It was always kept locked to prevent official visitors walking in unexpectedly.)

"I have business to talk about," Mr Bumble told Mrs Mann as he entered the house. He was a big fat man, often bad-tempered, and was full of self-importance. He did not like to be kept waiting at a locked gate.

Mrs Mann took his hat and coat, placed a chair for him, and expressed great concern for his comfort. "You've had a long walk, Mr Bumble" she said, "and you must be thirsty. " She took out a bottle from the cupboard.

"No, thank you, Mrs Mann. Not a drop. " He waved the bottle away.

"Just a little drop, Mr Bumble, with cold water," said Mrs Mann persuasively.

Mr Bumble coughed.

"What is it?" He asked, looking at the bottle with interest.

"Gin. I keep it for the children's medicine drink."

"You give the children gin, Mrs Mann?" asked Mr Bumble, watching as she mixed his drink.

"Only with medicine, sir. I don't like to see the m suffer. "

"You're a good woman, Mrs Mann. " Mr Bumble drank half his glass immediately. " I'll tell the board about you. Now - the reason why I'm here. Oliver Twist is nine years old today. We've never been able to discover anything about his parents. "

"Then how did he get his name?"

"I gave it to him," said Mr Bumble proudly. "We follow the alphabet. The last one was an S-Swubble. Then it was T, so this one is Twist. The next one will be Unwin. Anyway, Oliver Twist is now old enough to return to the workhouse. Bring him here, please. " While Mrs Mann went to get him, Mr Bumble finished the rest of his gin.

Oliver, his face and hands now almost clean, was led into the room.

"Will you come along with me, Oliver?" asked Mr Bumble in a loud voice.

Oliver was very glad to be free of Mrs Mann's violence, but he said nothing because she was angrily shaking her finger at him. However, as the gate closed behind Oliver, he burst into tears. He was leaving behind the other children, the only friends he had, and he realized at that moment how lonely he was in the world.

Mr Bumble walked on with long steps, with Oliver on his short little legs running beside him. The feeling of contentment produced by gin-and-water had now disappeared, and the beadle was in a bad mood once more.

Back at the workhouse, Oliver was taken to see the board. He stood in front of ten fat men who were sitting around a table.

"What's your name, boy?" asked a particularly fat man with a very round, red face.

Oliver was frightened at the sight of so many people, and started to cry.

"Why are you crying?"

The beadle hit him on the back, and so naturally Oliver cried even more.

"The boy is a fool," one member of the board announced.

"You know you have no father or mother," said the first man, "and that you have been brought up with other orphans?"

"Yes, sir," replied Oliver, crying bitterly.

"Why is the boy crying?" repeated the other man, puzzled.

"You have come here to be educated," continued the fat man, "so you will start working here tomorrow at six o'clock. "

Oliver was led away to a large room, where, on a rough hard bed, he cried himself to sleep.

The room in the workhouse where the boys were fed was a large stone hall, and at one end the master and two women served the food. This consisted of a bowl of thin soup three times a day, with a piece of bread on Sundays. The boys ate everything and were always hungry. The bowls never needed washing. The boys polished the m with their spoons until They shone. After three months of this slow starvation, one of the boys told the others he was so hungry that one night he might eat the boy who slept next to him. He had a wild hungry eye, and the other boys believed him. After a long discussion, They decided that one of the m should ask for more food after supper that evening, and Oliver was chosen

The evening arrived; the soup was served, and the bowls were empty again in a few seconds. Oliver went up to the master, with his bowl in his hand. He felt very frightened, but also desperate with hunger.

"Please, sir, I want some more. " The master was a fat, healthy man, but he turned very pale. He looked at the little boy in front of him with amazement. Nobody else spoke.

"What?" he asked at last, in a faint voice.

"Please, sir," replied Oliver, "I want some more. "

"The master hit him with the serving spoon, then seized Oliver's arms and shouted for the beadle. The beadle came quickly, heard the dreadful news, and immediately ran to tell the board.

"He asked for more?" Mr Limbkins, the fattest board member, asked in horror. "Bumble—is this really true?"

"That boy will be hanged ! " said the man who earlier had called Oliver a fool. "You see if I'm not right. "

Oliver was led away to be locked up, and a reward was offered to anybody who would take him away and use him for work.

 **Notes**

[1]workhouse—public institution for reception of paupers in a parish or group of parishes. The inhabitants of workhouses were subjected to most brutal exploitation. In the following pages Dickens gives a realistic picture of the horrible existence in workhouse.

[2]wedding ring: symbol for marriage

 **Questions**

1. How did the author describe Oliver Twist's childhood?

2. What was the author's intention of this chapter?

奥利弗的童年

奥利弗·特威斯特出生在一家济贫院里，他来到这个艰难的人世的那一刻，是否能活过三分钟都是很难说的。他躺在一张小硬板床上，挣扎着开始呼吸。

他出生时在场的两个人没有给他什么帮助，这使得奥利弗要独自承担他的第一场战斗。其中一个是位老妇人，她几乎总是喝得醉醺醺的；另一个则是当地一位忙碌的医生，这位医生没有得到足够的报酬，所以对奥利弗能否活下来并不很在意。在济贫院这个只有穷人和无家可归的人待的地方，死亡毕竟是一件非常平常的事。

不管怎样，奥利弗总算尽力吸进了第一口气，然后，他以响亮的哭声向济贫院里其他的人宣告自己的到来。他的母亲从枕头上抬起了年轻而苍白的脸，用微弱的声音说："让我看一眼孩子，我就可以死了。"

正在火炉上烤手取暖的医生转过身来，好心地对她说："别说什么死不死的了。"他把孩子递过去让她抱在怀里。她用冰冷而毫无血色的嘴唇怜爱地在孩子的额头上亲了一下，然后急切地在屋里四处环顾一圈，便向后倒去，咽了气。"可怜的东西！"老看护说着，急忙将一个绿色的小玻璃瓶揣回长裙子的兜里。

这时医生开始穿外衣。"这孩子太弱，恐怕会有麻烦，"他说，"如果真是这样，给他喂点牛奶，好让他别哭。"然后，他又转过脸看了一眼死去的女人，说："这母亲长得还挺漂亮。她是从哪儿来的？"

"她是昨天夜里被送到这儿来的，"老妇人回答道。"她倒在马路上，被人发现了。她脚上那双鞋子已经磨得破破烂烂的了，由此可以看出她是从很远的地方来的。她从哪儿来，要到哪儿去，叫什么名字，没人知道。"

医生拉起那年轻女人的左手，摇摇头，伤心地说："又是老一套。没有结婚戒指，果然如此。唉！晚安。"

奥利弗就这样被留下了，由那位醉醺醺的看护一个人看着。他光着身子，裹在毕生第一块毯子里，既可以是国王的儿子，也可以是乞丐的儿子。可后来老妇人给他穿上了由于年头太久而发了黄的粗棉布衣服，这时，他看上去和他的身份完全一致了——一个济贫院的孤儿，准备好了去过一种充满苦难、饥饿和被忽视的生活。

奥利弗大声哭着。假如他已经知道自己是一个济贫院的孤儿，他可能会哭得更响些。

在济贫院里没有专人照顾婴儿，所以奥利弗被送进了附近一家专门的"育婴堂"。在这里，奥利弗与其他三十多个孩子每天在地上滚爬着，没有过多的衣物和食物来麻烦他们。曼太太"照顾"着这些孩子，这个老女人非常有经验。她知道什么对孩子们有好处，知道吃饱肚子对孩子们的身体是非常有害的。同时她也知道什么对她自己有好处，于是她把人家给孩子们的伙食费都留给自己。负责孤儿事务的地方董事会有时会来检查孩子们的健康状况，可他们往往在前一天派执事去通告他们要来访问，执事是一种地方警察。所以，无论他们什么时候来，孩子们准是个个头净脚净的。

奥利弗就是这样长大的，因此，他到了九岁时，还非常苍白瘦小，比同龄孩子矮一大截。尽管常常遭到曼太太的毒打，他的意志却很坚强。这大概也是他竟然能活到九岁的缘故吧。

奥利弗九岁生日的这天，执事班布尔先生来育婴堂看曼太太。曼太太透过楼前的窗户看见他站在大门口，慌忙转向和她一起干活的女孩，说道：

"赶快！把奥利弗和其他孩子都带到楼上洗洗！"然后她匆忙跑去开大门。（为了防止官方人员料想不及的来访，这大门常常是锁着的。）

"我有点事要跟你谈，"班布尔先生跟曼太太说着，走进了屋子。他是个身材肥胖、脾气暴躁、妄自尊大的人。他可不喜欢被关在门外长时间地等候。

曼太太接过了他的帽子和外衣，替他端过一把椅子，并且对他是否舒适表示了极大的关心。

"班布尔先生，您大老远地走来，一定是渴了。"她说着从橱子里拿出了一个瓶子。

"不，谢谢，曼太太，我一滴都不喝。"他挥手推开瓶子。

"只稍稍来一点儿，班布尔先生，这是加了冰水的。"她极力地劝说着。

班布尔先生咳嗽了一声。"是什么？"他问道，并饶有兴趣地看着瓶子。

"杜松子酒，我这是留着给孩子们吃药用的。"

"曼太太，你给孩子们喝杜松子酒？"班布尔先生看着她给自己兑酒，问道。

"只是吃药的时候给他们喝上一点儿，先生。我不忍心看着他们受罪。"

"曼太太，你真是个好心的女人。"班布尔先生马上喝下了半杯，"我会在董事会那里替你美言的。现在言归正传，说说我今天来这儿的目的。奥利弗·特威斯特今天已经整整九岁了，迄今为止，我们没有打听到关于他父母的任何消息。"

"那么，他是怎么有了这个姓的？"

"这姓是我给他起的，"班布尔先生自豪地说，"我们是按照字母表的顺序给他们安排姓氏的，前一个是 S，叫斯瓦勃（Swubble），轮到他是字母 T，所以就叫特威斯特（Twist），下一个叫恩温（Unwin）。不管怎么说，奥利弗已经长大了，该回到济贫院去了。请把他带到这儿来。"曼太太去带奥利弗时，班布尔先生喝干了杯子里剩下的杜松子酒。

奥利弗手和脸差不多洗干净了，他被带了进来。

"你愿意跟我走吗，奥利弗？"班布尔先生大声问。

奥利弗特别渴望能尽早逃脱曼太太的暴虐统治，可他却没吭声，因为这时她正恶狠狠地向他暗暗摇着手指头。可是当大门在奥利弗身后关上时，他突然涕泪横流。他就要离开其他的孩子们了，而这些孩子是他仅有的朋友，他顿时感到自己在这个世界上是多么孤独。

班布尔先生在前面大步流星地走着，奥利弗挪动短腿一路小跑地跟在旁边。喝了加水的杜松子酒所产生的心满意足的感觉这会儿已荡然无存，这位执事的情绪又不好了。

回到了济贫院，奥利弗被带去见董事会的人。十个体态臃肿、肥头大耳的人围坐在一张桌子周围，他站在他们面前。

"小子，你叫什么名字？"其中一个长着滚圆红脸的特别胖的人问道。

奥利弗被眼前这么多的人给吓哭了。

"你哭什么？"

执事在奥利弗的背上揍了一下，当然这一下使他哭得更厉害了。

"他是个傻子。"一位董事大声说。

"你知道你没有父母，是和那些孤儿一起长大的吗？"第一位先生说。

"我知道，先生。"奥利弗伤心地回答道。

"这孩子哭什么？"另外那位先生莫名其妙地问。

"你是到这儿来受教育的，"那个胖子接着说，"所以从明天早晨六点钟起，你得在这儿干活。"

奥利弗又从这儿被带到了一间大屋子里。他躺在屋里一张粗糙的木板床上，哭着哭着就睡着了。

济贫院里男孩子们吃饭的地方是一间有石板墙石板地的大屋子，在屋子的一头，管事的和两位女佣负责给孩子们打饭。其实这一日三餐顿顿只是一碗稀粥，只有在星期天才加一片面包。孩子们把碗里的东西吃得一干二净，还是饥肠辘辘的。他们的碗根本不用刷洗。孩子们用勺子把碗刮得锃亮。这样缓慢的挨饿持续了三个月后，一天，一个男孩跟别的男孩子说他太饿了，没准哪天晚上他会吃了睡在他边上的人。他那饥饿得发狂的眼神让别的男孩无法不相信他的话。经过长时间的商量，他们决定必须有一个人在当天晚饭后，去请求多给点儿吃的。结果，奥利弗被选中了。

天黑了，开晚饭了，没有几秒钟，孩子们的碗就又一干二净了。奥利弗站了起来，手里捧着碗，心惊胆战地朝管事的走了过去。由于极度饥饿，他横下了一条心。

"劳驾，先生。我还想要一点儿。"

管事的是一个脑满肠肥的壮汉，但他一下子显得很吃惊，脸都白了。他惊讶地看着站在他面前的这个小男孩。这时屋里鸦雀无声。

"什么？"他终于回过味来，用无力的声音问道。

"劳驾，先生，"奥利弗又说了一遍，"我还想要一点儿。"

管事的用盛粥的勺子向奥利弗打去，过后又抓住他的胳膊大声地叫唤着执事。执事马上赶来了，得知了这件可怕的事，并立即跑去向董事会汇报。

"他想要更多的饭吃？"董事会头号大胖子利姆金斯先生震惊地问，"班布尔——难道真是这样吗？"

"这孩子将来是要上绞刑架的！"起初说奥利弗是个傻子的那位先生嚷嚷着，"你就看我说得对不对吧。"

奥利弗被带走，锁在一间屋子里。董事会宣布，谁把这孩子领去干活，谁就会得到奖赏。

References

[1]Brooks, Cleanth. Understanding Fiction [M].Beijing: Foreign Language Teaching and Research Press, 2005.

Unit 12　William Makepeace Thackeray (1811—1863)

Life

Thackeray, an only child, was born in Calcutta, British India, where his father, Richmond Thackeray 1781—1815), was secretary to the Board of Revenue in the British East India Company. His mother, Anne Becher (1792—1864), was the second daughter of Harriet Becher and John Harman Becher, who was also a secretary (writer) for the East India Company.

Richmond died in 1815, which caused Anne to send her son to England in 1816, while she remained in British India. The ship on which he travelled made a short stopover at St. Helena, where the imprisoned Napoleon was pointed out to him. Once in England he was educated at schools in Southampton and Chiswick, and then at Charterhouse School, where he became a close friend of John Leech. Thackeray disliked Charterhouse, and parodied it in his fiction as "Slaughterhouse." Nevertheless, Thackeray was honoured in the Charterhouse Chapel with a monument after his death. Illness in his last year there, during which he reportedly grew to his full height of six foot three, postponed his matriculation at Trinity College, Cambridge, until February 1829. Never too keen on academic studies, Thackeray left Cambridge in 1830, but some of his earliest published writing appeared in two university periodicals, *The Snob* and *The Gownsman*.

Thackeray then travelled for some time on the continent, visiting Paris and Weimar, where he met Goethe. He returned to England and began to study law at the Middle Temple, but soon gave that up. On reaching the age of 21 he came into his inheritance from his father, but he squandered much of it on gambling and on funding two unsuccessful newspapers, The National Standard and The Constitutional, for which he had hoped to write. He also lost a good part of his fortune in the collapse of two Indian banks. Forced to consider a profession to support himself, he turned first to art, which he studied in Paris, but did not pursue it, except in later years as the illustrator of some of his own novels and other writings.

Thackeray's years of semi-idleness ended after he married, on 20 August 1836, Isabella Gethin Shawe (1816—1893), second daughter of Isabella Creagh Shawe and Matthew Shawe, a colonel who had died after distinguished service, primarily in India. The Thackerays had three children, all girls: Anne Isabella (1837—1919), Jane (who died at eight months old) and Harriet Marian (1840—1875), who married Sir Leslie Stephen, editor, biographer and philosopher.

Thackeray now began "writing for his life", as he put it, turning to journalism in an effort to support his young family. He primarily worked for Fraser's Magazine, a sharp-witted and sharp-tongued conservative publication for which he produced art criticism, short fictional sketches, and two longer fictional works, Catherine and *The Luck of Barry Lyndon*. Between 1837 and 1840 he also reviewed books for The Times. He was also a regular contributor to *The Morning Chronicle and The Foreign Quarterly Review*. Later, through his connection to the illustrator John Leech, he began writing for the newly created magazine Punch, in which he published *The Snob* Papers, later collected as The Book of Snobs. This work popularised the modern meaning of the word "snob."Thackeray was a regular contributor to Punch between 1843 and 1854.

Tragedy struck in Thackeray's personal life as his wife, Isabella, succumbed to depression after the birth of their third child, in 1840. Finding that he could get no work done at home, he spent more and more time away until September 1840, when he realised how grave his wife's condition was. Struck by guilt, he set out with his wife to Ireland. During the crossing she threw herself from a water-closet into the sea, but she was pulled from the waters. They fled back home after a four-week battle with her mother. From November 1840 to February 1842 Isabella was in and out of professional care, as her condition waxed and waned.

She eventually deteriorated into a permanent state of detachment from reality. Thackeray desperately sought cures for her, but nothing worked, and she ended up in two different asylums in or near Paris until 1845, after which Thackeray took her back to England, where he installed her with a Mrs Bakewell at Camberwell. Isabella outlived her husband by 30 years, in the end being cared for by a family named Thompson in Leigh-on-Sea at Southend until her death in 1894. After his wife's illness Thackeray became a de facto widower, never establishing another permanent relationship. He did pursue other women, however, in particular Mrs Jane Brookfield and Sally Baxter. In 1851 Mr Brookfield barred Thackeray from further visits to or correspondence with Jane. Baxter, an American twenty years Thackeray's junior whom he met during a lecture tour in New York City in 1852, married another man in 1855.

In the early 1840s Thackeray had some success with two travel books, *The Paris Sketch Book* and *The Irish Sketch Book*, the latter marked by hostility to Irish Catholics. However, as the book appealed to British prejudices, Thackeray was given the job of being Punch's Irish expert, often under the pseudonym Hibernis Hibernior. It was Thackeray, in other words, who was chiefly responsible for Punch's notoriously hostile and condescending depictions of the Irish during the Irish Famine (1845—1851).

Thackeray achieved more recognition with his Snob Papers, but the work that really established his fame was the novel *Vanity Fair,* which first appeared in serialised instalments beginning in January 1847. Even before *Vanity Fair* completed its serial run Thackeray had become a celebrity, sought after by the very lords and ladies whom he satirised. They hailed him as the equal of Dickens.

He remained "at the top of the tree," as he put it, for the rest of his life, during which he produced several large novels, notably *Pendennis, The Newcomes* and *The History of Henry Esmond*, despite various illnesses, including a near-fatal one that struck him in 1849 in the middle of writing Pendennis. He twice visited the United States on lecture tours during this period. Thackeray also gave lectures in London on the English humorists of the eighteenth century, and on the first four Hanoverian monarchs. The latter series was published in book form as *The Four Georges*.

In Oxford he stood unsuccessfully as an independent for Parliament. He was narrowly beaten by Cardwell, who received 1070 votes, as against 1005 for Thackeray.

In 1860 Thackeray became editor of the newly established Cornhill Magazine, but he was never comfortable in the role, preferring to contribute to the magazine as the writer of a column called Roundabout Papers.

Thackeray's health worsened during the 1850s and he was plagued by a recurring stricture of the urethra that laid him up for days at a time. He also felt that he had lost much of his creative impetus. He worsened matters by excessive eating and drinking, and avoiding exercise, though he enjoyed horseback-riding (he kept a horse). He has been described as "the greatest literary glutton who ever lived." His main activity apart from writing was "guttling and gorging."He could not break his addiction to spicy peppers, further ruining his digestion. On 23 December 1863, after returning from dining out and before dressing for bed, he suffered a stroke. He was found dead in his bed the following morning. His death at the age of fifty-two was entirely unexpected, and shocked his family, his friends and the reading public. An estimated 7,000 people attended his funeral at Kensington Gardens. He was buried on 29 December at Kensal Green Cemetery, and a memorial bust sculpted by Marochetti can be found in Westminster Abbey.

Plot of *Vanity Fair*

The story is framed by its preface and coda as a puppet show taking place at a fair; the cover illustration of the serial installments was not of the characters but of a troupe of comic actors at Speakers' Corner in Hyde Park. The narrator, variously a show manager or writer, appears at times within the work itself and is highly unreliable, repeating a tale of gossip at second or third hand.

Rebecca Sharp ("Becky") is a strong-willed, cunning, moneyless, young woman determined to make her way in society. After leaving school, Becky stays with Amelia Sedley ("Emmy"), who is a good-natured, simple-minded young girl, of a wealthy London family. There, Becky meets the dashing and self-obsessed Captain George Osborne (Amelia's betrothed) and Amelia's brother Joseph ("Jos") Sedley, a clumsy and vainglorious but rich civil servant home from the East India Company. Hoping to marry Sedley, the richest young man she has met, Becky entices him, but she fails. George Osborne's friend Captain William Dobbin loves Amelia, but only wishes her happiness, which is centred on George.

Becky Sharp says farewell to the Sedley family and enters the service of the crude and profligate baronet Sir Pitt Crawley, who has engaged her as a governess to his daughters. Her behaviour at Sir Pitt's house gains his favour, and after the premature death of his second wife, he proposes marriage to her. However he finds that she has secretly married his second son, Captain Rawdon Crawley. (Becky very much regrets having done that; however, when she married Rawdon she had no idea that his father's wife would die so soon after). Sir Pitt's elder half sister, the spinster Miss Crawley, is very rich, having inherited her mother's fortune, and the whole Crawley family compete for her favour so she will bequeath them her wealth. Initially her favourite is Rawdon Crawley. But his marriage with Becky enrages her. First she favours the family of Sir Pitt's brother, but when she dies, she has left her money to Sir Pitt's oldest son, also called Pitt.

Amelia's father, John Sedley, becomes bankrupt. George's rich father forbids George to marry Amelia, who is now poor. Dobbin persuades George to marry Amelia, and George is consequently disinherited. News arrives that Napoleon has escaped from Elba, so George Osborne, William Dobbin and Rawdon Crawley are deployed to Brussels, accompanied by Amelia and Becky, and Amelia's brother, Jos. George is embarrassed by the vulgarity of Mrs. Major O'Dowd, the wife of the head of the regiment. Already, the newly wedded Osborne is growing tired of Amelia, and he becomes increasingly attracted to Becky, which makes Amelia jealous and unhappy. He is also losing money to Rawdon at cards and billiards. At a ball in Brussels, George gives Becky a note inviting her to run away with him. But then the army have marching orders to the Battle of Waterloo, and George spends a tender night with Amelia and leaves. The noise of battle horrifies Amelia, and she is comforted by the brisk but kind Mrs. O'Dowd. Becky is indifferent and makes plans for whatever the outcome (if Napoleon wins, she would aim to become the mistress of one of his Marshals...). She also makes a profit selling her carriage and horses at inflated prices to Jos, seeking to flee Brussels.

George Osborne is killed at Quatre Bras, while Dobbin and Rawdon survive Waterloo. Amelia bears a posthumous son, who carries on the name George. She returns to live in genteel poverty with her parents, spending her life in memory of her husband and care of her son. Dobbin pays for a small annuity for Amelia and expresses his love for her by small kindnesses toward her and her son. She is too much in love with her husband's memory to return Dobbin's love. Saddened, he goes with his regiment to India for many years.

Becky also has a son, named Rawdon after his father. Becky is a cold, distant mother, although Rawdon loves his son. Becky continues her ascent first in post-war Paris and then in London where she is patronised by the rich and powerful Marquis of Steyne. She is eventually presented at court to the Prince Regent and charms him further at a game of "acting charades" where she plays the roles of Clytemnestra and Philomela. The elderly Sir Pitt Crawley dies and is succeeded by his son Pitt, who had married Lady Jane Sheepshanks, Lord Southdown's third daughter. Becky is on good terms with Pitt and Jane originally, but Jane is disgusted by Becky's attitude to her son and jealous of Becky's relationship with Pitt.

At the summit of their social success, Rawdon is arrested for debt, possibly at Becky's connivance. The financial success of the Crawleys had been a topic of gossip; in fact they were living on credit even when it ruined those who trusted them, such as their landlord, an old servant of the Crawley family. The Marquis of Steyne had given Becky money, jewels, and other gifts but Becky does not use them for expenses or to free her husband. Instead, Rawdon's letter to his brother is received by Lady Jane, who pays the £170 that prompted his imprisonment. He returns home to find Becky singing to Steyne and strikes him down on the assumption—despite her protestations of innocence—that they are having an affair. Steyne is indignant, having assumed the £1000 he had just given Becky was part of an arrangement with her husband. Rawdon finds Becky's hidden bank records and leaves her, expecting Steyne to challenge him to a duel. Instead Steyne arranges for Rawdon to be made Governor of Coventry Island, a pest-ridden location. Becky, having lost both husband and credibility, leaves England and wanders the continent, leaving her son in the care of Pitt and Lady Jane.

As Amelia's adored son George grows up, his grandfather Mr Osborne relents towards him (though not towards Amelia) and takes him from his impoverished mother, who knows the rich old man will give him a better start in life than she could manage. After twelve years abroad, both Joseph Sedley and Dobbin return. Dobbin professes his unchanged love to Amelia. Amelia is affectionate, but she cannot forget the memory of her dead husband. Dobbin mediates a reconciliation between Amelia and her father-in-law, who dies soon after. He had amended his will, bequeathing young George half his large fortune and Amelia a generous annuity.

After the death of Mr Osborne, Amelia, Jos, George and Dobbin go to Pumpernickel (Weimar in Germany), where they encounter the destitute Becky. Becky has fallen in life. She lives among card sharps and con artists, drinking heavily and gambling. Becky enchants Jos Sedley all over again, and Amelia is persuaded to let Becky join them. Dobbin forbids this, and reminds Amelia of her jealousy of Becky with her husband. Amelia feels that this dishonours the memory of her dead and revered husband, and this leads to a complete breach between her and Dobbin. Dobbin leaves the group and rejoins his regiment, while Becky remains with the group.

However, Becky has decided that Amelia should marry Dobbin, even though she knows Dobbin is her enemy. Becky shows Amelia George's note, kept all this time from the eve of the Battle of Waterloo, and Amelia finally realises that George was not the perfect man she always thought, and that she has rejected a better man, Dobbin. Amelia and Dobbin are reconciled and return to England. Becky and Jos stay in Europe. Jos dies, possibly suspiciously, after signing a portion of his money to Becky as life insurance, setting her up with an income. She returns to England, and manages a respectable life, although all her previous friends refuse to acknowledge her.

Comments on *Vanity Fair*

The novel is considered a classic of English literature, though some critics claim that it has structural problems; Thackeray sometimes lost track of the huge scope of his work, mixing up characters' names and minor plot details. The number of allusions and references it contains can make it difficult for modern readers to follow.

The subtitle, *A Novel without a Hero*, is apt because the characters are all flawed to a greater or lesser degree; even the most sympathetic have weaknesses, for example Captain Dobbin, who is prone to vanity and melancholy. The human weaknesses Thackeray illustrates are mostly to do with greed, idleness, and snobbery, and the scheming,deceit and hypocrisy which mask them. None of the characters are wholly evil, although Becky's manipulative, amoral tendencies make her come pretty close. However, even Becky, who is amoral and cunning, is thrown on her own resources by poverty and its stigma. (She is the orphaned daughter of a poor artist and an opera dancer.) Thackeray's tendency to highlight faults in all of his characters displays his desire for a greater level of realism in his fiction compared to the rather unlikely or idealised people in many contemporary novels.

The novel is a satire of society as a whole, characterised by hypocrisy and opportunism, but it is not a reforming novel; there is no suggestion that social or political changes or greater piety and moral reformism could improve the nature of society. It thus paints a fairly bleak view of the human condition. This bleak portrait is continued with Thackeray's own role as an omniscient narrator, one of the writers best known for using the technique. He continually offers asides about his characters and compares them to actors and puppets, but his cheek goes even as far as his readers, accusing all who may be interested in such "Vanity Fairs" as being either "of a lazy, or a benevolent, or a sarcastic mood." As Lord David Cecil remarked, "Thackeray liked people, and for the most part he thought them well-intentioned. But he also saw very clearly that they were all in some degree weak and vain, self-absorbed and self-deceived." Amelia begins as a warm-hearted and friendly girl, though sentimental and naive, but by the story's end she is portrayed as vacuous and shallow. Dobbin appears first as loyal and magnanimous, if unaware of his own worth; by the end of the story he is presented as a tragic fool, a prisoner of his own sense of duty who knows he is wasting his gifts on Amelia but is unable to live without her. The novel's increasingly grim outlook can take readers aback, as characters whom the reader at first holds in sympathy are shown to be unworthy of such regard.

The work is often compared to the other great historical novel of the Napoleonic Wars, Tolstoy's War and Peace. While Tolstoy's work has a greater emphasis on the historical detail and the effect the war has upon his protagonists, Thackeray instead uses the conflict as a backdrop to the lives of his characters. The momentous events on the continent do not always have an equally important influence on the behaviors of Thackeray's characters. Rather their faults tend to compound over time. This is in contrast to the redemptive power conflict has on the characters in War and Peace. For Thackeray, the Napoleonic wars as a whole can be thought of as one more of the vanities expressed in the title.

A common critical topic is to address various objects in the book and the characters' relationships with them, such as Rebecca's diamonds or the piano Amelia values when she thinks it came from George and dismisses upon learning that Dobbin provided it. Marxist and similar schools of criticism that go further and see Thackeray condemning consumerism and capitalism, however, largely overstate their case. Thackeray is pointed in his criticism of the commodification of women in the marriage market, but his variations on Ecclesiastes's "all is vanity" are more personal than institutional. He also has broad sympathy with a measure of comfort and financial and physical "snugness." At one point, the narrator even makes a "robust defense of his lunch": "It is all vanity to be sure: but who will not own to liking a little of it? I should like to know what well-constituted mind, merely because it is transitory, dislikes roast-beef ?"

Despite the clear implications of Thackeray's illustration on the topic, John Sutherland has argued against Becky having murdered Jos on the basis of Thackeray's criticism of the "Newgate novels" of Edward Bulwer-Lytton and other authors of Victorian crime fiction. Although what Thackeray principally objected to was glorification of a criminal's deeds, his intent may have been to entrap the Victorian reader with their own prejudices and make them think the worst of Becky Sharp even when they have no proof of her actions.

Major Charaters

Emmy Sedley (Amelia)

Amelia, called Emmy, is good-natured but passive and naïve. Not very beautiful, she is frequently ignored by men and women but is well-liked by most men who get to know her because of her personality. This popularity is then resented by other women. She begins the work as its heroine and marries the dashing George Osborne against his father's wishes, but the narrator is soon forced to admit "she wasn't a heroine" after all as she remains soppily devoted to him despite his neglect of her and his flirtation with Becky.

Becky Sharp (Rebecca)

Rebecca Sharp, called Becky, is Amelia's opposite, an intelligent young woman with a gift for satire. She is described as a short sandy haired girl who has green eyes and a great deal of wit. Fluent in both French and English, Becky has a beautiful singing voice, plays the piano, and shows great talent as an actress. Without a mother to guide her into marriage, Becky resolves that "I must be my own Mamma."She thereafter appears to be completely amoral and without conscience and has been called the work's "anti-heroine."

Rawdon Crawley

Rawdon, the younger of the two Crawley sons, is an empty-headed cavalry officer who is his wealthy aunt's favourite until he marries Becky Sharp, who is of a far lower class. He permanently alienates his aunt, who leaves her estate to Rawdon's elder brother Sir Pitt instead. Sir Pitt has by this time inherited their father's estate, leaving Rawdon destitute.

Sir Pitt Crawley, Baronet

Rawdon Crawley's elder brother is ignorant, boorish, and mean. He inherits the Crawley estate from his elderly father, and he also inherits from his wealthy aunt, Miss Crawley. Sir Pitt is very religious and has political aspirations, although not many people appreciate his intelligence or wisdom because there's not much there to appreciate. Somewhat pedantic and conservative, Sir Pitt does nothing to help Rawdon or Becky even when they fall on hard times. This is chiefly due to the influence of his wife Lady Jane who dislikes Becky because of her callous treatment of her son, and also because Becky repaid Lady Jane's earlier kindness by patronizing her and flirting with Sir Pitt.

Miss Matilda Crawley

The elderly Miss Crawley is everyone's favourite wealthy aunt. Sir Pitt and Rawdon both dote on her, although Rawdon is her favourite nephew and sole heir until he marries Becky. While Miss Crawley likes Becky and keeps her around to entertain her with sarcasm and wit, and while she loves scandal and particularly stories of unwise marriage, she does not want scandal or unwise marriage in her family. A substantial part of the early section of the book deals with the efforts the Crawleys make to kowtow to Miss Crawley in the hope of receiving a big inheritance.

George Osborne

George Osborne, his father, and his two sisters are close to the Sedley family until Mr. Sedley (the father of Jos and Amelia) goes bankrupt following some ill-advised speculation. Since George and Amelia were raised in close company and were childhood sweethearts, George defies his father in order to marry Amelia. Before father and son can be reconciled, George is killed at the battle of Waterloo, leaving the pregnant Amelia to carry on as well as she can.

William Dobbin

The best friend of George Osborne, William Dobbin is tall, ungainly, and not particularly handsome. He is a few years older than George but has been friends with him since his school days even though Dobbin's father is a fig-merchant and the Osbornes belong to the genteel class and have become independently wealthy.

Joseph Sedley

Amelia's older brother is a "nabob", who made a respectable fortune as a collector in India. Obese and self-important but very shy and insecure, he is attracted to Becky Sharp but circumstances prevent him from proposing. He never marries, but when he meets Becky again he is easily manipulated into falling in love with her. Jos is not a courageous or intelligent man, displaying his cowardice at the Battle of Waterloo by trying to flee and purchasing both of Becky's overpriced horses. Becky ensnares him again near the end of the book and, it is hinted, murders him for his life insurance.

Chapter XXXVI: How to Live Well on Nothing a Year

I suppose there is no man in this Vanity Fair of ours so little observant as not to think sometimes about the worldly affairs of his acquaintances, or so extremely charitable as not to wonder how his neighbour Jones, or his neighbour Smith, can make both ends meet at the end of the year. With the utmost regard for the family, for instance (for I dine with them twice or thrice in the season), I cannot but own that the appearance of the Jenkinses in the park, in the large barouche with the grenadier-footmen, will surprise and mystify me to my dying day: for though I know the equipage is only jobbed, and all the Jenkins people are on board wages, yet those three men and the carriage must represent an expense of six hundred a year at the very least—and then there are the splendid dinners, the two boys at Eton[1], the prize governess and masters for the girls, the trip abroad, or to Eastbourne or Worthing[2], in the autumn, the annual ball with a supper from Gunter's (who, by the way, upplies most of the first-rate dinners which J. gives, as I know very well, having been invited to one of them to fill a vacant place, when I saw at once that these repasts are very superior to the common run of entertainments for which the humbler sort of J.'s acquaintances get cards) —who, I say, with the most good-natured feelings in the world, can help wondering how the Jenkinses make out matters? What is Jenkins? We all know—Commissioner of the Tape and Sealing Wax Office, with 1200 pounds a year for a salary. Had his wife a private fortune? Pooh—Miss Flint—one of eleven children of a small squire in Buckinghamshire. All she ever gets from her family is a turkey at Christmas, in exchange for which she has to board two or three of her sisters in the off season, and lodge and feed her brothers when they come to town. How does Jenkins balance his income? I say, every friend of his must say, How is it that he has not been outlawed long since, and that he ever came back (as he did to the surprise of everybody) last year from Boulogne?[3]

"I" is here introduced to personify the world in general—the Mrs. Grundy of each respected reader's private circle—every one of whom can point to some families of his acquaintance who live nobody knows how. Many a glass of wine have we all of us drunk, I have very little doubt, hob-and-nobbing with the hospitable giver and wondering how the deuce he paid for it.

Some three or four years after his stay in Paris, when Rawdon Crawley and his wife were established in a very small comfortable house in Curzon Street, May Fair[4], there was scarcely one of the numerous friends whom they entertained at dinner that did not ask the above question regarding them. The novelist, it has been said before, knows everything, and as I am in a situation to be able to tell the public how Crawley and his wife lived without any income, may I entreat the public newspapers which are in the habit of extracting portions of the various periodical works now published not to reprint the following exact narrative and calculations—of which I ought, as the discoverer(and at some expense, too), to have the benefit? My son, I would say, were I blessed with a child—you may by deep inquiry and constant intercourse with him learn how a man lives comfortably on nothing a year. But it is best not to be intimate with gentlemen of this profession and to take the calculations at second hand, as you do logarithms, for to work them yourself, depend upon it, will cost you something considerable.

On nothing per annum then, and during a course of some two or three years, of which we can afford to give but a very brief history, Crawley and his wife lived very happily and comfortably at Paris. It was in this period that he quitted the Guards and sold out of the army[5]. When we find him again, his mustachios and the title of Colonel on his card are the only relics of his military profession.

It has been mentioned that Rebecca, soon after her arrival in Paris, took a very smart and leading position in the society of that capital, and was welcomed at some of the most distinguished houses of the restored French nobility. The English men of fashion in Paris courted her, too, to the disgust of the ladies their wives, who could not bear the parvenue. For some months the salons of the Faubourg St. Germain, in which her place was secured, and the splendours of the new Court, where she was received with much distinction, delighted and perhaps a little intoxicated Mrs. Crawley, who may have been disposed during this period of elation to slight the people—honest young military men mostly—who formed her husband's chief society.

But the Colonel yawned sadly among the Duchesses and great ladies of the Court. The old women who played ecarte made such a noise about a five-franc piece that it was not worth Colonel Crawley's while to sit down at a card-table. The wit of their conversation he could not appreciate, being ignorant of their language. And what good could his wife get, he urged, by making curtsies every night to a whole circle of Princesses? He left Rebecca presently to frequent these parties alone, resuming his own simple pursuits and amusements amongst the amiable friends of his own choice.

The truth is, when we say of a gentleman that he lives elegantly on nothing a year, we use the word "nothing" to signify something unknown; meaning, simply, that we don't know how the gentleman in question defrays the expenses of his establishment. Now, our friend the Colonel had a great aptitude for all games of chance: and exercising himself, as he continually did, with the cards, the dice-box, or the cue, it is natural to suppose that he attained a much greater skill in the use of these articles than men can possess who only occasionally handle them. To use a cue at billiards well is like using a pencil, or a German flute, or a small-sword—you cannot master any one of these implements at first, and it is only by repeated study and perseverance, joined to a natural taste, that a man can excel in the handling of either. Now Crawley, from being only a brilliant amateur, had grown to be a consummate master of billiards. Like a great General, his genius used to rise with the danger, and when the luck had been unfavourable to him for a whole game, and the bets were consequently against him, he would with consummate skill and boldness make some prodigious hits which would restore the battle, and come in a victor at the end, to the astonishment of everybody—of everybody, that is, who was a stranger to his play. Those who were accustomed to see it were cautious how they staked their money against a man of such sudden resources and brilliant and overpowering skill.

At games of cards he was equally skilful; for though he would constantly lose money at the commencement of an evening, playing so carelessly and making such blunders, that newcomers were often inclined to think meanly of his talent; yet when roused to action and awakened to caution by repeated small losses, it was remarked that Crawley's play became quite different, and that he was pretty sure of beating his enemy thoroughly before the night was over. Indeed, very few men could say that they ever had the better of him. His successes were so repeated that no wonder the envious and the vanquished spoke sometimes with bitterness regarding them. And as the French say of the Duke of Wellington[7], who never suffered a defeat, that only an astonishing series of lucky accidents enabled him to be an invariable winner; yet even they allow that he cheated at Waterloo[8], and was enabled to win the last great trick: so it was hinted at headquarters in England that some foul play must have taken place in order to account for the continuous successes of Colonel Crawley.

Though Frascati's and the Salon were open at that time in Paris, the mania for play was so widely spread that the public gambling-rooms did not suffice for the general ardour, and gambling went on in private houses as much as if there had been no public means for gratifying the passion. At Crawley's charming little reunions of an evening this fatal amusement commonly was practised—much to good-natured little Mrs. Crawley's annoyance. She spoke about her husband's passion for dice with the deepest grief; she bewailed it to everybody who came to her house. She besought the young fellows never, never to touch a box; and when young Green, of the Rifles, lost a very considerable sum of money, Rebecca passed a whole night in tears, as the servant told the unfortunate young gentleman, and actually went on her knees to her husband to beseech him to remit the debt, and burn the acknowledgement. How could he? He had lost just as much himself to Blackstone of the Hussars, and Count Punter of the Hanoverian Cavalry. Green might have any decent time; but pay?—of course he must pay to talk of burning IOU's was child's play.

Other officers, chiefly young—for the young fellows gathered round Mrs. Crawley—came from her parties with long faces, having dropped more or less money at her fatal card-tables. Her house began to have an unfortunate reputation. The old hands warned the less experienced of their danger. Colonel O'Dowd, of the—th regiment, one of those occupying in Paris, warned Lieutenant Spooney of that corps. A loud and violent fracas took place between the infantry Colonel and his lady, who were dining at the Cafe de Paris, and Colonel and Mrs. Crawley; who were also taking their meal there. The ladies engaged on both sides. Mrs. O'Dowd snapped her fingers in Mrs. Crawley's face and called her husband "no betther than a black-leg." Colonel Crawley challenged Colonel O'Dowd, C.B. The Commander-in-Chief hearing of the dispute sent for Colonel Crawley, who was getting ready the same pistols "which he shot Captain Marker," and had such a conversation with him that no duel took place. If Rebecca had not gone on her knees to General Tufto, Crawley would have been sent back to England; and he did not play, except with civilians, for some weeks after.

But, in spite of Rawdon's undoubted skill and constant successes, it became evident to Rebecca, considering these things, that their position was but a precarious one, and that, even although they paid scarcely anybody, their little capital would end one day by dwindling into zero. "Gambling," she would say, "dear, is good to help your income, but not as an income itself. Some day people may be tired of play, and then where are we?" Rawdon acquiesced in the justice of her opinion; and in truth he had remarked that after a few nights of his little suppers, gentlemen were tired of play with him, and, in spite of Rebecca's charms, did not present themselves very eagerly.

Easy and pleasant as their life at Paris was, it was after all only an idle dalliance and amiable trifling; and Rebecca saw that she must push Rawdon's fortune in their own country. She must get him a place or appointment at home or in the colonies, and she determined to make a move upon England as soon as the way could be cleared for her. As a first step she had made Crawley sell out of the Guards and go on half-pay. His function as aide-de-camp to General Tufto had ceased previously. Rebecca laughed in all companies at that officer, at his toupee (which he mounted on coming to Paris), at his waistband, at his false teeth, at his pretensions to be a lady-killer above all, and his absurd vanity in fancying every woman whom he came near was in love with him. It was to Mrs. Brent, the beetle-browed wife of Mr. Commissary Brent, to whom the general transferred his attentions now—his bouquets, his dinners at the restaurateurs', his opera-boxes, and his knick-knacks. Poor Mrs. Tufto was no more happy than before, and had still to pass long evenings alone with her daughters, knowing that her General was gone off scented and curled to stand behind Mrs. Brent's chair at the play. Becky had a dozen admirers in his place, to be sure, and could cut her rival to pieces with her wit. But, as we have said, she was growing tired of this idle social life: opera-boxes and restaurateur dinners palled upon her: nosegays could not be laid by as a provision for future years: and she could not live upon knick-knacks, laced handkerchiefs, and kid gloves. She felt the frivolity of pleasure and longed for more substantial benefits.

At this juncture news arrived which was spread among the many creditors of the Colonel at Paris, and which caused them great satisfaction. Miss Crawley, the rich aunt from whom he expected his immense inheritance, was dying; the Colonel must haste to her bedside. Mrs. Crawley and her child would remain behind until he came to reclaim them. He departed for Calais, and having reached that place in safety, it might have been supposed that he went to Dover[9]: but instead he took the diligence to Dunkirk, and thence travelled to Brussels, for which place he had a former predilection. The fact is, he owed more money at London than at Paris; and he preferred the quiet little Belgian city to either of the more noisy capitals.

Her aunt was dead. Mrs. Crawley ordered the most intense mourning for herself and little Rawdon. The Colonel was busy arranging the affairs of the inheritance. They could take the premier now, instead of the little entresol of the hotel which they occupied. Mrs. Crawley and the landlord had a consultation about the new hangings, an amicable wrangle about the carpets, and a final adjustment of everything except the bill. She went off in one of his carriages; her French bonne with her; the child by her side; the admirable landlord and landlady smiling farewell to her from the gate. General Tufto was furious when he heard she was gone, and Mrs. Brent furious with him for being furious; Lieutenant Spooney was cut to the heart; and the landlord got ready his best apartments previous to the return of the fascinating little woman and her husband. He serred the trunks which she left in his charge with the greatest care. They had been especially recommended to him by Madame Crawley. They were not, however, found to be particularly valuable when opened some time after.

But before she went to join her husband in the Belgic capital, Mrs. Crawley made an expedition into England, leaving behind her her little son upon the continent, under the care of her French maid.

The parting between Rebecca and the little Rawdon did not cause either party much pain. She had not, to say truth, seen much of the young gentleman since his birth. After the amiable fashion of French mothers, she had placed him out at nurse in a village in the neighbourhood of Paris, where little Rawdon passed the first months of his life, not unhappily, with a numerous family of foster-brothers in wooden shoes. His father would ride over many a time to see him here, and the elder Rawdon's paternal heart glowed to see him rosy and dirty, shouting lustily, and happy in the making of mud-pies under the superintendence of the gardener's wife, his nurse.

Rebecca did not care much to go and see the son and heir. Once he spoiled a new dove-coloured pelisse of hers. He preferred his nurse's caresses to his mamma's, and when finally he quitted that jolly nurse and almost parent, he cried loudly for hours. He was only consoled by his mother's promise that he should return to his nurse the next day; indeed the nurse herself, who probably would have been pained at the parting too, was told that the child would immediately be restored to her, and for some time awaited quite anxiously his return.

In fact, our friends may be said to have been among the first of that brood of hardy English adventurers who have subsequently invaded the Continent and swindled in all the capitals of Europe. The respect in those happy days of 1817—1818 was very great for the wealth and honour of Britons. They had not then learned, as I am told, to haggle for bargains with the pertinacity which now distinguishes them. The great cities of Europe had not been as yet open to the enterprise of our rascals. And whereas there is now hardly a town of France or Italy in which you shall not see some noble countryman of our own, with that happy swagger and insolence of demeanour which we carry everywhere, swindling inn-landlords, passing fictitious cheques upon credulous bankers, robbing coach-makers of their carriages, goldsmiths of their trinkets, easy travellers of their money at cards, even public libraries of their books—thirty years ago you needed but to be a Milor Anglais, travelling in a private carriage, and credit was at your hand wherever you chose to seek it, and gentlemen, instead of cheating, were cheated. It was not for some weeks after the Crawleys' departure that the landlord of the hotel which they occupied during their residence at Paris found out the losses which he had sustained: not until Madame Marabou, the milliner, made repeated visits with her little bill for articles supplied to Madame Crawley; not until Monsieur Didelot from Bouled' Or in the Palais Royal had asked half a dozen times whether cette charmante Miladi who had bought watches and bracelets of him was de retour. It is a fact that even the poor gardener's wife, who had nursed madame's child, was never paid after the first six months for that supply of the milk of human kindness with which she had furnished the lusty and healthy little Rawdon. No, not even the nurse was paid—the Crawleys were in too great a hurry to remember their trifling debt to her. As for the landlord of the hotel, his curses against the English nation were violent for the rest of his natural life. He asked all travellers whether they knew a certain Colonel Lor Crawley—avec sa femme une petite dame, tres spirituelle. [10] "Ah, Monsieur !" he would add— "ils m'ont affreusement vole." [11] It was melancholy to hear his accents as he spoke of that catastrophe.

Rebecca's object in her journey to London was to effect a kind of compromise with her husband's numerous creditors, and by offering them a dividend of ninepence or a shilling in the pound, to secure a return for him into his own country. It does not become us to trace the steps which she took in the conduct of this most difficult negotiation; but, having shown them to their satisfaction that the sum which she was empowered to offer was all her husband's available capital, and having convinced them that Colonel Crawley would prefer a perpetual retirement on the Continent to a residence in this country with his debts unsettled; having proved to them that there was no possibility of money accruing to him from other quarters, and no earthly chance of their getting a larger dividend than that which she was empowered to offer, she brought the Colonel's creditors unanimously to accept her proposals, and purchased with fifteen hundred pounds of ready money more than ten times that amount of debts.

Mrs. Crawley employed no lawyer in the transaction. The matter was so simple, to have or to leave, as she justly observed, that she made the lawyers of the creditors themselves do the business. And Mr. Lewis representing Mr. Davids, of Red Lion Square, and Mr. Moss acting for Mr. Manasseh of Cursitor Street (chief creditors of the Colonel's, complimented his lady upon the brilliant way in which she did business, and declared that there was no professional man who could beat her.

Rebecca received their congratulations with perfect modesty; ordered a bottle of sherry and a bread cake to the little dingy lodgings where she dwelt, while conducting the business, to treat the enemy's lawyers: shook hands with them at parting, in excellent good humour and returned straightway to the Continent, to rejoin her husband and son and acquaint the former with the glad news of his entire liberation. As for the latter, he had been considerably neglected during his mother's absence by Mademoiselle Genevieve, her French maid; for that young woman, contracting an attachment for a soldier in the garrison of Calais, forgot her charge in the society of this militaire, and little Rawdon very narrowly escaped drowning on Calais sands at this period, where the absent Genevieve had left and lost him.

And so, Colonel and Mrs. Crawley came to London: and it is at their house in Curzon Street, May Fair, that they really showed the skill which must be possessed by those who would live on the resources above named.

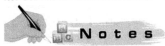 **Notes**

[1]College preparatory to Oxford for the sons of the aristocracy.

[2]English health resorts on the South coast.

[3]French port and health resort.

[4]Curzon Street and Mayfair are in aristocratic part of London.

[5]To become an officer one had to buy a commison; when retiring, the officer sold out his commission.

[6]French word, person of obscure, low social origin who has obtained wealth or position, an upstart.

[7]English military leader, who defeated Napoleon at the Battle of Waterloo in 1815.

[8]village in Belgium near which the forces of Britain and Prussia won a decisive battle against Napeleon in 1815.

[9]Dover: English port on the Channel serving the routes to the Continent.

[10]French: with his wife, a little lady, with high spirit.

[11]French: Ah, sir, they have robbed me terribly.

 **Questions**

1.According to the author, how do these people live on nothing?

2.How did the author describe their luxurious life?

3.What is the tone of the author in his description?

第三十六章　如何没有收入而过活

　　我想，在我们这名利场上的人，总不至于糊涂得对于自己朋友们的生活情况全不关心，凭他心胸怎么宽大，想到邻居里面像琼斯和斯密士这样的人一年下来居然能够收支相抵，总忍不住觉得诧异。譬如说，我对于琴根士一家非常的尊敬，因为在伦敦请客应酬最热闹的时候，我总在他家吃两三顿饭，可是我不得不承认，每当我在公园里看见他们坐着大马车，跟班的打扮得像穿特别制服的大兵，就免不了觉得纳闷，这个谜是一辈子也猜不透的了。我知道他们的马车是租来的，他们的佣人全是拿了工钱自理膳食的，可是这三个男佣人和马车一年至少也得六百镑才维持得起呢。他们又时常请客，酒菜是丰盛极了；两个儿子都在伊顿公学读书，家里另外给女儿们请着第一流的保姆和家庭教师。他们每到秋天便上国外游览，不到伊斯脱波恩便到窝丁；一年还要开一次舞会，酒席都是根脱饭馆预备的。我得补充一句，琴根士请客用的上等酒席大都叫他们包办。我怎么会知道的呢？原来有一回临时给他们拉去凑数，吃喝得真讲究，一看就知道比他们款待第二三流客人的普通酒菜精致许多。这么说来，凭你怎么马虎不管事，也免不了觉得疑惑，不知道琴根士他们到底是怎么一回事。琴根士本人是干哪一行的呢？我们都知道，他是照例行文局的委员，每年有一千二百镑的收入。他的妻子有钱吗？呸！她姓弗灵脱，父亲是白金汉郡的小地主，姊妹兄弟一共有十一个人。家里统共在圣诞节送她一只火鸡，她倒得在伦敦没有大应酬的时候供给两三个姊妹食宿，并且兄弟们到伦敦来的时候也得由她招待。琴根士究竟是怎么撑得起这场面的呢？我真想问问："他至今能够逍遥法外，究竟是怎么回事呀？去年他怎么还会从波浪涅回来呢？"他所有别的朋友一定也在那么猜测。去年他从波浪涅回来，大家都奇怪极了。

　　罗登·克劳莱夫妇在巴黎住了三四年后便回到英国，在梅飞厄的克生街上一所极舒服的小屋里住下来。在他们家里作客的许许多多朋友之中，差不多没有一个肚子里不在捉摸他们家用的来源。前面已经表过，写小说的人是无所不知的，因此我倒能够把克劳莱夫妇不花钱过日子的秘诀告诉大家。不幸现在的报纸常常随意把分期发表的小说摘录转载，所以我觉得担心，要请求各报的编辑先生不要抄袭我这篇情报和数字都绝顶准确的文章。既然发现内中情节的是我，出钱调查的是我，所得的利润当然也应该归我才对。如果我有个儿子，我一定对他说，孩子啊，倘若你要知道有些毫无收入的人怎么能过得那么舒服，只要常常跟他们来往和不断寻根究底地追问他们。不过我劝你少和靠这一行吃饭的家伙来往，你需要资料的话，尽不妨间接打听，就像你运用现成的对数表似的就行了。信我的话，倘若自己调查的话，得花不少钱呢。

克劳莱夫妇两手空空地在巴黎住了两三年，过得又快乐又舒服，可惜这段历史，我只能简单叙述一下。就在那时，克劳莱把军官的职位出卖，离开了禁卫队。我们和他重逢的时候，唯有他的胡子和名片上上校的名衔还沾着点军官的气息。

我曾经说过，利蓓加到达法国首都巴黎不久之后，便在上流社会出入，又时髦，又出风头，连好些光复后的王亲国戚都和她来往。许多住在巴黎的英国时髦人士也去奉承她，可是他们的妻子很不高兴，瞧着这个暴发户老大不入眼。在圣叶盂郊外一带的贵人家里，她的地位十分稳固，在灿烂豪华的新宫廷里，她也算得上有身份的贵客。克劳莱太太这么过了好几个月，乐得简直有些飘飘然。在这一段春风得意的日子里，大概她对于丈夫日常相与的一群老实的年轻军官很有些瞧不起。

上校混在公爵夫人和宫廷贵妇们中间，闷得直打呵欠。那些老太婆玩埃加脱，输了五法郎便大惊小怪，因此克劳莱上校觉得根本不值得斗牌。他又不懂法文，对于他们的俏皮话一句也听不懂。他的妻子天天晚上对着一大群公主屈膝行礼，这里面究竟有什么好处，他也看不出来。不久他让利蓓加独自出去作客，自己仍旧回到和他气味相投的朋友堆里来混，他是宁可过简单些的生活，找简单些的消遣的。

我们形容某某先生全无收入而过得舒服，事实上"全无收入"的意思就是"来路不明的收入"，也就是说这位先生居然能够开销这么一个家庭，简直使我们莫名其妙。我们的朋友克劳莱上校对于各种赌博，像玩纸牌、掷骰子、打弹子，没一样不擅长，而且他经过长期练习，自然比偶然赌一两场的人厉害得多。打弹子也和写字、击小剑、吹德国笛子一般，不但需要天赋的才能，而且应该有不懈的研究和练习，才能专精。克劳莱对于打弹子一道，本来是客串性质，不过玩得非常出色，到后来却成了技术高明的专家。他好像了不起的军事家，面临的危险愈大，他就愈有办法，往往一盘赌博下来，他手运一点也不好，所有的赌注都输了，然后忽然来几下子灵敏矫捷得出神入化的手法，把局势挽回过来，竟成了赢家。凡是对他赌博的本领不熟悉的人，看了没有不惊奇的。知道他有这么一手的人，和他赌输赢时便小心一些，因为他又机智，脑子又快，手又巧，别人再也赌不赢他。

斗牌的时候他也照样有本事。到黄昏初上场的时候他老是输钱，新和他交手的人见他随随便便，错误百出，都不怎么瞧得起他。可是接连几次小输之后，他生了戒心，抖擞起精神大战，大家看得出他的牌风和原来完全两样了，一晚下来，总能够把对手打得服服帖帖。说真的，在他手里赢过钱的人实在少得可怜。

他赢钱的次数那么多，无怪乎眼红的人、赌输的人，有时说起这事便要发牢骚。法国人曾经批评常胜将军威灵顿公爵，说他所以能常胜的缘故，无非是意外的运气，可是他们不得不承认他在滑铁卢之战的确耍过一些骗人的把戏，要不然那最后的一场比赛是赢不了的。同样的，在英国司令部，有好些人风言风语，总说克劳莱上校用了不老实的手段，才能保赢不输。

当时巴黎的赌风极盛，虽然弗拉斯加蒂和沙龙赌场都正式开放，可是一般人正在兴头上，觉得公共赌场还不过瘾，私人家里也公开聚赌，竟好像公共赌场从来就不存在，这股子赌劲没处发泄似的。在克劳莱家里，到黄昏往往有有趣的小聚会，也少不了这种有危险性的娱乐。克劳莱太太为人忠厚，为这件事心上很烦恼。她一谈起丈夫好赌的脾气就伤心得不得了，每逢家里有客，她总是唉声叹气的抱怨。她总哀求所有的小伙子不要挨近骰子匣。有一次来福枪联队里的葛里恩输了不少钱，害得利蓓加陪着流了一夜眼泪。这是她的佣人后来告诉那倒霉的输家的。据说她还向丈夫下跪，求他烧了债票，不要再去讨债。她丈夫不肯。那怎么行呢？匈牙利轻骑兵联队的勃拉克斯顿和德国汉诺伐骑兵联队里的本脱伯爵也赢了他那么多钱呢！葛里恩当然不必马上付钱，不妨过一个适当的时期再说，至于赌债，那是非还不可的。谁听说过烧毁债票呢？简直是孩子气！

到他们家去的军官多数年纪很轻，因为这些小伙子都爱追随在克劳莱太太身边。他们去拜访一次，多少总得在他们的牌桌上留下些钱，所以告别的时候都垂头丧气地拉长了脸。渐渐的克劳莱太太一家的声名便不大好听了。老手们时常警告没经验的人，说这里头的危险太大。当时驻扎在巴黎的第一联队的奥多上校就曾对联队里的斯卜内中尉下过劝告。有一次，步兵上校夫妇和克劳莱上校夫妇碰巧都在巴黎饭馆吃饭，两边就气势汹汹地大声吵闹起来了。两位太太都开了口。奥多太太冲着克劳莱太太的脸打响指，说她的丈夫"简直是个骗子"。克劳莱上校向奥多上校挑战，要跟他决斗。到他把"打死马克上尉"的手枪收拾停当，总司令已经风闻这次争辩，把克劳莱上校传去结结实实地训斥了一顿，结果也就没有决斗。倘若利蓓加不向德夫托将军下跪，克劳莱准会给调回英国去。此后几个星期里，他不敢赌了，最多找老百姓玩一下。

虽然罗登赌起来手法高明，百战百胜，利蓓加经过了这些挫折之后，觉得他们的地位并不稳。他们差不多什么账都不付，可是照这样下去，手头的一点儿款子总有一天会一文不剩。她常说："亲爱的，赌博只能贴补不足，不能算正经的收入。总有一天那些人赌厌了，咱们怎么办呢？"罗登觉得她的话不错；说实话，他发现先生们在他家里吃过几餐小晚饭之后，就不高兴再赌钱了，虽然利蓓加很迷人，他们还是不大愿意来。

他们在巴黎生活得又舒服又有趣，可是终究不过在偷安嬉耍，不是个久远之计。利蓓加明白她必须在本国替罗登打天下；或是在英国谋个出身，或是在殖民地上找个差使。她打定主意，一到有路可走的时候，就回英国。第一步，她先叫罗登把军官的职位出卖，只支半薪。他早已不当德夫托将军的副官了。利蓓加在不论什么应酬场上都讥笑那军官。她讥笑他的马（他进占巴黎时骑的就是它），还讥笑他的绑腰带、他的假牙齿。她尤其爱形容他怎么荒谬可笑，自以为是风月场上的老手，只当凡是和他接近的女人个个爱他。如今德夫托将军另有新欢，又去向军需处白瑞恩脱先生的凸脑门的妻子献殷勤儿了。花球、零星首饰、饭店里的酒席、歌剧院的包厢，都归这位太太受用。可怜的德夫托太太并没有比以前快乐；她明知丈夫洒了香水，卷了头发和胡子，在戏院里站在白瑞恩脱太太椅子背后讨好她，自己只能一黄昏一黄昏陪着女儿们闷在家里。蓓基身边有十来个拜倒在她裙下的人来顶替将军的位置，而且她谈吐俏皮，一开口就能把对手讥刺得体无完肤。可是我已经说过，她对于懒散的应酬生活已经厌倦了，坐包厢听戏和上馆子吃饭使她腻烦；花球不能作为日后衣食之计；她虽然有许多镂空手帕、羊皮手套，也不能靠着这些过日子。她觉得老是寻欢作乐空洞得很，渴望要些靠得住的资产。

正在紧要关头，上校在巴黎的债主们得到一个差强人意的消息，立刻传开了。他的有钱姑母克劳莱小姐病得很重，偌大的遗产快要传到他手里，因此他非得马上赶回去送终。克劳莱太太和她的孩子留在法国等他来接。他先动身到加莱；别人以为他平安到达那里之后，一定再向杜弗出发。不料他乘了邮车，由邓克刻转到布鲁塞尔去了。对于布鲁塞尔，他一向特别爱好。原来他在伦敦欠下的账比在巴黎的更多，嫌这两大首都太吵闹，宁可住在比利时的小城里，可以安逸些。

她姑妈死了，克劳莱太太给自己和儿子定做了全套的丧服。上校正忙着办理继承遗产的手续。如今他们住得起二楼的正房了，不必再住底层和二楼之间的那几间小屋子。克劳莱太太和旅馆主人商量该挂什么帘子，该铺什么地毯，为这事争得高兴。最后，什么都安排好了，只有账没有付。她动身的时候借用了他一辆马车，孩子和法国女佣人坐在她的身边一齐出发，旅馆主人夫妇，那两个好人，站在门口笑眯眯地给她送行。德夫托将军听说她已经离开法国，气得不得了，白瑞恩脱太太因为他生气，也就生他的气。斯卜内中尉难受得要命。旅馆主人以为那妩媚动人的太太和她丈夫不久就会回来，把他最好的房间都收拾整齐，又把她留下的箱子仔仔细细地锁好，因为是克劳莱太太特别嘱咐他留心照看的。可惜不久以后他们把箱子打开的时候，并没有发现什么值钱的东西。

克劳莱太太到比利时首都去找丈夫以前，先到英国去走了一趟，叫那法国女佣人带着儿子留在欧洲大陆。

利蓓加和小罗登分手的时候两边都不觉得割舍不下。说句实话，从这小孩子出世以来，她根本不大和他在一起。她学习法国妈妈们的好榜样，把他寄养在巴黎近郊的村子里。小罗登出世以后住在奶妈家里，和一大群穿木屐的奶哥哥在一起，日子过得相当快乐。他的爸爸常常骑了马去看望他。罗登看见儿子脸色红润，浑身肮脏，跟在他奶妈旁边（就是那花匠的妻子）做泥饼子，快乐得大呼小叫，心里不由得感到一阵做父亲的得意。

利蓓加不大高兴去看她的儿子，有一回孩子把她一件浅灰色的新外套给弄脏了。小罗登也宁可要奶妈，不要妈妈。他的奶妈老是兴高采烈的，像生身母亲似的疼他，因此他离开她的时候扯起嗓子哭了好几个钟头。后来他母亲哄他说第二天就让他回奶妈那儿去，他这才不哭了。奶妈也以为孩子就会被送回去，痴心等待了好些日子，倘若她知道从此分手，告别的时候一定也觉得伤心。

自从那时候起，就有一帮胆大妄为的英国流氓混进欧洲各个大都市去招摇撞骗，我们的这两位朋友，可以算是第一批骗子里面的角色。从1817年到1818年，英国人的日子过得实在富裕，大陆上的人对于他们的财富和道德非常尊敬。现在大家知道英国人有名的会斤斤计较和人讲价钱，据说当时他们还没有学会这套本领，欧洲的大城市也还没有给英国的流氓所盘踞。到如今差不多无论在法国和意大利哪个城市都有我们高贵的本国人，一看就是英国来的；他们态度骄横，走起路来那点架子摆得恰到好处。这些人欺骗旅馆老板，拿了假支票到老实的银行家那儿去诓钱，定了马车买了首饰不付账，和不懂事的过路客人斗牌，做了圈套赢他们的钱，甚至于还偷公共图书馆的书。三十年前，只要你是英国来的大爷，坐着自备马车到处游览，爱欠多少账都由你；那时的英国先生们不会哄人，只会上当。克劳莱一家离开法国好几个星期以后，那一向供他们食宿的旅馆老板才发现自己损失多么大。起初他还不知道，后来衣装铺子里的莫拉布太太拿着克劳莱太太的衣服账来找了她好几次，还有皇宫街金球珠宝店里的蒂拉洛先生也跑了六七回，打听那位问他买手表、镯子的漂亮太太究竟什么时候回来，他才恍然大悟。可怜的花匠老婆给太太当奶妈，把结实的小罗登抚养了一场，并且对他十分疼爱，也只拿到在最初六个月的工钱。克劳莱一家临行匆忙，哪里还记得这种没要紧的账目，所以奶妈的工钱也欠着。旅馆老板从此痛恨英国，一直到死，提起它便狠狠毒毒地咒骂。凡是有过往的客人住到他旅馆里来，他就问他们认识不认识一个克劳莱上校老爷——他的太太个子矮小，样子非常文雅。他总是说："唉，先生，他欠了我多少钱，害得我好苦！"他讲到那次倒霉的事件，声音真凄惨，叫人听着也觉得难受。

利蓓加回到伦敦，目的是和丈夫的一大群债主谈判。她情愿把丈夫所欠的债每镑中偿还九便士到一先令，作为他们让他回国的条件。至于她采取什么方法来进行这棘手的交涉，这里也不便细说。第一，她使债主们明了她丈夫名下只有这些钱，能够提出来还债的数目再也多不出了。第二，她向债主们解释，如果债务不能了结的话，克劳莱上校宁可一辈子住在欧洲大陆，永远不回国。第三，她向债主们证明克劳莱上校的确没有弄钱的去处，他们所能得到的款子绝没有希望超过她所建议的数目。那么一来，上校的债主们一致同意接受建议；她用了一千五百镑现款把债务完全偿清，实际上只还了全数的十分之一。

克劳莱太太办事不用律师。她说得很对，这件事简单得很，愿意不愿意随他们的便，因此她只让代表债主的几个律师自己去做交易。红狮广场台维滋先生的代表路易斯律师和可息多街马那息先生的代表莫斯律师（这两处是上校的主要债主）都恭维上校太太办事聪明能干，吃法律饭的人都比不过她。

利蓓加受了这样的奉承，全无骄色。她买了一瓶雪利酒和一个面包布丁，在她那间又脏又小的屋子里（她办事的时候住这样的屋子）款待对手的两个律师，分手的时候还跟他们拉手，客气得了不得。然后她马上回到大陆去找丈夫和儿子，向罗登报告他重获自由的好消息。至于小罗登呢，母亲不在的时候被她的法国女佣人叶尼薇爱芙丢来丢去地不当一回事。那年轻女人看中了一个加莱军营里的士兵，老是和他混在一起，哪里还想得着小罗登呢？有一回她把孩子丢在加莱海滩上自己走掉了，小罗登差点儿没被淹死。

这样，克劳莱上校夫妇回到伦敦，在梅飞厄的克生街上住下来。在那里，他们才真正施展出本领来；上面所谓没有收入而能过活的人，非要有这种能耐不可。

References

[1] 王守仁. 英国文学选读 [C]. 北京：高等教育出版社，2005.

Unit 13   Charlottë Brontë (1816—1855)

Life

Charlotte Brontë was born in 1816, the third daughter of the Rev. Patrick Brontë and his wife Maria. Her brother Patrick Branwell was born in 1817, and her sisters Emily and Anne in 1818 and 1820. In 1820, too, the Brontë family moved to Haworth, Mrs. Brontë died the following year.

In 1824 the four eldest Brontë daughters were enrolled as pupils at the Clergy Daughter's School at Cowan Bridge. The following year Maria and Elizabeth, the two eldest daughters, became ill, left the school and died: Charlotte and Emily, understandably, were brought home.

In 1831 Charlotte became a pupil at the school at Roe Head, but she left school the following year to teach her sisters at home. She returned to Roe Head School in 1835 as a governess: for a time her sister Emily attended the same school as a pupil, but became homesick and returned to Haworth. Ann took her place from 1836 to 1837.

In 1838, Charlotte left Roe Head School. In 1839 she accepted a position as governess in the Sidgewick family, but left after three months and returned to Haworth.

Upon her return to Haworth the three sisters, led by Charlotte, decided to open their own school after the necessary preparations had been completed. In 1842 Charlotte and Emily went to Brussels to complete their studies. After a trip home to Haworth, Charlotte returned alone to Brussels, where she remained until 1844.

Upon her return home the sisters embarked upon their project for founding a school, which proved to be a failure: their advertisements did not receive a single response from the public. The following year Charlotte discovered Emily's poems, and decided to publish a selection of the poems of all three sisters: 1846 brought the publication of their *Poems,* written under the pseudonyms of Currer, Ellis and Acton Bell whose first letters stand for their genuine names. Charlotte also completed *The Professor*, which was rejected for publication. The following year, however, Charlotte's *Jane Eyre*, Emily's *Wuthering Heights*, and Ann's *Agnes Grey* were all published, still under the Bell pseudonyms.

In 1848 Charlotte and Ann visited their publishers in London, and revealed the true identities of the "Bells." In the same year Branwell Brontë, by now an alcoholic and a drug addict, died, and Emily died shortly thereafter. Ann died the following year.

In 1849 Charlotte, visiting London, began to move in literary circles, making the acquaintance, for example, of Thackeray. In 1850 Charlotte edited her sister's various works, and met Mrs. Gaskell.

In 1854 Charlotte caught pneumonia. It was an illness which could have been cured, but she seems to have seized upon it (consciously or unconsciously) as an opportunity of ending her life, and after a lengthy and painful illness, she died, probably of dehydration.

1857 saw the posthumous publication of *The Professor*, which had been written in 1845—1846.

Major Works:

● *Poems* by Currer, Ellis and Acton Bell (1846).

● *Jane Eyre*: An Autobiography (1847).

● *Shirley*: A Tale (1849).

● *Villette* (1853).

● *The Professor*: A Tale (1857).

Plot of *Jane Eyre*

Introduction

The novel is a first-person narrative from the perspective of the title character. The novel's setting is somewhere in the north of England, during the reign of George III (1760—1820), and goes through five distinct stages: Jane's childhood at Gateshead Hall, where she is emotionally and physically abused by her aunt and cousins; her education at Lowood School, where she gains friends and role models but suffers privations and oppression; her time asgoverness at Thornfield Hall, where she falls in love with her Byronic employer, Edward Rochester; her time with the Rivers family, during which her earnest but cold clergyman cousin, St. John Rivers, proposes to her; and her reunion with, and marriage to, her beloved Rochester. During these sections the novel provides perspectives on a number of important social issues and ideas, many of which are critical of the status quo (see the Themes sectionbelow). Literary critic Jerome Beaty opines that the close first person perspective leaves the reader "too uncritically accepting of her worldview", and often leads reading and conversation about the novel towards supporting Jane, regardless of how irregular her ideas or perspectives are.

Jane Eyre is divided into 38 chapters, and most editions are at least 400 pages long. The original publication was in three volumes, comprising chapters 1 to 15, 16 to 27, and 28 to 38; this was a common publishing format during the 19th century (see three-volume novel).

Brontë dedicated the novel's second edition to William Makepeace Thackeray.

Jane's childhood

The novel begins with the titular character, Jane Eyre, aged 10, living with her maternal uncle's family, the Reeds, as a result of her uncle's dying wish. It is several years after her parents died of typhus. Mr. Reed, Jane's uncle, was the only one in the Reed family who was kind to Jane. Jane's aunt, Sarah Reed, dislikes her, treats her as a burden, and discourages her children from associating with Jane. Mrs. Reed and her three children are abusive to Jane, physically, emotionally, and spiritually. The nursemaid Bessie proves to be Jane's only ally in the household, even though Bessie sometimes harshly scolds Jane. Excluded from the family activities, Jane is incredibly unhappy, with only a doll and books for comfort.

One day, after her cousin John knocks her down and she attempts to defend herself, Jane is locked in the red room where her uncle died; there, she faints from panic after she thinks she has seen his ghost. She is subsequently attended to by the kindly apothecary, Mr. Lloyd, to whom Jane reveals how unhappy she is living at Gateshead Hall. He recommends to Mrs. Reed that Jane should be sent to school, an idea Mrs. Reed happily supports. Mrs. Reed then enlists the aid of the harsh Mr. Brocklehurst, director of Lowood Institution, a charity school for girls. Mrs. Reed cautions Mr. Brocklehurst that Jane has a "tendency for deceit", which he interprets as her being a "liar." Before Jane leaves, however, she confronts Mrs. Reed and declares that she'll never call her "aunt" again, that Mrs. Reed and her daughter, Georgiana, are the ones who are deceitful, and that she shall tell everyone at Lowood how cruelly Mrs. Reed treated her.

Lowood

At Lowood Institution, a school for poor and orphaned girls, Jane soon finds that life is harsh, but she attempts to fit in and befriends an older girl, Helen Burns, who is able to accept her punishment philosophically. During a school inspection by Mr. Brocklehurst, Jane accidentally breaks her slate, thereby drawing attention to herself. He then stands her on a stool, brands her a liar, and shames her before the entire assembly. Jane is later comforted by her friend, Helen. Miss Temple, the caring superintendent, facilitates Jane's self-defence and writes to Mr. Lloyd, whose reply agrees with Jane's. Jane is then publicly cleared of Mr. Brocklehurst's accusations.

The 80 pupils at Lowood are subjected to cold rooms, poor meals, and thin clothing. Many students fall ill when a typhus epidemic strikes, and Jane's friend Helen dies of consumption in her arms. When Mr. Brocklehurst's maltreatment of the students is discovered, several benefactors erect a new building and install a sympathetic management committee to moderate Mr. Brocklehurst's harsh rule. Conditions at the school then improve dramatically.

The name Lowood symbolizes the "low" point in Jane's life where she was maltreated. Helen Burns is a representation of Charlotte's elder sister Maria, who died of tuberculosis after spending time at a school where the children were mistreated.

Thornfield Hall

After six years as a student and two as a teacher at Lowood, Jane decides to leave, like her friend and confidante Miss Temple, who recently married. She advertises her services as a governess and receives one reply, from Alice Fairfax, housekeeper at Thornfield Hall. Jane takes the position, teaching Adèle Varens, a young French girl.

One night, while Jane is walking to a nearby town, a horseman passes her. The horse slips on ice and throws the rider. Despite the rider's surliness, Jane helps him to get back onto his horse. Later, back at Thornfield, she learns that this man is Edward Rochester, master of the house. Adèle is his ward, left in his care when her mother abandoned her.

At Jane's first meeting with him within Thornfield, Mr. Rochester teases her, accusing her of bewitching his horse to make him fall. He also talks strangely in other ways, but Jane is able to give as good as she gets. Mr. Rochester and Jane soon come to enjoy each other's company, and spend many evenings together.

Odd things start to happen at the house, such as a strange laugh, a mysterious fire in Mr. Rochester's room (from which Jane saves Rochester by rousing him and throwing water on him and the fire), and an attack on a house guest named Mr. Mason. Then Jane receives word that her aunt Mrs. Reed is calling for her, because she suffered a stroke after her son John died. Jane returns to Gateshead and remains there for a month, attending to her dying aunt. Mrs. Reed confesses to Jane that she wronged her, giving Jane a letter from Jane's paternal uncle, Mr. John Eyre, in which he asks for her to live with him and be his heir. Mrs. Reed admits to telling Mr. Eyre that Jane had died of fever at Lowood. Soon afterward, Mrs. Reed dies, and Jane helps her cousins after the funeral before returning to Thornfield.

Back at Thornfield, Jane broods over Mr. Rochester's rumoured impending marriage to the beautiful and talented, but snobbish and heartless, Blanche Ingram. However, one midsummer evening, Rochester baits Jane by saying how much he will miss her after getting married, but how she will soon forget him. The normally self-controlled Jane reveals her feelings for him. Rochester is then sure that Jane is sincerely in love with him, and he proposes marriage. Jane is at first sceptical of his sincerity, but eventually believes him and gladly agrees to marry him. She then writes to her Uncle John, telling him of her happy news.

As she prepares for her wedding, Jane's forebodings arise when a strange woman sneaks into her room one night and rips her wedding veil in two. As with the previous mysterious events, Mr. Rochester attributes the incident to Grace Poole, one of his servants. During the wedding ceremony, Mr. Mason and a lawyer declare that Mr. Rochester cannot marry because he is already married to Mr. Mason's sister, Bertha. Mr. Rochester admits this is true but explains that his father tricked him into the marriage for her money. Once they were united, he discovered that she was rapidly descending into madness, and so he eventually locked her away in Thornfield, hiring Grace Poole as a nurse to look after her. When Grace gets drunk, his wife escapes and causes the strange happenings at Thornfield.

It turns out that Jane's uncle, Mr. John Eyre, is a friend of Mr. Mason's and was visited by him soon after Mr. Eyre received Jane's letter about her impending marriage. After the marriage ceremony is broken off, Mr. Rochester asks Jane to go with him to the south of France, and live with him as husband and wife, even though they cannot be married. Refusing to go against her principles, and despite her love for him, Jane leaves Thornfield in the middle of the night.

Other employment

Jane travels as far from Thornfield as she can using the little money she had previously saved. She accidentally leaves her bundle of possessions on the coach and has to sleep on the moor, and unsuccessfully attempts to trade her handkerchief and gloves for food. Exhausted and hungry, she eventually makes her way to the home of Diana and Mary Rivers, but is turned away by the housekeeper. She collapses on the doorstep, preparing for her death. St. John Rivers— Diana and Mary's brother—and a clergyman save her. After she regains her health, St. John finds Jane a teaching position at a nearby village school. Jane becomes good friends with the sisters, but St. John remains aloof.

The sisters leave for governess jobs, and St. John becomes somewhat closer to Jane. St. John learns Jane's true identity and astounds her by telling her that her uncle, John Eyre, has died and left her his entire fortune of 20,000 pounds (equivalent to over £1.3 million in 2011). When Jane questions him further, St. John reveals that John Eyre is also his and his sisters' uncle. They had once hoped for a share of the inheritance but were left virtually nothing. Jane, overjoyed by finding that she has living and friendly family members, insists on sharing the money equally with her cousins, and Diana and Mary come back to live at Moor House.

Proposals

Thinking Jane will make a suitable missionary's wife, St. John asks her to marry him and to go with him to India, not out of love, but out of duty. Jane initially accepts going to India but rejects the marriage proposal, suggesting they travel as brother and sister. As soon as Jane's resolve against marriage to St. John begins to weaken, she mysteriously hears Mr. Rochester's voice calling her name. Jane then returns to Thornfield to find only blackened ruins. She learns that Mr. Rochester's wife set the house on fire and committed suicide by jumping from the roof. In his rescue attempts, Mr. Rochester lost a hand and his eyesight. Jane reunites with him, but he fears that she will be repulsed by his condition. "Am I hideous, Jane?", he asks. "Very, sir: you always were, you know", she replies. When Jane assures him of her love and tells him that she will never leave him, Mr. Rochester again proposes, and they are married. He eventually recovers enough sight to see their first-born son.

Comments on *Jane Eyre*

Morality

Jane refuses to become Mr. Rochester's paramour because of her "impassioned self-respect and moral conviction." She rejects St. John Rivers' religious fervour as much as the libertine aspects of Mr. Rochester's character. Instead, she works out a morality expressed in love, independence, and forgiveness.

God and religion

Throughout the novel, Jane endeavours to attain an equilibrium between moral duty and earthly happiness. She despises the hypocrisy of Mr. Brocklehurst, and sees deficiencies in St. John Rivers' indulgent yet detached devotion to his Christian duty. As a child, Jane admires Helen Burns' life philosophy of "turning the other cheek", which in turn helps her in adult life to forgive Aunt Reed and the Reed cousins for their cruelty. Although she does not seem to subscribe to any of the standard forms of popular Christianity, she honours traditional morality – particularly seen when she refuses to marry Mr. Rochester until he is widowed.

In her preface to the second edition of Jane Eyre, Brontë makes her beliefs clear, "conventionality is not morality" and "self-righteousness is not religion," declaring that narrow human doctrines, which serve only to elate and magnify a few, should not be substituted for the world-redeeming creed of Christ. Throughout the novel, Brontë presents contrasts between characters who believe in and practice what she considers a true Christianity, and those who pervert religion to further their own ends. Here are further examples:

Mr. Brocklehurst, who oversees Lowood Institution, is a hypocritical Christian. He professes aid and charity but does the opposite by using religion as a justification for punishment. For instance, he cites the Biblical passage "man shall not live by bread alone", to rebuke Miss Temple for having fed the girls an extra meal to compensate for their inedible breakfast of burnt porridge. He tells Miss Temple that she "may indeed feed their vile bodies, but you little think how you starve their immortal souls!"

Helen Burns is a complete contrast to Brocklehurst; she follows the Christian creed of "turning the other cheek" and by loving those who hate her. On her deathbed, Helen tells Jane "I'm going home to God, who loves me." Jane herself cannot quite profess Helen's absolute, selfless faith. Jane does not seem to follow a particular doctrine, but she is sincerely religious in a non-doctrinaire, general way; it is Jane, presumably, who places the stone with the word "Resurgam" (Latin for "I will rise again") on Helen's grave, some fifteen years after her friend's death. Jane is seen frequently praying and calling on God to assist her, especially with her struggles concerning Mr. Rochester; praying for his wellness and safety.

After Hannah, the Rivers' housekeeper, tried to turn the begging Jane away at the door, Jane later tells her that "if you are a Christian, you ought not consider poverty a crime."

The young evangelical clergyman St. John Rivers is a more conventionally religious figure. However, Brontë portrays his religious aspect ambiguously. Jane calls him "a very good man," yet she finds him cold and forbidding. In his determination to do good deeds (in the form of missionary work in India), St. John courts martyrdom. Moreover, he is unable to see Jane as a whole person, but views her only as a helpmate in his impending missionary work.

Mr. Rochester is a less than perfect Christian. He is, indeed, a sinner: he attempts to enter into a bigamous marriage with Jane and, when that fails, tries to persuade her to become his mistress. He also confesses that he has had three previous mistresses. However, at the end of the book Mr. Rochester repents his sinfulness, thanks God for returning Jane, and asks Him for the strength to lead a purer life. It is implied that Rochester's maiming and blindness were God's judgment for his sins, and that the partial recovery of his sight was due to his repentance. "God had tempered judgment with mercy."

Social class

Jane's ambiguous social position—a penniless yet decently educated orphan from a good family—leads her to criticise some discrimination based on class, though she makes class discriminations herself. Although she is educated, well-mannered, and relatively sophisticated, she is still a governess, a paid employee (middle class), and therefore relatively powerless. She respectfully defers to Rochester and his guests from the upper class, but she asks Leah, the housemaid (lower class), to get her a candle rather than get it herself, and has a servant girl when she is school mistress at the small village school in Morton. While Jane is always conscious of her social position (Rochester is master and she is employee) in everyday matters, at heart she sees herself as his equal, as evidenced in her passionate speech prior to Rochester's first proposal.

"... it is my spirit that addresses your spirit; just as if both had passed through the grave, and we stood at God's feet, equal,– as we are!"

Gender relations

A particularly important theme in the novel is the depiction of a patriarchal society. Jane attempts to assert her own identity within male-dominated society. Three of the main male characters, Mr. Brocklehurst, Mr. Rochester and St. John Rivers, try to keep Jane in a subordinate position and prevent her from expressing her own thoughts and feelings. Jane escapes Mr. Brocklehurst and rejects St. John, and she only marries Mr. Rochester once she is sure that their marriage is one between equals. Through Jane, Brontë opposes Victorian stereotypes about women, articulating her own feminist philosophy:

Women are supposed to be very calm generally, but women feel just as men feel; they need exercise for their faculties, and a field for their efforts as much as their brothers do; they suffer from too rigid a restraint, too absolute a stagnation, precisely as men would suffer; and it is narrow-minded in their more privileged fellow-creatures to say that they ought to confine themselves to making puddings and knitting stockings, to playing on the piano and embroidering bags. It is thoughtless to condemn them, or laugh at them, if they seek to do more or learn more than custom has pronounced necessary for their sex. (Chapter XII)

It is also interesting to note that while most readings of Jane Eyre dwell on the fact that Bertha is insane, it is not because she is insane that Rochester hates her (chapter. 27). The two specific claims that he makes against her, before she became insane, are that she was "intemperate and unchaste" and that he therefore felt degraded. Some feminist readings of the novel have taken this to mean that the strictures imposed on women contemporary to the book were such that stepping outside of them could have been construed as insane.

Other interpretations have seen this as evidence that Bertha was syphilitic, and that the romanticism of the book neglects the truth that Edward Rochester would have been as well. The book may use the syphilitic condition as a metaphor for the sexual predation and narcissistic projection of Edward Rochester; Edward says Bertha is "unchaste" in an attempt to relieve himself of the psychic pain of his having the disease himself and his own likely role in Bertha acquiring that condition as well as the fact he likely has the disease and risks infecting Jane. His psychological projection combined with his position of power distorts reality such that it gives Bertha no choice but to be "insane" (which may be combined with actual physical brain deterioration from the syphilis) if any challenge to his veracity would cause her greater problems, such as abandonment, starvation, etc.

Love and passion

A central theme in Jane Eyre is that of the clash between conscience and passion—which one is to be adhered to, and how to find a middle ground between the two. Jane, extremely passionate yet also dedicated to a close personal relationship with God, struggles between the two extremes for much of the novel. An instance of her leaning towards conscience over passion can be seen after it has been revealed that Mr. Rochester already has a wife, when Jane is begged to run away with Mr. Rochester and become his mistress. Up until that moment, Jane had been riding on a wave of emotion, forgetting all thoughts of reason and logic, replacing God with Mr. Rochester in her eyes, and allowing herself to be swept away in the moment. However, once the harsh reality of the situation sets in, Jane does everything in her power to refuse Mr. Rochester, despite almost every part of her rejecting the idea and urging her to just give in to Mr. Rochester's appeal. In the moment, Jane experiences an epiphany in regards to conscience, realising that "laws and principles are not for times when there is no temptation: they are for such moments as this." Jane finally comes to understand that all passion, as she had been living her life up until then, and all conscience, as she had leaned towards during her time at Lowood, is neither good nor preferable. In this case, Jane had allowed herself to lean too far in the direction of passion, and she is in danger of giving up all logic and reason in favour of temptation. However, Jane finally asserts that in times of true moral trial, such as the one she is in with Mr. Rochester at the moment, to forgo one's principles, to violate the "law given by God," would be too easy—and not something she is willing to do. Jane's struggles to find a middle ground between her passionate and conscience-driven sides frequently go back and forth throughout the novel, but in this case she has drawn the line as to where passion is taking too great a role in her life, and where she will not allow herself to forgo her moral and religious principles.

Feminism

The role and standing of women in the Victorian era is considered by Brontë in Jane Eyre, specifically in regard to Jane's independence and ability to make decisions for herself. As a young woman, small and of relatively low social standing, Jane encounters men during her journey, of good, bad, and morally debatable character. However, many of them, no matter their ultimate intentions, attempt to establish some form of power and control over Jane. One example can be seen in Mr. Rochester, a man who ardently loves Jane, but who frequently commands and orders Jane about. As a self-assured and established man, and her employer, Mr. Rochester naturally assumes the position of the master in their relationship. He sometimes demands rather than question Jane, tries to manipulate and assess her feelings towards him, and enjoys propping up Jane through excessive gifts and luxuries that only he would have been able to provide. Jane, however, believes in the importance of women's independence, and strives to maintain a position in life devoid of any debts to others. Her initial lack of money and social status unnerves her, as she realises that without the means to be an independent woman, she is bound to either struggle through life trying to make a living or marry and become dependent on a man. Even after Jane agrees to marry Mr. Rochester, and is swept up in the passion of the moment, the feminist elements of her personality still show through. She is uncomfortable with the showering of lavish gifts, as she resents that they will make her further reliant on and in debt to Mr. Rochester, and thus tries to resist them. Furthermore, Jane asserts that until she is married to Mr. Rochester, she will continue to be Adèle's governess and earn her keep. This plan, which was entirely radical and unheard of for the time, further illustrates Jane's drive to remain a somewhat independent woman. It was for this reason she suddenly remembered and wrote to her uncle who until now thought her dead. "... if I had but a prospect of one day bringing Mr. Rochester an accession of fortune, I could better endure to be kept by him now." This feminist undercurrent also presents itself in Jane's interaction with her long-lost cousin, St. John Rivers. St. John repressed Jane's feeling and controlled her excessively. She often felt that he "took away [her] liberty of mind."During her stay with her cousin, St. John proposes to Jane, by claiming her "as a soldier would a new weapon." Jane realises that she cannot marry a man who constantly forces her into submission and treats her like an object, and she refuses to marry him. Once again, her need for independence shines through.

The only time Jane truly feels ready to marry a man is when she is equal to him. In the end of Jane Eyre, Jane inherits a fortune from her uncle. This allows her to be economically independent from Mr. Rochester. Also, Mr. Rochester becomes lame and blind after the fire that ripped through his home. He now depends on Jane, rather than Jane depending on him. This change in the power dynamic of their relationship unites the two of them once again.

While the significant men present in Jane's life throughout the novel all try to, in some form or another, establish themselves as dominant over Jane, she in most cases remains resistant at least to a certain degree, refusing to submit fully or lose all of her independence. The only time Jane feels comfortable attaching herself to a man is when she knows that she is his financial, intellectual, and emotional equal. This final adherence to her strong convictions on the independence of women points out Brontë's similar views on the patriarchal Victorian society of the time.

Atonement and forgiveness

Much of the religious concern in Jane Eyre has to do with atonement and forgiveness. Mr. Rochester is tormented by his awareness of his past sins and misdeeds. He frequently confesses that he has led a life of vice, and many of his actions in the course of the novel are less than commendable. Readers may accuse him of behaving sadistically in deceiving Jane about the nature of his relationship (or rather, non-relationship) with Blanche Ingram to provoke Jane's jealousy. His confinement of Bertha may bespeak mixed motives. He is certainly aware that in the eyes of both religious and civil authorities, his marriage to Jane before Bertha's death would be bigamous. Yet, at the same time, Mr. Rochester makes genuine efforts to atone for his behaviour. For example, although he does not believe that he is Adèle's natural father, he adopts her as his ward and sees that she is well cared for. This adoption may well be an act of atonement for the sins he has committed. He expresses his self-disgust at having tried to console himself by having three different mistresses during his travels in Europe and begs Jane to forgive him for these past transgressions. However, Mr. Rochester can only atone completely – and be forgiven completely-after Jane has refused to be his mistress and left him. The destruction of Thornfield by fire finally removes the stain of his past sins; the loss of his left hand and of his eyesight is the price he must pay to atone completely for his sins. Only after this purgation can he be redeemed by Jane's love.

Search for home and family

Without any living family that she is aware of (until well into the story), throughout the course of the novel Jane searches for a place that she can call home. Significantly, houses play a prominent part in the story. (In keeping with a long English tradition, all the houses in the book have names). The novel's opening finds Jane living at Gateshead Hall, but this is hardly a home. Mrs. Reed and her children refuse to acknowledge her as a relation, treating her instead as an unwanted intruder and an inferior.

Shunted off to Lowood Institution, a boarding school for orphans and destitute children, Jane finds a home of sorts, although her place here is ambiguous and temporary. The school's manager, Mr. Brocklehurst, treats it more as a business and a place of correction than as school in loco parentis (in place of the parent). His emphasis on discipline and on spartan conditions at the expense of the girls' health make it the antithesis of the ideal home.

Jane subsequently believes she has found a home at Thornfield Hall. Anticipating the worst when she arrives, she is relieved when she is made to feel welcome by Mrs. Fairfax. She feels genuine affection for Adèle (who in a way is also an orphan) and is happy to serve as her governess. As her love for Mr. Rochester grows, she believes that she has found her ideal husband in spite of his eccentric manner and that they will make a home together at Thornfield. The revelation—as they are on the verge of marriage—that he is already legally married—brings her dream of home crashing down. Fleeing Thornfield, she literally becomes homeless and is reduced to begging for food and shelter. The opportunity of having a home presents itself when she enters Moor House, where the Rivers sisters and their brother, the Reverend St. John Rivers, are mourning the death of their father. She soon speaks of Diana and Mary Rivers as her own sisters, and is overjoyed when she learns that they are indeed her cousins. She tells St. John Rivers that learning that she has living relations is far more important than inheriting twenty thousand pounds. (She mourns the uncle she never knew. Earlier she was disheartened on learning that Mrs. Reed told her uncle that Jane had died and sent him away.) However, St. John Rivers' offer of marriage cannot sever her emotional attachment to Rochester. In an almost visionary episode, she hears Mr. Rochester's voice calling her to return to him. The last chapter begins with the famous simple declarative sentence, "Reader, I married him," (which inspired a 2016 story collection *Reader, I Married Him*) and after a long series of travails Jane's search for home and family ends in a union with her ideal mate.

Major Characters

Jane Eyre

She is an orphan and a girl with strong mind. In the novel, readers read a biographical description of Jane, from her childhood to her adulthood. She is a new woman image in 19th century. She is brave enough to express her feelings and thoughts. She is independent by supporting herself as a governess. She voices her desire for love based on equality and mutual attraction and understanding. Jane has overcome barriers in her way to happiness. During her life, she has to fight against the control and oppression of three men, i.e. Brocklehurst in Lowood School, Rochester and St. John Rivers. She is not a pretty girl. However, her character is charming and attractive. Such image has overturned the previous women images. Women images in the past are described as angels and they try their efforts to satisfy men. All of them are submissive. It seems that submission is a virtue for women of 19th century. So the image a Jane is significant for later writers who depict women characters. After all, appearance is not the only standard to comment on women.

Rochester

He is Jane's lover, a dark, passionate, brooding man. As a traditional romantic hero, Rochester has lived a troubled life. He married an insane woman who is locked in the house. But he shows great affection for Jane. At last, he and Jane are together after overcoming many difficulties.

Introduction to Chapter XXXVII

Chapter 37 is getting near to the end of the story. Jane returns to Thornfield and she finds that Bertha died in fire and Rochester became handicapped. He decided to stay with Rochester and marry him when he is in the greatest difficulty. In this chapter, Jane and Rochester express mutual affection for each other. Jane tells Rochester her experience when she ran away from Thornfield on the wedding day. Rochester proposes to Jane and she agrees to be Rochester's wife.

Chapter XXXVII

Very early the next morning I heard him up and astir[1], wandering from one room to another. As soon as Mary came down I heard the question: "Is Miss Eyre here?" Then: "Which room did you put her into? Was it dry? Is she up? Go and ask if she wants anything; and when she will come down."

I came down as soon as I thought there was a prospect of breakfast. Entering the room very softly, I had a view of him before he discovered my presence. It was mournful, indeed, to witness the subjugation of that vigorous spirit to a corporeal infirmity[2].He sat in his chair—still, but not at rest: expectant evidently; the lines of now habitual sadness marking his strong features. His countenance reminded one of a lamp quenched, waiting to be re-lit—and alas! It was not himself that could now kindle the luster[3] of animated expression: he was dependent on another for that office[4]! I had meant to be gay and careless, but the powerlessness of the strong man touched my heart to the quick[5]: still I accosted[6] him with what vivacity I could. "It is a bright, sunny morning, sir," I said. "The rain is over and gone, and there is a tender shining[7] after it: you shall have a walk soon."

I had wakened the glow: his features beamed.

"Oh, you are indeed there, my skylark! Come to me. You are not gone: not vanished? I heard one of your kind[8] an hour ago, singing high over the wood: but its song had no music for me, any more than the rising sun had rays. All the melody on earth is concentrated in my Jane's tongue to my ear (I am glad it is not naturally a silent one): all the sunshine I can feel is in her presence."

The water stood in my eyes to hear this avowal[9] of his dependence; just as if a royal eagle, chained to a perch, should be forced to entreat a sparrow to become its purveyor[10]. But I would not be lachrymose[11]: I dashed off the salt drops, and busied myself with preparing breakfast.

Most of the morning was spent in the open air. I led him out of the wet and wild wood into some cheerful fields: I described to him how brilliantly green they were; how the flowers and hedges looked refreshed; how sparklingly blue was the sky. I sought a seat for him in a hidden and lovely spot, a dry stump of a tree; nor did I refuse to let him, when seated, place me on his knee. Why should I, when both he and I were happier near than apart? Pilot[12] lay beside us: all was quiet. He broke out suddenly while clasping me in his arms.

"Cruel, cruel deserter! Oh, Jane, what did I feel when I discovered you had fled from Thornfield, and when I could nowhere find you; and, after examining your apartment, ascertained that you had taken no money, nor anything which could serve as an equivalent! A pearl necklace I had given you lay untouched in its little casket; your trunks were left corded[13] and locked as they had been prepared for the bridal tour. What could my darling do, I asked, left destitute[14] and penniless? And what did she do? Let me hear now."

Thus urged, I began the narrative of my experience for the last year. I softened considerably what related to the three days of wandering and starvation, because to have told him all would have been to inflict unnecessary pain: the little I did say lacerated[15] his faithful heart deeper than I wished.

I should not have left him thus, he said, without any means of making my way: should have told him my intention. I should have confided in him: he would never have forced me to be his mistress. Violent as he had seemed in his despair, he, in truth, loved me far too well and too tenderly to constitute[16] himself my tyrant: he would have given me half his fortune, without demanding so much as a kiss in return, rather than I should have flung myself friendless on the wide world. I had endured, he was certain, more than I had confessed to him.

"Well, whatever my sufferings had been, they were very short," I answered: and then I proceeded to tell him how I had been received at Moor House; how I had obtained the office of schoolmistress and the accession of fortune, the discovery of my relations, followed in due order. Of course, St. John Rivers' name came in frequently in the progress of my tale. When I had done, that name was immediately taken up.

"This St. John, then, is your cousin?"

"Yes."

"You have spoken of him often: do you like him?"

"He was a very good man, sir; I could not help liking him."

"A good man. Does that mean a respectable well-conducted[17] man of fifty? Or what does it mean?"

"St John was only twenty-nine, sir."

" 'Jeune encore[18],' as the French say. Is he a person of low stature, phlegmatic[19], and plain. A person whose goodness consists rather in his guiltlessness of vice, than in his prowess in virtue[20]."

"He is untiringly active. Great and exalted deeds are what he lives to perform."

"But his brain? That is probably rather soft? He means well: but you shrug your shoulders to hear him talk?"

"He talks little, sir: what he does say is ever to the point. His brain is first-rate, I should think not impressible, but vigorous."

"Is he an able man, then?"

"Truly able."

"A thoroughly educated man?"

"St. John is an accomplished and profound scholar."

"His manners, I think, you said are not to your taste?—priggish and parsonic[21]?"

"I never mentioned his manners; but, unless I had a very bad taste, they must suit it; they are polished, calm, and gentlemanlike."

"His appearance,—I forget what description you gave of his appearance;—a sort of raw curate, half strangled with his white neckcloth, and stilted up on his thick-soled high-lows[22], eh?"

"St. John dresses well. He is a handsome man: tall, fair, with blue eyes, and a Grecian profile."

(Aside.) "Damn him!" —(To me.) "Did you like him, Jane?"

"Yes, Mr. Rochester, I liked him: but you asked me that before."

I perceived, of course, the drift of my interlocutor[23]. Jealousy had got hold of him: she stung him; but the sting was salutary: it gave him respite[24] from the gnawing fang[25] of melancholy. I would not, therefore, immediately charm the snake.

"Perhaps you would rather not sit any longer on my knee, Miss Eyre?" was the next somewhat unexpected observation.

"Why not, Mr. Rochester?"

"The picture you have just drawn is suggestive of a rather too overwhelming contrast. Your words have delineated very prettily a graceful Apollo: he is present to your imagination,—tall, fair, blue-eyed, and with a Grecian profile. Your eyes dwell on a Vulcan[26],—a real blacksmith, brown, broad-shouldered: and blind and lame into the bargain."

"I never thought of it, before; but you certainly are rather like Vulcan, sir."

"Well, you can leave me, ma'am: but before you go" (and he retained me by a firmer grasp than ever), "you will be pleased just to answer me a question or two." He paused.

"What questions, Mr. Rochester?"

Then followed this cross-examination.

"St. John made you schoolmistress of Morton before he knew you were his cousin?"

"Yes."

"You would often see him? He would visit the school sometimes?"

"Daily."

"He would approve of your plans, Jane? I know they would be clever, for you are a talented creature!"

"He approved of them—yes."

"He would discover many things in you he could not have expected to find? Some of your accomplishments are not ordinary."

"I don't know about that."

"You had a little cottage near the school, you say: did he ever come there to see you?"

"Now and then?"

"Of an evening?"

"Once or twice."

A pause.

"How long did you reside with him and his sisters after the cousinship was discovered?"

"Five months."

"Did Rivers spend much time with the ladies of his family?"

"Yes; the back parlour was both his study and ours: he sat near the window, and we by the table."

"Did he study much?"

"A good deal."

"What?"

"Hindostanee[27]."

"And what did you do meantime?"

"I learnt German, at first."

"Did he teach you?"

"He did not understand German."

"Did he teach you nothing?"

"A little Hindostanee."

"Rivers taught you Hindostanee?"

"Yes, sir."

"And his sisters also?"

"No."

"Only you?"

"Only me."

"Did you ask to learn?"

"No."

"He wished to teach you?"

"Yes."

A second pause.

"Why did he wish it? Of what use could Hindostanee be to you?"

"He intended me to go with him to India."

"Ah! Here I reach the root of the matter. He wanted you to marry him?"

"He asked me to marry him."

"That is a fiction—an impudent invention to vex me."

"I beg your pardon, it is the literal truth: he asked me more than once, and was as stiff about urging his point as ever you could be."

"Miss Eyre, I repeat it, you can leave me. How often am I to say the same thing? Why do you remain pertinaciously[28] perched on my knee, when I have given you notice to quit?"

"Because I am comfortable there."

"No, Jane, you are not comfortable there, because your heart is not with me: it is with this cousin—this St. John. Oh, till this moment, I thought my little Jane was all mine! I had a belief she loved me even when she left me: that was an atom of sweet in much bitter. Long as we have been parted, hot tears as I have wept over our separation, I never thought that while I was mourning her, she was loving another! But it is useless grieving. Jane, leave me: go and marry Rivers."

"Shake me off, then, sir,—push me away, for I'll not leave you of my own accord[29]."

"Jane, I ever like your tone of voice: it still renews hope, it sounds so truthful. When I hear it, it carries me back a year. I forget that you have formed a new tie. But I am not a fool—go—"

"Where must I go, sir?"

"Your own way—with the husband you have chosen."

"Who is that?"

"You know—this St. John Rivers."

"He is not my husband, nor ever will be. He does not love me: I do not love him. He loves (as he CAN love, and that is not as you love) a beautiful young lady called Rosamond. He wanted to marry me only because he thought I should make a suitable missionary's wife, which she would not have done. He is good and great, but severe; and, for me, cold as an iceberg. He is not like you, sir: I am not happy at his side, nor near him, nor with him. He has no indulgence for me—no fondness. He sees nothing attractive in me; not even youth—only a few useful mental points.—

Then I must leave you, sir, to go to him?"

I shuddered involuntarily, and clung instinctively closer to my blind but beloved master. He smiled.

"What, Jane! Is this true? Is such really the state of matters between you and Rivers?"

"Absolutely, sir! Oh, you need not be jealous! I wanted to tease you a little to make you less sad: I thought anger would be better than grief. But if you wish me to love you, could you but see how much I DO love you, you would be proud and content. All my heart is yours, sir: it belongs to you; and with you it would remain, were fate to exile the rest of me from your presence for ever." Again, as he kissed me, painful thoughts darkened his aspect.

"My scared vision! My crippled strength!" he murmured regretfully.

I caressed, in order to soothe him. I knew of what he was thinking, and wanted to speak for him, but dared not. As he turned aside his face a minute, I saw a tear slide from under the sealed eyelid, and trickle down the manly cheek. My heart swelled.

"I am no better than the old lightning-struck chestnut-tree in Thornfield orchard," he remarked ere long[30]. "And what right would that ruin have to bid a budding woodbine[31] cover its decay with freshness?"

"You are no ruin, sir—no lightning-struck tree: you are green and vigorous. Plants will grow about your roots, whether you ask them or not, because they take delight in your bountiful shadow; and as they grow they will lean towards you, and wind round you, because your strength offers them so safe a prop."

Again he smiled: I gave him comfort.

"You speak of friends, Jane?" he asked.

"Yes, of friends," I answered rather hesitatingly: for I knew I meant more than friends, but could not tell what other word to employ. He helped me.

"Ah! Jane. But I want a wife."

"Do you, sir?"

"Yes, is it news to you?"

"Of course, you said nothing about it before."

"Is it unwelcome news?"

"That depends on circumstances, sir—on your choice."

"Which you shall make for me, Jane. I will abide by your decision."

"Choose then, sir—HER WHO LOVES YOU BEST."

"I will at least choose—HER I LOVE BEST. Jane, will you marry me?"

"Yes, sir."

"A poor blind man, whom you will have to lead about by the hand?"

"Yes, sir."

"A crippled man, twenty years older than you, whom you will have to wait on?"

"Yes, sir."

"Truly, Jane?"

"Most truly, sir."

"Oh! my darling! God bless you and reward you!"

"Mr. Rochester, if ever I did a good deed in my life—if ever I thought a good thought—if ever I prayed a sincere and blameless prayer—if ever I wished a righteous wish,—I am rewarded now. To be your wife is, for me, to be as happy as I can be on earth."

"Because you delight in sacrifice."

"Sacrifice! What do I sacrifice? Famine for food, expectation for content[32]. To be privileged to put my arms round what I value—to press my lips to what I love—to repose on what I trust: is that to make a sacrifice? If so, then certainly I delight in sacrifice."

"And to bear with my infirmities, Jane: to overlook my deficiencies."

"Which are none, sir, to me. I love you better now, when I can really be useful to you, than I did in your state of proud independence, when you disdained[33] every part but that of the giver and protector."

"Hitherto[34] I have hated to be helped—to be led: henceforth[35], I feel I shall hate it no more. I did not like to put my hand into a hireling's, but it is pleasant to feel it circled by Jane's little fingers. I preferred utter loneliness to the constant attendance of servants; but Jane's soft ministry will be a perpetual joy. Jane suits me: do I suit her?"

"To the finest fibre of my nature, sir."

"The case being so, we have nothing in the world to wait for: we must be married instantly."

He looked and spoke with eagerness: his old impetuosity[36] was rising.

"We must become one flesh without any delay, Jane: there is but the licence[37] to get—then we marry."

"Mr. Rochester, I have just discovered the sun is far declined from its meridian, and Pilot is actually gone home to his dinner. Let me look at your watch."

"Fasten it into your girdle[38], Janet, and keep it henceforward: I have no use for it."

"It is nearly four o'clock in the afternoon, sir. Don't you feel hungry?"

"The third day from this must be our wedding-day, Jane. Never mind fine clothes and jewels, now: all that is not worth a fillip[39]."

"The sun has dried up all the rain-drops, sir. The breeze is still: it is quite hot."

"Do you know, Jane, I have your little pearl necklace at this moment fastened round my bronze scrag[40] under my cravat[41]? I have worn it since the day I lost my only treasure, as a memento of her."

"We will go home through the wood: that will be the shadiest way."

He pursued his own thoughts without heeding me.

"Jane! you think me, I daresay, an irreligious dog: but my heart swells with gratitude to the beneficent God of this earth just now. He sees not as man sees, but far clearer: judges not as man judges, but far more wisely. I did wrong: I would have sullied my innocent flower—breathed guilt on its purity: the Omnipotent snatched it from me. I, in my stiff-necked rebellion, almost cursed the dispensation[42]: instead of bending to the decree, I defied it. Divine justice pursued its course; disasters came thick on me[43]: I was forced to pass through the valley of the shadow of death. HIS chastisements are mighty; and one smote[44] me which has humbled me for ever. You know I was proud of my strength: but what is it now, when I must give it over to foreign guidance, as a child does its weakness? Of late, Jane—only—only of late—I began to see and acknowledge the hand of God in my doom. I began to experience remorse, repentance; the wish for reconcilement to my Maker. I began sometimes to pray: very brief prayers they were, but very sincere.

"Some days since: nay, I can number them—four; it was last Monday night, a singular mood came over me: one in which grief replaced frenzy—sorrow, sullenness. I had long had the impression that since I could nowhere find you, you must be dead. Late that night—perhaps it might be between eleven and twelve o'clock—ere I retired to my dreary rest, I supplicated[45] God, that, if it seemed good to Him, I might soon be taken from this life, and admitted to that world to come, where there was still hope of rejoining Jane.

"I was in my own room, and sitting by the window, which was open: it soothed me to feel the balmy[46] night-air; though I could see no stars and only by a vague, luminous haze, knew the presence of a moon. I longed for thee, Janet! Oh, I longed for thee both with soul and flesh! I asked of God, at once in anguish and humility, if I had not been long enough desolate, afflicted, tormented; and might not soon taste bliss and peace once more. That I merited all I endured, I acknowledged—that I could scarcely endure more, I pleaded; and the alpha and omega of my heart's wishes[47] broke involuntarily from my lips in the words— 'Jane! Jane! Jane!'"

"Did you speak these words aloud?"

"I did, Jane. If any listener had heard me, he would have thought me mad: I pronounced them with such frantic energy."

"And it was last Monday night, somewhere near midnight?"

"Yes; but the time is of no consequence: what followed is the strange point. You will think me superstitious,—some superstition I have in my blood, and always had: nevertheless, this is true— true at least it is that I heard what I now relate.

"As I exclaimed 'Jane! Jane! Jane!' a voice—I cannot tell whence the voice came, but I know whose voice it was—replied, 'I am coming: wait for me;' and a moment after, went whispering on the wind the words— 'Where are you?'"

"I'll tell you, if I can, the idea, the picture these words opened to my mind: yet it is difficult to express what I want to express. Ferndean[48] is buried, as you see, in a heavy wood, where sound falls dull, and dies unreverberating. Where are you?' seemed spoken amongst mountains; for I heard a hill-sent echo repeat the words. Cooler and fresher at the moment the gale seemed to visit my brow: I could have deemed that in some wild, lone scene, I and Jane were meeting. In spirit, I believe we must have met. You no doubt were, at that hour, in unconscious sleep, Jane: perhaps your soul wandered from its cell to comfort mine; for those were your accents—as certain as I live— they were yours!"

Reader, it was on Monday night—near midnight—that I too had received the mysterious summons: those were the very words by which I replied to it. I listened to Mr. Rochester's narrative, but made no disclosure in return. The coincidence struck me as too awful and inexplicable to be communicated or discussed. If I told anything, my tale would be such as must necessarily make a profound impression on the mind of my hearer: and that mind, yet from its sufferings too prone to gloom, needed not the deeper shade of the supernatural. I kept these things then, and pondered them in my heart.

"You cannot now wonder," continued my master, "that when you rose upon me so unexpectedly last night, I had difficulty in believing you any other than a mere voice and vision, something that would melt to silence and annihilation, as the midnight whisper and mountain echo had melted before. Now, I thank God! I know it to be otherwise. Yes, I thank God!"

He put me off his knee, rose, and reverently[49] lifting his hat from his brow, and bending his sightless eyes to the earth, he stood in mute devotion. Only the last words of the worship were audible.

"I thank my Maker, that, in the midst of judgment, he has remembered mercy. I humbly entreat my Redeemer[50] to give me strength to lead henceforth a purer life than I have done hitherto!"

Then he stretched his hand out to be led. I took that dear hand, held it a moment to my lips, then let it pass round my shoulder: being so much lower of stature than he, I served both for his prop and guide. We entered the wood, and wended[51] homeward.

Notes

[1] get up

[2] 看到他那么旺盛的精神竟受制于肉体上的残弱。subjugation (to): surrender; corporeal: 肉体的，身体的。infirmity: 虚弱；病症

[3] 光辉

[4] function

[5] 深深地触痛了我的心。quick: 痛处

[6] 走近跟……讲话

[7] 柔和明媚的阳光

[8] 你的同类，指云雀。因上文罗切斯特将简比成云雀，"同类"便由此而来。

[9] 公开表示；坦率承认

[10] provider

[11] 爱哭的

[12] 罗切斯特养的狗

[13] 用绳捆扎好的

[14] 匮乏的，一无所有

[15] 撕裂；折磨

[16] 构成；形成

[17] well-behaved

[18]（法语）still young

[19] 迟钝的；冷漠的

[20] 一个人，其好处仅仅在于没有罪过，而并非品行出众。prowess：杰出的才能，高超的本领

[21] 古板自负的，一副牧师腔

[22] 一个没有经验的助理牧师，差点让自己的白领巾给勒死，踩着一双厚底高帮靴。curate：助理牧师

[23] 对话者

[24] pause

[25]（毒蛇的）毒牙

[26] 伏尔甘，古罗马宗教信奉的火神，最初象征破坏性的火，如火山和火灾，后来成为铁匠的守护神。

[27] 印度斯坦语

[28] 固执地；执着地

[29] of one's willingness

[30] 不久。ere：在……之前

[31] 五叶铁丝莲；忍冬

[32] Sacrifice famine for food, sacrifice expectation for content. 牺牲饥饿以得到食物，牺牲渴望以得到满足。

[33] contempt

[34] 到目前为止；迄今

[35] 从此以后

[36] 急躁；冲动

[37] marriage license

[38]（女子的）紧身褡

[39] 微不足道的东西

[40] 脖子

[41]（旧式的）领结或领带

[42] 天命；神的安排

[43] 灾难接连落到我的头上

[44]（past tense of "smite"）hit, punish

[45] 恳求；乞求

[46] 芬芳的；柔和的

[47] all the wishes in my heart. alpha:the first; omega: the last one

[48] 桑菲尔德庄园被烧毁后，罗切斯特的住所。

[49] 恭敬地，虔敬地

[50] maker; Jesus Christ

[51] 行，走

 Questions

1. In the eyes of Jane, what great changes have taken place to Rochester?

2. What had happened to Jane when she left Thornfield?

3. There is a sharp contrast between Jane's description of St. John Rivers and Rochester's imagination of St. John. What is the difference?

4. Why does Jane frequently mention St. John?

5. From the end of this chapter, what do you think of the end of the story?

Analysis of Chapter XXXVII

Jane returns to Thornfield and discovers it was ruined in fire. She and Rochester live in Ferndean, during which Jane and Rochester are able to marry at last.

It is possible to question *Jane Eyre's* feminism on the grounds that Jane only becomes Rochester's full equal (as she claims to be in the novel's epilogue-like last chapter) when he is physically infirm and dependent on her to guide him and read to him−in other words, when he is physically incapable of mastering her. However, it is also possible that Jane now finds herself Rochester's equal not because of the decline Rochester has suffered but because of the autonomy that she has achieved by coming to know herself more fully.

No woman was ever nearer to her mate than I am: ever more absolutely bone of his bone, and flesh of his flesh. I know no weariness of my Edward's society: he knows none of mine, any more than we each do of the pulsation of the heart that beats in our separate bosoms; consequently, we are ever together.

Another problem that troubles some critics is the fact that Jane finds happiness in the novel only through marriage, suggesting that marriage constitutes the only route to contentment for women. It could be argued that, in returning to Rochester, Jane sacrifices her long-sought autonomy and independence. Another way of looking at Jane's marriage is that she does not sacrifice everything, but enters into a relationship in which giving and taking occur in equal measure. Indeed, in order to marry Rochester Jane has had to reject another marriage, a marriage that would have meant a much more stifling and suppressed life for her. Moreover, in declining to marry St. John, Jane comes to the realization that part of being true to "who she is" means being true to her emotions and passions; part of what makes her *herself* is manifested in her relationships with *others*—in the giving of herself to other human beings. By entering into marriage, Jane does indeed enter into a "bond," but in many ways this "bond" is also the "escape" that Jane has sought all along.

Brontë seems to suggest a way in which a woman's quest for love and a feeling of belonging need not encroach upon her sense of self—need not restrict her intellectual, spiritual, and emotional independence. Indeed, Brontë suggests that it is only after coming to know oneself and one's own strength that one can enter wholly into a well-rounded and loving relationship with another.

《简·爱》 第三十七章（节选）

第二天一早，我听见他起来走动了，从一个房间摸到另一个房间。玛丽一下楼，我就听见他问："爱小姐在这儿吗？"接着又问："你把她安排在哪一间？里面干燥吗？她起来了吗？去问问是不是需要什么，什么时候下来？"

我一想到还有一顿早餐，便下楼去了。我轻手轻脚进了房间，他还没有发现我，我就已瞧见他了。说实话目睹那么生龙活虎的人沦为一个恹恹的弱者，真让人心酸。他坐在椅子上——虽然一动不动，却并不安分，显然在企盼着。如今，习惯性的愁容，已镌刻在他富有特色的脸庞上。他的面容令人想起一盏熄灭了的灯，等待着再度点亮——唉！现在他自己已无力恢复生气勃勃、光彩照人的表情了，不得不依赖他人来完成。我本想显得高高兴兴、无忧无虑，但是这个强者那么无能为力的样子，使我心碎了。不过我还是尽可能轻松愉快地跟他打了招呼：

"是个明亮晴朗的早晨呢，先生，"我说，"雨过天晴，你很快可以去走走了。"

我已唤醒了那道亮光，他顿时容光焕发了。

"呵，你真的还在，我的云雀！上我这儿来。你没有走，没有飞得无影无踪呀？一小时之前，我听见你的一个同类在高高的树林里歌唱，可是对我来说，它的歌声没有音乐，就像初升的太阳没有光芒。凡我能听到的世间美妙的音乐，都集中在简的舌头上，凡我能感到的阳光，全都聚在她身上。"

听完他表示对别人的依赖，我不禁热泪盈眶。他仿佛是被链条锁在栖木上的一头巨鹰，竟不得不企求一只麻雀为它觅食。不过，我不喜欢哭哭啼啼，抹掉带咸味的眼泪，便忙着去准备早餐了。

大半个早上是在户外度过的。我领着他走出潮湿荒凉的林子，到了令人心旷神怡的田野。我向他描绘田野多么苍翠耀眼，花朵和树篱多么生机盎然，天空又多么湛蓝闪亮。我在一个隐蔽可爱的地方，替他找了个座位，那是一个干枯的树桩。坐定以后，我没有拒绝他把我放到他膝头上。既然他和我都觉得紧挨着比分开更愉快，那我又何必要拒绝呢？派洛特躺在我们旁边，四周一片寂静。他正把我紧紧地搂在怀里时突然嚷道：

"狠心呀，狠心的逃跑者！呵，简，我发现你从桑菲尔德出走，而又到处找不着你，细看了你的房间，断定你没有带钱，或者可以当钱用的东西，我心里是多么难受呀！我送你的一条珍珠项链，原封不动地留在小盒子里。你的箱子捆好了上了锁，像原先准备结婚旅行时一样。我自问，我的宝贝成了穷光蛋，身边一个子儿也没有，她该怎么办呢？她干了些什么呀？现在讲给我听听吧。"

于是在他的敦促之下，我开始叙述去年的经历了。我大大淡化了三天的流浪和挨饿的情景，因为把什么都告诉他，只会增加他不必要的痛苦。但是我确实告诉他了一丁点儿，也撕碎了他那颗忠实的心，其严重程度超出了我的预料。

他说，我不应该两手空空地离开他，我应该把我的想法跟他说说。我应当同他推心置腹，他决不会强迫我做他的情妇。尽管他绝望时性情暴烈，但事实上，他爱我至深至亲，绝不会变成我的暴君。与其让我把自己举目无亲地抛向茫茫人世，他宁愿送我一半财产，而连吻一下作为回报的要求都不提。他确信，我所忍受的比我说给他听的要严重得多。

"嗯，我受的苦再多，时间都不长。"我回答。随后我告诉他如何被接纳进沼泽居；如何得到教师的职位，以及获得财产、发现亲戚等，按时间顺序一一叙述。当然随着故事的进展，圣·约翰·里弗斯的名字频频出现。我一讲完自己的经历，这个名字便立即提出来了。

"那么，这位圣·约翰是你的表兄了？"

"是的。"

"你常常提到他，你喜欢他吗？"

"他是个大好人，先生，我不能不喜欢他。"

"一个好人？那意思是不是一个体面而品行好的五十岁男人？不然那是什么意思？"

"圣·约翰只有二十九岁，先生。"

"Jeune encor，就像法国人说的。"他是个矮小、冷淡、平庸的人吗？是不是那种长处在于没有过错，而不是德行出众的人？"

"他十分活跃，不知疲倦，他活着就是要成就伟大崇高的事业。"

"但他的头脑呢？大概比较软弱吧。他本意很好，但听他谈话你会耸肩。"

"他说话不多，先生。但一开口总是一语中的。我想他的头脑是一流的，不易打动，却十分活跃。"

"那么他很能干了？"

"确实很能干。"

"一个受过良好教育的人？"

"圣·约翰是一个造诣很深、学识渊博的学者。"

"他的风度，我想你说过，不合你的口味？""一本正经，一副牧师腔调。"

"我从来没有提起过他的风度。但除非我的口味很差，不然是很合意的。他的风度优雅、沉着，一副绅士派头。"

"他的外表——我忘了你是怎么样描述他的外表的了——那种没有经验的副牧师，扎着白领巾，弄得气都透不过来；穿着厚底高帮靴，顶得像踏高跷似的，是吧？"

"圣·约翰衣冠楚楚，是个漂亮的男子，高个子，白皮肤，蓝眼睛，鼻梁笔挺。"

（旁白）"见他的鬼！——"（转向我）"你喜欢他吗，简？"

"是的，罗切斯特先生，我喜欢他。不过你以前问过我了。"

当然，我觉察出了说话人的用意。妒忌已经攫住了他，刺痛着他。这是有益于身心的，让他暂时免受忧郁的咬啮。因此我不想立刻降服嫉妒这条毒蛇。

"也许你不愿意在我膝头上坐下去了，爱小姐？"接着便是这有些出乎意料的话。

"为什么不愿意呢，罗切斯特先生？"

"你刚才所描绘的图画，暗示了一种过分强烈的对比。你的话已经巧妙地勾勒出了一个漂亮的阿波罗。他出现在你的想象之中，——'高个子，白皮肤，蓝眼睛，笔挺的鼻梁。'而你眼下看到的是一个火神——一个地道的铁匠，褐色的皮肤，宽阔的肩膀，瞎了眼睛，又瘸了腿。"

"我以前可从来没有想到过这点，不过你确实像个火神，先生。"

"好吧——你可以离开我了，小姐。但你走之前（他把我搂得更紧了），请你回答我一两个问题，"他顿了一下。

"什么问题。罗切斯特先生？"

接踵而来的便是这番盘问：

"圣·约翰还不知道你是他表妹，就让你做莫尔顿学校的教师？"

"是的。"

"你常常见到他吗？他有时候来学校看看吗？"

"每天如此。"

"他赞同你的计划吗，简？——我知道这些计划很巧妙，因为你是一个有才干的家伙。"

"是的，——他赞同了。"

"他会在你身上发现很多预料不到的东西，是吗？你身上的某些才艺不同寻常。"

"这我不知道。"

"你说你的小屋靠近学校，他来看过你吗？"

"不常来。"

"晚上来吗？"

"来过一两次。"

他停顿了一下。

"你们彼此的表兄妹关系发现后，你同他和他妹妹们又住了多久？"

"五个月。"

"里弗斯同家里的女士们在一起的时候很多吗？"

"是的，后客厅既是他的书房，也是我们的书房。他坐在窗边，我们坐在桌旁。"

"他书读得很多吗？"

"很多。"

"读什么？"

"印度斯坦语。"

"那时候你干什么呢？"

"起初学德语。"

"他教你吗？"

"他不懂德语。"

"他什么也没有教你吗？"

"教了一点儿印度斯坦语。"

"里弗斯教你印度斯坦语？"

"是的，先生。"

"也教他妹妹们吗？"

"没有。"

"光教你？"

"光教我。"

"是你要求他教的吗？"

"没有。"

"他希望教你？"

"是的。"

他又停顿了一下。

"他为什么希望教你？印度斯坦语对你会有什么用处？"

"他要我同他一起去印度。"

"呵！这下我触到要害了。他要你嫁给他吗？"

"他求我嫁给他。"

"那是虚构的，胡编乱造来气气我。"

"请你原谅，这是千真万确的事实。他不止一次地求过我，而且在这点上像你一样寸步不让。"

"爱小姐，我再说一遍，你可以离开我了。这句话我说过多少次了？我已经通知你可以走了，为什么硬赖在我膝头上？"

"因为在这儿很舒服。"

"不，简，你在这儿不舒服，因为你的心不在我这里，而在你的这位表兄，圣·约翰那里了，呵，在这之前，我以为我的小简全属于我的，相信她就是离开我了也还是爱我的，这成了无尽的苦涩中的一丝甜味，尽管我们别了很久，尽管我因为别离而热泪涟涟，我从来没有料到，我为她悲悲泣泣的时候，她却爱着另外一个人！不过，心里难过也毫无用处，简，走吧，去嫁给里弗斯吧！"

"那么，甩掉我吧，先生，一把把我推开，因为我可不愿意自己离开你。"

"简，我一直喜欢你说话的声调，它仍然唤起新的希望，它听起来又那么真诚。我一听到它，便又回到了一年之前。我忘了你结识了新的关系。不过我不是傻瓜，走吧。"

"我得上哪儿去呢，先生？"

"随你自己便吧，上你看中的丈夫那儿去。"

"谁呀？"

"你知道，这个圣·约翰·里弗斯。"

"他不是我丈夫，也永远不会是，他不爱我，我也不爱他。他爱（他可以爱，跟你的爱不同）一个名叫罗莎蒙德的年轻漂亮小姐。他要娶我只是由于以为我配当一个传教士的妻子，其实我是不行的。他不错，也很了不起，但十分冷峻，对我来说同冰山一般冷。他跟你不一样，先生。在他身边，接近他，或者同他在一起，我都不会愉快。他没有迷恋我——没有溺爱我。在我身上，他看不到吸引人的地方，连青春都看不到——他所看到的只不过心理上的几个有用之处罢了。那么，先生，我得离开你上他那儿去了？"

我不由自主地哆嗦了一下，本能地把我亲爱的瞎眼主人搂得更紧了。他微微一笑。

"什么，简！这是真的吗？这真是你与里弗斯之间的情况吗？"

"绝对如此，先生。呵，你不必嫉妒！我想逗你一下让你少伤心些。我认为愤怒比忧伤要好。不过要是你希望我爱你，你就只要瞧一瞧我确实多么爱你，你就会自豪和满足了。我的整个心儿是你的，先生，它属于你，即使命运让我身体的其余部分永远同你分离，我的心也会依然跟你在一起。"

他吻我的时候，痛苦的想法使他的脸又变得阴沉了。

"我烧毁了的视力！我伤残了的体力！"他遗憾地咕哝着。

我抚摸着他给他以安慰。我知道他心里想些什么，并想替他说出来，但我又不敢。他的脸转开的一刹那，我看到一滴眼泪从他封闭着的眼睑滑下来，流到了富有男子气的脸颊上。我的心膨胀起来了。

"我并不比桑菲尔德果园那棵遭雷击的老栗子树好多少，"没有过多久，他说，"那些残枝，有什么权利吩咐一棵爆出新芽的忍冬花以自己的鲜艳来掩盖它的腐朽呢？"

"你不是残枝，先生——不是遭雷击的树。你碧绿而茁壮。不管你求不求，花草会在你根子周围长出来，因为它们乐于躲在你慷慨的树荫下。长大了它们会偎依着你，缠绕着你，因为你的力量给了它们可靠的支撑。"

他再次笑了起来，我又给了他安慰。

"你说的是朋友吗，简？"他问。

"是的，是朋友，"我迟迟疑疑地回答。我知道我的意思超出了朋友，但无法判断要用什么字。他帮了我忙。

"呵？简。可是我需要一个妻子。"

"是吗，先生？"

"是的，对你来说是桩新闻吗？"

"当然，先前你对此什么也没说。"

"是一桩不受欢迎的新闻？"

"那就要看情况了，先生——要看你的选择。"

"你替我选择吧，简。我会遵从你的决定。"

"先生，那就挑选最爱你的人。"

"我至少会选择我最爱的人，简。你肯嫁给我吗？"

"肯的，先生。"

"一个可怜的瞎子，你得牵着手领他走的人。"

"是的，先生。"

"一个比你大二十岁的瘸子，你得侍候他的人。"

"是的，先生。"

"当真，简？"

"完全当真，先生。"

"呵，我的宝贝？愿上帝祝福你，报答你！"

"罗切斯特先生，如果我平生做过一件好事——如果我有过一个好的想法——如果我做过一个真诚而没有过错的祷告——如果我曾有过一个正当的心愿——那么现在我得到了酬报。对我来说，做你的妻子是世上最愉快的事了。"

"因为你乐意做出牺牲。"

"牺牲！我牺牲了什么啦？牺牲饥饿而得到食品，牺牲期待而得到满足。享受特权搂抱我珍重的人——亲吻我热爱的人——寄希望于我信赖的人。那能叫牺牲吗？如果说这是牺牲，那我当然乐于做出牺牲了。"

"还要忍受我的体弱，简，无视我的缺陷。"

"我毫不在乎，先生。现在我确实对你有所帮助了，所以比起当初你能自豪地独立自主，除了施主与保护人，把什么都不放在眼里时，要更爱你了。"

"我向来讨厌要人帮助——要人领着，但从今天起我觉得我不再讨厌了。我不喜欢把手放在雇工的手里，但让简的小小的指头挽着，却很愉快。我不喜欢佣人不停地服侍我，而喜欢绝对孤独。但是简温柔体贴的照应却永远是一种享受。简适合我，而我适合她吗？"

"你与我的天性丝丝入扣。"

"既然如此，就根本没有什么好等的了，我们得马上结婚。"

他的神态和说话都很急切，他焦躁的老脾气又发作了。

"我们必须毫不迟疑地化为一体了，简。只剩下把证书拿到手——随后我们就结婚——"

"罗切斯特先生，我刚发现，日色西斜，太阳早过了子午线。派洛特实际上已经回家去吃饭了，让我看看你的手表。"

"把它别在你腰带上吧，珍妮特，今后你就留着，反正我用不上。"

"差不多下午四点了，先生。你不感到饿吗？"

"从今天算起第三天，该是我们举行婚礼的日子了，简。现在，别去管豪华衣装和金银首饰了，这些东西都一钱不值。"

"太阳已经晒干了雨露，先生。微风止了，气候很热。"

"你知道吗，简，此刻在领带下面青铜色的脖子上，我戴着你小小的珍珠项链。自从失去仅有的宝贝那天起，我就戴上它了，作为对她的怀念。"

"我们穿过林子回家吧，这条路最阴凉。"

他顺着自己的思路去想，没有理会我。

"简！我想，你以为我是一条不敬神的狗吧，可是这会儿我对世间仁慈的上帝满怀感激之情。他看事物跟人不一样，要清楚得多；他判断事物跟人不一样，而要明智得多。我做错了，我会玷污清白的花朵——把罪孽带给无辜，要不是上帝把它从我这儿抢走的话。我倔强地对抗，险些儿咒骂这种处置方式，我不是俯首听命，而是全不放在眼里。神的审判照旧进行，大祸频频临头。我被迫走过死荫的幽谷，他的惩罚十分严厉，其中一次惩罚是使我永远甘于谦卑。你知道我曾对自己的力量非常自傲，但如今它算得了什么呢？我不得不依靠他人的指引，就像孩子的孱弱一样。最近，简——只不过是最近——我在厄运中开始看到并承认上帝之手。我开始自责和忏悔，情愿听从造物主。有时我开始祈祷了，祷告很短，但很诚恳。"

"已经有几天了，不，我能说出数字来——四天。那是上星期一个晚上——我产生了一种奇怪的心情：忧伤，也就是悲哀和阴沉代替了狂乱。我早就想，既然到处找不着你，那你一定已经死了。那天深夜——也许在十一二点之间——我闷闷不乐地去就寝之前，祈求上帝，要是他觉得这么做妥当的话，可以立刻把我从现世收去，准许我踏进未来的世界，那儿仍有希望与简相聚。"

"我在自己的房间，坐在敞开着的窗边，清香的夜风沁人心脾。尽管我看不见星星，只是凭着一团模糊发亮的雾气，才知道有月亮。我盼着你，珍妮特！呵，无论是肉体还是灵魂，我都盼着你。我既痛苦而又谦卑地问上帝，我那么凄凉、痛苦、备受折磨，是不是已经够久了，会不会很快就再能尝到幸福与平静。我承认我所忍受的一切是应该的——我恳求，我实在不堪忍受了。我内心的全部愿望不由自主地崩出了我的嘴巴，化作这样几个字——‘简！简！简！’”

“你大声说了这几个字吗？”

“我说了，简。谁要是听见了，一定会以为我在发疯，我疯也似的使劲叫着那几个字。”

“而那是星期一晚上，半夜时分！”

“不错，时间倒并不重要，随后发生的事儿才怪呢。你会认为我迷信吧——从气质来看，我是有些迷信，而且一直如此。不过，这回倒是真的——我现在说的都是我听到的，至少这一点是真的。

“我大叫着‘简！简！简！’的时候，不知道哪儿传来了一个声音，但听得出是谁的，这个声音回答道，‘我来了，请等一等我！’过了一会儿，清风送来了悄声细语——‘你在哪儿呀？’

“要是我能够，我会告诉你这些话在我的心灵中所展示的思想和画面，不过要表达自己的想法并不容易。你知道，芬丁庄园深藏在密林里，这儿的声音很沉闷，没有回荡便会消失。‘你在哪儿呀？’这声音似乎来自于大山中间，因为我听到了山林的回声重复着这几个字。这时空气凉爽清新，风似乎也朝我额头吹来。我会认为我与简在荒僻的野景中相会。我相信，在精神上我们一定已经相会了。毫无疑问，当时你睡得很熟，说不定你的灵魂脱离了它的躯壳来抚慰我的灵魂。因为那正是你的口音——千真万确——是你的！”

读者呀，正是星期一晚上——将近午夜——我也接到了神秘的召唤，而那些也正是我回答的话。我倾听着罗切斯特先生的叙述，却并没有向他吐露什么，我觉得这种巧合太令人畏惧、令人费解了，因而既难以言传，也无法议论。要是我说出什么来，我的经历也必定会在聆听者的心灵中留下深刻的印象，而这饱受痛苦的心灵容易忧伤了，不需要再笼罩更深沉的超自然阴影了。于是我把这些纵情留在心里，反复思量。

“这会儿你不会奇怪了吧，”我主人继续说，“那天晚上你出乎意料地在我当前冒出来时，我难以相信你不只是一个声音和幻象，不只是某种会销声匿迹的东西，就像以前已经消失的夜半耳语和山间回声那样。现在我感谢上帝，我知道这回可不同了。是的，我感谢上帝！”

他把我从膝头上放下来。虔敬地从额头摘下帽子，向大地低下了没有视力的眼睛，虔诚地默默站立着，只有最后几句表示崇拜的话隐约可闻。

“我感谢造物主，在审判时还记着慈悲。我谦恭地恳求我的救世主赐予我力量，让我从今以后过一种比以往更纯洁的生活！”随后他伸出手让我领着，我握住了那只可爱的手，在我的嘴唇上放了一会儿，随后让它挽住我肩膀，我个子比他矮得多，所以既做了支撑，又当了向导。我们进了树林，朝家里走去。

References

[1] 宋兆霖 . 勃朗特姐妹全集 [C]. 石家庄：河北教育出版社，1996.

[2] 杨静远 . 勃朗特姐妹研究 [M]. 北京：中国社会科学出版社，1993.

Unit 14   Emily Brontë (1818—1848)

Life

Emily Brontë was born on 30 July 1818 in the village of Thornton, West Riding of Yorkshire, in Northern England, to Maria Branwell and an Irish father, Patrick Brontë. She was the younger sister of Charlotte Brontë and the fifth of six children. In 1820, shortly after the birth of Emily's younger sister Anne, the family moved eight miles away to Haworth, where Patrick was employed as perpetual curate; here the children developed their literary talents.

After the death of their mother on 15 September 1821 from cancer, when Emily was three years old, the older sisters Maria, Elizabeth and Charlotte were sent to the Clergy Daughters' School at Cowan Bridge, where they encountered abuse and privations later described by Charlotte in Jane Eyre. At the age of six on 25 November 1824, Emily joined her sisters at school for a brief period. When a typhoid epidemic swept the school, Maria and Elizabeth caught it. Maria, who may actually have had tuberculosis, was sent home, where she died. Emily was subsequently removed from the school, in June 1825, along with Charlotte and Elizabeth. Elizabeth died soon after their return home.

The three remaining sisters and their brother Patrick Branwell were thereafter educated at home by their father and aunt Elizabeth Branwell, their mother's sister. Despite the lack of formal education, Emily and her siblings had access to a wide range of published material; favourites included Sir Walter Scott, Byron, Shelley, and Blackwood's Magazine.

In their leisure time the children began to write fiction at home, inspired by a box of toy soldiers Branwell had received as a gift and created a number of fantasy worlds (including "Angria") which featured in stories they wrote—all "very strange ones" according to Charlotte—and enacted about the imaginary adventures of their toy soldiers along with the Duke of Wellington and his sons, Charles and Arthur Wellesley. Little of Emily's work from this period survives, except for poems spoken by characters. When Emily was 13, she and Anne withdrew from participation in the Angria story and began a new one about Gondal, a fictional island whose myths and legends were to preoccupy the two sisters throughout their lives. With the exception of their Gondal poems and Anne's lists of Gondal's characters and place-names, the writings on Gondal were not preserved. Some "diary papers" of Emily's have survived in which she describes current events in Gondal, some of which were written, others enacted with Anne. One dates from 1841, when Emily was twenty-three: another from 1845, when she was twenty-seven.

At seventeen, Emily attended the Roe Head Girls' School, where Charlotte was a teacher but managed to stay only a few months before being overcome by extreme homesickness. Charlotte later stated that: "Liberty was the breath of Emily's nostrils; without it she perished. The change from her own home to a school and from her own very noiseless, very secluded but unrestricted and unartificial mode of life, to one of disciplined routine (though under the kindest auspices), was what she failed in enduring... I felt in my heart she would die, if she did not go home, and with this conviction obtained her recall." She returned home and Anne took her place. At this time, the girls' objective was to obtain sufficient education to open a small school of their own.

Adulthood

Emily became a teacher at Law Hill School in Halifax beginning in September 1838, when she was twenty. Her health broke under the stress of the 17-hour work day and she returned home in April 1839. Thereafter she became the stay-at-home daughter, doing most of the cooking, ironing, and cleaning. She taught herself German out of books and also practised the piano.

In 1842, Emily accompanied Charlotte to the Héger Pensionnat in Brussels, Belgium, where they attended the girls' academy run by Constantin Héger. They planned to perfect their French and German in anticipation of opening their school. Nine of Emily's French essays survive from this period. Héger seems to have been impressed with the strength of Emily's character, and made the following assertion:

She should have been a man—a great navigator. Her powerful reason would have deduced new spheres of discovery from the knowledge of the old; and her strong imperious will would never have been daunted by opposition or difficulty, never have given way but with life. She had a head for logic, and a capability of argument unusual in a man and rarer indeed in a woman... impairing this gift was her stubborn tenacity of will which rendered her obtuse to all reasoning where her own wishes, or her own sense of right, was concerned.

The two sisters were committed to their studies and by the end of the term had attained such competence in French that Madame Héger made a proposal for both to stay another half-year, even offering to dismiss the English master, according to Charlotte, so that she could take his place, while Emily was to teach music as she had by that time become a competent piano teacher. However, the illness and death of their aunt meant that they returned to Haworth and though they did try to open a school at their home, they were unable to attract students to the remote area.

In 1844, Emily began going through all the poems she had written, recopying them neatly into two notebooks. One was labelled "Gondal Poems"; the other was unlabelled. Scholars such as Fannie Ratchford and Derek Roper have attempted to piece together a Gondal storyline and chronology from these poems. In the autumn of 1845, Charlotte discovered the notebooks and insisted that the poems be published. Emily, furious at the invasion of her privacy, at first refused, but relented when Anne brought out her own manuscripts and revealed to Charlotte that she had been writing poems in secret as well. As co-authors of Gondal stories, Anne and Emily were accustomed to read their Gondal stories and poems to each other, while Charlotte was excluded from their privacy. Around this time she had written one of her the most famous poems "No coward soul is mine", probably as an answer to the violation of her privacy and her own transformation into a published writer. Despite Charlotte's later claim, it wasn't her last poem.

In 1846, the sisters' poems were published in one volume as Poems by Currer, Ellis, and Acton Bell. The Brontë sisters had adopted pseudonyms for publication, preserving their initials: Charlotte was "Currer Bell", Emily was "Ellis Bell" and Anne was "Acton Bell." Charlotte wrote in the "Biographical Notice of Ellis and Acton Bell" that their "ambiguous choice" was "dictated by a sort of conscientious scruple at assuming Christian names positively masculine, while we did not like to declare ourselves women, because... we had a vague impression that authoresses are liable to be looked on with prejudice."Charlotte contributed 19 poems, and Emily and Anne each contributed 21. Although the sisters were told several months after publication that only two copies had sold, they were not discouraged (of their two readers, one was impressed enough to request their autographs). The Athenaeum reviewer praised Ellis Bell's work for its music and power, singling out his poems as the best: "Ellis possesses a fine, quaint spirit and an evident power of wing that may reach heights not here attempted", and The Critic reviewer recognised "the presence of more genius than it was supposed this utilitarian age had devoted to the loftier exercises of the intellect."

Personality and character

Emily Brontë remains a mysterious figure and a challenge to biographers because information about her is sparse, due to her solitary and reclusive nature. She does not seem to have made any friends outside her family. Her closest friend was her sister Anne. Together they shared their own fantasy world, Gondal, and, according to Charlotte's friend Ellen Nussey, in childhood they were "like twins", "inseparable companions" and "in the very closest sympathy which never had any interruption." In 1845 Anne took Emily to visit some of the places she had come to know and love in the five years she spent as governess. A plan to visit Scarborough fell through and instead the sisters went to York where Anne showed her sister York Minster. During the trip Emily and Anne acted out some of their Gondal characters.

Charlotte Brontë remains the primary source of information about Emily, although as an elder sister, writing publicly about her shortly after her death, she is not a neutral witness. Stevie Davies believes that there is what might be called Charlotte's smoke-screen and argues that Emily evidently shocked her, to the point where she may even have doubted her sister's sanity. After Emily's death, Charlotte rewrote her character, history and even poems on a more acceptable (to her and the bourgeois reading public) model. According to Lucasta Miller, in her analysis of Brontë biographies, "Charlotte took on the role of Emily's first mythographer." In the Preface to the Second Edition of *Wuthering Heights*, in 1850, Charlotte wrote:

My sister's disposition was not naturally gregarious; circumstances favoured and fostered her tendency to seclusion; except to go to church or take a walk on the hills, she rarely crossed the threshold of home. Though her feeling for the people round was benevolent, intercourse with them she never sought; nor, with very few exceptions, ever experienced. And yet she knew them: knew their ways, their language, their family histories; she could hear of them with interest, and talk of them with detail, minute, graphic, and accurate; but with them, she rarely exchanged a word.

Emily's unsociability and extremely shy nature have subsequently been reported many times. According to Norma Crandall, her "warm, human aspect" was "usually revealed only in her love of nature and of animals." In a similar description, Literary news (1883) states: "[Emily] loved the solemn moors, she loved all wild, free creatures and things", and critics attest that her love of the moors is manifest in Wuthering Heights. Over the years, Emily's love of nature has been the subject of many anecdotes. A newspaper dated 31 December 1899, gives the folksy account that "with bird and beast [Emily] had the most intimate relations, and from her walks she often came with fledgling or young rabbit in hand, talking softly to it, quite sure, too, that it understood."The following anecdote is also related:

Once she was bitten by a dog that she saw running by in great distress, and to which she offered water. The dog was mad. She said no word to any one, but herself burned the lacerated flesh to the bone with the red hot poker, and no one knew of it until the red scar was accidentally discovered some weeks after, and sympathetic questioning brought out this story.

In *Queens of Literature of the Victorian Era* (1886), Eva Hope summarises Emily's character as "a peculiar mixture of timidity and Spartan-like courage", and goes on to say, "She was painfully shy, but physically she was brave to a surprising degree. She loved few persons, but those few with a passion of self-sacrificing tenderness and devotion. To other people's failings she was understanding and forgiving, but over herself she kept a continual and most austere watch, never allowing herself to deviate for one instant from what she considered her duty."

Emily's health probably was weakened by the harsh local climate and by unsanitary conditions at home, the source of water being contaminated, by runoff, from the church's graveyard. Branwell died suddenly, on Sunday, September 24, 1848. At his funeral service, a week later, Brontë caught a severe cold which quickly developed into inflammation of the lungs and led to tuberculosis. Though her condition worsened steadily, she rejected medical help and all offered remedies, saying that she would have "no poisoning doctor" near her. On the morning of 19 December 1848, Charlotte, fearing for her sister, wrote this:

She grows daily weaker. The physician's opinion was expressed too obscurely to be of use—he sent some medicine which she would not take. Moments so dark as these I have never known—I pray for God's support to us all.

At noon, Emily was worse; she could only whisper in gasps. With her last audible words she said to Charlotte, "If you will send for a doctor, I will see him now" but it was too late. She died that same day at about two in the afternoon. According to Mary Robinson, an early Emily's biographer, it happened while she was sitting on the sofa. However, Charlotte's letter to William Smith Williams where she mentions Emily's dog lying at the side of her dying-bed, makes this statement unlikely.

It was less than three months since Branwell's death, which led Martha Brown, a housemaid, to declare that "Miss Emily died of a broken heart for love of her brother." Emily had grown so thin that her coffin measured only 16 inches wide. The carpenter said he had never made a narrower one for an adult. She was interred in the Church of St Michael and All Angels family capsule, Haworth, West Yorkshire, England. Emily Brontë never knew the extent of fame she achieved with her one and only novel, *Wuthering Heights*, as she died a year after its publication, aged 30.

Plot of *Wuthering Heights*

Opening

In 1801, Lockwood, a wealthy young man from the South of England who is seeking peace and recuperation, rents Thrushcross Grange in Yorkshire. He visits his landlord, Heathcliff, who lives in a remote moorland farmhouse, Wuthering Heights. There Lockwood finds an odd assemblage: Heathcliff seems to be a gentleman, but his manners are uncouth; the reserved mistress of the house is in her mid-teens; and a young man who seems to be a member of the family, yet dresses and speaks as if he is a servant.

Snowed in, Lockwood is grudgingly allowed to stay and is shown to a bedchamber where he notices books and graffiti left by a former inhabitant named Catherine. He falls asleep and has a nightmare in which he sees the ghostly Catherine trying to enter through the window. He cries out in fear, rousing Heathcliff, who rushes into the room. Lockwood is convinced that what he saw was real. Heathcliff, believing Lockwood to be right, examines the window and opens it, hoping to allow Catherine's spirit to enter. When nothing happens, Heathcliff shows Lockwood to his own bedroom and returns to keep watch at the window.

At sunrise, Heathcliff escorts Lockwood back to Thrushcross Grange. Lockwood asks the housekeeper, Nelly Dean, about the family at Wuthering Heights, and she tells him the tale.

Heathcliff 's childhood (Chapters 4 to 17)

Thirty years earlier, the owner of Wuthering Heights is Mr. Earnshaw, who lives with his teenage son Hindley and younger daughter Catherine. On a trip toLiverpool, Earnshaw encounters a homeless boy, described as a "dark-skinned gypsy in aspect." He adopts the boy and names him Heathcliff. Hindley feels that Heathcliff has supplanted him in his father's affections and becomes bitterly jealous. Catherine and Heathcliff become friends and spend hours each day playing on the moors. They grow close.

Hindley is sent to college. Three years later Earnshaw dies and Hindley becomes the landowner; he is now master of Wuthering Heights. He returns to live there with his new wife, Frances. He allows Heathcliff to stay but only as a servant.

A few months after Hindley's return, Heathcliff and Catherine walk to Thrushcross Grange to spy on the Lintons, who live there. After being discovered they try to run away but are caught. Catherine is injured by the Lintons' dog and taken into the house to recuperate, while Heathcliff is sent home. Catherine stays with the Lintons. The Lintons arelanded gentry and Catherine is influenced by their fine appearance and genteel manners. When she returns to Wuthering Heights her appearance and manners are more ladylike, and she laughs at Heathcliff's unkempt appearance. The next day, knowing that the Lintons are to visit, Heathcliff tries to dress up, in an effort to impress Catherine, but he and Edgar Linton get into an argument and Hindley humiliates Heathcliff by locking him in the attic. Catherine tries to comfort Heathcliff, but he vows revenge on Hindley.

The following year, Frances Earnshaw gives birth to a son, named Hareton, but she dies a few months later. Hindley descends into drunkenness. Two more years pass, and Catherine and Edgar Linton become friends, while she becomes more distant from Heathcliff. Edgar visits Catherine while Hindley is away and they declare themselves lovers soon afterwards.

Catherine confesses to Nelly that Edgar has proposed marriage and she has accepted, although her love for Edgar is not comparable to her love for Heathcliff, whom she cannot marry because of his low social status and lack of education. She hopes to use her position as Edgar's wife to raise Heathcliff's standing. Heathcliff overhears her say that it would "degrade" her to marry him (but not how much she loves him), and he runs away and disappears without a trace.

Distraught over Heathcliff's departure, Catherine makes herself ill. Nelly and Edgar begin to pander to her every whim to prevent her from becoming ill again.

Three years pass. Edgar and Catherine marry and go to live together at Thrushcross Grange, where Catherine enjoys being "lady of the manor." Six months later, Heathcliff returns, now a wealthy gentleman. Catherine is delighted, but Edgar is not. Edgar's sister, Isabella, soon falls in love with Heathcliff, who despises her, but encourages the infatuation as a means of revenge. One day, he embraces Isabella, leading to an argument with Edgar. Upset, Catherine locks herself in her room and begins to make herself ill again.

Heathcliff takes up residence at Wuthering Heights and spends his time gambling with Hindley and teaching Hareton bad habits. Hindley dissipates his wealth and mortgages the farmhouse to Heathcliff to pay his debts. Heathcliff elopes with Isabella Linton. Two months later, they return to Wuthering Heights. Heathcliff hears that Catherine is ill and, with Nelly's help, visits her secretly. However, Catherine is pregnant. The following day she gives birth to a daughter, Cathy, shortly before dying.

After Catherine's funeral, Isabella leaves Heathcliff, takes refuge in the South of England and gives birth to a son, Linton. Hindley dies six months after Catherine, and Heathcliff thus finds himself master of Wuthering Heights.

Heathcliff's maturity (Chapters 18 to 31)

Twelve years pass. Catherine's daughter Cathy has become a beautiful, high-spirited girl. Edgar learns that his sister Isabella is dying, so he leaves to retrieve her son Linton in order to adopt and educate him. Cathy, who has rarely left home, takes advantage of her father's absence to venture further afield. She rides over the moors to Wuthering Heights and discovers that she has not one but two cousins: Hareton, in addition to Linton. She also lets it be known that her father has gone to fetch Linton. When Edgar returns with Linton, a weak and sickly boy, Heathcliff insists that he live at Wuthering Heights.

Three years pass. Walking on the moors, Nelly and Cathy encounter Heathcliff, who takes them to Wuthering Heights to see Linton and Hareton. Heathcliff hopes that Linton and Cathy will marry, so that Linton will become the heir to Thrushcross Grange. Linton and Cathy begin a secret friendship, echoing the childhood friendship between their respective parents, Heathcliff and Catherine.

The following year, Edgar becomes very ill and takes a turn for the worse while Nelly and Cathy are out on the moors, where Heathcliff and Linton trick them into entering Wuthering Heights. Heathcliff keeps them captive to enable the marriage of Cathy and Linton to take place. After five days, Nelly is released and later, with Linton's help, Cathy escapes. She returns to the Grange to see her father shortly before he dies.

Now master of both Wuthering Heights and Thrushcross Grange, Cathy's father-in-law, Heathcliff, insists on her returning to live at Wuthering Heights. Soon after she arrives Linton dies. Hareton tries to be kind to Cathy, but she withdraws from the world.

At this point, Nelly's tale catches up to the present day (1801). Time passes and, after being ill for a period, Lockwood grows tired of the moors and informs Heathcliff that he will be leaving Thrushcross Grange.

Ending (Chapters 32 to 34)

Eight months later, Lockwood returns to the area by chance. Given that his tenancy at Thrushcross Grange is still valid, he decides to stay there again. He finds Nelly living at Wuthering Heights and enquires what has happened since he left. She explains that she moved to Wuthering Heights to replace the housekeeper, Zillah, who had left.

Hareton has an accident and is confined to the farmhouse. During his convalescence, he and Cathy overcome their mutual antipathy and become close. While their friendship develops, Heathcliff begins to act strangely and has visions of Catherine. He stops eating and, after four days, is found dead in Catherine's old room. He is buried next to Catherine.

Lockwood learns that Hareton and Cathy plan to marry on New Year's Day. As he gets ready to leave, he passes the graves of Catherine, Edgar and Heathcliff and pauses to contemplate the quiet of the moors.

Comments on *Wuthering Heights*

There is the realistic story of the relations between the oppressor and the oppressed and the revenge that results from these relations. Heathcliff in the novel is at first the oppressed person and then be becomes himself the oppressor, but at the end of the book, the oppressed turned oppressor weakens and breaks down. The final failure of Heathcliff suggests, according to Arnold Kettle a modern British critic, Heathcliff has at last "come to see the pointlessness of his fight to revenge himself on the world of power and property through its own values," for Kettle comprehends in profundity that the novel is not merely a story of personal love and revenge but "an expression in the imaginative terms of art of the stresses and tensions and conflicts, personal and spiritual, of nineteenth-century capitalist society."

Wuthering Heights belongs to the tradition of Gothic novels. The choice of the Gothic style suits well the theme of the novel. Gothic literature has always been associated with the abnormal and absurd. The setting is often in a remote or an alien soil. Actions take place in ruined, deserted castles. Old and empty house that once with creepers and grasses. Gothic novels pursue the creation of a grotesque atmosphere through the depiction of a rather bizarre and terrifying natural environment. The Gothic literature re presented by Horace Walpole's *The Castle of Otranto*; Mary Shelley's *Frankenstein* and Mathew Lewis's *The Monk*.

Wuthering Heights has a contemporary setting but it bears a similar strange Gothic quality. There were steep hills and precipitous slopes stretching far and deep ridges stood high like some giants on the landscape. Leafless trees stood on bare rocks and strong winds howled across the moor.

The gothic novel strives to create feelings of horror caused by the terrifying transformation of human character. It deals with the unconventional, the uncommon aspects of human mature. *Wuthering Heights* provides an effective environment in which the dark side of human nature is put under careful examination. Human passion can be constructive and destructive as well. In the novel, various human weaknesses are exposed: Catherine is selfish, Edgar weak, Heathcliff Savage, Isabella ill tempered and Cathy willful. Their weakness generates fearful results that nearly destroy every character involved. But Emily did not condemn the characters. Emily seemed to emphasize that it was fate that drove them together, and under a special environment, human love is a source of tragic disaster.

It is noticeable that the narration of the story is unconventional. Different from the first person singular or the third person omniscient, the story is told chiefly by two characters in the story: Mr. Lockwood, one of the tenants of Heathcliff, and Nelly Dean, a Housekeeper in the service of Catherine, in addition some supplementary aids, like Catherine's diary. The unusual way of narration adds much to the truthfulness of the story and the complexity of its plot.

While you are reading the selection, try to sense the above-mentioned personalities of characters and its literary features.

Major Characters

Heathcliff

He is a foundling taken in by Mr. Earnshaw and raised with his children. Of unknown descent, he seems to represent wild and natural forces, which often seem amoral and dangerous for society. His almost inhuman devotion to Catherine is the moving force in his life. Second, his vindictive hatred for all those who stand between him and his beloved makes him cruel but magnificent readers can never forget that at the heart of the grown man lies the abandoned, hungry child of the streets of Liverpool.

Mr. Earnshaw

He is the father of Catherine and Hindley, a plain, fairly well-off farmer with few pretensions but a kind heart. He is a stern father. He takes in Heathcliff despite his family's protests.

Catherine (or Cathy) Earnshaw

She is Mr. Earnshaw's daughter and Hindley's sister. She is also Heathcliff's foster sister and beloved. She marries Edgar Linton and has a daughter, also named Catherine. Catherine is beautiful and charming, but she is never as civilized as she pretends to be. In her heart she is always a wild girl playing on the moors with Heathcliff. She regards it as her right to be loved by all, and has an unruly temper. Heathcliff usually calls her Cathy; Edgar usually calls her Catherine.

Hindley Earnshaw

He is the only son of Mr. and Mrs. Earnshaw, and Catherine's older brother. He is a bullying, discontented boy who grows up to be a violent alcoholic when his beloved wife, Frances, dies. He hates Heathcliff because he felt his father's affection for him has been taken away by another boy, and Heathcliff in return hates him even more.

Edgar Linton

He is Isabella's older brother, who marries Catherine Earnshaw and fathers Catherine Linton. In contrast to Heathcliff, he is a gently bred, refined man, a patient husband and a loving father. His faults are certain effeminacy (女人气), and a tendency to be cold and unforgiving when his dignity is hurt.

Isabella Linton

She is Edgar's younger sister, and marries Heathcliff to become Isabella Heathcliff; her son is named Linton Heathcliff. Before she marries Heathcliff, she is a rather shallow-minded young lady, pretty and quick-witted but a little foolish (as can be seen by her choice of husbands). Her unhappy marriage brings out an element of cruelty in her character: when her husband treats her brutally, she rapidly grows to hate him with all her heart.

Ellen (or Nelly) Dean

She is one of the main narrators. She has been a servant with the Earnshaws and the Lintons for all her life, and knows them better than anyone else. She is independently minded and high spirited, and retains an objective viewpoint on those she serves. She is called Nelly by those who are on the most equalitarian terms with her: such as Mr. Earnshaw, the older Catherine, Heathcliff.

Lockwood

He is the narrator of the novel. Heathcliff's tenant at Thrushcross Grange. He is a gentleman from London, in distinct contrast to the other rural characters. He is not particularly sympathetic and tends to patronize his subjects. That is to say, he treats the servants lower than him as if he were a master.

Next generation

Hareton Earnshaw

He is the son of Hindley; he marries the younger Catherine. For most of the novel, he is rough and rustic and uncultured, having been carefully kept from all civilizing influences by Heathcliff. He grows up to be superficially like Heathcliff, but is really much more sweet-tempered and forgiving. He never blames Heathcliff for having disinherited him.

Catherine (or Cathy) Linton

She is the daughter of the older Catherine and Edgar Linton. She marries Linton Heathcliff to become Catherine Heathcliff, and then marries Hareton to be Catherine EarnshawShe has all her mother's charm without her wildness, although she is by no means submissive and spiritless. Edgar calls her Cathy.

Linton Heathcliff

He is the son of Heathcliff and Isabella. He combines the worst characteristics of both parents, and is effeminate, weakly, and cruel. He uses his status as an invalid to manipulate the tender-hearted younger Catherine. His father despises him. Linton marries Catherine and dies soon after.

Introduction to Chapter 15

Chapter 15 is the climax of the whole novel. There is the final meeting of Cathy and Heathcliff. Their love is passionate and wild, however, to be tortured by the betrayal of the love for Heathcliff, Cathy only wants to die. Cathy died and Heathcliff starts his mad revenge on those who are the barriers of Cathy and him. First he marries Isabella, sister of Linton but he doesn't love her. He tortures her because it is her brother married Cathy. He snatches Linton's heritage by asking Linton's daughter to marry his sick son. So this chapter is turning point of the story. After this chapter, Heathcliff turns himself from a person being oppressed to an oppressor.

Chapter 15

Another week over and I[1] am so many days nearer health, and spring! I have now heard all my neighbour's[2] history, at different sittings[3], as the housekeeper[4] could spare time from more important occupations. I'll continue it in her own words, only a little condensed. She is, on the whole, a very fair narrator, and I don't think I could improve her style.

In the evening, she said, the evening of my visit to the Heights[5], I knew, as well as if I saw him, that Mr. Heathcliff was about the place[6]; and I shunned going out, because I still carried his letter[7] in my pocket, and didn't want to be threatened or teased any more. I had made up my mind not to give it till my master went somewhere, as I could not guess how its receipt would affect Catherine. The consequence was, that it did not reach her before the lapse of three days. The fourth was Sunday, and I brought it into her room after the family were gone to church. There was a manservant left to keep the house with me, and we generally made a practice of locking the doors during the hours of service[8]; but on that occasion the weather was so warm and pleasant that I set them wide open, and, to fulfill my engagement[9], as I knew who would be coming, I told my companion that the mistress wished very much for some oranges, and he must run over to the village and get a few, to be paid for on the morrow. He departed, and I went up-stairs.

Mrs. Linton sat in a loose white dress, with a light shawl over her shoulders, in the recess of the open window, as usual. Her thick, long hair had been partly removed[10] at the beginning of her illness, and now she wore it simply combed in its natural tresses over her temples and neck. Her appearance was altered, as I had told Heathcliff; but when she was calm, there seemed unearthly beauty in the change. The flash of her eyes had been succeeded by a dreamy and melancholy softness; they no longer gave the impression of looking at the objects around her: they appeared always to gaze beyond, and far beyond - you would have said out of this world. Then, the paleness of her face—its haggard aspect having vanished as she recovered flesh—and the peculiar expression arising from her mental state, though painfully suggestive of their causes, added to the touching interest which she awakened[11]; and—invariably to me, I know, and to any person who saw her, I should think—refuted more tangible proofs of convalescence, and stamped her as one doomed to decay.

A book lay spread on the sill before her, and the scarcely perceptible wind fluttered its leaves at intervals. I believe Linton had laid it there: for she never endeavoured to divert herself with reading, or occupation of any kind, and he would spend many an hour in trying to entice her attention to some subject which had formerly been her amusement. She was conscious of his aim, and in her better moods endured his efforts placidly, only showing their uselessness by now and then suppressing a wearied sigh, and checking him at last with the saddest of smiles and kisses. At other times, she would turn petulantly away, and hide her face in her hands, or even push him off angrily; and then he took care to let her alone, for he was certain of doing no good.

Gimmerton chapel[12] bells were still ringing; and the full, mellow flow of the beck in the valley came soothingly on the ear. It was a sweet substitute for the yet absent murmur of the summer foliage, which drowned that music about the Grange when the trees were in leaf. At Wuthering Heights it always sounded on quiet days following a great thaw or a season of steady rain. And of Wuthering Heights Catherine was thinking as she listened: that is, if she thought or listened at all; but she had the vague, distant look I mentioned before, which expressed no recognition of material things either by ear or eye.

"There's a letter for you, Mrs. Linton," I said, gently inserting it in one hand that rested on her knee. "You must read it immediately, because it wants an answer. Shall I break the seal?" "Yes," she answered, without altering the direction of her eyes. I opened it—it was very short. "Now," I continued, "read it." She drew away her hand, and let it fall. I replaced it in her lap, and stood waiting till it should please her to glance down; but that movement was so long delayed that at last I resumed— "Must I read it, ma'am? It is from Mr. Heathcliff."

There was a start and a troubled gleam of recollection, and a struggle to arrange her ideas. She lifted the letter, and seemed to peruse it; and when she came to the signature she sighed: yet still I found she had not gathered its import, for, upon my desiring to hear her reply, she merely pointed to the name, and gazed at me with mournful and questioning eagerness.

"Well, he wishes to see you," said I, guessing her need of an interpreter. "He's in the garden by this time, and impatient to know what answer I shall bring."

As I spoke, I observed a large dog lying on the sunny grass beneath raise its ears as if about to bark, and then smoothing them back, announce, by a wag of the tail, that some one approached whom it did not consider a stranger. Mrs. Linton bent forward, and listened breathlessly. The minute after a step traversed the hall; the open house was too tempting for Heathcliff to resist walking in: most likely he supposed that I was inclined to shirk my promise, and so resolved to trust to his own audacity. With straining eagerness Catherine gazed towards the entrance of her chamber. He did not hit the right room directly: she motioned me to admit him, but he found it out ere I could reach the door, and in a stride or two was at her side, and had her grasped in his arms.

He neither spoke nor loosed his hold for some five minutes, during which period he bestowed more kisses than ever he gave in his life before, I daresay: but then my mistress had kissed him first, and I plainly saw that he could hardly bear, for downright agony, to look into her face! The same conviction had stricken him as me, from the instant he beheld her, that there was no prospect of ultimate recovery there—she was fated, sure to die.

"Oh, Cathy! Oh, my life! how can I bear it?" was the first sentence he uttered, in a tone that did not seek to disguise his despair. And now he stared at her so earnestly that I thought the very intensity of his gaze would bring tears into his eyes; but they burned with anguish: they did not melt.

"What now?" said Catherine, leaning back, and returning his look with a suddenly clouded brow: her humour was a mere vane for constantly varying caprices. "You and Edgar have broken my heart, Heathcliff! And you both come to bewail the deed to me, as if you were the people to be pitied! I shall not pity you, not I. You have killed me—and thriven on it, I think. How strong you are! How many years do you mean to live after I am gone?"

Heathcliff had knelt on one knee to embrace her; he attempted to rise, but she seized his hair, and kept him down.

"I wish I could hold you,'" she continued, bitterly, "till we were both dead! I shouldn't care what you suffered. I care nothing for your sufferings. Why shouldn't you suffer? I do! Will you forget me? Will you be happy when I am in the earth? Will you say twenty years hence, 'That's the grave of Catherine Earnshaw? I loved her long ago, and was wretched to lose her; but it is past. I've loved many others since: my children are dearer to me than she was; and, at death, I shall not rejoice that I are going to her: I shall be sorry that I must leave them!' Will you say so, Heathcliff?"

"Don't torture me till I'm as mad as yourself," cried he, wrenching his head free, and grinding his teeth.

The two, to a cool spectator, made a strange and fearful picture. Well might Catherine deem that heaven would be a land of exile to her, unless with her mortal body she cast away her moral character also. Her present countenance had a wild vindictiveness in its white cheek, and a bloodless lip and scintillating eye; and she retained in her closed fingers a portion of the locks she had been grasping. As to her companion, while raising himself with one hand, he had taken her arm with the other; and so inadequate was his stock of gentleness to the requirements of her condition, that on his letting go I saw four distinct impressions left blue in the colourless skin.

"Are you possessed with a devil," he pursued, savagely, "to talk in that manner to me when you are dying? Do you reflect that all those words will be branded in my memory, and eating deeper eternally after you have left me? You know you lie to say I have killed you: and, Catherine, you know that I could as soon forget you as my existence[13]! Is it not sufficient for your infernal selfishness, that while you are at peace I shall writhe in the torments of hell?"

"I shall not be at peace," moaned Catherine, recalled to a sense of physical weakness by the violent, unequal throbbing of her heart, which beat visibly and audibly under this excess of agitation. She said nothing further till the paroxysm was over; then she continued, more kindly—

"I'm not wishing you greater torment than I have, Heathcliff. I only wish us never to be parted: and should a word of mine distress you hereafter, think I feel the same distress underground, and for my own sake, forgive me! Come here and kneel down again! You never harmed me in your life. Nay, if you nurse anger, that will be worse to remember than my harsh words! Won't you come here again? Do!"

Heathcliff went to the back of her chair, and leant over, but not so far as to let her see his face, which was livid with emotion. She bent round to look at him; he would not permit it: turning abruptly, he walked to the fireplace, where he stood, silent, with his back towards us. Mrs. Linton's glance followed him suspiciously: every movement woke a new sentiment in her. After a pause and a prolonged gaze, she resumed; addressing me in accents of indignant disappointment:—

"Oh, you see, Nelly, he would not relent a moment to keep me out of the grave. THAT is how I'm loved! Well, never mind. That is not MY Heathcliff. I shall love mine yet; and take him with me: he's in my soul. And," added she musingly, "the thing that irks me most is this shattered prison[14], after all. I'm tired of being enclosed here. I'm wearying to escape into that glorious world[15], and to be always there: not seeing it dimly through tears, and yearning for it through the walls of an aching heart: but really with it, and in it. Nelly, you think you are better and more fortunate than I; in full health and strength: you are sorry for me—very soon that will be altered. I shall be sorry for you. I shall be incomparably beyond and above you all. I WONDER he won't be near me!" She went on to herself. "I thought he wished it[16]. Heathcliff, dear! you should not be sullen now. Do come to me, Heathcliff."

In her eagerness she rose and supported herself on the arm of the chair. At that earnest appeal he turned to her, looking absolutely desperate. His eyes, wide and wet, at last flashed fiercely on her; his breast heaved convulsively. An instant they held asunder[17], and then how they met I hardly saw, but Catherine made a spring, and he caught her, and they were locked in an embrace from which I thought my mistress would never be released alive: in fact, to my eyes, she seemed directly insensible. He flung himself into the nearest seat, and on my approaching hurriedly to ascertain if she had fainted, he gnashed at me, and foamed like a mad dog, and gathered her to him with greedy jealousy. I did not feel as if I were in the company of a creature of my own species: it appeared that he would not understand, though I spoke to him; so I stood off, and held my tongue, in great perplexity.

A movement of Catherine's relieved me a little presently: she put up her hand to clasp his neck, and bring her cheek to his as he held her; while he, in return, covering her with frantic caresses, said wildly—

"You teach me now how cruel you've been—cruel and false. Why did you despise me? Why did you betray your own heart, Cathy? I have not one word of comfort. You deserve this. You have killed yourself[18]. Yes, you may kiss me, and cry; and wring out my kisses and tears: they'll blight you—they'll damn you. You loved me—then what right had you to leave me? What right—answer me—for the poor fancy you felt for Linton? Because misery and degradation, and death, and nothing that God or Satan could inflict would have parted us, you, of your own will, did it. I have not broken your heart—you have broken it; and in breaking it, you have broken mine. So much the worse for me that I am strong. Do I want to live? What kind of living will it be when you—oh, God! would you like to live with your soul in the grave?"

"Let me alone. Let me alone," sobbed Catherine. "If I've done wrong, I'm dying for it. It is enough! You left me too: but I won't upbraid you! I forgive you. Forgive me!"

"It is hard to forgive, and to look at those eyes, and feel those wasted hands," he answered. "Kiss me again; and don't let me see your eyes! I forgive what you have done to me. I love my murderer—but your! How can I?"

They were silent—their faces hid against each other, and washed by each other's tears. At least, I suppose the weeping was on both sides; as it seemed Heathcliff could weep on a great occasion like this.

I grew very uncomfortable, meanwhile; for the afternoon wore fast away, the man whom I had sent off returned from his errand, and I could distinguish, by the shine of the western sun up the valley, a concourse thickening outside Gimmerton chapel porch.

"Service is over," I announced. "My master will be here in half an hour."

Heathcliff groaned a curse, and strained Catherine closer: she never moved.

Ere long I perceived a group of the servants passing up the road towards the kitchen wing. Mr. Linton was not far behind; he opened the gate himself and sauntered slowly up, probably enjoying the lovely afternoon that breathed as soft as summer.

"Now he is here,' I exclaimed. 'For heaven's sake, hurry down! You'll not meet any one on the front stairs. Do be quick; and stay among the trees till he is fairly in."

"I must go, Cathy," said Heathcliff, seeking to extricate himself from his companion's arms. "But if I live, I'll see you again before you are asleep. I won't stray five yards from your window."

"You must not go!" she answered, holding him as firmly as her strength allowed. 'You shall not, I tell you.'

"For one hour," he pleaded earnestly.

"Not for one minute," she replied.

"I must—Linton will be up immediately," persisted the alarmed intruder.

He would have risen, and unfixed her fingers by the act—she clung fast, gasping: there was mad resolution in her face.

"No!" she shrieked. "Oh, don't, don't go. It is the last time! Edgar will not hurt us. Heathcliff, I shall die! I shall die!"

"Damn the fool! There he is," cried Heathcliff, sinking back into his seat. "Hush, my darling! Hush, hush, Catherine! I'll stay. If he shot me so, I'd expire with a blessing on my lips."

And there they were fast again[19]. I heard my master mounting the stairs—the cold sweat ran from my forehead: I was horrified.

"Are you going to listen to her ravings?" I said, passionately. "She does not know what she says. Will you ruin her, because she has not wit to help herself? Get up! You could be free instantly. That is the most diabolical deed that ever you did. We are all done for[20]—master, mistress, and servant."

I wrung my hands, and cried out; and Mr. Linton hastened his step at the noise. In the midst of my agitation, I was sincerely glad to observe that Catherine's arms had fallen relaxed, and her head hung down.

"She's fainted, or dead," I thought: "so much the better. Far better that she should be dead, than lingering a burden and a misery-maker to all about her."

Edgar sprang to his unbidden guest, blanched with astonishment and rage. What he meant to do I cannot tell; however, the other stopped all demonstrations, at once, by placing the lifeless-looking form in his arms.

"Look there!" he said. "Unless you be a fiend, help her first—then you shall speak to me!"

He walked into the parlour, and sat down. Mr. Linton summoned me, and with great difficulty, and after resorting to many means, we managed to restore her to sensation; but she was all bewildered; she sighed, and moaned, and knew nobody. Edgar, in his anxiety for her, forgot her hated friend. I did not. I went, at the earliest opportunity, and besought him to depart; affirming that Catherine was better, and he should hear from me in the morning how she passed the night.

"I shall not refuse to go out of doors," he answered; "but I shall stay in the garden: and,

Nelly, mind you keep your word to-morrow. I shall be under those larch-trees. Mind! or I pay another visit, whether Linton be in or not.."

He sent a rapid glance through the half-open door of the chamber, and, ascertaining that what I stated was apparently true, delivered the house of his luckless presence[21].

Notes

[1] Mr.Lockwood, Mr. Heathcliff's tenant at Thrushcross Grange.

[2] Mr. Heathcliff

[3] during our different conversation

[4] Nelly Dean, Catherine's servant

[5] Nelly Dean's visit to Wuthering Heights a week before

[6] I knew, as surely as if I saw him, that Mr. Heathcliff was prowling about Thrushcross Grange in the hope of getting a chance to break in and talk to Catherine.

[7] Heathcliff's letter to Catherine. He had made Nelly agree to carry to her mistress.

[8] religious service

[9] Nelly had engaged to carry Heathcliff's letter to Catherine and arrange for their meeting.

[10] partly cut off

[11] make her pitous

[12] a church

[13] I can not forget you just as I can not forget my existence.

[14] this world, which is a shattered prison for me

[15] the next world

[16] I am surprised he won't be near me! I thought he wished to be near me.

[17] they kept away from each other

[18] This refers to Catherine's luckless marriage with Edgar Linton.

[19] And there they held each other fast again.

[20] ruined; finished

[21] the presence of Heathcliff

 ## Questions

1. Can you describe Cathy's illness?

2. What words show Cathy and Heathcliff's love is wild and mad?

3. In this chapter what personality does Ellen have as an on-looker, to readers?

4. What does the last paragraph mean?

Analysis of Chapter 15

The selection here is taken from Chapter 15, which depicts the final meeting between Heathcliff and Catherine. This meeting is the climax of the whole story. What follows the meeting is Heathcliff's uncontrollable revenge on those who he thinks are related to his love failure.

This part is narrated by Nelly Ellen. She is the housekeeper in the service of Catherine and her observation and narration are usually objective and unbiased. One Sunday Ellen visits Wuthering Heights. She finds excuses for not being able to give Heathcliff's letter to Catherine, for she kept it in her pocket for 3 days. The fourth day, Sunday, most of the people went to church and Ellen found it is a perfect chance for her to complete the assignment. She gave Catherine Heathcliff's letter.

Catherine was changed by her sickness: there is a vivid description of Cathy in serious illness. She was beautiful in an unearthly way and her eyes *"appeared always to gaze beyond, and far beyond. You would have said out the world."* Judging from her mental and physical state, Ellen draws a conclusion, Catherine doomed to decay. Having been in her service for many years, Ellen was quite familiar with Catherine and Linton, so *"A book lay spread on the sill before her"*– "I" believe *Linton had laid it there*; And Catherine's attitude toward Linton changes according to her mood and feelings. She is bad tempered, however, Linton tries everything to make her happy. There is a concise depiction of scene at Wuthering Heights. " The ringing bell in chapel; murmur of the summer foliage when the trees were in leaf was now substituted by the Chapel bells' sound." In a few words the author depicts the quiet winter days of Wuthering Heights; a great thaw or a season of steady rain (spring) and murmur of summer foliage (sounds of trees in leaf in summer). Ellen gives the letter to Catherine (a conversation between the House keeper and Catherine). After she has learnt it was a letter from Heathcliff, her reaction to the sudden visit of her former lover is realistically portrayed. Here Cathy was astonished and confused. It was Ellen who gave her an interpretation of the letter by saying *"He wishes to see you. He is in the garden by this time and impatient to know what answer I shall bring."* Ellen had left the door open, so Heathcliff walked in and Catherine eagerly waited for him to find the right room she lives. "In stride", "had her grasped in his arms", and "hold for 5 minutes without speaking" show

Heathcliff's deep yearning and affection for Catherine. His manner of showing his love for Cathy is so passionate and almost crazy about her. Their reunion was bitter-sweet: though passionately glad to be reunited, embrace, kisses and sweet words such as *"O Cathy My life! How can I bear it"* can't prevent Heathcliff from expressing his sufferings to Cathy. It is a bitter scene. In the eyes of Ellen *"The two, to a cool spectator made a strange and fearful picture."* Catherine accused Heathcliff of having killed her, and Heathcliff warned her not to say such things when he would be tortured by them after her death besides, she had been at fault by abandoning him. She asked him to forgive her, since she would not "be at peace" after death, and he answered: "It is hard to forgive, and to look at those eyes, and feel those wasted hands... I love my murderer but yours! (but your murderer) How can I (How can I be your murderer?)?" They held each other closely and wept until Ellen warned them that Linton was returning by saying that *service is over; my master will be here in half an hour.* Heathcliff wanted to leave, but Catherine insisted that he stay, since she was dying and would never see him again. He consented to stay, and "in the midst of the agitation, [Ellen] was sincerely glad to observe that Catherine's arms had fallen relaxed... She's fainted or dead, so much the better...(she loses consciousness)." Linton came in, Heathcliff handed him Catherine's body and told him to take care of her: "Unless you be a fiend, help her first, then you shall speak to me!" He told Nelly he would wait outside for news of Catherine's welfare (health information), and left. (Heathcliff promise to come again the next day without consideration of the existence of Linton.); here the subtle action shows delicate and considerate thoughts of Heathcliff for Catherine: "I" *stated: she's fainted or die.* While before Heathcliff left, it says *delivered the house of his luckless presence* which means the presence of Heathcliff has disburdened Mr. and Mrs. Linton and Ellen, for his stay was luckless to them all, because it was his presence that accelerate Catherine's death.

 **中文译文**

《呼啸山庄》 第十五章

又过了一个星期——我更接近了健康和春天！我现在已经听完了我的邻居的全部历史，因为这位管家可以从比较重要的工作中腾出空闲常来坐坐。我要用她自己的话继续讲下去，只是压缩一点。总的来说，她是一个说故事的能手，我可不认为我能把她的风格改得更好。

晚上，（她说）：就是我去山庄的那天晚上，我知道希斯克厉夫先生又在附近，就像是我看到了他；我不出去，因为我还把他的信搁在口袋里，而且不愿再被吓唬或被揶揄了。我决定现在不交这信，一直等到我主人到什么地方去后再说，因为我拿不准凯瑟琳收到这信后会怎么样。结果是，这信过了三天才到她的手里。第四天是星期日，等到全家都去教堂后，我就把信带到她屋里。还有一个男仆留下来同我看家。我们经常在做礼拜时把门锁住，可是那天天气是这么温暖宜人，我就把门都打开，而且，我既然知道谁会来，为了履行我的诺言，我就告诉我的同伴说女主人非常想吃橘子，他得跑到村里去买几个，明天再付钱。他走了，我就上了楼。

林惇夫人穿着一件宽大的白衣服，和往常一样，坐在一个敞开着窗子的凹处，肩上披着一条薄薄的肩巾。她那厚厚的长发在她初病时曾剪去一点，现在她简单地梳梳，顺其自然地披在她的鬓角和脖子上。正如我告诉过希斯克厉夫的一样，她的外表是改变了；但当她是宁静的时候，在这种变化中仿佛具有非凡的美。她眼里的亮光已经变成一种梦幻的、忧郁的温柔；她的眼睛不再给人这种印象：她是在望着她四周的东西；而且显现出总是在凝视着远方，遥远的地方——你可以说是望着世外。还有她脸上的苍白——她恢复之后，那种憔悴的面貌消失了——还有从她心境中所产生的特别表情，虽然很凄惨地暗示了原因，却使她格外令人爱怜；这些现象——对于我，我知道，对于别的看见她的人都必然认为——足以反驳那些说是正在康复的明证，却标明她是注定要凋谢了。

一本书摆在她面前的窗台上，打开着，简直令人感觉不到的风间或掀动着书页。我相信是林惇放在那儿的：因为她从来不想读书，或干任何事，他得花上许多钟头来引起她注意那些以前曾使她愉快的事物。她明白他的目的，在她心情较好时，就温和地听他摆布；只是时不时地压下一声疲倦的叹息，表示这些是没有用的，到最后就用最悲惨的微笑和亲吻来制止他。在其他时候，她就突然转身，用手掩着脸，或者甚至愤怒地把他推开；然后他就小心翼翼地让她自己待着，因为他确信自己是无能为力的了。

吉默吞的钟还在响着；山谷里那涨满了的水溪传来的潺潺流水声非常悦耳。这美妙的声音代替了现在还没有到来的夏日树叶飒飒声，等到树上结了果子，这声音就湮没了田庄附近的那种音乐。在呼啸山庄附近，在风雪或雨季之后的平静日子里，这小溪总是这样响着的。在凯瑟琳倾听时，那就是，如果她是在想着或倾听着的话；她所想的就是呼啸山庄！可是她有着我以前提到过的那种茫然的、捉摸不到的神气，这表明她的耳朵或眼睛简直不能辨识任何外界的东西。

"有你一封信，林惇夫人，"我说，轻轻把信塞进她摆在膝上的一只手里。"你得马上看它，因为等着回信呢。我把封漆打开好吗？""好吧，"她回答，没改变她的目光的方向。我打开它——信很短。"现在，"我接着说，"看吧。"她缩回她的手，任这信掉到地上。我又把它放在她的怀里，站着等她乐意朝下面看看的时候；可是她总是不动，终于我说——

"要我念吗，太太？是从希斯克厉夫先生那儿来的。"

她一惊，露出一种因回忆而苦恼的神色，竭力使自己镇定下来。她拿起信，仿佛是在阅读；当她看到签名的地方，她叹息着；但我还是发现她并没有领会到里面的意思，因为我急着要听她的回信，她却只指着署名，带着悲哀的、疑问的热切神情盯着我。

"唉，他想见见你，"我说，"心想她需要一个人给她解释，这时候他在花园里，急想知道我将给他带去什么样的回信呢"。

在我说话的时候，我看见躺在下面向阳的草地上的一只大狗竖起了耳朵，仿佛正要吠叫，然后耳朵又向后平下去。它摇摇尾巴算是宣布有人来了，而且它不把这个人当作陌生人看待。林惇夫人向前探身，上气不接下气地倾听着。过了一分钟，有脚步声穿过大厅；这开着门的房子对于希斯克厉夫是太诱惑了，他不能不走进来：大概他以为我有意不履行诺言，就决定随心所欲地大胆行事了。凯瑟琳带着紧张的热切神情，盯着她卧房的门口。他并没有马上发现应该走进哪间屋子：她示意要我接他进来，可是我还没走到门口，他已经找到了，而且大步走到她身边，把她搂在自己怀里了。

有五分钟左右，他没说话，也没放松他的拥抱，在这段时间我敢说他给予的吻比他有生以来所给的还多：但是先吻他的是我的女主人，我看得清清楚楚，他由于真正的悲痛，简直不能直瞅她的脸！他一看见她，就跟我同样地确信，她是没有最后复原的希望了——她命中注定，一定要死了。

"啊，凯蒂！啊，我的命！我怎么受得了啊？"这是他说出的第一句话，那声调并不想掩饰他的绝望。现在他这么热切地盯着她，他的凝视是这么热烈，我想他会流泪的。但是那对眼睛却燃烧着极度的痛苦——并没化作泪水。

"现在还要怎么样呢？"凯瑟琳说，向后仰着，以突然阴沉下来的脸色回答他的凝视——她的性子不过是她那时常变动的精神状态的风向标而已。"你和埃德加把我的心都弄碎了，希斯克厉夫！你们都为那件事来向我哀告，好像你们才是该被怜悯的人！我不会怜悯你的，我才不。你已经害了我——而且，我想，还因此心满意足吧。你多强壮呀！我死后你还打算活多少年啊？"

希斯克厉夫本来是用一条腿跪下来搂着她的。他想站起来，可是她抓着他的头发，又把他按下去。

"但愿我能抓住你不放，"她辛酸地接着说，"一直到我们两个都死掉！我不应该管你受什么苦。我才不管你的痛苦哩。你为什么不该受苦呢？我可在受呀！你会忘掉我吗？等我埋在土里的时候，你会快乐吗？二十年后你会不会说，'那是凯瑟琳·恩萧的坟。很久以前我爱过她，而且为了失去她而难过；可是这都过去了。从那以后我又爱过好多人：我的孩子对于我可比她要亲多了；而且，到了死的时候，我不会因为我要去她那儿就高兴——我会很难过，因为我得离开他们了！'你会不会这么说呢，希斯克厉夫？"

"不要把我折磨得跟你自己一样地发疯吧，"他叫，扭开他的头，咬着牙。

在一个冷静的旁观者看来，这两个人形成了一幅奇异而可怕的图画。凯瑟琳很有理由认为天堂对于她就是流放之地，除非她的精神也随同她的肉体一起抛开。在她现在的面容上，那白白的双颊、没有血色的唇，以及闪烁的眼睛都显出一种狂野的要复仇的心情；在她的握紧的手指中间还留有她刚才抓住的一把头发。至于她的同伴，他一只手撑住自己，一只手握着她的胳膊；他对她那种温存，对于她当时的健康状况是很不适合的。在他松手时，我看见在那没有血色的皮肤上留下了四条清清楚楚的紫痕。

"你是不是被鬼缠住了，"他凶暴地追问着，"在你要死的时候还这样跟我说话？你想没想到所有这些话都要烙在我的记忆里，而且在你丢下我之后，将要永远更深地啮食着我？你明知道你说的我害死你的话是说谎；而且，凯瑟琳，你知道我只要活着就不会忘掉你！当你得到安息的时候，我却要在地狱的折磨里受煎熬，这还不够使你那狠毒的自私心得到满足吗？"

"我不会得到安息的，"凯瑟琳哀哭着，感到她身体的衰弱，因为在这场过度的激动下，她的心猛烈地、不规则地跳动着，甚至跳得能觉察出来。她说不出话来，直到这阵激动过去，才又接着说，稍微温和一些了。

"我并不愿意你受的苦比我受的还大，希斯克厉夫。我只愿我们永远不分离：如果我有一句话使你今后难过，想想我在地下也感到一样的难过，看在我自己的份上，饶恕我吧！过来，再跪下去！你一生从来没有伤害过我。是啊，如果你生了气，那今后你想起你的气愤就要比想起我那些粗暴的话更难受！你不肯再过来吗？来呀！"

希斯克厉夫走到她椅子背后，向前探身，却让她看不见他那因激动而变得发青的脸。她回过头望他；他不许她看；他突然转身，走到炉边，站在那儿，沉默着，背对着我们。林惇夫人的目光疑惑不解地跟着他：每一个动作在她心里都唤起一种新的感情。在一阵沉默和长久的凝视之后，她又讲话了；带着愤慨的失望声调对我说——

"啊，你瞧，耐莉，他都不肯暂时发发慈悲好让我躲开坟墓。我就是这样被人爱啊！好吧，没关系。那不是我的希斯克厉夫。我还是要爱我那个；我带着他：他是在我灵魂里。而且，"她沉思地又说，"使我最厌烦的到底还是这个破碎的牢狱，我不愿意被关在这儿了。我多想躲避到那个愉快的世界里，永远在那儿：不是泪眼模糊地看到它，不是在痛楚的心境中渴望着它；可是真的跟它在一起，在它里面。耐莉，你以为你比我好些、幸运些；完全健康有力；你为我难过——不久这就要改变了。我要为你们难过。我将要无可比拟地超越你们，在你们所有的人之上。我奇怪他不肯挨近我？"她自言自语地往下说，"我以为他是愿意的。希斯克厉夫，亲爱的！现在你不该沉着脸。到我这儿来呀，希斯克厉夫。"

她异常激动地站起身来，身子靠着椅子的扶手。听了那真挚的乞求，他转身向她，神色是完全不顾一切了。他睁大着双眼，含着泪水，终于猛地向她一闪，胸口激动地起伏着。他们各自站住一刹那，然后我简直没看清他们是怎么合在一起的，只见凯瑟琳向前一跃，他就把她擒住了，他们拥抱得紧紧地，我想我的女主人绝不会被活着放开了：事实上，据我看，她仿佛立刻就不省人事了。他投身到最近处的椅子上，我赶忙走上前看看她是不是昏迷了，他就对我咬牙切齿，像个疯狗似的吐着白沫，带着贪婪的嫉妒神色把她抱紧。我简直不觉得我是在陪着一个跟我同类的动物：看来即使我跟他说话，他也不会懂；因此我只好非常惶惑地躲开，也不吭声。

凯瑟琳动弹了一下，这才使我立刻放了心：她伸出手搂住他的脖子，他抱住她，她把脸紧贴着他的脸；他回报给她无数疯狂的爱抚，又狂乱地说——

"你现在才使我明白你曾经多么残酷——残酷又虚伪。你过去为什么瞧不起我呢？你为什么欺骗你自己的心呢，凯蒂？我没有一句安慰的话。这是你应得的。你害死了你自己。是的，你可以亲吻我，哭，又逼出我的吻和眼泪：我的吻和眼泪要摧残你——要诅咒你。你爱过我——那么你有什么权力离开我呢？有什么权力——回答我——对林惇存有那种可怜的幻想？因为悲惨、耻辱和死亡，以及上帝或撒旦所能给的一切打击和痛苦都不能把我们分开，而你，却出于你自己的心意，这样做了。我没有弄碎你的心——是你弄碎了的；而在弄碎它的时候，你把我的心也弄碎了。因为我是强壮的，对于我就格外苦。我还要活吗？那将是什么样的生活，当你—— 啊，上帝！你愿意带着你的灵魂留在坟墓里吗？"

"别管我吧，别管我吧，"凯瑟琳抽泣着，"如果我曾经做错了，我就要为此而死去的。够啦！你也丢弃过我的，可我并不要责备你！我饶恕你。饶恕我吧！"

"看看这对眼睛，摸摸这双消瘦的手，要饶恕是很难的，"他回答，"再亲亲我吧；别让我看见你的眼睛！我饶恕你对我做过的事。我爱害了我的人——可是害了你的人呢？我又怎么能够饶恕他？"

他们沉默着——脸紧贴着，用彼此的眼泪在冲洗着。至少，我猜是双方都在哭泣；在这样一个不同寻常的场合中，就连希斯克厉夫仿佛也都哭泣了。

同时我越来越心焦；因为下午过去得很快，我支使出去的人已经完成使命回来了，而且我从照在山谷的夕阳也能分辨出吉默吞教堂门外已有一大堆人涌出了。

"做完礼拜了，"我宣布，"我的主人要在半个钟头内到家啦。"

希斯克厉夫哼出一声咒骂，把凯瑟琳抱得更紧，她一动也不动。

不久我看见一群仆人走过大路，向厨房那边走去。林惇先生在后面不远；他自己开了大门，慢慢溜达过来，大概是要享受这风和日丽、宛如夏日的下午。

"现在他到这儿来了，"我大叫，"看在老天爷的份上，快下去吧！你在前面楼梯上不会遇到什么人的。快点吧，在树林里待着，等他进来你再走。"

"我一定得走了，凯蒂，"希斯克厉夫说，想从他的伴侣的胳臂中挣脱出来，"可是如果我还活着，在你睡觉以前，我还要来看你的。我不会离开你的窗户五码之外的。"

"你绝不能走！"她回答，尽她的全力紧紧地抓住他，"我告诉你，你不要走。"

"只走开一个钟头，"他热诚地恳求着。

"一分钟也不行。"她回答。

"我非走不可——林惇马上就要来了。"这受惊的闯入者坚持着。

他想站起来，要松开她的手指——但她紧紧搂住，喘着气：在她脸上表现出疯狂的决心。

"不！"她尖叫，"啊，别，别走。这是最后一次了！埃德加不会伤害我们的。希斯克厉夫，我要死啦！我要死啦！"

"该死的混蛋！他来了，"希斯克厉夫喊着，倒在他的椅子上，"别吵，我亲爱的！别吵，别吵，凯瑟琳！我不走了。如果他就这么拿枪崩了我，我也会在嘴唇上带着祝福咽气的。"

他们又紧紧地搂在一起。我听见我主人上楼了——我的脑门上直冒冷汗；我吓坏了。

"你就听她的胡话吗？"我激动地说，"她不知道她说什么。就因为她神志丧失，不能自主，你要毁了她吗？起来！你马上就可以挣脱的。这是你所做过的最恶毒的事。我们——主人，女主人，仆人——可都给毁啦！"

我绞着手，大叫；林惇先生一听见声音，加快了脚步，在我的震动之中，我衷心喜欢的看见凯瑟琳的胳臂松落下来，她的头也垂下来。"她是昏迷了，或是死了，"我想，"这样还好些。与其活着成为周围人的负担，成为不幸的制造者，那还不如让她死了的好。"

埃德加冲向这位不速之客，脸色因惊愕与愤怒而发白。他打算怎么样，我也不知道；可是，另一个人把那看来已没有生命的东西往他怀里一放，立刻停止了所有的示威行动。

"瞧吧！"他说，"除非你是一个恶魔，不然就去救救她吧——然后你再跟我说话！"

他走到客厅里坐下来。林惇先生召唤我去，费了好大劲，用了好多方法，我们才使她醒过来；可是她完全精神错乱了；她叹息，呻吟，谁也不认识。埃德加一心为她焦急，也忘了她那可恨的朋友。我可没有忘。我找了个最早的机会劝他离开：肯定地说凯瑟琳已经好些了，他明天早晨可以听我告诉他她这一夜过得怎么样。

"我不会拒绝出这个门的。"他回答，"可是我要待在花园里。耐莉，记着明天你要遵守诺言。我将在那些落叶松下面，记住！不然我还要来，不管林惇在不在家。"

他急急地向卧房的半开的门里投去一瞥，证实了我所说的是真实的，这不吉利的人才离开了这所房子。

References

[1] 朱虹 . 英国小说的黄金时代 [M]. 北京：中国社会科学出版社，1997.

[2] 勃朗特 . 呼啸山庄 [M]. 杨苡，译 . 南京：译林出版社，1990.

Unit 15   Robert Browning (1812—1889)

Life

Robert Browning (1812—1889) was an English poet and playwright whose mastery of the dramatic monologue made him one of the foremost Victorian poets. His poems are known for their irony,characterization, dark humour, social commentary, historical settings, and challenging vocabulary and syntax.

Browning's early career began promisingly, but was not a success. The long poem Pauline brought him to the attention of Dante Gabriel Rossetti, and was followed by Paracelsus, which was praised by Wordsworth and Dickens, but in 1840 the difficult Sordello, which was seen as wilfully obscure,  brought his poetry into disrepute. His reputation took more than a decade to recover, during which time he moved away from the Shelleyan forms of his early period and developed a more personal style.

In 1846 Browning married the older poet Elizabeth Barrett, who at the time was considerably better known than himself. So started one of history's most famous literary marriages. They went to live in Italy, a country he called "my university", and which features frequently in his work. By the time of her death in 1861, he had published the crucial collection *Men and Women*. The collection *Dramatis Personae* and the book-length epic poem *The Ring and the Book* followed, and made him a leading British poet. He continued to write prolifically, but his reputation today rests largely on the poetry he wrote in this middle period.

When Browning died in 1889, he was regarded as a sage and philosopher-poet who through his writing had made contributions to Victorian social and political discourse—as in the poem Caliban upon Setebos, which some critics have seen as a comment on the theory of evolution, which had recently been put forward by Darwin and others. Unusually for a poet, societies for the study of his work were founded while he was still alive. SuchBrowning Societies remained common in Britain and the United States until the early 20th century.

Browning's admirers have tended to temper their praise with reservations about the length and difficulty of his most ambitious poems, particularly *The Ring and the Book*. Nevertheless, they have included such eminent writers asHenry James, Oscar Wilde, George Bernard Shaw, G. K. Chesterton, Ezra Pound, Jorge Luis Borges, and Vladimir Nabokov. Among living writers, Stephen King's *The Dark Tower* series and A.S. Byatt's *Possession* refer directly to Browning's work.

Today Browning's critically most esteemed poems include the monologues *Childe Roland to the Dark Tower Came, Fra Lippo Lippi, Andrea Del Sarto, and My Last Duchess*. His most popular poems include *Porphyria's Lover, How They Brought the Good News from Ghent to Aix*, the diptych *Meeting at Night*, the patriotic *Home Thoughts from Abroad*, and the children's poem *The Pied Piper of Hamelin*. His abortive dinner-party recital of *How They Brought The Good News* was recorded on an Edison wax cylinder, and is believed to be the oldest surviving recording made in the United Kingdom of a notable person.

My Last Duchess

Historical background

The poem is preceded by "Ferrara", indicating that the speaker is most likely Alfonso II d'Este, the fifth Duke ofFerrara (1533—1598), who, at the age of 25, married Lucrezia di Cosimo de' Medici, the 14-year-old daughter of Cosimo I de' Medici, Grand Duke of Tuscany, and Eleonora di Toledo. Lucrezia was not well educated, and the Medicis could be considered "nouveau riche" in comparison to the venerable and distinguished Este family (the Duke's remark regarding his gift of a "nine-hundred-years-old name" clearly indicates that he considered his bride beneath him socially). She came with a sizeable dowry, and the couple married in 1558. He then abandoned her for two years before she died on 21 April 1561, at age 17. There was a strong suspicion of poisoning. The Duke then sought the hand of Barbara, eighth daughter of the Holy Roman Emperor Ferdinand I and Anna of Bohemia and Hungary and the sister of the Count of Tyrol, Ferdinand II. The count was in charge of arranging the marriage; the chief of his entourage, Nikolaus Madruz, a native of Innsbruck, was his courier. Madruz is presumably the silent listener in the poem.

The other characters named in the poem, painter Frà Pandolf and sculptor Claus of Innsbruck, are fictional.

Story

The poem is set during the late Italian Renaissance. The speaker (presumably the Duke of Ferrara) is giving the emissary of the family of his prospective new wife (presumably a third or fourth since Browning could have easily written "second" but did not do so) a tour of the artworks in his home. He draws a curtain to reveal a painting of a woman, explaining that it is a portrait of his late wife; he invites his guest to sit and look at the painting. As they look at the portrait of the late Duchess, the Duke describes her happy, cheerful and flirtatious nature, which had displeased him. He says, "She had a heart—how shall I say? —too soon made glad..." He goes on to say that his complaint of her was that "that was not her husband's presence only" that made her happy. Eventually, "I gave commands; then all smiles stopped together." This could be interpreted as either the Duke had given commands to the Duchess to stop smiling or commands for her to be killed. He now keeps her painting hidden behind a curtain that only he is allowed to draw back, meaning that now she only smiles for him. In *My Last Duchess*, the Duke of Ferrara is addressing the envoy of the Count of Tyrol. Although he is on his best behaviour, the Duke of Ferrara demonstrates many sociopathic tendencies as he recalls the time he shared with his now-deceased Duchess. Even in death the Duke wished to hide her away behind the curtain where no other man could admire her beauty. The Duke then resumes an earlier conversation regarding wedding arrangements, and in passing points out another work of art, a bronze statue of Neptune taming a sea-horse by Claus of Innsbruck, so making his late wife but just another work of art.

In an interview, Browning said, "I meant that the commands were that she should be put to death ... Or he might have had her shut up in a convent."

My Last Duchess

Ferrara

That's my last Duchess painted on the wall,

Looking as if she were alive. I call

That piece a wonder, now: Frà Pandolf's [1]hands

Worked busily a day, and there she stands.

Will't [2]please you sit and look at her? I said

Frà Pandolf' by design[3], for never read

Strangers like you that pictured countenance[4],

The depth and passion of its earnest glance,

But to myself they turned (since none puts by[5],

The curtain I have drawn for you, but I)

And seemed as they would ask me, if they durst[6],

How such a glance came there; so, not the first

Are you to turn and ask thus. Sir, 't[7] was not

Her husband's presence only, called[8] that spot

Of joy into the Duchess' cheek: perhaps

Frà Pandolf chanced to say, "Her mantle laps

Over my lady's wrist too much," or "Paint

Must never hope to reproduce the faint

Half-flush that dies along her throat:'" such stuff

Was courtesy[9], she thought, and cause enough

For calling up that spot of joy. She had

A heart—how shall I say?—too soon made glad,

Too easily impressed; she liked whate'er[10]

She looked on, and her looks went everywhere.

Sir, 't was all one! my favour at her breast,

The dropping of the daylight in the West,

The bough of cherries some officious[11] fool

Broke in the orchard for her, the white mule

She rode with round the terrace—all and each

Would draw from her alike the approving speech,

Or blush, at least. She thanked men, —good! but thanked

Somehow—I know not how—as if she ranked

my gift of a nine-hundred-years-old name

With anybody's gift. Who'd stoop to blame

This sort of trifling? Even had you skill

In speech—(which I have not)—to make your will

Quite clear to such an one, and say, 'Just this

Or that in you disgusts me; here you miss,

Or there exceed the mark' —and if she let

Herself be lessoned so, nor plainly set

Her wits to yours, forsooth[12], and made excuse,

—E'en then would be some stooping[13]; and I choose

Never to stoop. Oh, sir, she smiled, no doubt,

Whene'er I passed her; but who passed without

Much the same smile? This grew; I have commands;

Then all smiles stopped together. There she stands

As if alive. Will't please you rise? We'll meet

The company below then. I repeat,

The Count[14] your master's known munificence

Is ample warrant[15] that no just pretence

Of mine for dowry[16] will be disallowed;

Though his fair daughter's self, as I avowed

At starting, is my object. Nay, we'll go

Together down, sir. Notice Neptune[17], though,

Taming a sea-horse, thought a rarity[18],

Which Claus of Innsbruck[19] cast in bronze for me!

Notes

[1] 潘道夫教士

[2] Will it

[3] 有意识的

[4] 表情，外表

[5] 放在一边

[6] dare 的过去分词

[7] it's

[8] caused

[9] 礼貌，好意

[10] whatever

[11] 过于殷勤的

[12] 确实，的确

[13] 弯腰

[14] 伯爵；宽宏大量

[15] 保障；要求

[16] 嫁妆

[17] 海神

[18] 罕见，稀有

[19] 人名；地名

 Questions

1. What did the Duchess look like?

2. Can you infer the Duchess' characters through the description?

3. What is the significance of the poem?

Analysis of the poem

My Last Duchess is written in iambic pentameter and abides by the pattern of the heroic couplet. This poem is loosely based on historical events involving Alfonso, the Duke of Ferrara, who lived in the 16th century. The main themes are power, influence, marriage, aristocracy and egoism.

In this poem, Browning use dramatic monologue to express his views. A dramatic monologue is a piece of spoken verse that offers great insight into the feelings of the speaker, a form invented and practiced principally by Robert Browning. They were favored by many poets in the Victorian period, in which a character in fiction or in history delivers a speech explaining his or her feelings, actions, or motives. The monologue is usually directed toward a silent audience, with the speaker's words influenced by a critical situation.

There's no doubt that *My Last Duchess* is one of the greatest masterpieces throughout the world, not only because it is a poem that best exemplifies Robert Browning's use of the dramatic monologue, but also it combined writing skill with characteristics of character perfectly.

中文译文

我已故的公爵夫人

墙上的这幅画是我的前公爵夫人，
看起来就像她活着一样。如今，
我称它为奇迹：潘道夫的手笔
经一日忙碌，从此她就在此站立。
你愿坐下看看她吗？我有意提起
潘道夫，因为外来的生客（例如你）
凡是见了画中描绘的面容、
那真挚的眼神的深邃和热情，
没有一个不转向我（因为除我外
再没有别人把画上的帘幕拉开），
似乎想问我可是又不大敢问；
是从哪儿来的——这样的眼神？
你并非第一个人回头这样问我。
先生，不仅仅是她丈夫的在座
使公爵夫人面带欢容，可能
潘道夫偶然说过："夫人的披风
盖住她的手腕太多，"或者说：
"隐约的红晕向颈部渐渐隐没，
这绝非任何颜料所能复制。"
这种无聊话，却被她当成好意，
也足以唤起她的欢心。她那颗心——
怎么说好呢？——要取悦容易得很，
也太易感动。她看到什么都喜欢，
而她的目光又偏爱到处观看。

先生，她对什么都一样！她胸口上
佩戴的我的赠品，或落日的余光；
过分殷勤的傻子在园中攀折
给她的一枝樱桃，或她骑着
绕行花圃的白骡——所有这一切
都会使她同样地赞美不绝，
或至少泛起红晕。她感激人。好的！
但她的感激（我说不上怎么搞的）
仿佛把我赐她的九百年的门第
与任何人的赠品并列。谁愿意
屈尊去谴责这种轻浮举止？即使
你有口才（我却没有）能把你的意志
给这样的人儿充分说明："你这点
或那点令我讨厌。这儿你差得远，
而那儿你超越了界限。"即使她肯听
你这样训诫她而毫不争论，
毫不为自己辩解，——我也觉得
这会有失身份，所以我选择
绝不屈尊。哦，先生，她总是在微笑，
每逢我走过；但是谁人走过得不到
同样慷慨的微笑？发展至此，
我下了令：于是一切微笑都从此制止。
她站在那儿，像活着一样。请你起身
客人们在楼下等。我再重复一声：
你的主人——伯爵先生闻名的大方
足以充分保证：我对嫁妆
提出任何合理要求都不会遭拒绝；
当然，如我开头声明的，他美貌的小姐
才是我追求的目标。别客气，让咱们
一同下楼吧。但请看这海神尼普顿
在驯服海马，这是件珍贵的收藏，
是克劳斯为我特制的青铜铸像。

Unit 16   Thomas Hardy (1840—1928)

Life

Thomas Hardy was born on 2 June 1840 in Higher Bockhampton (then Upper Bockhampton), a hamlet in the parish of Stinsford to the east of Dorchester in Dorset, England, where his father Thomas (1811—1892) worked as a stonemason and local builder, and married his mother Jemima (née Hand; 1813—1904) in Beaminster, towards the end of 1839. Jemima was well-read, and she educated Thomas until he went to his first school at Bockhampton at the age of eight. For several years he attended Mr. Last's Academy for Young Gentlemen in Dorchester, where he learned Latin

and demonstrated academic potential. Because Hardy's family lacked the means for a university education, his formal education ended at the age of sixteen, when he became apprenticed to James Hicks, a local architect.

Hardy trained as an architect in Dorchester before moving to London in 1862; there he enrolled as a student at King's College London. He won prizes from the Royal Institute of British Architects and the Architectural Association. He joined Arthur Blomfield's practice as assistant architect in April 1862 and worked with Blomfield on All Saints' parish church in Windsor, Berkshire in 1862—1864. A reredos, possibly designed by Hardy, was discovered behind panelling at All Saints' in August 2016. In the mid-1860s, Hardy was in charge of the excavation of part of the graveyard of St. Pancras Old Church prior to its destruction when the Midland

Railway was extended to a new terminus at St. Pancras.

Hardy never felt at home in London, because he was acutely conscious of class divisions and his social inferiority. During this time he became interested in social reform and the works of John Stuart Mill. He was also introduced by his Dorset friend Horace Moule to the works of Charles Fourier and Auguste Comte. After five years, concerned about his health, he returned to Dorset, settling in Weymouth, and decided to dedicate himself to writing.

In 1870, while on an architectural mission to restore the parish church of St Juliot in Cornwall, Hardy met and fell in love with Emma Gifford, whom he married in Kensington in the autumn of 1874. In 1885 Thomas and his wife moved into Max Gate, a house designed by Hardy and built by his brother. Although they later became estranged, Emma's subsequent death in 1912 had a traumatic effect on him and after her death, Hardy made a trip to Cornwall to revisit places linked with their courtship; his Poems 1912—1913 reflect upon her death. In 1914, Hardy married his secretary Florence Emily Dugdale, who was 39 years his junior. However, he remained preoccupied with his first wife's death and tried to overcome his remorse by writing poetry. In 1910, Hardy had been awarded the Order of Merit and was also for the first time nominated for the Nobel Prize in Literature. He would be nominated for the prize in eleven more years.

Hardy became ill with pleurisy in December 1927 and died at Max Gate just after 9 pm on 11 January 1928, having dictated his final poem to his wife on his deathbed; the cause of death was cited, on his death certificate, as "cardiac syncope", with "old age" given as a contributory factor. His funeral was on 16 January at Westminster Abbey, and it proved a controversial occasion because Hardy had wished for his body to be interred at Stinsford in the same grave as his first wife, Emma. His family and friends concurred; however, his executor, Sir Sydney Carlyle Cockerell, insisted that he be placed in the abbey's famous Poets' Corner. A compromise was reached whereby his heart was buried at Stinsford with Emma, and his ashes in Poets' Corner. Hardy's estate at death was valued at £95,418.

Shortly after Hardy's death, the executors of his estate burnt his letters and notebooks, but twelve documents survived, one of them containing notes and extracts of newspaper stories from the 1820s, and research into these has provided insight into how Hardy used them in his works. In the year of his death Mrs Hardy published *The Early Life of Thomas Hardy, 1841—1891*, compiled largely from contemporary notes, letters, diaries, and biographical memoranda, as well as from oral information in conversations extending over many years.

Hardy's work was admired by many younger writers, including D. H. Lawrence, John Cowper Powys, and Virginia Woolf. In his autobiography *Goodbye to All That (1929),* Robert Graves recalls meeting Hardy in Dorset in the early 1920s and how Hardy received him and his new wife warmly, and was encouraging about his work.

Hardy's birthplace in Bockhampton and his house Max Gate, both in Dorchester, are owned by the National Trust.

Plot of *Tess of the D'Urbervilles*

Phase the first: the maiden (1–11)

The novel is set in impoverished rural England, Thomas Hardy's fictional Wessex, during the Long Depression of the 1870s. Tess is the oldest child of John and Joan Durbeyfield, uneducated peasants; however, John is given the impression by Parson Tringham that he may have noble blood, since "Durbeyfield" is a corruption of "D'Urberville", the surname of a noble Norman family, then extinct. The news immediately goes to John's head.

That same day, Tess participates in the village May Dance, where she meets Angel Clare, youngest son of Reverend James Clare, who is on a walking tour with his two brothers. He stops to join the dance and partners several other girls. Angel notices Tess too late to dance with her, as he is already late for a promised meeting with his brothers. Tess feels slighted.

Tess's father gets too drunk to drive to the market that night, so Tess undertakes the journey herself. However, she falls asleep at the reins, and the family's only horse encounters a speeding wagon and is fatally wounded. Tess feels so guilty over the horse's death that she agrees, against her better judgement, to visit Mrs d'Urberville, a rich widow who lives in a rural mansion near the town of Trantridge, and "claim kin." She is unaware that, in reality, Mrs d'Urberville's husband Simon Stoke adopted the surname even though he was unrelated to the real d'Urbervilles.

Tess does not succeed in meeting Mrs d'Urberville, but chances to meet her libertine son, Alec, who takes a fancy to Tess and secures her a position as poultry keeper on the estate. Tess dislikes Alec but endures his persistent unwanted attention to earn enough to replace her family's horse. The threat that Alec presents to Tess's virtue is obscured for Tess by her inexperience and almost daily commonplace interactions with him. Late one night, walking home from town with some other Trantridge villagers, Tess inadvertently antagonizes Car Darch, Alec's most recently discarded favourite, and finds herself in physical danger. When Alec rides up and offers to "rescue" her from the situation, she accepts. Instead of taking her home, he rides through the fog until they reach an ancient grove in a forest called "The Chase", where he informs her that he is lost and leaves on foot to get his bearings. Alec returns to find Tess asleep, and it is implied that he rapes her, although there remains a degree of ambiguity.

Mary Jacobus, a commentator on Hardy's works, speculates that the ambiguity may have been forced on the author to meet the requirements of his publisher and the "Grundyist" readership of his time.

Phase the second: maiden no more (12–15)

Tess goes home to her father's cottage, where she keeps almost entirely to her room. The following summer, she gives birth to a sickly boy who lives only a few weeks. On his last night alive, Tess baptises him herself, because her father would not allow the parson to visit, stating that he didn't want the parson to "pry into their affairs." The child is given the name "Sorrow" and Tess arranges his burial in the "shabby corner" of the churchyard reserved for unbaptised infants. Tess adds a homemade cross to the grave with flowers in an empty marmalade jar.

Phase the third: the rally (16–24)

More than two years after the Trantridge debacle, Tess, now twenty, has found employment outside the village, where her past is not known. She works for Mr. and Mrs. Crick as amilkmaid at Talbothays Dairy. There, she befriends three of her fellow milkmaids, Izz, Retty, and Marian, and meets again Angel Clare, now an apprentice farmer who has come to Talbothays to learn dairy management. Although the other milkmaids are in love with him, Angel singles out Tess, and the two fall in love.

Phase the fourth: the consequence (25–34)

Angel spends a few days away from the dairy, visiting his family at Emminster. His brothers Felix and Cuthbert, both ordained Church of England ministers, note Angel's coarsened manners, while Angel considers them staid and narrow-minded. The Clares have long hoped that Angel would marry Mercy Chant, a pious schoolmistress, but Angel argues that a wife who knows farm life would be a more practical choice. He tells his parents about Tess, and they agree to meet her. His father, the Reverend James Clare, tells Angel about his efforts to convert the local populace, mentioning his failure to tame a young miscreant named Alec d'Urberville.

Angel returns to Talbothays Dairy and asks Tess to marry him. This puts Tess in a painful dilemma: Angel obviously thinks her a virgin and she shrinks from confessing her past. Such is her love for him that she finally agrees to the marriage, explaining that she hesitated because she had heard he hated old families and thought he would not approve of her d'Urberville ancestry. However, he is pleased by this news because he thinks it will make their match more suitable in the eyes of his family.

As the marriage approaches, Tess grows increasingly troubled. She writes to her mother for advice; Joan tells her to keep silent about her past. Her anxiety increases when a man from Trantridge, named Groby, recognises her and crudely alludes to her history. Angel overhears and flies into an uncharacteristic rage. Tess, deciding to tell Angel the truth, writes a letter describing her dealings with d'Urberville and slips it under his door. When Angel greets her with the usual affection the next morning, she thinks he has forgiven her; later she discovers the letter under his carpet and realises that he has not seen it. She destroys it.

The wedding goes smoothly, apart from the omen of a cock crowing in the afternoon. Tess and Angel spend their wedding night at an old d'Urberville family mansion, where Angel presents his bride with diamonds that belonged to his godmother. When he confesses that he once had a brief affair with an older woman in London, Tess is moved to tell Angel about Alec, thinking he will understand and forgive.

Phase the fifth: the woman pays (35—44)

Angel is appalled by the revelation, and makes it clear that Tess is reduced in his eyes. He spends the wedding night on a sofa. After a few awkward days, a devastated Tess suggests they separate, saying that she will return to her parents. Angel gives her some money and promises to try to reconcile himself to her past, but warns her not to try to join him until he sends for her. After a brief visit to his parents, Angel takes a ship to Brazil to start a new life. Before he leaves, he encounters Tess's milkmaid friend Izz and impulsively asks her to come with him as his mistress. She accepts, but when he asks her how much she loves him, she admits "Nobody could love 'ee more than Tess did! She would have laid down her life for 'ee. I could do no more!" Hearing this, he abandons the whim, and Izz goes home weeping bitterly.

Tess returns home for a time but, finding this unbearable, decides to join Marian at a starve-acre farm called Flintcomb-Ash; they are later joined by Izz. On the road, she is again recognised and insulted by Groby, who proves to be her new employer. At the farm, the three former milkmaids perform hard physical labour.

One day, Tess attempts to visit Angel's family at the parsonage in Emminster, hoping for practical assistance. As she nears her destination, she encounters Angel's older brothers, with Mercy Chant. They do not recognise her, but she overhears them discussing Angel's unwise marriage, and dares not approach them. On the way, she overhears a wandering preacher and is shocked to discover that it is Alec d'Urberville, who has been converted to Methodismunder the Reverend James Clare's influence.

Phase the sixth: the convert (45–52)

Alec and Tess are each shaken by their encounter, and Alec begs Tess never to tempt him again as they stand beside an ill-omened stone monument called the Cross-in-Hand. However, Alec soon comes to Flintcomb-Ash to ask Tess to marry him, and she tells him she is already married. He begins stalking her, despite repeated rebuffs, returning at Candlemas and again in early spring, when Tess is hard at work feeding a threshing machine. He tells her he is no longer a preacher and wants her to be with him. When he insults Angel, she slaps him, drawing blood. Tess then learns from her sister, Liza-Lu, that her father, John, is ill and that her mother is dying. Tess rushes home to look after them. Her mother soon recovers, but her father unexpectedly dies from a heart condition.

The family is evicted from their home, as Durbeyfield held only a life lease on their cottage. Alec, having followed her to her home village, tells Tess that her husband is never coming back and offers to house the Durbeyfields on his estate. Tess refuses his assistance. She had earlier written Angel apsalm-like letter, full of love, self-abasement, and pleas for mercy; now, however, she finally admits to herself that Angel has wronged her and scribbles a hasty note saying that she will do all she can to forget him, since he has treated her so unjustly.

The Durbeyfields plan to rent some rooms in the town of Kingsbere, ancestral home of the d'Urbervilles, but arrive to find that the rooms have already been rented to another family. All but destitute, they are forced to take shelter in the churchyard, under the D'Urberville window. Tess enters the church and in the d'Urberville Aisle, Alec reappears and importunes Tess again. In despair, she looks at the entrance to the d'Urberville vault and wishes herself dead.

In the meantime, Angel has been very ill in Brazil and, his farming venture having failed, heads home to England. On the way, he confides his troubles to a stranger, who tells him that he was wrong to leave his wife; what she was in the past should matter less than what she might become. Angel begins to repent his treatment of Tess.

Phase the seventh: fulfilment (53–59)

Upon his return to his family home, Angel has two letters waiting for him: Tess's angry note and a few cryptic lines from "two well-wishers" (Izz and Marian), warning him to protect his wife from "an enemy in the shape of a friend." He sets out to find Tess and eventually locates Joan, now well-dressed and living in a pleasant cottage. After responding evasively to his enquiries, she tells him Tess has gone to live in Sandbourne, a fashionable seaside resort. There, he finds Tess living in an expensive boarding house under the name "Mrs. d'Urberville." When he asks for her, she appears in startlingly elegant attire and stands aloof. He tenderly asks her forgiveness, but Tess, in anguish, tells him he has come too late; thinking he would never return, she yielded at last to Alec d'Urberville's persuasion and has become his mistress. She gently asks Angel to leave and never come back. He departs, and Tess returns to her bedroom, where she falls to her knees and begins a lamentation. She blames Alec for causing her to lose Angel's love a second time, accusing Alec of having lied when he said that Angel would never return to her.

The landlady, Mrs. Brooks, tries to listen in at the keyhole, but withdraws hastily when the argument becomes heated. She later sees Tess leave the house, then notices a spreading red spot—a bloodstain—on the ceiling. She summons help, and Alec is found stabbed to death in his bed.

Angel, totally disheartened, has left Sandbourne; Tess hurries after him and tells him that she has killed Alec, saying that she hopes she has won his forgiveness by murdering the man who ruined both their lives. Angel doesn't believe her at first, but grants his forgiveness and tells her that he loves her. Rather than head for the coast, they walk inland, vaguely planning to hide somewhere until the search for Tess is ended and they can escape abroad from a port. They find an empty mansion and stay there for five days in blissful happiness, until their presence is discovered one day by the cleaning woman.

They continue walking and, in the middle of the night, stumble upon Stonehenge, where Tess lies down to rest on an ancient altar. Before she falls asleep, she asks Angel to look after her younger sister, Liza-Lu, saying that she hopes Angel will marry her after she is dead. At dawn,

Angel sees that they are surrounded by police. He finally realises that Tess really has committed murder and asks the men in a whisper to let her awaken naturally before they arrest her. When she opens her eyes and sees the police, she tells Angel she is "almost glad" because "now I shall not live for you to despise me." Her parting words are, "I am ready."

Tess is escorted to Wintoncester (Winchester) prison. The novel closes with Angel and Liza-Lu watching from a nearby hill as the black flag signalling Tess's execution is raised over the prison. Angel and Liza-Lu then join hands and go on their way.

Comments on *Tess of the D'Urbervilles*

Hardy's writing often explores what he called the "ache of modernism", and this theme is notable in Tess, which, as one critic noted, portrays "the energy of traditional ways and the strength of the forces that are destroying them." In depicting this theme Hardy uses imagery associated with hell when describing modern farm machinery, as well as suggesting the effete nature of city life as the milk sent there must be watered down because townspeople cannot stomach whole milk. Angel's middle-class fastidiousness makes him reject Tess, a woman whom Hardy presents as a sort of Wessex Eve, in harmony with the natural world. When he parts from her and goes to Brazil, the handsome young man gets so ill that he is reduced to a "mere yellow skeleton." All these instances have been interpreted as indications of the negative consequences of man's separation from nature, both in the creation of destructive machinery and in the inability to rejoice in pure and unadulterated nature.

On the other hand, Marxist critic Raymond Williams in *The English Novel From Dickens to Lawrence* questions the identification of Tess with a peasantry destroyed by industrialisation. Williams sees Tess not as a peasant, but as an educated member of the rural working class, who suffers a tragedy through being thwarted, in her aspirations to socially rise and her desire for a good life (which includes love and sex), not by industrialism, but by the landed bourgeoisie (Alec), liberal idealism (Angel) and Christian moralism in her family's village.

Another important theme of the novel is the sexual double standard to which Tess falls victim; despite being, in Hardy's view, a truly good woman, she is despised by society after losing her virginity before marriage. Hardy plays the role of Tess's only true friend and advocate, pointedly subtitling the book "a pure woman faithfully presented" and prefacing it with Shakespeare's words from *The Two Gentlemen of Verona*: "Poor wounded name! My bosom as a bed/ Shall lodge thee." However, although Hardy clearly means to criticise Victorian notions of female purity, the double standard also makes the heroine's tragedy possible, and thus serves as a mechanism of Tess's broader fate. Hardy variously hints that Tess must suffer either to atone for the misdeeds of her ancestors, or to provide temporary amusement for the gods, or because she possesses some small but lethal character flaw inherited from her ancestors.

Because of the numerous pagan and neo-Biblical references made about her, Tess has been viewed variously as an Earth goddess or as a sacrificial victim. For example, early in the novel, she participates in a festival for Ceres, the goddess of the harvest, and when she baptises her dead child she chooses a passage from Genesis, the book of creation, rather than the more traditional New Testament verses. Then at the end, when Tess and Angel come to Stonehenge, which was commonly believed in Hardy's time to be a pagan temple, she willingly lies down on a stone supposedly associated with human sacrifice.

Tess has also been seen as a personification of nature and her association with animals throughout the novel emphasizes this idea. Tess's misfortunes begin when she falls asleep while driving Prince to market, and causes the horse's death; at Trantridge, she becomes a poultry-keeper; she and Angel fall in love amid cows in the fertile Froom valley; and on the road to Flintcombe-Ashe, she kills some wounded pheasants to end their suffering.

However, Tess emerges as a powerful character not because of this symbolism but because "Hardy's feelings for her were strong, perhaps stronger than for any of his other invented personages."

Major Characters

Tess Durbeyfield

She is the main character of the book. It is a book of hers. Through all the scenes and all the seasons of the year, our attention is focused on what happens to her. At the beginning, Tess, a sixteen-years-old girl is enjoying herself on holiday. Because of her physical attraction and innocence, she is seduced by Alec. Later she falls in love with Angel, but her confession of the past in the night of marriage brings the dreaded disaster. Angel's reappearance and his forgiveness set her in disgrace and shame. She kills Alec and she is executed.

Love and responsibility are Tess's leading characteristics. She will do in her power for those she loves, under all difficulties, and at the expense of her own wishes and comfort. Having got into difficulties, her pride and guilt prevent her from appealing for help, until it is too late. Yet she is not perfect. Still young and inexperienced, she idealizes Angel and accepts what he says and does without question. Nevertheless, Tess is indeed "a pure woman", loving and true, too young to be always wise, but ruined far more through the fault of Angel than through her own.

Angel

He is enraptured by Tess's beauty and being in the dairy-farm. He falls in love with her. In spring, when love naturally grows passionate, Angel embraces Tess uncontrollably. Once having done so, he decides, disregarding the wishes of his parents and brothers, to marry her. Fascinated as he is by her virginal beauty, he believes Tess to be absolutely chaste and pure like nature's very daughter.

The sleep-walking scene, symbolic of the working of the subconscious mind, reveals his intense love for Tess and the terrible disappointment caused by the discovery of her past. After his strange travel to Brazil, ashamed of his own weaknesses, he is struck with remorse for his past actions. He has now a clearer knowledge of his love for Tess, of her innocence, of his true self and that of Tess. The conflict thus resolved, he decides to return to Tess.

Angel is the main cause of Tess's tragedy. He has the inconsistencies, preconceptions, idealism, intellectualism, irrationality and impulsiveness of an ardent young man. Like Tess, though he goes astray, he has a general tendency to goodness, and chastened by experience he soberly accepts his new responsibility, the care of Liza-Lu.

Alec Stoke-D'Urberville

He is the villain of this novel, with his rolling and lascivious eye, diamond ring and black moustachios conventional of stage melodrama. He is thoroughly sensual, violent and headstrong, and determined on getting her own way at all costs. Tess's resistance to the fulfillment of his desires is puny when compared to his cunning maneuvers and ultimately fails. As Tess's first lover, he is frequently regarded as another of Hardy's Sadan figures.

Alec never seeks Tess out as a loving, equal partner. Clearly he assumes a cultural right, by virtue of class and gender, to possess Tess's body. Later, after he has proposed to Tess, he reveals his motive tobe not love but a desire for power when he states: "I was your master once! I will be your master again."

Introduction to Chapter 58

Chapter 58 is approaching to the end of the story. After Tess murdered Alec, she and Angel Clare are busy in escape. They live in an estate and enjoy several happy days. Their peace is interrupted by the care-taker. Tess follows Angel's advice and goes on walking to the South. They arrive at the old Stonehenge and Tess is exhausted and unwilling to walk forward. Tess tells Angel to get married after her death. While she is lying on the stone slate, the police arrest her and "the justice is done." This chapter show two lovers powerlessness in face of destiny. Tess is determined to be a tragic character.

Chapter 58

The night was strangely solemn and still. In the small hours[1] she whispered to him the whole story of how he had walked in his sleep with her in his arms across the Froom stream[2], at the imminent risk of both their lives, and laid her down in the stone coffin at the ruined abbey. He had never known of that till now.

"Why didn't you tell me next day?" he said. "It might have prevented much misunderstanding and woe[3]."

"Don't think of what's past!" said she. "I am not going to think outside of now. Why should we! Who knows what tomorrow has in store?"

But it apparently had no sorrow. The morning was wet and foggy, and Clare, rightly informed that the caretaker[4] only opened the windows on fine days, ventured to creep out of their chamber, and explore the house, leaving Tess asleep. There was no food on the premises[5], but there was water, and he took advantage of the fog to emerge from the mansion, and fetch tea, bread, and butter from a shop in a little place two miles beyond, as also a small tin kettle and spirit-lamp[6], that they might get fire without smoke. His re-entry awoke her; and they breakfasted on what he had brought.

They were indisposed to stir abroad[7], and the day passed, and the night following, and the next, and next; till, almost without their being aware, five days had slipped by in absolute seclusion, not a sight or sound of a human being disturbing their peacefulness, such as it was. The changes of the weather were their only events, the birds of the New Forest their only company. By tacit consent[8] they hardly once spoke of any incident of the past subsequent to their wedding-day. The gloomy intervening time seemed to sink into chaos, over which the present and prior times closed as if it never had been. Whenever he suggested that they should leave their shelter, and go forwards towards Southampton or London, she showed a strange unwillingness to move.

"Why should we put an end to all that's sweet and lovely!" she deprecated[9]. "What must come will come." And, looking through the shutter-chink[10]: "All is trouble outside there; inside here content."

He peeped out also. It was quite true; within was affection, union, error forgiven: outside was the inexorable[11].

"And—and," she said, pressing her cheek against his; "I fear that what you think of me now may not last. I do not wish to outlive your present feeling for me. I would rather not. I would rather be dead and buried when the time comes for you to despise me, so that it may never be known to me that you despised me."

"I cannot ever despise you."

"I also hope that. But considering what my life has been I cannot see why any man should, sooner or later, be able to help despising me.... How wickedly mad I was! Yet formerly I never could bear to hurt a fly or a worm, and the sight of a bird in a cage used often to make me cry."

They remained yet another day. In the night the dull sky cleared, and the result was that the old caretaker at the cottage awoke early. The brilliant sunrise made her unusually brisk; she decided to open the contiguous[12] mansion immediately, and to air it thoroughly on such a day. Thus it occurred that, having arrived and opened the lower rooms before six o'clock, she ascended to the bedchambers, and was about to turn the handle of the one wherein they lay. At that moment she fancied she could hear the breathing of persons within. Her slippers and her antiquity had rendered her progress a noiseless one so far, and she made for instant retreat; then, deeming that her hearing might have deceived her, she turned around, to the door and softly tried the handle. The lock was out of order, but a piece of furniture had been moved forward on the inside, which prevented her opening the door more than an inch or two. A stream of morning light through the shutter-chink fell upon the faces of the pair, wrapped in profound slumber, Tess's lips being parted like a half-opened flower near his cheek. The caretaker was so struck with their innocent appearance, and with the elegance of Tess's gown hanging across a chair, her silk stockings beside it, the pretty parasol, and the other habits[13] in which she bad arrived because she had none else, that her first indignation at the effrontery[14] of tramps and vagabonds gave way to a momentary sentimentality over this genteel elopement, as it seemed. She closed the door, and withdrew as softly as she had come, to go and consult with her neighbours on the odd discovery.

Not more than a minute had elapsed after her withdrawal when Tess woke, and then Clare. Both had a sense that something had disturbed them, though they could not say what; and the uneasy feeling which it engendered grew stronger. As soon as he was dressed he narrowly scanned the lawn through the two or three inches of shutter-chink.

"I think we will leave at once," said he. "It is a fine day. And I cannot help fancying somebody is about the house. At any rate, the woman will be sure to come to-day."

She passively assented, and putting the room in order they took up the few articles that belong to them, and departed noiselessly. When they had got into the Forest she turned to take a last look at the house.

"Ah, happy house-good-bye!" she said. "My life can only be a question of a few weeks. Why should we not have stayed there?"

"Don't say it, Tess! We shall soon get out of this district altogether. We'll continue our course as we've begun it, and keep straight north. Nobody will think of looking for us there. We shall be looked for at the Wessex ports if we are sought at all. When we are in the north we will get to a port and away."

Having thus persuaded her the plan was pursued, and they kept a bee line[15] northward. Their long repose at the manor-house[16] lent them walking power now; and towards mid-day they found that they were approaching the steepled city of Melchester[17], which lay directly in their way. He decided to rest her in a clump of trees during the afternoon, and push onward under cover of darkness. At dusk Clare purchased food as usual, and their night march began, the boundary between Upper and Mid-Wessex being crossed about eight o'clock.

To walk across country without much regard to roads was not new to Tess, and she showed her old agility in the performance. The intercepting city, ancient Melchester, they were obliged to pass through in order to take advantage of the town bridge for crossing a large river that obstructed them. It was about midnight when they went along the deserted streets, lighted fitfully by the few lamps, keeping off the pavement that it might not echo their footsteps. The graceful pile of cathedral architecture rose dimly on their left hand, but it was lost upon them now. Once out of the town they followed the turnpike-road[18], which after a few miles plunged across an open plain.

Though the sky was dense with cloud a diffused light from some fragment of a moon had hitherto helped them a little. But the moon had now sunk, the clouds seemed to settle almost on their heads, and the night grew as dark as a cave. However, they found their way along, keeping as much on the turf as possible that their tread might not resound, which it was easy to do, there being no hedge or fence of any kind. All around was open loneliness and black solitude, over which a stiff breeze blew.

They had proceeded thus gropingly two or three miles further when on a sudden Clare became conscious of some vast erection close in his front, rising sheer from the grass. They had almost struck themselves against it.

"What monstrous place is this?" said Angel.

"It hums," said she. "Hearken[19]!"

He listened. The wind, playing upon the edifice, produced a booming tune, like the note of some gigantic one-stringed harp. No other sound came from it, and lifting his hand and advancing a step or two, Clare felt the vertical surface of the structure. It seemed to be of solid stone, without joint or moulding[20]. Carrying his fingers onward he found that what he had come in contact with was a colossal rectangular pillar; by stretching out his left hand he could feel a similar one adjoining. At an indefinite height overhead something made the black sky blacker, which had the semblance of a vast architrave uniting the pillars horizontally. They carefully entered beneath and between; the surfaces echoed their soft rustle; but they seemed to be still out of doors. The place was roofless. Tess drew her breath fearfully, and Angel, perplexed, said: "What can it be?"

Feeling sideways they encountered another tower-like pillar, square and uncompromising as the first; beyond it another and another. The place was all doors and pillars, some connected above by continuous architraves[21].

"A very Temple of the Winds[22]," he said.

The next pillar was isolated; others composed a trilithon[23]; others were prostrate, their flanks forming a causeway wide enough for a carriage; and it was soon obvious that they made up a forest of monoliths[24] grouped upon the grassy expanse of the plain. The couple advanced further into this pavilion of the night till they stood in its midst.

"It is Stonehenge[25]!" said Clare.

"The heathen[26] temple, you mean?"

"Yes. Older than the centuries; older than the d'Urbervilles! Well, what shall we do, darling? We may find shelter further on." But Tess, really tired by this time, flung herself upon an oblong slab that lay close at hand, and was sheltered from the wind by a pillar. Owing to the action of the sun during the preceding day the stone was warm and dry, in comforting contrast to the rough and chill grass around, which had damped her skirts and shoes.

"I don't want to go any further, Angel," she said stretching out her hand for his. "Can't we bide[27] here?"

"I fear not. This spot is visible for miles by day, although it does not seem so now."

"One of my mother's people was a shepherd hereabouts, now I think of it. And you used to say at Talbothays that I was a heathen. So now I am at home."

He knelt down beside her outstretched form, and put his lips upon hers.

"Sleepy are you, dear? I think you are lying on an altar."

"I like very much to be here," she murmured. "It is so solemn and lonely—after my great happiness—with nothing but the sky above my face. It seems as if there were no folk in the world but we two; and I wish there were not—except Liza-Lu."

Clare thought she might as well rest here till it should get a little lighter, and he flung his overcoat upon her, and sat down by her side.

"Angel, if anything happens to me, will you watch over Liza-Lu for my sake?" she asked, when they had listened a long time to the wind among the pillars.

"I will."

"She is so good and simple and pure. O, Angel—I wish you would marry her if you lose me, as you will do shortly. O, if you would!"

"If I lose you I lose all! And she is my sister-in-law[28]."

"That's nothing, dearest. People marry sister-laws continually about Marlott; and Liza-Lu is so gentle and sweet, and she is growing so beautiful. O I could share you with her willingly when we are spirits! If you would train her and teach her, Angel, and bring her up for your own self!... She has all the best of me without the bad of me; and if she were to become yours it would almost seem as if death had not divided us... .Well, I have said it. I won't mention it again."

She ceased, and he fell into thought. In the far north-east sky he could see between the pillars a level streak of light. The uniform concavity[29] of black cloud was lifting bodily like the lid of a pot, letting in at the earth's edge the coming day, against which the towering monoliths and trilithons began to be blackly defined.

"Did they sacrifice to God here?" asked she.

"No," said he.

"Who to?"

"I believe to the sun. That lofty stone set away by itself is in the direction of the sun, which will presently rise behind it."

"This reminds me, dear," she said. "You remember you never would interfere with any belief of mine before we were married? But I knew your mind all the same, and I thought as you thought - not from any reasons of my own, but because you thought so. Tell me now, Angel, do you think we shall meet again after we are dead? I want to know."

He kissed her to avoid a reply at such a time.

"O, Angel—I fear that means no!" said she, with a suppressed sob. "And I wanted so to see you again—so much, so much! What not even you and I, Angel, who love each other so well?" Like a greater than himself, to the critical question at the critical time he did not answer[30]; and they were again silent. In a minute or two her breathing became more regular, her clasp of his hand relaxed, and she fell asleep. The band of silver paleness along the east horizon made even the distant parts of the Great Plain appear dark and near; and the whole enormous landscape bore that impress of reserve, taciturnity[31], and hesitation which is usual just before day. The eastward pillars and their architraves stood up blackly against the light, and the great flame-shaped Sun-stone beyond them; and the Stone of Sacrifice midway. Presently the night wind died out, and the quivering little pools in the cup-like hollows of the stones lay still. At the same time something seemed to move on the verge of the dip eastward—a mere dot. It was the head of a man approaching them from the hollow beyond the Sun-stone. Clare wished they had gone onward, but in the circumstances decided to remain quiet. The figure came straight towards the circle of pillars in which they were.

He heard something behind him, the brush of feet. Turning, he saw over the prostrate columns another figure; then before he was aware, another was at hand on the right, under a trilithon, and another on the left. The dawn shone full on the front of the man westward, and Clare could discern from this that he was tall, and walked as if trained. They all closed in with evident purpose. Her story then was true! Springing to his feet, he looked around for a weapon, loose stone, means of escape, anything. By this time the nearest man was upon him.

"It is no use, sir," he said. "There are sixteen of us on the Plain, and the whole country is reared."

"Let her finish her sleep!" he implored in a whisper of the men as they gathered round.

When they saw where she lay, which they had not done till then, they showed no objection, and stood watching her, as still as the pillars around. He went to the stone and bent over her, holding one poor little hand; her breathing now was quick and small, like that of a lesser creature than a woman[32]. All waited in the growing light, their faces and hands as if they were silvered, the remainder of their figures dark, the stones glistening green-gray, the Plain still a mass of shade. Soon the light was strong, and a ray shone upon her unconscious form, peering under her eyelids and waking her.

"What is it, Angel?" she said, starting up. "Have they come for me?"

"Yes, dearest," he said. "They have come."

"It is as it should be," she murmured. "Angel, I am almost glad, yes, glad! This happiness could not have lasted. It was too much. I have had enough; and now I shall not live for you to despise me!" She stood up, shook herself, and went forward, neither of the men having moved.

"I am ready." she said quietly.

 Notes

[1] 早上一两点钟

[2] 佛鲁姆河。新婚之夜，Angel 梦游时抱着 Tess 走过佛鲁姆河，将她放在石棺上，后来又将她抱回。当时 Tess 醒着，但 Angel 却对此并不知晓。

[3] 不幸；痛苦

[4] 看门人

[5] 房屋，指 Angel 和 Tess 在逃亡途中暂时栖身的一座空房子。

[6] 酒精灯

[7] 他们都不想外出。

[8] 默准

[9] 反对

[10] 百叶窗窗缝

[11] 冷酷无情

[12] 邻居的

[13] 衣服

[14] 放肆

[15]straight line

[16] 庄园，即他们暂时栖身的空屋

[17] 尖塔之城梅尔切斯特

[18] 收税路

[19] hear

[20] 浇铸

[21] 柱顶过梁

[22] 风神庙

[23] 三根相连的巨石柱

[24] 独块巨石

[25] 巨石阵。英国南部索尔兹伯里附近一处史前巨石建筑遗址。

[26] 异教徒

[27] 停留

[28] 英国国会及法律禁止与已故妻子的妹妹结婚。该法律于 1906 年废止。

[29] 凹陷处

[30] 据《新约·约翰福音》记载，当耶稣被带到控告他的祭司长和长老们面前时，他拒绝回答他们的任何问题。

[31] 沉默寡言

[32] 不是妇女，而是小姑娘。

 Questions

1. Why do Tess and Angel escape?

2. Why is Tess unwilling to escape?

3. Why does Tess ask Angel to marry her sister, Liza-Lu after her death?

4. How is Tess arrested by the police?

5. What do you think about the end of the story?

Analysis of Chapter 58

Tess of the D'Urbervilles is Hardy's masterpiece. In Chapter 58, Tess tells Angel about how he carried her while sleepwalking, and he regrets that did not tell him about this earlier, for it might have prevented much misunderstanding and woe. Tess is unwilling to leave their shelter and go forward, for she wonders why they must put an end to all that sweet and lovely. She says that what must come will come. Angel decides that they must finally leave the mansion, but Tess wishes to stay, for she believes she will not last more than several weeks. Angel plans to take Tess north, where they sail from Wessex. They travel northward and reach Stonehenge. Tess wishes to remain there, for Angel used to say that she was a heathen and thus Stonehenge is appropriate for her. Tess asks Angel to look after Liza-Lu if he loses her and to marry her. Tess falls asleep there, as she sleeps a party come for her. Tess admits that she is almost glad, for her happiness could not have lasted. She tells them that she is ready.

《德伯家的苔丝》 第五十八章

那天的夜晚尤其阴沉，尤其宁静。半夜过后，苔丝悄悄地向他讲述了他梦游的故事，说他怎样在睡梦里抱着她，冒着两个人随时都会掉进河里淹死的危险，从佛卢姆河的桥上走过，把她放在寺庙废墟中的一个石头棺材里。直到现在苔丝告诉了他，他才知道了这件事。

"第二天你为什么不告诉我呢？"他说，"如果你告诉了我，许多误会和痛苦也许就避免了。"

"过去了的事就不要再想了吧！"她说，"除了我们的此时此刻而外，我什么都不去想。我们不要去想！又有谁知道明天会发生什么事呢？"

不过第二天显然没有悲伤痛苦。早上潮湿多雾，克莱尔昨天已经听人说过，看管房子的人只是在天晴的时候才来开窗户，所以他就把苔丝留在房间里继续睡觉，自己大胆地走出房间，把整座房子查看了一遍，屋内虽然没有食物，但是有火。于是他就利用闹雾的天气，走出屋外，到两三英里以外的一个小地方的店铺里，买了茶点、面包和黄油，还买了一个铁皮水壶和一个酒精灯，这样他们就有了不冒烟的火了。他回来时把苔丝惊醒了；于是他们就一起吃他买回来的东西，当了一顿早饭。

他们都不想到外面去，只是待在屋里；白天过去了，夜晚来临了，接着是另一天，然后又是另一天；在不知不觉中，他们差不多就这样在绝对隐蔽的地方度过了五天，看不见一个人影，也听不到一点人声，没有谁来打扰他们的平静。天气变化是他们唯一的大事，陪伴他们的也只有新林的鸟儿。他们都心照不宣，几乎一次也没有提起过婚后的任何一件事情。他们中间那段悲伤的日子似乎在天地开辟之前的混沌中消失了，现在的和过去的欢乐时光又重新连接起来，仿佛从来就没有中断似的。每当他提出离开他们躲藏的屋子到南桑普顿或者伦敦去，她总是令人奇怪地表示不愿意离开。

"一切都是这样恩爱甜蜜，我们为什么要结束它呢！"她恳求说，"要来的总是躲不掉的。"她从百叶窗的缝隙中看着外面说："你看，屋外都是痛苦，屋内才是美满啊。"

他也向外面看去。她说得完全对：屋内是爱情、和谐、宽恕，屋外却是冷酷、无情。

"而且——而且，"她把自己的脸贴在他的脸上说，"你现在这样对待我，我担心也许不会长久。我希望永远拥有你现在这份情意。我不愿意失去它。我情愿在你瞧不起我的那一天到来的时候，我已经死了，埋掉了，那样我就永远不会知道你瞧不起我了。"

"我永远也不会瞧不起你的。"

"我也希望如此，可是一想到我这一生的遭遇，我总以为别人早晚都要瞧不起我的。……我真是一个可恶的疯子呀！可是从前，我连一只苍蝇、一条小虫都不敢伤害，看见关在笼子里的小鸟，也常常要悲伤流泪。"

他们在那座屋子里又待了一天。晚上，阴沉的天气晴朗了，因此照看房子的老太太很早就在她的茅屋里醒了。灿烂的朝阳使她精神异常爽快，于是决定立即就去把那座屋子的窗户打开，在这样好的天气里让空气流通。因此在六点钟以前，她就来到那座屋子，把楼下房间的窗户打开了，接着又上楼去开卧室的窗户；她来到克莱尔和苔丝躲藏的那个房间，就用手去转动门上的把手。就在这个时候，她认为自己听见房间里有人呼吸的声音。她脚上穿着便鞋，年纪又大，所以走到房间门口也没有弄出一点儿声音。她听见声音，就急忙退了回去。后来，她想也许是自己听错了，就又转身走到门口，轻轻地转动门上的把手。门锁已经坏了，但是有一件家具被搬过来，从里面把门挡住。老太太无法完全把门打开，只打开了一两英寸。早上太阳的光线穿过百叶窗的缝隙，照射在一对正在酣睡着的人的脸上，苔丝的嘴半张着，就像是在克莱尔的脸旁半开的一朵鲜花。照看房子的老太太看见他们睡在那儿，样子是那样纯真；她看见苔丝挂在椅子上的长袍，看见长袍旁边的丝织长袜和漂亮的小阳伞，还有苔丝没有别的可穿而穿来的其他几件衣服，被它们的华美高雅深深打动了；她最初以为他们是妓女流氓，心里十分生气，现在看来他们好像是上流社会一对私奔的情侣，于是心中的愤怒便化作了一阵怜爱。她把门关上，像来的时候那样轻轻地离开，找她的邻居商量她的奇怪发现去了。

老太太走后不到一分钟，苔丝就醒了，接着克莱尔也醒了。他们两个人都觉得出现过打扰他们的事，但是他们又说不清楚是什么事；因此他们心中产生的不安情绪也就越来越强烈了。克莱尔穿好衣服，立即从百叶窗上两三寸宽的窄缝中向外仔细观察。

"我想我们要立即离开了，"他说，"今天是一个晴天。我总觉得房子里有什么人来过。无论如何，那个老太太今天肯定是要来的。"

苔丝只好同意，于是他们收拾好房间，带上属于他们的几件物品，不声不响地离开了那座屋子。在他们走进新林的时候，苔丝回过头去，向那座屋子望了最后一眼。

"啊，幸福的屋子啊——再见吧！"她说，"我只能活上几个礼拜了。我们为什么不待在那儿呢？"

"不要说这种话，苔丝！不久我们就要完全离开这个地方了。我们要按照我们当初的路线走，一直朝北走。谁也不会想到上那儿去缉拿我们的。他们要是缉拿我们，一定是在威塞克斯各个港口寻找。等我们到了北边，我们就可以从一个港口离开。"

苔丝被说服以后，他们就按计划行事，径直朝北走。他们在那座屋子里休息了这样长的时间，现在走路也有了力气；到了中午，他们走到了恰好挡住他们去路的尖塔城梅尔彻斯特的附近。克莱尔决定下午让苔丝在一个树丛里休息，到了晚上在黑夜的掩护下赶路。克莱尔在黄昏时又像往常一样去买了食物，开始在夜晚中往前走。到了八点左右，他们就走过了上威塞克斯和中威塞克斯之间的边界。

苔丝早就习惯在乡野里走路而不管道路如何，因此她走起路来就显得轻松自如。他们必须从阻挡着他们的那座古老城市梅尔彻斯特穿过去，这样他们就可以从城里那座桥上通过挡住他们去路的大河。到了午夜时候，街道上空无一人，他们借着几盏闪烁不定的街灯走着，避开人行道，免得走路的脚步声引起回响。朦胧中出现在他们左边的那座堂皇雄伟的大教堂，现在已经从他们的眼前消失了。他们出了城，沿着收税栅路走，往前走了几英里，就进了他们要穿过的广阔平原。

先前虽然天上乌云密布，但是月亮仍然洒下散光，对他们走路多少有一些帮助。现在月亮已经落下去了，乌云似乎就笼罩在他们的头上，天黑得伸手不见五指。但是他们摸索着往前走，尽量走在草地上，免得脚步发出响声。这是容易做到的，因为在他们周围，既没有树篱，也没有任何形式的围墙。他们四周的一切都是空旷的寂静和黑夜的孤独，还有猛烈的风不停地吹着。

他们就这样摸索着又往前走了两三英里，克莱尔突然感觉到，他的面前有一座巨大的建筑物，在草地上顶天而立。他们几乎撞到了它的上面。

"这是一个什么古怪地方呢？"安琪尔说。

"还在嗡嗡响呢，"她说，"你听！"

他听了听。风在那座巨大的建筑物中间吹着，发出一种嗡嗡的音调，就像是一张巨大的单弦竖琴发出的声音。除了风声，他们听出还有其他的声音。克莱尔把一双手伸着，向前走了一两步，摸到了那座建筑物垂直的表面。它似乎是整块的石头，没有接缝，也没有花边。他继续用手摸去，发现摸到的是一根巨大的方形石柱；他又伸出左手摸去，摸到附近还有一根同样的石柱。在他的头顶上，高高的空中还有一件物体，使黑暗的天空变得更加黑暗了，它好像是把两根石柱按水平方向连接起来的横梁。他们小心翼翼地从两根柱子中间和横梁底下走了进去；他们走路的沙沙声从石头的表面发出回声，但他们似乎仍然还在门外。这座建筑是没有屋顶的。苔丝感到害怕，呼吸急促起来，而安琪尔也感到莫名其妙，就说——

"这里是什么地方呢？"

他们向旁边摸去，又摸到一根和第一根石柱同样高大坚硬的方形石柱，然后又摸到一根，再摸到一根。这儿全是门框和石柱，有的石柱上面还架着石梁。

"这是一座风神庙！"克莱尔说。

下面一根石柱孤零零地矗立着；另外有些石柱都是两根竖着的石柱上面横着一根石柱；还有一些石柱躺在地上，它们的两边形成了一条通道，宽度足以通过马车；不久他们就弄明白了，原来在这块平原的草地上竖立的石柱，一起形成了一片石林。他们两个人继续往前走，一直走进黑夜中这个由石柱组成的亭台中间。

"原来是史前神庙。"克莱尔说。

"你是说这是一座异教徒的神庙？"

"是的。比纪元前还要古老；也比德贝维尔家族还要古老！啊，我们怎么办哪，亲爱的？再往前走我们也许就可以找到一个栖身的地方了。"

但是苔丝这一次倒是真正累了，看见附近有一块长方形石板，石板的一头有石柱把风挡住，于是她就在石板上躺下来。由于白天太阳的照射，这块石板既干燥又暖和，和周围粗糙冰冷的野草相比舒服多了，那时候她的裙子和鞋子已经被野草上的露水弄湿了。

"我再也不想往前走了，安琪尔，"她把手伸给克莱尔说，"我们不能在这儿过一夜吗？"

"恐怕不行。这个地点现在虽然觉得别人看不见，但是在白天，好几英里以外都能够看见的。"

"现在我想起来了，我母亲娘家有一个人是这儿附近的一个牧羊人。在泰波塞斯你曾经说我是一个异教徒，所以我现在算是回了老家啦。"

克莱尔跪在躺着的苔丝身旁，用自己的嘴唇吻着她的嘴唇。

"亲爱的，想睡了吧？我想你正躺在一个祭坛上。"

"我非常喜欢躺在这儿，"她嘟哝着说，"这儿是这样庄严，这样僻静，头上只有一片苍天——我已经享受过巨大的幸福了。我觉得，世界上除了我们两个而外，仿佛没有其他的人了；我希望没有其他的人，不过丽莎·露除外。"

克莱尔心想，她不妨就躺在这儿休息，等到天快亮的时候再走；于是他把自己的外套脱下来盖在她的身上，在她的身旁坐下。

"安琪尔，要是我出了什么事，你能不能看在我的份上照看丽莎·露？"风声在石柱中间响着，他们听了好久，苔丝开口说。

"我会照顾她的。"

"她是那样善良、那样天真、那样纯洁。啊，安琪尔——要是你失去了我，我希望你会娶了她。啊，要是你能够娶她的话！"

"要是我失去了你，我就失去了一切！她是我的姨妹啊。"

"那是没有关系的，亲爱的。在马洛特村一带时常有跟小姨子结婚的；丽莎·露是那样温柔、甜美，而且还越长越漂亮了。啊，当我们大家都变成了鬼魂，我也乐意和她一起拥有你啊！安琪尔，你只要训练她、教导她，你就可以把她也培养得和你自己一样了！……我的优点她都有，我的坏处她一点儿也没有；如果她将来做了你的妻子，我就是死了，我们也是无法分开的了。……唉，我已经说过了。我不想再提了。"

她住了口，克莱尔听了也陷入了深思。从远处东北方向的天上，他看见石柱中间出现了一道水平的亮光。满天的乌云像一个大锅盖，正在整个地向上揭起，把姗姗来迟的黎明从大地的边上放进来，因此矗立在那儿的孤独石柱和两根石柱加一根横梁的牌坊，也露出了黑色的轮廓。

"他们就是在这儿向天神献祭吗？"她问。

"不！"他说。

"那么向谁呢？"

"我认为是向太阳献祭的。那根高高的石头柱子不就是朝着太阳的方向安放的吗？一会儿太阳就从它的后面升起来了。"

"亲爱的，这让我想起一件事来，"她说，"在我们结婚以前，你说你永远不会干涉我的信仰，你还记不记得？其实我一直明白你的思想，像你一样去思考——而不是从我自己的判断去思考，因为你怎样想，我就怎样想。现在告诉我吧，安琪尔，你认为我们死后还能见面吗？我想知道这件事。"

他吻她，免得在这种时候去回答这个问题。

"啊，安琪尔——恐怕你的意思是不能见面了！"她尽力忍着哽咽说，"我多想再和你见面啊——我想得多厉害啊，多厉害啊！怎么，安琪尔，即使像你和我这样相爱，都还不能再见面吗？"

安琪尔也像一个比他自己更伟大的人物一样，在这样一个关键时候对于这样一个关键问题，不作回答，于是他们两个人又都沉默起来。过了一两分钟，苔丝的呼吸变得更加均匀了，她握着安琪尔的那只手放松了，因为她睡着了。东方的地平线上出现了一道银灰色的光带，大平原上远处的部分在那道光带的映衬下，变得更加黑暗了，也变得离他更近了。那一片苍茫的整个景色，露出了黎明到来之前的常有的特征，冷漠、含蓄、犹豫。东边的石柱和石柱上方的横梁，迎着太阳矗立着，显得黑沉沉的。在石柱的外面可以看见火焰形状的太阳石，也可以看见在石柱和太阳石之间的牺牲石。晚风很快就停止了，石头上由杯形的石窝形成的小水潭也不再颤抖了。就在这个时候，东边低地的边缘上似乎有什么东西在移动——是一个黑色的小点。那是一个人的头，正在从太阳石后面的洼地向他们走来。克莱尔后悔没有继续往前走，但是现在只好决定坐着不动。那个人影径直向他们待的那一圈石柱走来。

他听见他的后面传来声音，那是有人走路的脚步声。他转过身去，看见躺在地上的柱子后面出现了一个人影；他还看见在他附近的右边有一个，在他左边的横梁下也有一个。曙光完全照在从西边走来的那个人的脸上，克莱尔在曙光里看见他个子高大，走路像军人的步伐。他们所有的人显然是有意包围过来的。苔丝说的话应验了！克莱尔跳起来，往四周看去，想寻找一件武器，寻找一件松动的石头，或者寻找一种逃跑的方法什么的，就在这个时候，那个离他最近的人来到了他的身边。

"这是没有用的，先生，"他说，"在这个平原上我们有十六个人，这儿整个地区都已经行动起来了。"

"让她把觉睡完吧！"在他们围拢来的时候，他小声地向他们恳求说。

直到这个时候，他们才看见她睡觉的地方，因此就没有表示反对，而是站在一旁守着，一动也不动，像周围的柱子一样。他走到她睡觉的那块石头跟前，握住她那只可怜的小手；那时候她的呼吸快速而又细弱，和一个比女人还要弱小的动物的呼吸一样。天越来越亮了，所有的人都在那儿等着，他们的脸和手都仿佛镀上了一层银灰色，而他们身体的其他部分则是黑色的，石头柱子闪耀着灰绿色的光，平原仍然是一片昏暗。不久天大亮了，太阳的光线照射在苔丝没有知觉的身上，透过她的眼睑射进她的眼里，把苔丝唤醒了。

"怎么啦，安琪尔？"她醒过来说，"他们已经来抓我了吧？"

"是的，最亲爱的，"他说，"他们已经来啦。"

"他们是该来啦，"她嘟哝着说，"安琪尔，我一直感到高兴——是的，一直感到高兴！这种幸福是不能长久的，因为它太过分了。我已经享够了这种幸福；现在我不会活着等你来轻视我了！"

她站起来，抖了抖身子，就往前走，而其他的人一个也没有动。

"现在可以走了。"她从容地说。

References

[1] 钱青.英国 19 世纪文学史 [M].北京：外语教学与研究出版社，2006.

Unit 17   James Joyce (1882—1904)

Life

James Augustine Aloysius Joyce (2 February 1882—13 January 1941) was an Irish novelist and poet. He contributed to the modernist avant-garde and is regarded as one of the most influential and important authors of the 20th century.

Joyce is best known for *Ulysses* (1922), a landmark work in which the episodes of Homer's Odyssey are paralleled in an array of contrasting literary styles, perhaps most prominent among these the stream of consciousness technique he utilised. Other well-known works are the short-story collection *Dubliners* (1914), and the novels *A Portrait of the Artist as a Young Man* (1916) and *Finnegans Wake* (1939). His other writings include three books of poetry, a play, occasional journalism and his published letters.

Joyce was born in 41 Brighton Square, Rathgar, Dublin—about half a mile from his mother's birthplace in Terenure—into a middle-class family on the way down. A brilliant student, he excelled at the Jesuit schools Clongowes and Belvedere, despite the chaotic family life imposed by his father's alcoholism and unpredictable finances. He went on to attend University College Dublin.

In 1904, in his early twenties, Joyce emigrated permanently to continental Europe with his partner (and later wife)Nora Barnacle. They lived in Trieste, Paris and Zurich. Though most of his adult life was spent abroad, Joyce's fictional universe centres on Dublin, and is populated largely by characters who closely resemble family members, enemies and friends from his time there. *Ulysses* in particular is set with precision in the streets and alleyways of the city. Shortly after the publication of *Ulysses*, he elucidated this preoccupation somewhat, saying, "For myself, I always write about Dublin, because if I can get to the heart of Dublin I can get to the heart of all the cities of the world. In the particular is contained the universal."

Plot of *Eveline*

A nineteen-year-old girl, Eveline struggles with poverty and the difficulties of supporting her family. She works very hard, at a store and also at home. She is planning to leave Ireland forever; her means of escape is a sailor named Frank, who promises her a new life. Frank treats her with tenderness, and he entertains her with stories about his travels around the world. Still, she loves her father and regrets the idea of leaving him in his old age. She remembers her mother's death, when she promised her mother to keep the home together as long as she could. In the end, however, she is too paralyzed and too frightened to leave Dublin.

Major Character

It is a short story about a girl called Eveline. She works hard all day at the shop bullied by her supervisor, at home doing all the housework and looking after two brothers; Being the breadwinner and the woman of the house, she has so many responsibilities. She is passive. She seems to see Frank only as harsh "protector" for a kind one. Eveline is incapable of becoming wiser. We know her future will be one of those some "commonplace sacrifices" like her mother.

Eveline

She sat at the window watching the evening invade the avenue. Her head was leaned against the window curtains and in her nostrils was the odour of dusty cretonne. She was tired.

Few people passed. The man out of the last house passed on his way home; she heard his footsteps clacking along the concrete pavement and afterwards crunching on the cinder path before the new red houses. One time there used to be a field there in which they used to play every evening with other people's children. Then a man from Belfast bought the field and built houses in it—not like their little brown houses but bright brick houses with shining roofs. The children of the avenue used to play together in that field—the Devines, the Waters, the Dunns, little Keogh the cripple, she and her brothers and sisters. Ernest, however, never played: he was too grown up. Her father used often to hunt them in out of the field with his blackthorn stick[1]; but usually little Keogh used to keep nix and call out when he saw her father coming. Still they seemed to have been rather happy then. Her father was not so bad then; and besides, her mother was alive. That was a long time ago; she and her brothers and sisters were all grown up her mother was dead. Tizzie Dunn was dead, too, and the Waters had gone back to England. Everything changes. Now she was going to go away like the others, to leave her home.

Home! She looked round the room, reviewing all its familiar objects which she had dusted once a week for so many years, wondering where on earth all the dust came from. Perhaps she would never see again those familiar objects from which she had never dreamed of being divided.

She had consented to go away, to leave her home. Was that wise? She tried to weigh each side of the question. In her home anyway she had shelter and food; she had those whom she had known all her life about her. Of course she had to work hard, both in the house and at business. What would they say of her in the Stores when they found out that she had run away with a fellow? Say she was a fool, perhaps; and her place would be filled up by advertisement. Miss Gavan would be glad. She had always had an edge on her, especially whenever there were people listening.

"Miss Hill, don't you see these ladies are waiting?"

"Look lively, Miss Hill, please."

She would not cry many tears at leaving the Stores.

But in her new home, in a distant unknown country, it would not be like that. Then she would be married—she, Eveline. People would treat her with respect then. She would not be treated as her mother had been. Even now, though she was over nineteen, she sometimes felt herself in danger of her father's violence. She knew it was that that had given her the palpitations. When they were growing up he had never gone for her like he used to go for Harry and Ernest, because she was a girl but latterly he had begun to threaten her and say what he would do to her only for her dead mother's sake. And now she had nobody to protect her. Ernest was dead and Harry, who was in the church decorating business, was nearly always down somewhere in the country. Besides, the invariable squabble for money on Saturday nights had begun to weary her unspeakably. She always gave her entire wages—seven shillings—and Harry always sent up what he could but the trouble was to get any money from her father. He said she used to squander the money, that she had no head, that he wasn't going to give her his hard-earned money to throw about the streets, and much more, for he was usually fairly bad on Saturday night. In the end he would give her the money and ask her had she any intention of buying Sunday's dinner. Then she had to rush out as quickly as she could and do her marketing, holding her black leather purse tightly in her hand as she elbowed her way through the crowds and returning home late under her load of provisions. She had hard work to keep the house together and to see that the two young children who had been left to hr charge went to school regularly and got their meals regularly. It was hard work—a hard life—but now that she was about to leave it she did not find it a wholly undesirable life.

She was about to explore another life with Frank. Frank was very kind, manly, open-hearted. She was to go away with him by the night-boat to be his wife and to live with him in Buenos Ayres[2] where he had a home waiting for her. How well she remembered the first time she had seen him; he was lodging in a house on the main road where she used to visit. It seemed a few weeks ago. He was standing at the gate, his peaked cap pushed back on his head and his hair tumbled forward over a face of bronze. Then they had come to know each other. He used to meet her outside the Stores every evening and see her home. He took her to see The Bohemian Girl[3] and she felt elated as she sat in an unaccustomed part of the theatre with him. He was awfully fond of music and sang a little. People knew that they were courting and, when he sang about the lass that loves a sailor, she always felt pleasantly confused. He used to call her Poppens out of fun. First of all it had been an excitement for her to have a fellow and then she had begun to like him. He had tales of distant countries. He had started as a deck boy at a pound a month on a ship of the Allan Line going out to Canada. He told her the names of the ships he had been on and the names of the different services. He had sailed through the Straits of Magellan[4] and he told her stories of the terrible Patagonians[5]. He had fallen on his feet in Buenos Ayres, he said, and had come over to the old country just for a holiday. Of course, her father had found out the affair and had forbidden her to have anything to say to him.

"I know these sailor chaps," he said.

One day he had quarreled with Frank and after that she had to meet her lover secretly.

The evening deepened in the avenue. The white of two letters in her lap grew indistinct. One was to Harry; the other was to her father. Ernest had been her favourite but she liked Harry too. Her father was becoming old lately, she noticed; he would miss her. Sometimes he could be very nice. Not long before, when she had been laid up for a day, he had read her out a ghost story and made toast for her at the fire. Another day, when their mother was alive, they had all gone for a picnic to the Hill of Howth. She remembered her father putting on her mother's bonnet to make the children laugh.

Her time was running out but she continued to sit by the window, leaning her head against the window curtain, inhaling the odour of dusty cretonne. Down far in the avenue she could hear a street organ playing. She knew the air Strange that it should come that very night to remind her of the promise to her mother, her promise to keep the home together as long as she could. She remembered the last night of her mother's illness; she was again in the close dark room at the other side of the hall and outside she heard a melancholy air of Italy. The organ-player had been ordered to go away and given sixpence. She remembered her father strutting back into the sickroom saying: "Damned Italians! Coming over here!"

As she mused the pitiful vision of her mother's life laid its spell on the very quick of her being—that life of commonplace sacrifices closing in final craziness. She trembled as she heard again her mother's voice saying constantly with foolish insistence:

"Derevaun Seraun! Derevaun Seraun!"

She stood up in a sudden impulse of terror. Escape! She must escape! Frank would save her. He would give her life, perhaps love, too. But she wanted to live. Why should she be unhappy? She had a right to happiness. Frank would take her in his arms, fold her in his arms. He would save her.

She stood among the swaying crowd in the station at the North Wall. He held her hand and she knew that he was speaking to her, saying something about the passage over and over again. The station was full of soldiers with brown baggages. Through the wide doors of the sheds she caught a glimpse of the black mass of the boat, lying in beside the quay wall, with illumined portholes. She answered nothing. She felt her cheek pale and cold and, out of a maze of distress, she prayed to God to direct her, to show her what was her duty. The boat blew a long mournful whistle into the mist. If she went, tomorrow she would be on the sea with Frank, steaming towards Buenos Ayres. Their passage had been booked. Could she still draw back after all he had done for her? Her distress awoke a nausea in her body and she kept moving her lips in silent fervent prayer.

A bell clanged upon her heart. She felt him seize her hand:

"Come!"

All the seas of the world tumbled about her heart. He was drawing her into them: he would drown her. She gripped with both hands at the iron railing.

"Come!"

No! No! No! It was impossible. Her hands clutched the iron in frenzy. Amid the seas she sent a cry of anguish.

"Eveline! Evvy!"

He rushed beyond the barrier and called to her to follow. He was shouted at to go on but he still called to her. She set her white face to him, passive, like a helpless animal. Her eyes gave him no sign of love or farewell or recognition.

 N o t e s

[1] 李木手杖

[2] 布宜诺斯艾利斯，城市名，阿根廷的首都。

[3] 波西米亚女孩

[4] 麦哲伦海峡，南美智利以南的一个海峡。

[5] 南美洲南端的巴塔哥尼亚印第安人。

 Q u e s t i o n s

1. Why did she want to escape?

2. Why didn't she escape?

3. If you were Eveline, what would you choose, to leave or not to leave home?

Analysis of *Eveline*

Eveline focuses on the theme of escape. She has been given a chance, yet in the end, the girl finds herself incapable of escape. Eveline has a complex psychological world. She lingers on the question whether to run away from home or not. On one hand, she want to leave home, because she feels lonely and unhappy. Her father was not kind any longer, and mother was not alive. She had to work hard, both in the house and at business. She was in danger of her father's violence and threats and she always spent her entire wages (7 shillings) on the whole family. The most important reason is that she wants to marry Frank and that means a new life, where she will be treated with respect. Eveline has learnt from her mother's experience—she sacrifices and ends life in craziness, so Eveline does not want to repeat her mother's life—she wants to escape.

However she can't make a decision to leave home. Home, for her means shelter and food. She had those whom she had known all her life about her and she has fear of being said as a fool to run away with a fellow. She was tortured by her promise to her mother—keep the home together as long as she could. The last reason is that she has a fear of being drowned in the seas. Maybe Frank is also a symbol of danger in her world.

Powerlessness, Imprisonment and paralysis are themes of the story. Eveline, a young woman, is in some way imprisoned. The imprisonment is often caused by a combination of circumstances: poverty, social pressure and family situation.

In this story, the 19 year old girl, Eveline's mental world symbolizes the dream's disillusionment and Frank is a symbol of new life and new experience or maybe a potential danger in the life of Eveline.

 中文译文

伊芙琳

她临窗而坐，看着夜色慢慢降临在林荫道上。她脑袋靠在窗帘上，嗅得出它肮脏的霉味。她累了。

有几个人走过，最后一个下班的人走在回家的路上，听得见水泥板人行道上响着他啪啪的脚步声，然后是踏在那幢新的红砖房子前面小径的沙沙声。那儿曾经是一块空旷地，每天傍晚他们常和别家的孩子在那儿玩耍。后来从贝尔法斯特来了一个人，买了这块地，建了一幢房——不像他们这样的小灰色房子，而是明亮的砖房，有光闪闪的屋顶。街上的孩子们以前总在那空地上做游戏，有狄怀恩家的、瓦特家的、但恩家的，还有拐子小吉奥，她和她的兄弟姐妹们。然而，恩尼斯从来不玩——他太大了。她父亲总是用藤条才能把他们赶回家去。尽管如此，那时大家似乎都很快活，父亲也不见得脾气那么坏。现在，她和兄弟姐妹们早已长大成人，母亲去世了，但恩也不在人间了，瓦特一家搬回了英格兰——一切都变了样。如今，她也要像其他人一样走了，要离开她的家。

啊，家！她的目光扫视屋里四围，仔细观察这么多年来她每礼拜掸扫一遍灰尘的每一件熟悉的家具和陈设。她老是觉得奇怪——这些灰尘是从什么鬼地方来的？也许她再也见不到这些东西了，她从未想过有跟它们分手的一天。

她已经答应离家出走。这明智吗？她努力衡量利弊。在家里，她好歹头上有片瓦顶

着，有顿饭充饥肠，还有这些与她生活密切相关的熟悉东西。当然啰，她得卖力做工，不管在家里还是在外头，都得拼命干。一旦店里人发现她与人私奔了，会说些什么闲话呢？也许会议论她傻，而报纸会登个广告，雇人来顶她的空位。嘉雯小姐会幸灾乐祸，她对她说话总那么刻薄苛求，特别是有人在旁听的时候更是如此。

"希尔小姐，你没看见这些女顾客在等着买东西吗？"

"手脚放麻利点，希尔小姐！"

她对离开店铺一点也不觉得不安和留恋。

可是，在那个新的家，在遥远异国的家，情况就迥然不同了。她——伊夫琳，将要结婚，人们会敬重她，她不用忍受和母亲同样的遭遇。她已经十九岁了，可是还时常处于父亲粗暴举止的威胁下，她常常为之心惊肉跳。长大后，父亲不会像殴打哈里和恩尼斯那样揍她了，因为她毕竟是个大姑娘。但近来父亲也开始恐吓她说，为了对得起死去的妈妈，要教训她一顿。现在没有人保护她了：恩尼斯死了，哈里是教堂的装修工，总是在乡下的什么地方干活。而且，那固定不变的每礼拜六晚上为了钱引起的争吵，也使她不厌其烦。她把干活挣来的钱（每周七先令）全部交给父亲，哈里也尽量往家里多寄点钱。但是从父亲手里拿一个毫子也不容易，他说她花钱大手大脚，一点头脑也没有，说他不想把自己辛辛苦苦挣来的钱让女儿扔到大街上，等等。所以一到礼拜六晚上，父亲的脾气总是特别不好。一场争吵之后，他掏出钱来，问女儿到底还想不想去买礼拜天的面包。她只好尽快跑步去做她的买办。她手里紧捏着黑皮钱袋子，一边用胳膊肘在人群里挤开一条路，很迟很迟，她才挎着沉甸甸的粮食口袋回到家里。维持这个家，还照顾下面两个小弟妹，让他们能继续上学，不让他们有一天饿肚皮，对她的确不是件简单的事。真艰难啊——艰难的生活！可是，如今当她即将告别这种生活，反而觉得生活并不那么令人不快了。

她就要和弗兰克一起开拓另一种新的生活。弗兰克既善良又有男子气概，还慷慨大方，她要和他乘夜班船走，去当他的妻子，一道在布宜诺斯艾利斯生活。在那儿，他早已为她准备了一个新的家。初次见他的情景她记得多清楚啊；那时他在大路上，一所她常去拜访的房子暂住。想起来就跟几个礼拜前的事儿一样。他站在大门边，尖顶帽子向脑后推着，头发翻在前面，盖住古铜色的脸庞。接着他们认识了对方。每天傍晚他都在仓库外面等她，送她回家。他带着她去看波希米亚姑娘，当她跟他坐在剧院里那个陌生的座位区，她是那么开心。他对音乐极其痴迷，自己还唱一点儿。别人都知道他俩是在谈恋爱，而且，当他唱到那个爱上水手的少女，她总是感觉又快活又迷糊。他过去老是开玩笑叫她的绰号。刚一开始，身边有个小伙子让她兴奋，后来她就开始喜欢他了。他有来自遥远国度的故事。他是在爱轮轮船公司的一艘跑加拿大线的船上，从一个月领一英镑的甲板手开始做起的。他跟她列数他上过的船和干过的活儿。他跟她讲他穿越麦哲伦海峡和遇到可怕的巴塔哥尼亚人的故事。他曾在布宜诺斯艾利斯安然脱险，他说，然后就来到了这个古老的国度，只待一个假期。自然，她父亲发现了这一切，接着便严禁她再跟他说一句话。

"我清楚这些海上的小子们是怎么一回事儿。"他说。

有一天他跟弗兰克吵了一架，从那之后，她就只能跟她的恋人悄悄地相会了。

街上的夜色更深了。她腿上那两封原本是呈白色的信慢慢地看不清了。一封是给哈里的，另一封给她的父亲。恩尼斯一直是她最爱的哥哥，但是她也喜欢哈里。她父亲最近老了许多，她注意到了；他会想念她的。有时候他也可以很好。不是太久以前，她因病躺倒了一整天，他给她读了一个鬼故事，还在火边给她烤了土司。还有一天，那是他们的母亲还在世的时候，一家人跑到豪特山野餐。她记得她父亲戴上了她母亲的软帽来逗孩子们笑。

她没剩什么时间了，但她还是坐在窗边，把头抵着窗帘，吸着棉布灰尘的气味。从大街的远处她可以听到有人拉着街头风琴。她识得那旋律。出奇的是那一个晚上响起的也是这个旋律，让她想起了对母亲的承诺，她许诺会尽力让这个家尽可能长地不散掉。她想起母亲病重的最后一夜；她在厅的那一边的那个封闭、幽暗的房间里，而外面传来了一支意大利的悲哀旋律。他们勒令那风琴手走得远远的，塞给了他六便士。她记得父亲撑回病房，嘴里说着："意大利人都该死！跑到这儿来了！"

当她眼前浮现着她母亲去世的那最后一小会儿——就是她平凡的生命终于在最后的疯狂闭幕中牺牲掉的那一刻，她颤抖着，好像耳畔又响起母亲愚顽的坚持重复着的声音：

"德日王色朗！德日王色朗！"

她在惊怖的推动中一下子站起来。逃！她一定得逃！弗兰克会拯救她的。他会给她生命，或许，还有爱。可她想要活着。为什么她就该不快活？她有权幸福。弗兰克会拥她入怀，紧紧抱住她。他会拯救她。

她站在北墙区码头摇晃攒动的人群里。他拉着她的手，她知道他在跟她说着些关于船票的什么话，翻来覆去的。码头上满是背着棕色行囊的士兵。穿过候船室的道道阔门，她瞥到轮船的巨大黑影，停靠在码头垣边，上面是一个个亮堂堂的舷窗。她没有答他的话。她感觉到自己的脸颊苍白寒冷，而且，出于让她困惑的苦恼，她祈祷神指引她，指示她什么才是她的职责。船上一声悲怆的汽笛透入雾层。如果走，明天她就跟弗兰克在海上，在船冒出的蒸汽中驶向布宜诺斯艾利斯。他们已经订好了船票。在他为她做了这一切以后她还可以反悔吗？她的苦恼在她身体里唤起一阵反胃，而她在无声又炙热的祷告中不停地动着嘴唇。

铃声叮咚打在她的心上。她感觉到他一把抓住她的手：

"来！"

全世界全部的海都在她的心头翻滚。他正拉着她往那里面去。他会淹死她的。她用两手抓住铁栏杆。

"来呀！"

不！不！不！不可能的。她狂暴地死死抠住那铁条。向着海中间发出一声痛苦的大喊。

"伊芙琳！伊芙！"

他冲过大堤，喊着叫她跟上来。他被人吼着催着往前走，可他还是在叫她。她把白白的脸庞转向他，被动的，像只无助的动物。她的眼睛没有给他或是爱或是告别或是认识他的任何信号。

Unit 18　Oscar Wilde (1854—1900)

Oscar Fingal O'Flahertie Wills Wilde (16 October 1854—30 November 1900) was an Irish playwright, novelist, essayist, and poet. After writing in different forms throughout the 1880s, he became one of London's most popular playwrights in the early 1890s. He is remembered for his epigrams, his novel The Picture of Dorian Gray, his plays, as well as the circumstances of his imprisonment and early death.

Wilde's parents were successful Anglo-Irish Dublin intellectuals. Their son became fluent in French and German early in life. At university, Wilde read Greats; he proved himself to be an outstanding classicist, first at Dublin, then at Oxford. He became known for his involvement in the rising philosophy of aestheticism, led by two of his tutors, Walter Pater and John Ruskin. After university, Wilde moved to London into fashionable cultural and social circles.

As a spokesman for aestheticism, he tried his hand at various literary activities: he published a book of poems, lectured in the United States and Canada on the new "English Renaissance in Art", and then returned to London where he worked prolifically as a journalist. Known for his biting wit, flamboyant dress and glittering conversation, Wilde became one of the best-known personalities of his day.

At the turn of the 1890s, he refined his ideas about the supremacy of art in a series of dialogues and essays, and incorporated themes of decadence, duplicity, and beauty into his only novel, *The Picture of Dorian Gray* (1890). The opportunity to construct aesthetic details precisely, and combine them with larger social themes, drew Wilde to write drama. He wrote *Salome* (1891) in French in Paris but it was refused a licence for England due to the absolute prohibition of Biblical subjects on the English stage. Unperturbed, Wilde produced four society comedies in the early 1890s, which made him one of the most successful playwrights of late Victorian London.

At the height of his fame and success, while his masterpiece, *The Importance of Being Earnest* (1895), was still on stage in London, Wilde had the Marquess of Queensberry prosecuted for criminal libel. The Marquess was the father of Wilde's lover, Lord Alfred Douglas. The charge carried a penalty of up to two years in prison. The trial unearthed evidence that caused Wilde to drop his charges and led to his own arrest and trial for gross indecencywith men. After two more trials he was convicted and imprisoned for two years' hard labour.

In 1897, in prison, he wrote *De Profundis*, which was published in 1905, a long letter which discusses his spiritual journey through his trials, forming a dark counterpoint to his earlier philosophy of pleasure. Upon his release he left immediately for France, never to return to Ireland or Britain. There he wrote his last work, *The Ballad of Reading Gaol* (1898), a long poem commemorating the harsh rhythms of prison life. He died destitute in Paris at the age of 46.

Comments on *The Picture of Dorian Gray*

Some commentaters have suggested that *The Picture of Dorian Gray* was influenced by the British Prime Minister Benjamin Disraeli's (anonymously published) first novel *Vivian Grey* (1826) as, "a kind of homage from one outsider to another." The name of Dorian Gray's love interest, Sibyl Vane, may be a modified fusion of the title of Disraeli's best known novel (Sybil) and Vivian Grey's love interest Violet Fane, who, like Sibyl Vane, dies tragically. There is also a scene in Vivian Grey in which the eyes in the portrait of a "beautiful being" move when its subject dies.

The Picture of Dorian Gray originally was a short novel submitted to Lippincott's Monthly Magazine for serial publication. In 1889, J. M. Stoddart, an editor for Lippincott, was in London to solicit short novels to publish in the magazine. On 30 August 1889, Stoddart dined with Oscar Wilde, Sir Arthur Conan Doyle and T. P. Gill at the Langham Hotel, and commissioned short novels from each writer. Conan Doyle promptly submitted *The Sign of the Four* (1890) to Stoddart, but Wilde was more dilatory; Conan Doyle's second Sherlock Holmes novel was published in the February 1890 edition ofLippincott's Monthly Magazine, yet Stoddart did not receive Wilde's manuscript for *The Picture of Dorian Gray* until 7 April 1890, nine months after having commissioned the novel from him.

The literary merits of *The Picture of Dorian Gray* impressed Stoddart, but, as an editor, he told the publisher, George Lippincott, "in its present condition there are a number of things an innocent woman would make an exception to...." Among the pre-publication deletions that Stoddart and his editors made to the text of Wilde's original manuscript were: (i) passages alluding to homosexuality and to homosexual desire; (ii) all references to the fictional book title Le Secret de Raoul and its author, Catulle Sarrazin; and (iii) all "mistress" references to Gray's lovers, Sibyl Vane and Hetty Merton.

The Picture of Dorian Gray was published on 20 June 1890, in the July issue of Lippincott's Monthly Magazine. British reviewers condemned the novel's immorality, and said condemnation was so controversial that the W H Smith publishing house withdrew every copy of the July 1890 issue of Lippincott's Monthly Magazine from its bookstalls in railway stations. Consequent to the harsh criticism of the 1890 magazine edition, Wilde ameliorated the homoerotic references, in order to simplify the moral message of the story. In the magazine edition (1890), Basil tells Lord Henry how he "worships" Dorian, and begs him not to "take away the one person that makes my life absolutely lovely to me." In the magazine edition, Basil concentrates upon love, whereas, in the book edition (1891), Basil concentrates upon his art, saying to Lord Henry, "the one person who gives my art whatever charm it may possess: my life as an artist depends on him."

The magazine edition of *The Picture of Dorian Gray* (1890) was expanded from thirteen to twenty chapters; and the magazine edition's final chapter was divided into two chapters, the nineteenth and twentieth chapters of the book edition of *The Picture of Dorian Gray* (1891). Wilde's textual additions were about "fleshing out of Dorian as a character" and providing details of his ancestry that made his "psychological collapse more prolonged and more convincing."

The introduction of the James Vane character to the story develops the socio-economic background of the Sibyl Vane character, thus emphasising Dorian's selfishness and foreshadowing James's accurate perception of the essentially immoral character of Dorian Gray; thus, he correctly deduced Dorian's dishonourable intent towards Sibyl. The sub-plot about James Vane's dislike of Dorian gives the novel a Victorian tinge of class struggle. With such textual changes, Oscar Wilde meant to diminish the moralistic controversy about the novel *The Picture of Dorian*

Gray.

In the 19th century, the critical reception of the novel *The Picture of Dorian Gray* (1890) was poor. The book critic of *The Irish Times* said, *The Picture of Dorian Gray* was "first published to some scandal." Such book reviews achieved for the novel a "certain notoriety for being 'mawkish and nauseous', 'unclean', 'effeminate' and 'contaminating'." Such moralistic scandal arose from the novel's homoeroticism, which offended the sensibilities (social, literary, and aesthetic) of Victorian book critics. Yet, most of the criticism was personal, attacking Wilde for being a hedonist with a distorted view of conventional morality of Victorian Britain. In the 30 June 1890 issue, the Daily Chronicle the book critic said that Wilde's novel contains "one element ... which will taint every young mind that comes in contact with it." In the 5 July 1890 issue, of the Scots Observer, the reviewer asked, "Why must Oscar Wilde 'go grubbing in muck-heaps?'" In response to such criticism, Wilde obscured the homoeroticism of the story and expanded the personal background of the characters.

Major Characters

Dorian Gray

He is a handsome, narcissistic young man enthralled by Lord Henry's "new" hedonism. He indulges in every pleasure and virtually every "sin", studying its effect upon him, which eventually leads to his death.

Basil Hallward

He is a deeply moral man, the painter of the portrait, and infatuated with Dorian, whose patronage realises his potential as an artist. The picture of Dorian Gray is Basil's masterpiece.

Lord Henry "Harry" Wotton

He is an imperious aristocrat and a decadent dandy who espouses a philosophy of self-indulgent hedonism. Initially Basil's friend, he neglects him for Dorian's beauty. The character of witty Lord Harry is a critique of Victorian culture at the Fin de siècle-of Britain at the end of the 19th century. Lord Harry's libertine world view corrupts Dorian, who then successfully emulates him. To the aristocrat Harry, the observant artist Basil says, "You never say a moral thing, and you never do a wrong thing." Lord Henry takes pleasure in impressing, influencing, and even misleading his acquaintances (to which purpose he bends his considerable wit and eloquence) but appears not to observe his own hedonistic advice, preferring to study himself with scientific detachment. His distinguishing feature is total indifference to the consequences of his actions. Scholars generally accept the character is partly inspired by Wilde's friend Lord Ronald Gower.

Sibyl Vane

She is a talented actress and singer, she is the beautiful girl, of a poor family, with whom Dorian falls in love. Her love for Dorian ruins her acting ability, because she no longer finds pleasure in portraying fictional love as she is now experiencing real love in her life. She kills herself on learning that Dorian no longer loves her; at that, Lord Henry likens her to Ophelia, in Hamlet.

James Vane

He is Sibyl's brother, a sailor who leaves for Australia. He is very protective of his sister, especially as their mother cares only for Dorian's money. Believing that Dorian means to harm Sibyl, James hesitates to leave, and promises vengeance upon Dorian if any harm befalls her. After Sibyl's suicide, James becomes obsessed with killing Dorian, and stalks him, but a hunter accidentally kills James. The brother's pursuit of vengeance upon the lover (Dorian Gray), for the death of the sister (Sibyl) parallels that of Laertes vengeance against Prince Hamlet.

Alan Campbell

He is a chemist and one-time friend of Dorian who ended their friendship when Dorian's libertine reputation devalued such a friendship. Dorian blackmails Alan into destroying the body of the murdered Basil Hallward; Campbell later shoots himself dead.

Lord Fermor

He is Lord Henry's uncle, who tells his nephew, Lord Henry Wotton, about the family lineage of Dorian Gray.

Adrian Singleton

He is A youthful friend of Dorian's, whom he evidently introduced to opium addiction, which induced him to forge a cheque and made him a total outcast from his family and social set.

Victoria, Lady Wotton

She is Lord Henry's wife, whom he treats disdainfully; she divorces him.

Introduction to the *Preface to The Picture of Dorain Gray*

Consequent to the harsh criticism of the magazine edition of the novel, the textual revisions to *The Picture of Dorian Gray* included a preface in which Wilde addressed the criticisms and defended the reputation of his novel. To communicate how the novel should be read, in the Preface, Wilde explains the role of the artist in society, the purpose of art, and the value of beauty. It traces Wilde's cultural exposure to Taoism and to the philosophy of Chuang Tsǔ (Zhuang Zhou). Earlier, before writing the preface, Wilde had written a book review of Herbert Giles's translation of the work of Zhuang Zhou. The preface was first published in the 1891 edition of the novel; nonetheless, by June 1891, Wilde was defending *The Picture of Dorian Gray* against accusations that it was a bad book.

In the essay *The Artist as Critic*, Oscar Wilde said that:

The honest ratepayer and his healthy family have no doubt often mocked at the dome-like forehead of the philosopher, and laughed over the strange perspective of the landscape that lies beneath him. If they really knew who he was, they would tremble. For Chuang Tsǔ spent his life in preaching the great creed of Inaction, and in pointing out the uselessness of all things.

Preface to *The Picture of Dorian Gray*

The artist is the creator of beautiful things. To reveal art and conceal the artist is art's aim. The critic is he who can translate into another manner or a new material his impression of beautiful things.

The highest as the lowest form of criticism is a mode of autobiography. Those who find ugly meanings in beautiful things are corrupt without being charming. This is a fault.

Those who find beautiful meanings in beautiful things are the cultivated. For these there is hope. They are the elect to whom beautiful things mean only beauty.

There is no such thing as a moral or an immoral book. Books are well written, or badly written. That is all.

The nineteenth century dislike of realism is the rage of Caliban[1] seeing his own face in a glass.

The nineteenth century dislike of romanticism is the rage of Caliban not seeing his own face in a glass. The moral life of man forms part of the subject-matter of the artist, but the morality of art consists in the perfect use of an imperfect medium.

No artist desires to prove anything. Even things that are true can be proved. No artist has ethical sympathies. An ethical sympathy in an artist is an unpardonable mannerism of style. No artist is ever morbid. The artist can express everything.

Thought and language are to the artist instruments of an art. Vice and virtue are to the artist materials for an art. From the point of view of form, the type of all the arts is the art of the musician. From the point of view of feeling, the actor's craft is the type. All art is at once surface and symbol. Those who go beneath the surface do so at their peril.

Those who read the symbol do so at their peril. It is the spectator, and not life, that art really mirrors. Diversity of opinion about a work of art shows that the work is new, complex, and vital. When critics disagree, the artist is in accord with himself. We can forgive a man for making a useful thing as long as he does not admire it. The only excuse for making a useless thing is that one admires it intensely.

All art is quite useless.

 N o t e s

[1] The character in Shakespeare's Tempest is halfman, half-monster.

 Q u e s t i o n s

1.What did the author want to express in this preface?

2.Do you agree with the author's idea about art?

3.Try to learn as much as possible about aestheticism.

 中文译文

《道林·格雷的画像》 序言

艺术家是美的作品的创造者。艺术的宗旨是展示艺术本身，同时把艺术家隐藏起来或将新的材料表达出来。

自传体是批评的最高形式，也是最低形式。在美的作品中发现丑恶含义的人是堕落

的，而且堕落得一无可爱之处。这是一种罪过。

在美的作品中发现美的含义的人是有教养的。这种人是有希望的。认为美的作品仅仅意味着美的人才是上帝的选民。

书无所谓道德的或不道德的。书有写得好的或写得糟的。仅此而已。

十九世纪对现实主义的憎恶，犹如从镜子里照见自己面孔的凯列班的狂怒。

十九世纪对浪漫主义的憎恶，犹如从镜子里照不见自己面孔的凯列班的狂怒。人的精神生活只是艺术家创作题材的一部分，艺术的道德则在于完美地运用并不完美的手段。

艺术家并不企求证明任何事情。即使是天经地义的事情也是可以证明的。艺术家没有伦理上的好恶。艺术家如在伦理上有所臧否，那是不可原谅的矫揉造作。艺术家从来没有病态的。艺术家可以表现一切。

思想和语言是艺术家艺术创作的手段。邪恶与美德是艺术家艺术创作的素材。从形式着眼，音乐家的艺术是各种艺术的典型；从感觉着眼，演员的技艺是典型。一切艺术同时既有外观，又有象征。有人要钻到外观底下去，那由他自己负责。

有人要解释象征意义，那由他自己负责。其实，艺术这面镜子反映的是照镜者，而不是生活。对一件艺术品的看法不一，说明这件作品新颖、复杂、重要。批评家们尽可意见分歧，艺术家不会自相矛盾。一个人做了有用的东西可以原谅，只要他不自鸣得意。一个人做了无用的东西，只要他视若至宝，也可宽宥。

一切艺术都是毫无用处的。

The Nightingale and the Rose

A nightingale overhears a student complaining that his professor's daughter will not dance with him, as he is unable to give her a red rose. The nightingale visits all the rose-trees in the garden, and one of the roses tells her there is a way to produce a red rose, but only if the nightingale is prepared to sing the sweetest song for the rose all night with her heart pressing into a thorn, sacrificing her life. Seeing the student in tears, and valuing his human life above her bird life, the nightingale carries out the ritual. She impales herself on the rose-tree's thorn so that her heart's blood can stain the rose. The student takes the rose to the professor's daughter, but she again rejects him because another man has sent her some real jewels and "everybody knows that jewels cost far more than flowers." The student angrily throws the rose into the gutter, returns to his study of metaphysics, and decides not to believe in true love anymore.

Comments on *The Nightingale and the Rose*

Words would always be Wilde's most powerful defense, and no other writer in the English language has used them with the same elegance. He made an art form of the single and the perfectly poised, contradictory phrase. The beautiful scenery with flowers, rich colors, romance and beauties unfolded before us.

Another technique Oscar Wilde used is his ingenious design. There was no red rose in the student's garden, which suggested that the student had no true love in his heart. The process of looking for the red rose was full of difficulties, which implies the true love is not easy to obtain. Sometimes it needs the life's devotion as depicted Nightingale. Consequently, the true love is so precious and hard to obtain. Despite the life cost of the bird, the student threw away the red rose in the gutter in the end, then the student returned to his reading. As a student, he neither had money nor practical skills to nourish his love. So he could do nothing but return to his world and read his book. So the perfectness of word choice and ingenious design are in accordance to his idea of aestheticism.

Oscar wanted to express the pursuit of beauty and true love. Short as the Nightingale's life remains in the world, yet her image lives everlasting in our heart. She sings for her love and dies for her dream. This is the true meaning of life and reflects Oscar's view of beauty and life.

The Nightingale and the Rose

"She said that she would dance with me if I brought her red roses," cried the young Student, "but in all my garden there is no red rose."

From her nest in the oak tree the Nightingale heard him and she looked out through the leaves and wondered.

"No red rose in all my garden." he cried, and his beautiful eyes filled with tears." Ah, I have read all that the wise men have written, and all the secrets of philosophy are mine, yet for a red rose my life is made wretched."

"Here at last is a true lover," said the Nightingale. "Night after night have I sung of him, and now I see him."

"The Prince gives a ball tomorrow night," murmured the young student," and my love will be there. If bring her a red rose she will dance with me till dawn. I shall hold her in my arms, and she will lean her head upon my shoulder. But there is no red rose in my garden, so I shall sit lonely and my heart will break."

"Here, indeed, is the true lover," said the nightingale. Surely love is a wonderful thing. It is more precious than emeralds and opals.

"The musicians will play upon their stringed instruments," said the young Student, "and my love will dance to the sound of the harp and the violin. She will dance in his hands, and wept."

"Why is he weeping?'" asked a green Liard, as he ran past him with his face in his tail in the air.

"Why, indeed?" whispered a Daisy to his neighbor, in a soft, low voice.

"He is weeping for a red rose," said the Nightingale.

"For a red rose?" they cried, " how very ridiculous." and the little Lizard who was something of a cynic, laughed outright. But the Nightingale understood the Student's sorrow, and sat silent in the Oak-tree.

Suddenly she spread her brown wings for flight, and soared into the air. She passed through the grove like a shadow and like a shadow and like a shadow she sailed across the garden.

In the centre of the grass-plot stood a beautiful Rose-tree, and when she saw it she flew over to it. "Give me a red rose", she cried, "and I will sing you my sweetest song."

But the Tree shook its head.

"MY ROSES ARE WHITE," It answered, "as white as the foam of the sea, and whiter than the snow upon the mountain. But go to my brother who grows round the old sun-dial, and perhaps will give you what you want."

So the Nightingale flew over to the Rose-tree that was growing round the old sun-dial.

"Give me a red rose," she cried, "and I will sing you my sweetest song." But the Tee shook its head.

"My roses are yellow," it answered, "as yellow as the hair of the maiden, and yellower than the daffodil [1] that blooms in the meadow. But go to my brother who brother who grows beneath the Student's window, and perhaps he will give you what you want."

So the Nightingale flew over to the Rose-tree That was growing beneath the Student's window.

"Give me a red rose," she cried, " and I will sing you my sweetest song." But the Tree Shook its head.

"My roses are red," it answered, " as red as the feet of the dove, and redder than the great fans of coral[2]. But the winter has chilled my veins, and the frost has nipped my buds, and the storm has broken my branches, and I shall have no roses at all this year."

"One red rose is all that I want," cried the Nightingale, "only one red rose. Is there no way by which I can get it?"

"There is a way." said the Tree, "but it is so terrible that I dare not tell it to you."

"Tell it to me." said the Nightingale, "I am not afraid."

"If you want a red rose," said the Tree. "you must build it out of music by moonlight, and stain it with your own heart's blood. You must sing to me with your breast against a thorn. All night long you must sing to me, and the thorn must pierce your heart, and your life-blood must flow into my veins, and become mine."

"Death is a great price to pay for a red rose," cried the Nightingale,m "and life is very dear to all. Yet love is better than life, and what is the heart of a bird compared to the heart of a man?"

So she spread her wings for flight, and soared into the air. She swept over the garden like a shadow, and like a shadow she sailed through the grove.

The young Student was still lying on the grass, and the tears were not yet dry in his beautiful eyes. "Be happy," cried the Nightingale, "be happy, you shall have your red rose I will build it out of music by moonlight, and stain it with my own heart's blood. All that I ask you be a true lover."

The Student looked up from the grass, and listened, but he could not understand what the Nightingale was saying to him. But the Oak-tree understood and felt sad, for he was very fond of the little Nightingale. "Sing me one last song," he whispered. "I shall feel lonely when you are gone."

So the Nightingale sang to the Oak-tree, and her voice was like water bulling from a silver jar. When she had finished her song, the Student got up.

"She has form," he said to himself, as he walked away. "That cannot be denied. But has she got feeling? I am afraid not. In fact, like most artists, she is all style without any sincerity." And he went to his room, and lay down on his bed , and after a time, he fell asleep.

And when the Moon shone in the heaven, the Nightingale flew to the Rose-tree, and set her breast against the thorn. All night long she sang with her breast against the thorn, and cold crystal Moon leaned down and listened. All night long she sang, and the thorn went into her breast, and her life-blood ebbed away from her.

She sang first of love in the heart of a boy and a girl. And on the topmost spray of the Rose-tree there blossomed a marvelous rose, petal following petal, as song followed song.

But the Tree cried to the Nightingale pressed closer against the thorn, "Press closer, little Nightingale pressed closer against the thorn, and louder and louder are the song, for she sang of the birth of passion in the soul of a man and a maid."

And a delicate flush of pink came into the leaves of the rose, like the flush in the face of the bridegroom when he kissed the lips of the bride. But the thorn had not yet reached her heart so the rose's heart remained white.

And the Tree cried to the Nightingale to press closer against the thorn. "Press closer, little Nightingale," cried the Tree, "or the Day will come before the rose is finished."

So the Nightingale pressed closer against the thorn, and the thorn touched her heart, and a fierce pang of pain shot through her. Bitter, bitter was the pain, and wilder and wilder grew her song, for she sang of the Love that is perfected by Death, of the Love that dies not in the tomb.

And the marvelous rose became crimson[3]. Crimson was the girdle[4] of pearls, and crimson as a ruby was the heart.

But the Nightingale's voice grew fainter and a film came over her eyes. Fainter and fainter grew her song, and she felt something chocking her in her throat.

Then she gave last burst of music. The white Moon heard it, and she forgot the dawn, and lingered on in the sky .The Red Rose heard it, and trembled, and trembled all over with ecstasy[5], and opened its in the cold morning air.

"Look, look," cried the Tree, "the rose is finished now." But the Nightingale made no answer, for she was lying dead in the grass, with the thorn in her heart.

And at noon the Student opened his window and looked out.

"Why, what a wonderful piece of luck." he cried, "here is the reddest rose I have ever seen." And he leaned down and plucked it.

Then he put on his hat, and ran up to Professor's daughter with the rose in his hand.

"You said that you would dance with me if I brought you a red rose," cried the Student. "Here is the reddest rose in all the world. You will wear it tonight next your heart, and as we dance together it will tell you how I love you."

But the girl frowned.

"I am afraid it will not go with my dress." she answered, "and besides, the Chamberlain's nephew has sent me some jewels, and everybody knows that jewels cost more than flowers."

"Well, upon my word, you are very ungrateful," said the Student angrily; and he threw the rose into the street, where it fell into the gutter[6].

"What a silly thing Love is." said the Student as he walked away, "In fact it is quite unpractical, and as in this age to be practical is everything, I shall go back to Philosophy."

So he returned to his room to his room and pulled out a great dusty book, and began to read.

Notes

[1] 水仙花

[2] 珊瑚色

[3] 深红色

[4] 围绕

[5] 狂喜

[6] 排水沟

Questions

1. How can Wilde describe the beauty of the rose?

2. What did Wilde want to express in this story?

3. What is aestheticism according to this story?

中文译文

夜莺与玫瑰

"她说我若为她采得红玫瑰，便与我跳舞。"青年学生哭着说，"但我全园里何曾有一朵红玫瑰？"

夜莺在橡树上巢中听见，从叶丛里往外看，心中诧异。

青年哭道："我园中并没有红玫瑰！"他秀眼里满含着泪珠。"呀！幸福倒靠着这些区区小东西！古圣贤书我已读完，哲学的玄秘我已彻悟，然而因为求一朵红玫瑰不得，我的生活便这样难堪。"

夜莺叹道："真情人竟在这里。我夜夜歌唱他，如今我见着他了。"

青年又低声自语："王子今晚宴会跳舞，我的爱人也将与会。我若为她采得红玫瑰，她就和我跳舞直到天明，我若为她采得红玫瑰，我将把她抱在怀里，她的头，在我肩上枕着，她的手，在我手中握着。但我园里没有红玫瑰，我只能寂寞地坐着，我的心将要粉碎了。"

"这真是个真情人。"夜莺又说着。

青年说："乐师们将在乐坛上弹弄丝竹，我那爱人也将按着弦琴的音节舞蹈。"

绿色的小壁虎说："他为什么哭泣？"说完就竖起尾巴从他跟前跑过。

金盏花亦向她的邻居低声探问："唉，怎么？"夜莺说："他为着一朵红玫瑰哭泣。"

他们叫道："为着一朵红玫瑰！真笑话！"那小壁虎本来就刻薄，于是大笑。

然而夜莺了解那青年烦恼里的秘密，她静坐在橡树枝上细想"爱"的玄妙。

忽然她张起棕色的双翼，冲天飞去。她穿过那树林如同影子一般，如同影子一般的，她飞出了花园。

草地当中站着一株艳美的玫瑰树，她看见那树，向前飞去。

她叫道："给我一朵鲜红玫瑰，我为你唱我最婉转的歌。"

可是那树摇头。

"我的玫瑰是白的，"那树回答她，"白如海涛的泡沫，白过山巅上的雪。请你到古日晷旁找我兄弟，或者他能应你所求。"

于是夜莺飞到日晷旁边那丛玫瑰上。

她又叫道："给我一朵鲜红玫瑰，我为你唱最醉人的歌。"

可是那树摇头。

"我的玫瑰是黄的，"那树回答她，"黄如琥珀座上人鱼神的头发，黄过割草人未割以前的金水仙。请你到那边青年窗下找我兄弟，或者他能应你所求。"

于是夜莺飞到青年窗下那丛玫瑰上。

她仍旧叫道："给我一朵鲜红玫瑰，我为你唱最甜美的歌。"

可是那树摇头。

那树回答她道："我的玫瑰是红的，红如白鸽的脚趾，红过海底岩下扇动的珊瑚。但是严冬已冻僵了我的血脉，寒霜已啮伤了我的萌芽，暴风已打断了我的枝干，今年我不能再开了。"

夜莺央告说："一朵红玫瑰就够了。只要一朵红玫瑰！请问有什么法子没有？"

那树答道："有一个法子，只有一个，但是太可怕了，我不敢告诉你。""告诉我吧，"夜莺勇敢地说，"我不怕。"

那树说道："你若要一朵红玫瑰，你需在月色里用音乐制成，然后用你自己的心血染她。你需将胸口顶着一根尖刺，为我歌唱。你需整夜地为我歌唱，那刺需刺入你的心头，你生命的血液得流到我的心房里变成我的。"

夜莺叹道："拿死来买一朵红玫瑰，代价真不小，谁的生命不是宝贵的？然而'爱'比生命更可贵，一个鸟的心又怎能和人的心比？"

忽然她张起棕色的双翼，冲天飞去。她穿过那花园如同影子一般，她荡出了那树林子。

那青年仍旧僵卧在草地上方才她离去的地方，他那副秀眼里的泪珠还没有干。

夜莺喊道："高兴吧，快乐吧；你将要采到你那朵红玫瑰了。我将用月下的歌音制成她，用我心脏的血液染红它。我向你所求的报酬，仅是要你做一个真挚的情人。"

青年从草里抬头侧耳静听，但是他不懂夜莺对他所说的话。

那橡树却是懂得，他觉得悲伤，因为他极爱怜那枝上结巢的小夜莺。他轻声说道："唱一首最后的歌给我听罢，你离去后，我要感到无限的寂寥了。"

于是夜莺为橡树歌唱，她恋别的音调就像在银瓶里涌溢的水浪一般的清越。她唱罢时，那青年站起身。他一面走出那树林，一面自语道："那夜莺的确有些姿态。这是人所不能否认的；但是她有感情吗？我怕没有。实在她就像许多美术家一般，尽是仪式，没有诚心。"于是他回到自己室中，躺在他的小草垫的床上想念他的爱人；过了片时他就睡去。

待月亮升到天空，放出她的光艳时，那夜莺也就来到玫瑰枝边，将胸口插在刺上。她胸前插着尖刺，整夜地歌唱，那晶莹的月亮倚在云边静听。她整夜地，啭着歌喉，那刺越插越深，她生命的血液渐渐溢去。最先她歌颂的是稚男幼女心胸里爱恋的诞生。于是那玫瑰的顶尖枝上结了一苞卓绝的玫瑰蕾，歌儿一首连着一首地唱，花瓣一片跟着一片地开。

但是那树还催迫着夜莺紧插那枝刺。"靠紧那刺，小夜莺。"那树连声的叫唤。

于是夜莺越紧插入那尖刺，越扬声地唱她的歌，因她这回所歌颂的是男子与女子性灵里烈情的诞生。如今那玫瑰瓣上生了一层娇嫩的红晕，如同初吻新娘时新郎的绛颊。但是那刺还未插到夜莺的心房，所以那花心尚留着白色，因为只有夜莺的心血可以染红玫瑰花心。

那树复催迫着夜莺紧插那枝刺，"靠紧那刺，小夜莺，"那树连声的叫唤，"不然，玫瑰还没开成，晓光就要闯来了。"

于是夜莺紧紧插入那枝刺，那刺居然插入了她的心，但是一种奇痛穿过她的全身。那卓绝的玫瑰于是变作鲜红，如同东方的天色。花的外瓣红同烈火，花的内心赤如绛玉。

夜莺的声音越唱越模糊了，她的双翅拍动起来，她的眼上起了一层薄膜。她的歌声模糊了，她觉得喉间哽咽了。于是她献出绝唱，白色的残月听见，忘记天晓，挂在空中停着。那玫瑰听见，凝神战栗着，在清冷的晓风里瓣瓣地开放。

那树叫道："看，这玫瑰已制成了。"然而夜莺并不回答，她已躺在乱草里死去，那刺还插在心头。日午时青年开窗往外看。

他叫道："怪事，真是难遇的幸运，这儿有朵红玫瑰，这样好的玫瑰，我生来从没有见过。"说着便俯身下去折了这花。于是他戴上帽子，跑往教授家去，手里拈着红玫瑰。青年叫道，"你说过我若为你采得红玫瑰，你便同我跳舞。这里有一朵全世界最珍贵的红玫瑰。你可以将她插在你的胸前，我们同舞的时候，这花便能告诉你，我怎样地爱你。"那女郎只皱着眉头。她答说，"我怕这花不能配上我的衣裳；而且大臣的侄子送我许多珠宝首饰，人人都知道珠宝比花草贵重。"

青年怒道："我敢说你是个无情义的人。"她便将玫瑰掷在街心，掉在车辙里，让一个车轮轧过。

青年走着自语道："爱好傻呀。在这个世界里，首先要有实用的东西，我还是回到我的哲学和玄学书上去吧。"于是他回到房中取出一本笨重的、满堆着尘土的大书埋头细读。

Unit 19　D. H. Lawrence (1885—1930)

Life

David Herbert Richards Lawrence (11 September 1885—2 March 1930) was an English novelist, poet, playwright, essayist, literary critic and painter. His collected works represent, among other things, an extended reflection upon the dehumanising effects of modernity and industrialisation. Some of the issues Lawrence explores are emotional health, vitality, spontaneity and instinct.

Lawrence's opinions earned him many enemies and he endured official persecution, censorship, and misrepresentation of his creative work throughout the second half of his life, much of which he spent in a voluntary exile which he called his "savage pilgrimage." At the time of his death, his public reputation was that of a pornographer who had wasted his considerable talents. E. M. Forster, in an obituary notice, challenged this widely held view, describing him as, "The greatest imaginative novelist of our generation." Later, the influential Cambridgecritic F. R. Leavis championed both his artistic integrity and his moral seriousness, placing much of Lawrence's fiction within the canonical "great tradition" of the English novel.

He was the fourth child of Arthur John Lawrence, a barely literate miner at Brinsley Colliery, and Lydia, a former pupil teacher who, owing to her family's financial difficulties, had to do manual work in a lace factory, Lawrence spent his formative years in the coal mining town of Eastwood, Nottinghamshire. The house in which he was born, in Eastwood, 8a Victoria Street, is now the D. H.

Lawrence Birthplace Museum. His working-class background and the tensions between his parents provided the raw material for a number of his early works. Lawrence would return to this locality and often wrote about nearby Underwood, calling it; "the country of my heart," as a setting for much of his fiction. Despite common misconception he is not related to T. E. Lawrence.

In the autumn of 1908 the newly qualified Lawrence left his childhood home for London. While teaching in Davidson Road School, Croydon, he continued writing. Some of the early poetry, submitted by Jessie Chambers, came to the attention of Ford Madox Ford, then known as Ford Hermann Hueffer and editor of the influential The English Review. Hueffer then commissioned the story Odour of Chrysanthemums which, when published in that magazine, encouragedHeinemann, a London publisher, to ask Lawrence for more work. His career as a professional author now began in earnest, although he taught for another year. Shortly after the final proofs of his first published novel, The White Peacock, appeared in 1910, Lawrence's mother died of cancer. The young man was devastated, and he was to describe the next few months as his "sick year." It is clear that Lawrence had an extremely close relationship with his mother, and his grief became a major turning point in his life, just as the death of Mrs. Morel is a major turning point in his autobiographical novel Sons and Lovers, a work that draws upon much of the writer's provincial upbringing.

After the traumatic experience of the war years, Lawrence began what he termed his "savage pilgrimage", a time of voluntary exile. He escaped from Britain at the earliest practical opportunity, to return only twice for brief visits, and with his wife spent the remainder of his life travelling. Thiswanderlust took him to Australia, Italy, Ceylon , the United States, Mexico and the South of France.

Lawrence abandoned Britain in November 1919 and headed south, first to the Abruzzo region in central Italy and then onwards to Capri and the Fontana Vecchia in Taormina, Sicily. From Sicily he made brief excursions to Sardinia, Monte Cassino, Malta, Northern Italy, Austria and Southern Germany. Many of these places appeared in his writings. New novels included *The Lost Girl* (for which he won the James Tait Black Memorial Prize for fiction), *Aaron's Rodand the fragment titled Mr Noon* (the first part of which was published in the Phoenix anthology of his works, and the entirety in 1984). He experimented with shorter novels or novellas, such as *The Captain's Doll, The Fox* and *The Ladybird*. In addition, some of his short stories were issued in the collection *England, My England and Other Stories*. During these years he produced a number of poems about the natural world in *Birds, Beasts and Flowers*. Lawrence is widely recognised as one of the finest travel writers in the English language. *Sea and Sardinia*, a book that describes a brief journey undertaken in January 1921, is a recreation of the life of the inhabitants of Sardinia. Less well known is the memoir of Maurice Magnus, *Memoirs of the Foreign Legion*, in which Lawrence recalls his visit to the monastery of Monte Cassino. Other non-fiction books include two responses to *Freudian psychoanalysis and Movements in European History*, a school textbook that was published under a pseudonym, a reflection of his blighted reputation in Britain.

Lawrence continued to write despite his failing health. In his last months he wrote numerous poems, reviews and essays, as well as a robust defence of his last novel against those who sought to suppress it. His last significant work was a reflection on the Book of Revelation, titled *Apocalypse*. After being discharged from a sanatorium, he died on 2 March 1930 at the Villa Robermond in Vence, France, from complications of tuberculosis, without even reaching the age of 45. Frieda Weekley commissioned an elaborate headstone for his grave bearing a mosaic of his adopted emblem of the phoenix. After Lawrence's death, Frieda lived with Angelo Ravagli on the ranch in Taos and eventually married him in 1950. In 1935 Ravagli arranged, on Frieda's behalf, to have Lawrence's body exhumed and cremated and his ashes brought back to the ranch to be interred there in a small chapel amid the mountains of New Mexico.

Sons and Lovers

Sons and Lovers is a 1913 novel by the English writer D. H. Lawrence, originally published by B.W. HuebschPublishers. The Modern Library placed it ninth on their list of the 100 best novels of the 20th century. While the novel initially received a lukewarm critical reception, along with allegations of obscenity, it is today regarded as a masterpiece by many critics and is often regarded as Lawrence's finest achievement.

Plot of *Sons and Lovers*

Part I

The refined daughter of a "good old burgher family", Gertrude Coppard meets a rough-hewn miner, Walter Morel, at a Christmas dance and falls into a whirlwind romance characterised by physical passion. But soon after her marriage to Walter, she realises the difficulties of living off his meagre salary in a rented house. The couple fight and drift apart and Walter retreats to the pub after work each day. Gradually, Mrs. Morel's affections shift to her sons beginning with the oldest, William.

As a boy, William is so attached to his mother that he doesn't enjoy the fair without her. As he grows older, he defends her against his father's occasional violence. Eventually, he leaves their Nottinghamshire home for a job in London, where he begins to rise up into the middle class. He is engaged, but he detests the girl's superficiality. He dies and Mrs. Morel is heartbroken, but when Paul catches pneumonia she rediscovers her love for her second son.

Part II

Both repulsed by and drawn to his mother, Paul is afraid to leave her but wants to go out on his own, and needs to experience love. Gradually, he falls into a relationship with Miriam, a farmer's daughter who attends his church. The two take long walks and have intellectual conversations about books but Paul resists, in part because his mother disapproves. At Miriam's family's farm, Paul meets Clara Dawes, a young woman with, apparently, feminist sympathies who has separated from her husband, Baxter.

After pressuring Miriam into a physical relationship, which he finds unsatisfying, Paul breaks with her as he grows more intimate with Clara, who is more passionate physically. But even she cannot hold him and he returns to his mother. When his mother dies soon after, he is alone.

Lawrence summarised the plot in a letter to Edward Garnett on 12 November 1912:

It follows this idea: a woman of character and refinement goes into the lower class, and has no satisfaction in her own life. She has had a passion for her husband, so her children are born of passion, and have heaps of vitality. But as her sons grow up she selects them as lovers–first the eldest, then the second. These sons are urged into life by their reciprocal love of their mother–urged on and on. But when they come to manhood, they can't love, because their mother is the strongest power in their lives, and holds them. It's rather like Goethe and his mother and Frau von Stein and Christiana–As soon as the young men come into contact with women, there's a split. William gives his sex to a fribble, and his mother holds his soul. But the split kills him, because he doesn't know where he is. The next son gets a woman who fights for his soul–fights his mother. The son loves his mother–all the sons hate and are jealous of the father. The battle goes on between the mother and the girl, with the son as object. The mother gradually proves stronger, because of the ties of blood. The son decides to leave his soul in his mother's hands, and, like his elder brother go for passion. He gets passion. Then the split begins to tell again. But, almost unconsciously, the mother realises what is the matter, and begins to die. The son casts off his mistress, attends to his mother dying. He is left in the end naked of everything, with the drift towards death.

Comments on *Sons and Lovers*

On the one hand, the context of *Sons and Lovers* includes the background of this novel as well as the author D.H. Lawrence's life experiences. Living in a highly industrialized world during the twentieth century, the westerners keep their attention on the acquirement of knowledge instead of pursuing their lust and desire which extinguishes their human nature gradually. However, Lawrence is the exception who writes from his inner world without hesitation. He was born in the year of 1885, and his father was a coal miner while his mother was a well educated middle class woman. This book actually is the autobiography of Lawrence's early life. And he uses this novel to show his concern with the ever-increasing environmental contaminations as well as his dissatisfaction on the indelible social class distinctions. Moreover, it also expresses the conflict between the marriage and sex. In his novel, Lawrence is deeply engaged by the questions of how individuals are shaped by their social environments, how historical forces influence on people's lives, how class, wealth, and gender help to determine people's fates. Most of his novels are rooted in a realistically rendered social setting and in a precise historical time. His novel is a mirror of the times which reveals social injustices in every aspect of life.

On the other hand, one of the major features of his novel is that he depicts lots of beautiful sceneries and they often fit the situation well. And through the way of describing, the characters' moods become more vivid and rich.

For example, in the first chapter Lawrence describes the scenery in front of the Morel's house: "The sky overhead throbbed and pulsed with light. The glow sank quickly off the field; the earth and the hedges smoked dusk." This sentence not only shows the quick change of the weather but also the life which can change in a blink of an eye. Many years before, Mrs. Morel was still a high educated pretty lady rounded by numerous gentlemen, and now she is struggled with poverty, mistreats by his uneducated husband. When she sees this scene at this moment, she is overwhelmed by lots of different feelings include regret, desperate, sadness and hopelessness.

These sentences are good because of the bleak nightfall scenes fit well with the complicated feelings of Mrs. Morel.

Another major feature of his novel is his great psychology describing. He uses different ways to fulfill the character by describe the heart monologue, remembering, feeling and so on. For instance, Mrs. Morel said to herself once: "I wait, −I wait, and what I wait for can never come."from this sentence we could see a desperate housewife sighs deeply for her hopeless life. And it also shows that women used to have such a low position, they are mostly functioned as a machine for raising their children and there is no meaning in life when they get married.

Major Characters

Walter Morel

He is a collier, who had been a handsome, dashing youngman when he got married. But after a few years of marriage he proved to be an irresponsible breadwinner and drunkard, and his wife hated him for what he had once meant to her and for what he now was.

Mrs. Morel

She is the mother. She was a good parent; her children loved her. The oldest son, William, was successful in his work but he longed to go to London, where he had promise of a better job. After he had gone, Mrs. Morel turned to Paul for the companionship and love she had found in William.

Paul

He liked to paint. More sensitive than his brothers and sisiter, he was closer to Mrs. Morel than any of the others.

Miriam Leivers

she was a strange girl, but her inner charm attracted Paul. Mrs. Morel, like any others, did not care for Miriam.

Clara Dawes

She was separated from her husband, Baxter Dawes. She was five years Paul's senior, but a beautiful woman whose loveliness charmed him. Although Clara became his mistress, she refused to divorce her husband and marry Paul.

Introduction to Chapter 12

For this chapter, Paul had passion for Clara. They had such a good time together. But his mother still felt very uncomfortable with Paul's love.

Chapter 12 Passion (excerpt)

He was walking to the station—another mile! The train was near Nottingham. Would it stop before the tunnels? But it did not matter; it would get there before dinner-time. He was at Jordan's. She would come in half an hour. At any rate, she would be near. He had done the letters. She would be there. Perhaps she had not come. He ran downstairs. Ah! he saw her through the glass door. Her shoulders stooping a little to her work made him feel he could not go forward; he could not stand. He went in. He was pale, nervous, awkward, and quite cold. Would she misunderstand him? He could not write his real self with this shell.

"And this afternoon," he struggled to say. "You will come?"

"I think so," she replied, murmuring.

He stood before her, unable to say a word. She hid her face from him. Again came over him the feeling that he would lose consciousness. He set his teeth and went upstairs. He had done everything correctly yet, and he would do so. All the morning things seemed a long way off, as they do to a man under chloroform. He himself seemed under a tight band of constraint. Then there was his otherself, in the distance, doing things, entering stuff in a ledger, and he watched that far-off him carefully to see he made no mistake.

But the ache and strain of it could not go on much longer. He worked incessantly. Still it was only twelve o'clock. As if he had nailed his clothing against the desk, he stood there and worked, forcing every stroke out of himself. It was a quarter to one; he could clear away. Then he ran downstairs.

"You will meet me at the Fountain at two o'clock," he said.

"I can't be there till half-past."

"Yes!" he said.

She saw his dark, mad eyes.

"I will try at a quarter past."

And he had to be content. He went and got some dinner. All the time he was still under chloroform, and every minute was stretched out indefinitely. He walked miles of streets. Then he thought he would be late at the meeting-place. He was at the Fountain at five past two. The torture of the next quarter of an hour was refined beyond expression. It was the anguish of combining the living self with the shell. Then he saw her. She came! And he was there.

"You are late," he said.

"Only five minutes," she answered.

"I'd never have done it to you," he laughed.

She was in a dark blue costume. He looked at her beautiful figure.

"You want some flowers," he said, going to the nearest florist's.

She followed him in silence. He bought her a bunch of scarlet, brick-red carnations. She put them in her coat, flushing.

"That's a fine colour!" he said.

"I'd rather have had something softer," she said.

He laughed.

"Do you feel like a blot of vermilion walking down the street?" he said.

She hung her head, afraid of the people they met. He looked sideways at her as they walked. There was a wonderful close down on her face near the ear that he wanted to touch. And a certain heaviness, the heaviness of a very full ear of corn that dips slightly in the wind, that there was about her, made his brain spin. He seemed to be spinning down the street, everything going round.

As they sat in the tramcar[1], she leaned her heavy shoulder against him, and he took her hand. He felt himself coming round from the anaesthetic[2], beginning to breathe. Her ear, half-hidden among her blonde hair, was near to him. The temptation to kiss it was almost too great. But there were other people on top of the car. It still remained to him to kiss it. After all, he was not himself, he was some attribute of hers, like the sunshine that fell on her.

He looked quickly away. It had been raining. The big bluff of the Castle rock was streaked with rain, as it reared above the flat of the town. They crossed the wide, black space of the Midland Railway, and passed the cattle enclosure that stood out white. Then they ran down sordid Wilford Road.

She rocked slightly to the tram's motion, and as she leaned against him, rocked upon him.

He was a vigorous, slender man, with exhaustless energy. His face was rough, with rough-hewn features, like the common people's; but his eyes under the deep brows were so full of life that they fascinated her. They seemed to dance, and yet they were still trembling on the finest balance of laughter. His mouth the same was just going to spring into a laugh of triumph, yet did not. There was a sharp suspense about him. She bit her lip moodily. His hand was hard clenched over hers.

They paid their two halfpennies at the turnstile and crossed the bridge. The Trent was very full. It swept silent and insidious[3] under the bridge, travelling in a soft body. There had been a great deal of rain. On the river levels were flat gleams of flood water. The sky was grey, with glisten of silver here and there. In Wilford churchyard the dahlias were sodden with rain—wet black-crimson balls. No one was on the path that went along the green river meadow, along the elm-tree colonnade.

There was the faintest haze over the silvery-dark water and the green meadow-bank, and the elm-trees that were spangled with gold. The river slid by in a body, utterly silent and swift, intertwining among itself like some subtle, complex creature. Clara walked moodily beside him.

"Why," she asked at length, in rather a jarring tone, "did you leave Miriam?"

He frowned.

"Because I WANTED to leave her," he said.

"Why?"

"Because I didn't want to go on with her. And I didn't want to marry."

She was silent for a moment. They picked their way down the muddy path. Drops of water fell from the elm-trees.

"You didn't want to marry Miriam, or you didn't want to marry at all?" she asked.

"Both," he answered, "both!"

They had to manoeuvre to get to the stile, because of the pools of water.

"And what did she say?" Clara asked.

"Miriam? She said I was a baby of four, and that I always HAD battled her off."

Clara pondered over this for a time.

"But you have really been going with her for some time?" she asked.

"Yes."

"And now you don't want any more of her?"

"No. I know it's no good."

She pondered again.

"Don't you think you've treated her rather badly?" she asked.

"Yes; I ought to have dropped it years back. But it would have been no good going on. Two wrongs don't make a right."

"How old ARE you?" Clara asked.

"Twenty-five."

"And I am thirty," she said.

"I know you are."

"I shall be thirty-one—or AM I thirty-one?"

"I neither know nor care. What does it matter!"

They were at the entrance to the Grove. The wet, red track, already sticky with fallen leaves, went up the steep bank between the grass. On either side stood the elm-trees like pillars along a great aisle, arching over and making high up a roof from which the dead leaves fell. All was empty and silent and wet. She stood on top of the stile, and he held both her hands. Laughing, she looked down into his eyes. Then she leaped. Her breast came against his; he held her, and covered her face with kisses.

They went on up the slippery, steep red path. Presently she released his hand and put it round her waist.

"You press the vein in my arm, holding it so tightly," she said.

They walked along. His finger-tips felt the rocking of her breast. All was silent and deserted. On the left the red wet plough-land showed through the doorways between the elm-boles and their branches. On the right, looking down, they could see the tree-tops of elms growing far beneath them, hear occasionally the gurgle of the river. Sometimes there below they caught glimpses of the full, soft-sliding Trent, and of water-meadows dotted with small cattle.

"It has scarcely altered since little Kirke White used to come," he said.

But he was watching her throat below the ear, where the flush was fusing into the honey-white, and her mouth that pouted disconsolate[4]. She stirred against him as she walked, and his body was like a taut string.

Halfway up the big colonnade of elms, where the Grove rose highest above the river, their forward movement faltered to an end. He led her across to the grass, under the trees at the edge of the path. The cliff of red earth sloped swiftly down, through trees and bushes, to the river that glimmered and was dark between the foliage. The far-below water-meadows were very green. He and she stood leaning against one another, silent, afraid, their bodies touching all along. There came a quick gurgle from the river below.

"Why," he asked at length, "did you hate Baxter Dawes?"

She turned to him with a splendid movement. Her mouth was offered him, and her throat; her eyes were half-shut; her breast was tilted as if it asked for him. He flashed with a small laugh, shut his eyes, and met her in a long, whole kiss. Her mouth fused with his; their bodies were sealed and annealed. It was some minutes before they withdrew. They were standing beside the public path.

"Will you go down to the river?" he asked.

She looked at him, leaving herself in his hands. He went over the brim of the declivity and began to climb down.

"It is slippery," he said.

"Never mind," she replied.

The red clay went down almost sheer. He slid, went from one tuft of grass to the next, hanging on to the bushes, making for a little platform at the foot of a tree. There he waited for her, laughing with excitement. Her shoes were clogged with red earth. It was hard for her. He frowned. At last he caught her hand, and she stood beside him. The cliff rose above them and fell away below. Her colour was up, her eyes flashed. He looked at the big drop below them.

"It's risky," he said; "or messy, at any rate. Shall we go back?"

"Not for my sake," [5] she said quickly.

"All right. You see, I can't help you; I should only hinder. Give me that little parcel and your gloves. Your poor shoes!"

They stood perched on the face of the declivity, under the trees.

"Well, I'll go again," he said.

Away he went, slipping, staggering, sliding to the next tree, into which he fell with a slam that nearly shook the breath out of him. She came after cautiously, hanging on to the twigs and grasses. So they descended, stage by stage, to the river's brink. There, to his disgust, the flood had eaten away the path, and the red decline ran straight into the water. He dug in his heels and brought himself up violently. The string of the parcel broke with a snap; the brown parcel bounded down, leaped into the water, and sailed smoothly away. He hung on to his tree.

"Well, I'll be damned!" he cried crossly. Then he laughed. She was coming perilously down.

"Mind!" he warned her. He stood with his back to the tree, waiting. "Come now," he called, opening his arms.

She let herself run. He caught her, and together they stood watching the dark water scoop at the raw edge of the bank. The parcel had sailed out of sight.

"It doesn't matter," she said.

He held her close and kissed her. There was only room for their four feet.

"It's a swindle!" [6] he said. "But there's a rut where a man has been, so if we go on I guess we shall find the path again."

The river slid and twined its great volume. On the other bank cattle were feeding on the desolate flats. The cliff rose high above Paul and Clara on their right hand. They stood against the tree in the watery silence.

"Let us try going forward," he said; and they struggled in the red clay along the groove a man's nailed boots had made. They were hot and flushed. Their barkled shoes hung heavy on their steps. At last they found the broken path. It was littered with rubble from the water, but at any rate it was easier. They cleaned their boots with twigs. His heart was beating thick and fast.

 **N o t e s**

[1] 有轨电车

[2] 麻醉的，麻药

[3] 阴险的，潜伏的

[4] 惆怅的，孤独的

[5] 不要为了我的缘故

[6] 骗局，欺骗

 Q u e s t i o n s

1. How does Lawrence describe the passion between them?

2. What is the purpose of environment description?

3. How do you understand Paul's love for Clara?

 **中文译文**

第十二章　激情（节选）

他朝车站走去——还有一英里！火车快到诺丁汉姆了。火车会在隧道前面停吗？不过这也没什么，它在午饭前总会开到的。他到了乔丹厂。半小时后她才会来的。不管怎么说，她快来了。他办完了来往的信件。她应该到了。也许她就没来。他奔下楼梯。啊！透过玻璃门他看到了她。她正俯着身子在干活，这让他觉得他不能贸然上前去打扰她，可他又忍不住不去。终于，他进去了，他的脸色苍白，神情紧张局促，但他却装出十分镇静的样子。她不会误解他吧？他在表面上不能露出本来面目啊！

"今天下午，"他艰难地说，"你会来吗？"

"我想会的。"她喃喃答道。

他站在她面前，竟然一句话也说不出来，她把脸从他面前扭开。那种没有知觉的感觉仿佛又笼罩了他，他紧咬着牙上了楼。他把每件事都干得很完善，他还要这么干下去。整个上午他好像被打了一剂麻醉药似的，看什么都像隔得老远，恍恍惚惚的，他自己仿佛被一个紧身箍紧紧地憋得喘不过气来。他的另一个自我则在远处干活，在分类账上记着账，他全神贯注地监视着远处的自我，生怕他弄出什么差错来。

可他不能老是这样痛苦而又紧张。他一直不停地干着，可表还是才指在十二点钟。他的衣服仿佛都被钉在桌子上，他就那样站在那儿不停地干着，强迫自己写着每一笔。好不容易到了十二点三刻，他可以结束了。于是他奔下了楼。

"两点钟在喷泉那儿跟我见面。"他说。

"我得要两点半才能到那儿呢。"

"好吧！"他说。

她看了他一眼，看到了那双有些痴狂的黑眼睛。

"我尽量在两点一刻到。"

他只得同意。然后他去吃了午饭。这一段时间他仿佛被打了麻醉药，每一分钟都无限地延长了。他在街上不停地走着，不知走了多少英里。后来，想起自己可能不能按时赶到约会地点了。两点过五分，他赶到了喷泉。接下来的那一刻钟对他来说简直是一种无法忍受的酷刑，这是一种强压住自己本性使他不至于忘形的痛苦。他终于看见她了。她来了！他早已在等她了。

"你迟到了。"他说。

"只晚了五分钟。"她答道。

"我对你可从来没有迟到过。"他笑着说。

她穿着一身深蓝色的衣服，他看着她那窈窕的身段。

"你需要几朵花。"说着，他就朝最近的花店走去。

她在后面默默地跟着他，他给她买了一束石竹花，有鲜红的，有朱红的。她脸色通红，把花别在衣服上。

"这颜色很漂亮！"他说。

"我倒宁愿要那种色彩柔和些的。"她说。

他笑了。

"你是否觉得你在街上走着就像一团火？"他说。

她低着头，生怕碰上别人。他们并肩走着，他侧过脸来看着她，她颊边那缕可爱的头发遮住了耳朵，他真想去摸一下。她有一种丰腴的韵味，就像风中那微微低垂的饱满的稻穗一样，这让他感到一阵目眩。他在路上晕晕乎乎地走着，仿佛在飞转，周围一切都在身边旋转。

乘电车时，她那浑圆的肩膀斜靠在他身上，他握住了她的手。他感觉自己仿佛从麻醉中苏醒过来，开始呼吸了。她那半掩在金发中的耳朵离他很近。他真想吻吻它，可是车上还有别人。她的耳朵会留着让他去吻的。尤其是，他仿佛不是他自己，而是她的什么附属品，就好像照耀在她身上的阳光。

他赶紧移开了眼光。外面一直在下着雨，城堡下巨大的峭岩高耸在小镇的平地上，雨水从上面直泻下来，留下一道水迹。电车穿过中部火车站那片宽广的黑沉沉的广场，经过了白色的牛场，然后沿着肮脏的威福路开去。

她的身子随着电车的行驶轻轻晃动着，由于她紧靠着他，他的身体也随之晃动。他是一个精力充沛、身材修长的男人，浑身好像有着使不完的精力。他的脸长得粗糙，五官粗犷，貌不出众，但浓眉下的那对眼睛却生气勃勃，不由得叫她着了迷。这双眼睛似乎在闪烁，然而实际却十分平静，目光与笑声保持着一定的协调。他的嘴巴也是如此，正要绽出得意的笑容却又戛然而止。他身上有一种显而易见的疑虑。她沉思般地咬着自己的嘴唇，他紧紧地握着她的手。

他们在旋转式栅门前付了两枚半便士，然后走上了桥。特伦特河水已经涨得很高，河水在桥下悄悄急速地流过。不久前的这场雨可不小，河面上是一大片粼光闪闪的洪水。天空也是灰蒙蒙的，到处闪耀着银光。威福教堂里的大丽菊由于浸透了雨水，成了一团湿漉漉的黑红色花球。河边草地和榆树廊边上的小道上看不到一个人影。

黑黑的河面上泛着银光，一股淡淡的薄雾弥漫在绿荫覆盖的堤岸和斑斑点点的榆树上空。河水浑然成一体，像怪物似的互相缠绕着，悄悄地以极快的速度飞奔而去。克莱拉一声不响地在他身边走着。

"为什么，"她慢慢地用一种相当刺耳的语调问他，"为什么你与米丽亚姆分手？"

他皱了皱眉。

"因为我想离开她。"他说。

"为什么？"

"因为我不愿意再和她继续下去，而且我也不想结婚。"

她沉默了片刻。他们沿着泥泞小道小心翼翼地走着，雨滴不停地从榆树上往下掉。

"你是不想跟米丽亚姆结婚呢，还是你根本不愿结婚？"

"两者兼而有之。"他答道，"兼而有之。"

因为路上积了一摊摊的水，他们只好跨上了阶梯。

"那么她怎么说呢？"克莱拉问。

"米丽亚姆吗？她说我只是一个四岁的小孩子，说我老是挣扎着想把她推开。"

克莱拉听后沉思了一会儿。"不过你和她交朋友的时间不算短了吧？"

"是的。"

"你现在不想再要她了？"

"是的，我知道这样下去没什么好处。"

她又陷入了深思。

"你不觉得你这样对她有点太狠心了吗？"她问。

"是有点。我应该早几年就和她分手，但再继续下去是一点好处也没有的，错上加错并不能得出正确的结论。"

"你多大了？"克莱拉问。

"二十五了。"

"我已经三十了。"她说道。

"我知道你三十了。"

"我就要三十一了，——也许我已经三十一了吧？"

"我不知道，也不在乎这个。这有什么关系！"

他们走进了园林的入口处，潮湿的红土路上沾满了落叶，穿过草丛一直通向陡峭的堤岸。两侧的榆树就像一条长廊两旁的柱子一般竖立在那儿，枝丫互相交叉，形成了一个高高的拱顶，枯叶就是从那上面落下来的。周围的一切都是那么空旷、寂静和潮湿。她站在最上面一层的台阶上，他握着她的双手，她则笑着望着他的双眼，然后跳了下来。她的胸脯紧贴在他的胸前。他搂住了她，在她脸上吻着。

他们一路沿着这条滑溜溜的陡峭的红土路走着。此时，她松开了他的手，让他搂住她的腰。

"你搂得这么紧，我胳膊上的血脉都不通了。"她说。

他们就这么走着。他的指尖可以感觉到她的乳房的晃动。四周静悄悄的，一个人也没有。左边，透过榆树干和枝丫间的缝隙可以看到湿漉漉的红色耕地。右边，往下看，可以看见远处下面的榆树树顶，还可以听见汩汩的流水声。间或还可以瞥见下面涨满了河水的特伦特河在静静地流淌着，以及点缀在浅滩上的那几头小牛。

"自从柯克·怀特小时候来过这儿以后，这儿几乎没有什么变化。"他说。

虽然他说着话，但他却一直盯着她不满地撅着的嘴巴以及耳朵下的脖子，脸上的红晕在脖子这儿与皮肤的蜜乳色交融在一起。她走路时，挨着他的身子微微晃动着，而他则挺得像根绷紧的弦。

走到榆树林的一半，就到了河边这片园林的最高处。他们踟蹰不前，停了下来。他带她穿过路旁树下的草地。红色的悬崖陡峭地斜向河流。河水掩映在一片树木和灌木丛下，闪着银光。下面远处的浅滩绿油油地绵延成一大片。他和她互相依偎着站在那儿，默默无言，心中惶惶不安。他们的身体一直紧紧地依偎着。河水在下面汩汩地流着。

"你为什么恨巴克斯特·道伍斯？"他终于问道。

她优雅地向他转过身来，向他仰起脖子，翘起嘴巴，双目微闭，她的胸向前倾俯，她像在邀请他来吻。他轻声笑了，随即闭上了眼，同她长长地热吻着。她的嘴和他的仿佛融为一体，两人紧紧地拥抱着，就这样过了许久才分开。他们一直站在这条暴露在众人眼里的小路边上。

"你想不想到下面河边上去？"他问。

她看了看他，任凭他扶着。他走到斜坡边上，开始往下爬。

"真滑。"他说。

"没关系。"她应道。

红土坡比较陡峭，他打着滑，从一簇野草丛滑到另外一簇，抓住灌木丛，向树根下的一小块平地冲去。他在树下等着她，兴奋地笑着。她的鞋上沾满了红土，这使她走起来非常困难。他皱起了眉头。最后他终于抓住了她的手，她就站在他身边了。他们头顶悬崖，脚踏峭壁。她的脸颊鲜红，双眼熠熠闪光。他看了看脚下的那一段陡坡。

"这太冒险了，"他说，"而且不管怎么说，也太脏了些，我们往回走吧！"

"可别是因为我的缘故啊。"她赶紧说。

"好吧，你瞧，我帮不了你，只会碍事。把你的小包和手套给我。瞧你这双可怜的鞋子！"

他们站在树下，在斜坡面上休息了一会儿。

"好了，我们又该出发了。"他说。

他离开了，连摔带滚地滑到了下一棵树旁，他的身体猛然撞到树上，吓得他半天喘不过气来。她在后面小心翼翼地跟着,紧紧揪着树枝和野草。就这样他们一步步地走到了河边。倒霉的是河水已经将小道给淹没了,红土斜坡直接伸到了河里。保罗脚跟深深隐入泥土,身子拼命往上爬。突然小包的绳子"啪"的一声断了,棕色的小包掉了下来,滚进了河里,顺水漂走了。他紧紧地抓着一棵树。

"哎呀,我真该死!"他怒气冲冲地大叫着。接着,又开始哈哈大笑起来,她正冒险往下走。

"小心!"他提醒着。他背靠着树站在那儿等着她。"来吧。"他张开双臂喊道。

她放心地往下跑,他抓住她,两人一起站在那儿看着黑黝黝的河水拍打着河岸,那个包早已漂得不见影子了。

"没关系。"她说。

他紧紧地搂住她吻着。这块地方刚刚能容纳得下四只脚。

"这是一个圈套!"他说,"不过那边有条野径,上面有人走过,所以如果咱们顺着沟往下走的话,我想我们一定能重新找到这条路。"

河水打着旋儿飞快地流着。河对岸,荒芜的浅滩上有牛在吃草。悬崖就矗立在保罗和克莱拉的右边。他们背靠树干,站在死水一般的寂静中。

"我们往前试着走走。"他说。于是他们在红土中沿着沟里某个人钉靴踩出来的脚印,挣扎着往前走去。他们走得浑身发热,满脸通红。他们的鞋上粘着厚厚的泥,沉重而艰难地走着。终于,他们找到了那条中断了的小道。路上布满了河边冲来的碎石头,不管怎样,在上面行走可比在泥泞中跋涉好多了。他们用树枝把靴子上的泥剔干净。他的心急促地狂跳着。

References

[1] 张伯香,龙江.英美经典小说赏析[C].武汉:武汉大学出版社,2005.

Unit 20   Virginia Woolf (1882—1941)

Life

Virginia Woolf was born in London, the daughter of Julia Jackson Duckworth, a member of the Duckworth publishing family, and Sir Leslie Stephen, a literary critic, and the founder of the *Dictionary of National Biography*. Leslie Stephen's first wife had been the daughter of the novelist William Makepeace Thackeray.

Woolf, who was educated at home, grew up at the family home at Hyde Park Gate. From her early age, she was extremely attached to her father. Woolf's youth was shadowed by series of emotional shocks. Woolf's mother died from influenza, when Virginia was in her early teens. Stella Duckworth, her half sister, took her mother's place, but died two years later. Woolf's father suffered a slow death from stomach cancer, he died in 1904. When Virginia's brother Thoby died in 1906, she had a prolonged mental breakdown.

Following the death of her father, Woolf moved with her sister and two brothers to the house in Bloomsbury.

The Voyage Out (1915) was Virginia Woolf's first novel. Set in South America, it tells of the emotions of tourists somewhere near the Amazon River. The whole scene is imaginary; Woolf had never been there, but the story can be read as an allegory of artistic creation. This work, which received mixed reviews, was followed by *Night and Day* (1919), a realistic novel about the lives of two friends, Katherine and Mary. *Jacob's Room* (1922) was based upon the life and death of her brother Thoby.

With *To the Lighthouse* (1927) and *The Waves* (1931) Woolf established herself as one of the leading writers of modernism. *The Waves* is perhaps Woolf's most difficult novel. It follows in soliloquies the lives of six persons from childhood to old age.

Much of her writing reflected her inner conflicts. Woolf developed innovative literary techniques in order to reveal women's experience and find an alternative to the dominating views of reality.

Mrs. Dalloway (1925) formed a web of boring and depressing thoughts of several groups of people. Like Joyce's *Ulysses*, the action takes place in a single day, in this case in June in 1923. There is little action, but much movement in time from present to past and back again. The central figure, Clarissa Dalloway, married to Richard Dalloway, is a wealthy London hostess, who spends her day in London preparing for her evening party. Clarissa recalls her life before World War I, her friendship with the unconventional Sally Seton, and her relationship with Peter Walsh. At her party she never meets the shell-shocked veteran Septimus Smith, one of the first Englishmen to enlist in the war. Sally returns as Lady Rossetter, Peter Walsh is still enamored with Mrs. Dalloway, the prime minister arrives, and Smith commits suicide.

After the final attack of mental illness, Woolf loaded her pockets full of stones and drowned herself in the river, near her Sussex home, on March 28, 1941. On her note to her husband she wrote: "I have a feeling I shall go mad. I cannot go on longer in these terrible times. I hear voices and cannot concentrate on my work. I have fought against it but cannot fight any longer. I owe all my happiness to you but cannot go on and spoil your life."

Virginia Woolf's concern with feminist themes is dominant in *A Room of One's Own* (1929). In it she made her famous statement: "A woman must have money and a room of her own if she is to write fiction."

As an essayist Woolf was prolific. She published some 500 essays in periodicals and collections, beginning 1905. To find her own voice, she read and wrote voraciously, but it was not until Woolf was middle-aged she felt confident in her craft. Characteristic for Woolf's essays are dialogic nature of style. A number of her writings are autobiographical. In the essay on the art of Walter Sickert, which was inspired by her visit in his retrospective show, Woolf asked how words can express colour, and answered that all great writers are great colorists: "Each of Shakespeare's plays has its dominant colour. And each writer differs of course as a colourist..." (Walter Sickert: *A Conversation,* 1934). Woolf's rejection of an authoritative voice links her essays to the tradition of Montaigne.

Plot of *Mrs. Dalloway*

Clarissa Dalloway goes around London in the morning, getting ready to host a party that evening. The nice day reminds her of her youth spent in the countryside in Bourton and makes her wonder about her choice of husband; she married the reliable Richard Dalloway instead of the enigmatic and demanding Peter Walsh, and she "had not the option" to be with Sally Seton. Peter reintroduces these conflicts by paying a visit that morning.

Septimus Warren Smith, a First World War veteran suffering from deferred traumatic stress, spends his day in the park with his Italian-born wife Lucrezia, where Peter Walsh observes them. Septimus is visited by frequent and indecipherable hallucinations, mostly concerning his dear friend Evans who died in the war. Later that day, after he is prescribed involuntary commitment to a psychiatric hospital, he commits suicide by jumping out of a window.

Clarissa's party in the evening is a slow success. It is attended by most of the characters she has met in the book, including people from her past. She hears about Septimus' suicide at the party and gradually comes to admire this stranger's act, which she considers an effort to preserve the purity of his happiness.

Comments on *Mrs. Dalloway*

In *Mrs Dalloway,* all of the action, except flashbacks, takes place on a day in June. It is an example of free indirect discourse storytelling (not stream of consciousness because this story moves between the consciousnesses of every character in a form of discourse): every scene closely tracks the momentary thoughts of a particular character.

Because of structural and stylistic similarities, *Mrs Dalloway* is commonly thought to be a response to James Joyce's *Ulysses*, a text that is often considered one of the greatest novels of the twentieth century.

The novel has two main narrative lines involving two separate characters; within each narrative there is a particular time and place in the past that the main characters keep returning to in their minds. For Clarissa, it is her charmed youth at Bourton keeps intruding into her thoughts on this day in London. For Septimus, it is his time as a soldier during the Great War keeps intruding, especially in the form of Evans, his comrade.

The novel follows the themes as Mental illness and feminism. Septimus, as the shell-shocked war hero, operates as a pointed criticism of the treatment of mental illness and depression.

Woolf goes beyond criticizing the treatment of mental illness. Using the characters of Clarissa and Rezia, she makes the argument that people can only interpret Septimus' shell-shock according to their cultural norms. Throughout the course of the novel Clarissa does not meet Septimus. Clarissa's reality is vastly different from that of Septimus; his presence in London is unknown to Clarissa until his death becomes idle chat at her party. Her use of Septimus as the stereotypically traumatized man from the war is her way of showing that there were still reminders of the First World War in 1923 London.

Themes

The novel has two main narrative lines involving two separate characters (Clarissa Dalloway and Septimus Smith); within each narrative there is a particular time and place in the past that the main characters keep returning to in their minds. For Clarissa, the "continuous present" (Gertrude Stein's phrase) of her charmed youth at Bourton keeps intruding into her thoughts on this day in London. For Septimus, the "continuous present" of his time as a soldier during the "Great War" keeps intruding, especially in the form of Evans, his fallen comrade.

Time and secular living

Time plays an integral role in the theme of faith and doubt in Mrs. Dalloway. The overwhelming presence of the passing of time and the impending fate of death for each of the characters is felt throughout the novel. As Big Ben arches over the city of London and rings for each half-hour, characters can't help but stop and notice the loss of life to time in regular intervals throughout the development of the story. Experiencing the vicious war, the notion of death constantly floats in Septimus' mind as he continues to see his friend Evans talking of such things. A constant stream of consciousness from the characters, especially Clarissa, can serve as a distraction from this passing of time and ultimate march towards death but each character has a constant reminder of the inevitability of these facts. However evident time and death may be throughout the novel, only a day passes over the course of the entire story, not nearly enough to be worried about death that much. Each individual moment in a character's life then is assumed to be as important as heroic journeys and other epics which also push the boundaries of death.

Constant connections to memories and overarching ideas made by simple things passing through the character's mind also demonstrate the meaning in every detail and the appreciation that can be drawn as a result. Clarissa even feels that her job (by throwing her parties) is to offer "the gift" of connections to the inhabitants of London. Here in lies Woolf's underlying message. Woolf's writing style crosses the boundaries of the past, present and future, emphasising her idea of time as a constant flow, connected only by some force (or divinity) within each person. There lies an evident contrast between the constant passing of time signalled by Big Ben and the random crossing of time in Woolf's writing. Although it seems random, it only demonstrates the infinite amount of possibilities that the world can offer once connected by the individuality of each person inside.

Mental illness

Septimus, as the shell-shocked war hero, operates as a pointed criticism of the treatment of mental illness and depression. Woolf criticises medical discourse through Septimus' decline and suicide; his doctors make snap judgments about his condition, talk to him mainly through his wife, and dismiss his urgent confessions before he can make them. Rezia remarks that Septimus "was not ill. Dr Holmes said there was nothing the matter with him."

Woolf goes beyond commenting on the treatment of mental illness. Using the characters of Clarissa and Rezia, she makes the argument that people can only interpret Septimus' shell shock according to their cultural norms. Throughout the course of the novel Clarissa does not meet Septimus. Clarissa's reality is vastly different from that of Septimus; his presence in London is unknown to Clarissa until his death becomes the subject of idle chatter at her party. By never having these characters meet, Woolf is suggesting that mental illness can be contained to the individuals who suffer from it without others, who remain unaffected, ever having to witness it. This allows Woolf to weave her criticism of the treatment of the mentally ill with her larger argument, which is the criticism of society's class structure. Her use of Septimus as the stereotypically traumatised veteran is her way of showing that there were still reminders of the First World War in London in 1923. These ripples affect Mrs. Dalloway and readers spanning generations. Shell shock, or post traumatic stress disorder, is an important addition to the early 20th century canon of post-war British literature.

There are similarities in Septimus' condition to Woolf's struggles with bipolar disorder. Both hallucinate that birds sing in Greek, and Woolf once attempted to throw herself out of a window as Septimus does. Woolf had also been treated for her condition at various asylums, from which her antipathy towards doctors developed. Woolf committed suicide by drowning, sixteen years after the publication of *Mrs. Dalloway*.

Woolf's original plan for her novel called for Clarissa to kill herself during her party. In this original version, Septimus (whom Woolf called Mrs. Dalloway's "double") did not appear at all.

Existential issues

When Peter Walsh sees a girl in the street and stalks her for half an hour, he notes that his relationship to the girl was "made up, as one makes up the better part of life." By focusing on characters' thoughts and perceptions, Woolf emphasises the significance of private thoughts on existential crisisrather than concrete events in a person's life. Most of the plot in Mrs Dalloway consists of realisations that the characters subjectively make.

Fueled by her bout of ill health, Clarissa Dalloway is emphasised as a woman who appreciates life. Her love of party-throwing comes from a desire to bring people together and create happy moments. Her charm, according to Peter Walsh who loves her, is a sense of joie de vivre, always summarised by the sentence: "There she was." She interprets Septimus Smith's death as an act of embracing life and her mood remains light, even though she hears about it in the midst of the party.

Feminism

As a commentary on inter-war society, Clarissa's character highlights the role of women as the proverbial "Angel in the House" and embodies sexual andeconomic repression and the narcissism of bourgeois women who have never known the hunger and insecurity of working women. She keeps up with and even embraces the social expectations of the wife of a patrician politician, but she is still able to express herself and find distinction in the parties she throws.

Her old friend Sally Seton, whom Clarissa admires dearly, is remembered as a great independent woman: She smoked cigars, once ran down a corridor naked to fetch her sponge-bag, and made bold, unladylike statements to get a reaction from people. When Clarissa meets her in the present day, Sally turns out to be a perfect housewife, having married a self-made rich man and given birth to five sons.

Bisexuality

Clarissa Dalloway is strongly attracted to Sally Seton at Bourton. Thirty four years later, Clarissa still considers the kiss they shared to be the happiest moment of her life. She feels about Sally "as men feel", but she does not recognise these feelings as signs of bisexuality.

Similarly, Septimus is haunted by the image of his dear friend Evans. Evans, his commanding officer, is described as being "undemonstrative in the company of women." The narrator describes Septimus and Evans behaving together like "two dogs playing on a hearth-rug" who, inseparable, "had to be together, share with each other, fight with each other, quarrel with each other...." Jean E. Kennard notes that the word "share" could easily be read in a Forsteranmanner, perhaps as in Forster's Maurice, which shows the word's use in this period to describe homosexual relations. Kennard is one to note Septimus' "increasing revulsion at the idea of heterosexual sex," abstaining from sex with Rezia and feeling that "the business of copulation was filth to him before the end."

Major Characters

Clarissa Dalloway

She is a fifty-one-year-old protagonist of the novel. She is the wife of Richard and mother of Elizabeth. She spends the day organizing a party that will be held that night while also reminiscing about the past. She is self-conscious about her role in London high society.

Richard Dalloway

He is the haughty husband of Clarissa. He is immersed in his work in government.

Elizabeth Dalloway

She is a seventeen-year-old daughter of Clarissa and Richard. She is said to look "oriental" and has great composure. Compared to her mother, she takes great pleasure in politics and modern history, hoping to be either a doctor or farmer in the future.

Septimus Warren Smith

He is a World War I veteran who suffers from "shell shock" and hallucinations of his deceased friend, Evans. Educated and decorated in the war, he is detached from society. He is married to Lucrezia from whom he has grown distant.

Lucrezia Smith

She is the Italian wife of Septimus. She is burdened by his mental illness and believes that she is judged because of it. During most of the novel she is homesick for family and country, which she left to marry Septimus after the Armistice.

Sally Seton

She had a strained relationship with her family and spent much time with Clarissa's family in her youth. Sally is married to Lord Rosseter and has five boys. She can be described as feisty as well as a youthful ragamuffin.

Peter Walsh

He is an old friend of Clarissa. In the past, she rejected his marriage proposal. Now he has returned to England from India and is one of the guests at Clarissa's party. He is planning to marry Daisy.

Introduction to Chapter I (an excerpt)

Clarissa Dalloway, an upper-class, fifty-two-year-old woman married to a politician, decides to buy flowers herself for the party she is hosting that evening instead of sending a servant to buy them. London is full of noise this Wednesday. Big Ben strikes. The king and queen are at the palace. It is a fresh mid-June morning, and Clarissa recalls one girlhood summer on her father's estate, Bourton. She sees herself at eighteen, standing at the window, feeling as if something awful might happen. Despite the dangers, Clarissa loves life. Her one gift, she feels, is an ability to know people by instinct.

She thinks affectionately of Peter, who once asked her to marry him. She refused. He made her cry when he said she would marry a prime minister and throw parties. Clarissa continues to feel the sting of his criticisms but now also feels anger that Peter did not accomplish any of his dreams.

Chapter I

(An Excerpt)

Mrs. Dalloway said she would buy the flowers herself.

For Lucy[1] had her work cut out for her. The doors would be taken off their hinges; Rumpelmayer's men[2] were coming. And then, thought Clarissa Dalloway, what a morning—fresh as if issued to children on a beach.

What a lark! What a plunge! For so it had always seemed to her, when, with a little squeak[3] of the hinges, which she could hear now, she had burst open the French windows[4] and plunged at Bourton[5] into the open air. How fresh, how calm, stiller than this of course, the air was in the early morning; like the flap of a wave; the kiss of a wave; chill and sharp and yet (for a girl of eighteen as she then was) solemn, feeling as she did, standing there at the open window, that something awful was about to happen; looking at the flowers, at the trees with the smoke winding off them and the rooks rising, falling; standing and looking until Peter Walsh said, "Musing among the vegetables?" —was that it?— "I prefer men to cauliflowers" —was that it? He must have said it at breakfast one morning when she had gone out on to the terrace — Peter Walsh. He would be back from India one of these days, June or July, she forgot which, for his letters were awfully dull; it was his sayings one remembered; his eyes, his pocket-knife, his smile, his grumpiness[6] and, when millions of things had utterly vanished — how strange it was! — a few sayings like this about cabbages.

She stiffened a little on the kerb[7], waiting for Durtnall's van[8] to pass. A charming woman, Scrope Purvis[9] thought her (knowing her as one does know people who live next door to one in Westminster[10]); a touch of the bird about her, of the jay[11], blue-green, light, vivacious[12], though she was over fifty, and grown very white since her illness. There she perched, never seeing him, waiting to cross, very upright.

For having lived in Westminster — how many years now? over twenty — one feels even in the midst of the traffic, or waking at night, Clarissa was positive, a particular hush, or solemnity; an indescribable pause; a suspense (but that might be her heart, affected, they said, by influenza) before Big Ben[13] strikes. There! Out it boomed. First a warning, musical; then the hour, irrevocable[14]. The leaden circles dissolved in the air. Such fools we are, she thought, crossing Victoria Street[15].

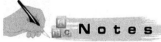 **N o t e s**

[1] 露西，达洛维夫人家里的女佣。

[2] Rumpelmayer 是店名。Rumpelmayer's men 是指前来卸门的工人。

[3] 嘎吱嘎吱的响声

[4] 落地窗

[5] 英格兰度假胜地，这里指达洛维夫人少女时代其父母的居住地。

[6] bad temper

[7] 人行道

[8] 某商号的运货车

[9] 大概是运货车的驾驶员或其他雇员。

[10] 威斯敏斯特，英国伦敦西部的贵族居住区，在泰晤士河北岸，区内有白金汉宫、议会大厦、首相府邸、政府各部门和威斯敏斯特大教堂。

[11] 松鸭

[12] 活泼的

[13] 大本钟，伦敦英国议会大厦钟楼上的大钟。

[14] 不可挽回的

[15] 维多利亚大街，在伦敦市中心。

 Questions

1. How does Woolf present *Mrs. Dalloway* to the reader?

2. How do you know about the personality of Peter Walsh?

3. What is the function of Big Ben?

Analysis of Chapter I (an excerpt)

Woolf wrote much of Mrs. Dalloway in free indirect discourse. We are generally immersed in the subjective mental world of various characters, although the book is written in the third person, referring to characters by proper names, as well as the pronouns he, she, and they. Woolf allows us to evaluate characters from both external and internal perspectives: We follow them as they move physically through the world, all the while listening to their most private thoughts. The subjective nature of the narrative demonstrates the unreliability of memory.

In this excerpt, Clarissa is full of happy thoughts as she sets off to buy flowers that beautiful June morning, but her rapture reminds her of a similar June morning thirty years earlier, when she stood at the window at Bourton and felt something awful might happen. Tragedy is never far from her thoughts, and from the first page of the book Clarissa has a sense of impending tragedy. Indeed, one of the central dilemmas Clarissa will face is her own mortality. Even as Clarissa rejoices in life, she struggles to deal with aging and death. Then, by accident, she reads two lines about death from an open book in a shop window: "Fear no more the heat of the sun/Nor the furious winter's rages." The words are from one of Shakespeare's later plays, *Cymbeline*, which is experimental since it has comic, romantic, and tragic elements, much like *Mrs. Dalloway*. The lines are from a funeral song that suggests death is a comfort after life's hard struggles.

Woolf reveals mood and character through unusual and complex syntax. The rush and movement of London are reflected in galloping sentences that go on for line after line in a kind of ecstasy. These sentences also reflect Clarissa's character, particularly her ability to enjoy life, since they forge ahead quickly and bravely, much as Clarissa does. As Clarissa sees the summer air moving the leaves like waves, sentences become rhythmic, full of dashes and semicolons that imitate the choppy movement of water. Parentheses abound, indicating thoughts within thoughts, sometimes related to the topic at hand and sometimes not.

《达洛维夫人》 第一章（选段）

达洛维夫人说她要自己去买花。

因为露西有很多事情要做。几扇屋门将从合页上卸下；朗波尔迈耶店里的工人要来。再说，克拉丽莎·达洛维想，今天早晨多么清新啊，好像是专为海滩上的孩子们准备的。

多有意思！多么痛快！因为她过去总有这样的感觉，每当合页吱扭一声，她现在还能听见那合页的轻微声响，她猛地推开伯尔顿村住宅的落地窗置身于户外的时候。早晨的空气多么清新，多么宁静，当然比现在要沉寂些；像微浪拍岸，像浮波轻吻，清凉刺肤。然而（对于当时的她，一个十八岁的姑娘来说）又有几分庄严肃穆；当时她站在敞开的落地窗前，预感到有某种可怕的事就要发生；她观赏着鲜花，观赏着烟雾缭绕的树丛和上下翻飞的乌鸦；他站着，看着，直到彼得·沃尔什说："对着蔬菜想什么心事呢？"是那么说的吧？"我感兴趣的是人，不是花椰菜。"是那么说的吧？这一定是他在那天吃早餐的时候说的，在她走到屋外的平台之后，彼得·沃尔什，他过些天就要从印度回来了，是六月还是七月，她记不清了，因为他的来信总是那么枯燥无味；倒是他常说的几句话让人忘不掉；她记得他的眼睛、他的折叠小刀、他的微笑、他的坏脾气，还有，在忘掉了成千上万件事情之后，还记得他说过的关于卷心菜的诸如此类的话。多奇怪呀！

她站在人行道的石沿上挺了挺身子，等着达特诺尔公司的小货车开过去。一个有魅力的女人，斯科洛普·派维斯这样评价她（他了解她的程度就跟威斯敏斯特市的居民了解自己紧邻的程度差不多）；她有几分像小鸟，像只樫鸟，蓝绿色，体态轻盈，充满活力，尽管她已经年过五十，而且自患病以来面色苍白。她站在人行道边上，从未看见过他，她在等着过马路，腰背挺直。

由于在威斯敏斯特住了，有多少年呢？二十多年了，克拉丽莎相信，你即使在车流之中，或在夜半醒来，总能感觉到一种特殊的寂静，或者说是肃穆；总能感觉到一种不可名状的停顿、一种牵挂（但有可能是因为她的心脏，据说是流行性感冒所致），等待着国会大厦上的大本钟敲响。听！那深沉洪亮的钟声响了。先是前奏，旋律优美；然后报时，铿锵有力。那深沉的音波逐渐消逝在空中。我们是如此愚蠢，穿过维多利亚街时她这样想。

References

[1] 弗吉尼亚·伍尔夫. 达洛维太太 [M]. 谷启楠，译. 北京：人民文学出版社，2005.